Contents at a Glance

Table of Contents

ASP.NET

BY EXAMPLE

201 West 103rd Street
Indianapolis, Indiana 46290

Steven A. Smith

ASP.NET by Example

Trademarks

Warning and Disclaimer

Publisher
David Culverwell

Executive Editor
Candy Hall

Acquisitions Editor
Michelle Newcomb

Development Editors
Robin Drake
Maureen McDaniel
Sarah Robbins

Managing Editor
Thomas F. Hayes

Senior Editor
Susan Ross Moore

Copy Editors
Margaret Berson
Michael Dietsch

Indexer
D&G Limited, LLC

Proofreader
D&G Limited, LLC

Technical Editor
Vincent W. Mayfield

Team Coordinator
Cindy Teeters

Media Developer
Michael Hunter

Interior Designer
Karen Ruggles

Cover Designer
Rader Design

Page Layout
D&G Limited, LLC

About the Authors

Steven A. Smith is a Managing Consultant and Internet Specialist for Software Architects, Inc., a Chicago-based consulting firm with offices in more than a dozen U.S. cities. Steve has been a "SARK" for more than four years and is currently working in the Cleveland office, focusing on highly scalable component-based architectures. In his spare time, Steve runs the #1 ASP.NET community site, ASPAlliance.com, and maintains a column there with dozens of articles on ASP and ASP.NET. He has also written a number of articles for ASPToday.com and continues to work as a technical reviewer for WROX, Prentice Hall, and QUE. Steve has an MCSE+Internet (4.0) certification and previously completed the MCSD. He is also a graduate of The Ohio State University with a degree in Computer Science Engineering. His development experience prior to .NET was mainly focused on ASP, Visual Basic, SQL Server, and COM+.

When he isn't bonding with his laptop computer, Steve enjoys biking, swimming, foosball, and spending time with his wife, Michelle, and their two dogs, Jaegerin and Mojo.

Steve can be reached at ssmith@aspalliance.com.

Nicholas Chase has been involved in Web site development for companies such as Lucent Technologies, Sun Microsystems, Oracle Corporation, and the Tampa Bay Buccaneers. Nick has been a high school physics teacher, a low-level radioactive waste facility manager, an online science fiction magazine editor, a multimedia engineer, and an Oracle instructor. More recently, he was the Chief Technology Officer of Site Dynamics Interactive Communications in Clearwater, Florida, and is the author of three books on Web development, including *Java and XML From Scratch* (Que). He loves to hear from readers and can be reached at nicholas@nicholaschase.com.

Glenn Cook has been programming and teaching ASP since 1997. His tutorials and award-winning source code continue to make his column at the AspAlliance, the #1 ASP.NET Community, one of the most popular in its history.

He is the founder of simpleCsharp.com and is a Senior Consultant with Fahrenheit Technology in Richmond, VA. He has lead projects for clients such as Land Rover, Charles Schwab, The Yellow Pages, Marriot, and most recently for CapitalOne.

When he's not playing with code, he is spending time with his family in the D.C./VA area.

Nathen Grass is a consultant with RDA Corporation (http://www.rdacustomsoftware.com) in Atlanta, Georgia. RDA builds custom software and Web-based applications to solve complex business problems for mid-market and large-scale companies. Nathen specializes in DNA architecture development using various Microsoft technologies and lately has been heavily involved in learning and developing on the .NET platform. Nathen can be reached at grass@rdacustomsoftware.com.

Vincent W. Mayfield is a Senior Software Engineer, Microsoft Certified Solutions Developer, and Vice President/Co-Founder of Bit-Wizards IT Solutions, Inc., of Fort Walton Beach, Florida. He has more than 12 years of experience developing software, and over 8 years developing applications for the Microsoft Windows Family of Operating Systems with C and C++. He has served in the U.S. Army Reserves and the U.S. Air Force, and is an FAA Commercial Instrument rated pilot. Vincent has authored/co-authored several programming books to include: Wait Group's *COM/DCOM Primer Plus*, *ActiveX Programming Unleashed*, and *Visual C++ 5.0 Developer's Guide*. Vincent holds a BS in Mathematics with Minors in Computer Science and Aerospace Science as well as a MS in International Relations. Bit-Wizards IT Solutions is a cutting-edge technology company that provides professional software engineering, e-commerce, wireless, Web, consulting, and information technology solutions.

Wynn Netherland is President of Houston, Texas-based Praexis, Inc., a software consulting firm specializing in developing hosted applications using .NET. Wynn has worked in Web development since 1995 and is currently working on his second .NET title. When he's not churning out code or chapters, he enjoys traveling and attending Astros games with his wife, Paula. He can be reached at wynn.netherland@praexis.com.

Scott Swigart is living proof that being a geek at age 12 pays off. He is currently a senior principal at 3 Leaf Solutions, where he spends the bulk of his time providing training and consulting services for .NET early adopters. Scott started working with .NET as soon as the first bits would complete an install. In addition to working with .NET early adopters, Scott is actively involved in various .NET projects for Microsoft.

William Wise holds a Master's degree in Software Engineering from Brandeis University, a Bachelor's degree in Philosophy and Religious Studies, and has done a fair amount of graduate work at the University of Virginia studying Christianity and Judaism in antiquity. Professionally, he has worked as a developer, trainer, network administrator, and database administrator and has developed a number of two-tier and three-tier applications to meet the business objectives of a variety of employers, primarily in the biotech business sector. His interests include playing guitar, reading Tolkien's fiction over and over, and learning the ins and outs of Linux. William currently resides in the historic community of Williamsburg, VA, along with his fiancé and several old, close friends.

Dedication

To my wife, Michelle, with my thanks.

Acknowledgments

I would like to thank two Michelles in my life: my wife, Dr. Michelle Smith, who has put up with many long hours devoted to my computer, and my editor, Michelle Newcomb. They have both been very patient with me while I have worked on this, my first print book. It's been a long road with a few surprises, and I've really appreciated the support. Thanks also to Chris, for many hours of diversion while I should have been concentrating.

Tell Us What You Think!

As the reader of this book, *you* are our most important critic and commentator. We value your opinion and want to know what we're doing right, what we could do better, what areas you'd like to see us publish in, and any other words of wisdom you're willing to pass our way.

As an Associate Publisher for Que, I welcome your comments. You can fax, e-mail, or write me directly to let me know what you did or didn't like about this book—as well as what we can do to make our books stronger.

Please note that I cannot help you with technical problems related to the topic of this book, and that due to the high volume of mail I receive, I might not be able to reply to every message.

When you write, please be sure to include this book's title and author as well as your name and phone or fax number. I will carefully review your comments and share them with the author and editors who worked on the book.

Fax: 317-581-4666

E-mail: feedback@quepublishing.com

Mail: Associate Publisher
              Que
              201 West 103rd Street
              Indianapolis, IN 46290 USA

Introduction

The *by Example* Series

How does the *by Example* series make you a better programmer? The *by Example* series teaches programming using the best method possible. After a concept is introduced, you'll see one or more examples of that concept in use. The text acts as a mentor by figuratively looking over your shoulder and showing you new ways to use the concepts you just learned. The examples are numerous. While the material is still fresh in your mind, you see example after example demonstrating ways to use the material you've just learned.

The philosophy of the *by Example* series is simple: The best way to teach computer programming is using multiple examples. Command descriptions, format syntax, and language references are not enough to teach a newcomer a programming language. Only by looking at many examples in which new commands are immediately used and by running sample programs can programming students get more than just a feel for the language.

How This Book Is Designed

This book is designed to quickly get you up to speed with using ASP.NET. The Microsoft .NET Framework and ASP.NET allow you to develop powerful distributed applications using an extensive library of functions, in one of many different programming languages. What began with Active Server Pages as a powerful new way to develop Internet applications has evolved into ASP.NET: a much more powerful, robust, secure, and extensible architecture.

This book is example-based. After a few introductory chapters that lay a conceptual foundation for the work we are going to do (and introduce you to ASP.NET), you'll find that every chapter is loaded with examples. I believe in the example-based approach to learning upon which this series is based. Whenever I get into a jam and need to learn a new programming technique, when I consult the documentation, the first thing I do is look for a good code example that fits my needs. It's one of the fastest ways to learn. One snippet of tight, well-documented code is worth ten paragraphs of "how to" explanations.

To further enhance the "by Example" approach, every example in this book is available online at the book's online resource center. You will be able to actually see the examples run on an ASP.NET server, as well as download the source code.

Using Other Resources

The Microsoft .NET architecture encompasses nearly every part of the Microsoft programming platform. Obviously, this book cannot hope to cover all or even very much of the .NET architecture, of which ASP.NET is a single part. You may find some areas of the book that refer to .NET architectural features without much further elaboration. You can find Microsoft's .NET documentation online at the following URL:

http://www.microsoft.com/net/

You can also find Microsoft's ASP.NET and Visual Studio.NET documentation online at the following Web sites:

ASP.NET: http://www.asp.net/

VS.NET: http://msdn.microsoft.com/vstudio/

Finally, although Appendix D features a C# Reference, you can find additional C# documentation from Microsoft at the following Web address:

http://msdn.microsoft.com/vstudio/nextgen/technology/csharpintro.asp

Who Should Use This Book

ASP.NET by Example is intended for people with some prior knowledge of Microsoft's Active Server Pages (ASP) technology who are familiar with programming and dynamic data-driven Internet applications. However, you do not need to be an expert with VBScript, JScript, or any other scripting language because they play a very limited part in the future of ASP that is ASP.NET. Furthermore, knowledge of ActiveX Data Objects (ADO) and knowledge of databases in general, including some SQL (Structured Query Language), is assumed. Some understanding of components and event-driven programming will be helpful as well.

What We Assume You Know

We assume that you know how to develop Web pages using HyperText Markup Language (HTML) and Active Server Pages (or a similar Web development language). You're familiar with either VBScript or JScript or more likely some of both, and you've probably developed at least one Component Object Model (COM) object, probably using Visual Basic. You may have used ASP 3.0 or COM+, but many of you are still working with Internet Information Server (IIS) 4.0 on Windows NT, and will only be upgrading to Windows 2000 as this book reaches the shelves.

What We Assume You Don't Know

If you already know all that, what can this book do for you? Well, we assume that you've heard of ASP.NET, the .NET architecture, VB Webforms, and other

Microsoft marketing hoopla over the last year, but that you haven't had the chance to work with any of it yet. We figure you're reading this book to learn

- How ASP.NET can help you as an Internet application developer to be more efficient and to build more powerful applications

- How the error handling in ASP.NET allows you to centralize your error handling into one page

- How ASP.NET will make your existing applications perform better by using compiled code

- How with ASP.NET a complete programming model is available for applications that allows for better tools and simpler form handling

This Book's Organization

This book is organized to maximize your transition to the ASP.NET development environment. The early chapters provide an introduction to the .NET Framework and describe the differences between ASP.NET and its predecessor, ASP 3.0. From there, the all-important knowledge of how to work with data (ADO.NET) is covered early, so that you can leverage this knowledge in the later chapters, which progressively cover more and more advanced topics. Almost every chapter includes many examples that will help you to understand the points being covered, and you can test the examples yourself online at the book's supporting Web site at http://aspauthors.com/aspnetbyexample/.

Specifically, Chapter 1 provides an overview of the .NET Framework, on which ASP.NET is built. Chapter 2 introduces the reader to ASP.NET, and Chapter 3 provides some guidelines and examples for migrating to ASP.NET. Chapter 4 introduces the reader to ADO.NET, which is used to access data in ASP.NET. Chapters 5 through 9 cover various controls, including List Controls, Rich Controls, Validation Controls, User Controls, and Intrinsic Controls. In Chapter 10 we'll look at how to manage ASP.NET applications. Chapter 11 describes Web Services, and exciting new technology that allows separate web applications to easily communicate with one another. Chapter 12 discusses how to build your on ASP.NET controls. Chapter 13 provides an overview of how to debug your ASP.NET applications. Finally, Chapter 14 provides a case study of an e-commerce site built with ASP.NET. In the appendixes you'll find references for the ASP.NET Object Model, the ADO.NET Object Model, the VB.NET and C# programming languages, and a quick reference to using Visual Studio. NET. We hope you find this useful as you continue to develop using the latest Microsoft has to offer.

Conventions Used In This Book

This book uses several common conventions to help teach ASP.NET. Here is a summary of these typographical conventions:

EXAMPLE

OUTPUT

- **Example.** Examples are the most important part of any *by Example* title. These provide working demonstrations of the points that are being covered by the text in each chapter. You'll see the Example icon beside each of those demonstrations.

- **Output.** The Output icon indicates a figure or code that shows the result of the preceding example. We supply the output so that you know what to expect when you run the example yourself.

- **Note.** Notes provide additional commentary or explanation that doesn't fit neatly into the surrounding text. You will find detailed explanations of how something works, or alternate ways of doing a task.

- **Tip.** Tips help you work more efficiently by providing shortcuts or hints about alternate and faster ways of accomplishing a task.

- **Caution.** Cautions provide a warning to you about situations that involve possible danger to your system or to your data.

- **Online Reference.** These notes provide you with URLs that you can visit to get more information or other resources relating to the topic being discussed.

- A special `monospaced` computer font indicates commands and computer output.

- Because this is a book that has a limited page width, some lines of code may be too long to fit on a single line. When you see a code continuation character (➥), you will know that the code has wrapped to the second line.

Online Resources

In addition to the contents of this book, you will find additional resources online at the book's Web site. The Web site includes online sample code, any updates to the book that may be necessary, and information for providing feedback or questions to the book's authors. You can find the book's support Web site at:

`http://aspauthors.com/aspnetbyexample/`

In addition, you will find a number of ASP.NET related Web sites on the inside of the back cover.

What's Next

OK, enough with the preliminary necessities! Let's take a look at what all the fuss is about with ASP.NET. In the first chapter, we'll provide you with an introduction to Microsoft's new development architecture, the .NET Framework. This provides the basis for all of ASP.NET (and, indeed, all Microsoft development in the near term). Following this introduction, we'll move into learning ASP.NET in particular.

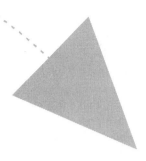

.NET Overview

"Keep on the lookout for novel ideas that others have used successfully. Your idea has to be original only in its adaptation to the problem you're working on."
—Thomas Edison

Thomas Edison did not invent the first electric light bulb or the first incandescent lamp. He did, however, invent the first practical and commercially successful electric incandescent lamp. He did not invent the first electrical power station. He improved the designs of existing generators and regulators to create the first commercially successful power station capable of delivering affordable power for electric lighting. He did not invent the telegraph. But he did invent the first duplex and multiplex telegraphy systems, enabling telegraphs to send and receive messages at the same time over the same wire.

Thomas Edison did not invent the Internet, wireless computer devices, or even .NET. He did, however, create a framework of core technologies that we have improved that make those technologies possible. .NET is not the next generation of the Internet. It is the first practical set of tools that will enable software developers to invent the next generation of the Internet. .NET is an original adaptation of many successful and novel technologies and ideas to solve a problem; businesses have found it very difficult and expensive to create profitable Internet solutions with the available development frameworks and architectures. The next generation of the Internet will be funded by businesses who demand solutions with a short development cycle, a quick return on their investment, long-term profitability, and that are secure and inexpensive to maintain and upgrade.

.NET has been designed with the Internet in mind from the ground up. .NET absorbs many successful ideas that have been in use for years, yet it is a radical departure from the client-server framework it replaces. It is based on time-tested, object-oriented software programming concepts, nonproprietary standards and protocols, and programming languages that many of you are already quite comfortable with. Comfortable or not, Microsoft has decided to make a clean break from the past, which means that nobody is completely immune from a learning curve if they care to follow Microsoft into the future. If you already own a copy of Windows 2000, or Windows XP, you will not need to purchase anything more from Microsoft to develop, test, and deploy your own software inventions on the .NET framework. The only thing you will need to invest in beyond that is your future.

If you don't buy into the hype, good for you! We encourage you to look beyond our biased enthusiasm to examine all the facts. When you gain a better understanding of what .NET is, and the role that ASP.NET has within this platform, most of you will recognize the changes and investments that you will need to make to create your own personal commercial success. The changes might even force you to take a closer look at what the competition offers, which can't hurt, regardless of your opinions about .NET. If you're starting to feel a bit overwhelmed, just look to the closest light socket and a bit of Edison's wisdom to guide you: "Opportunity is often missed because it is dressed in overalls and looks a lot like work."

This chapter will give you a high-level introduction to the key concepts and components that make up the .NET Framework. You will have a much shorter learning curve if you can think of ASP.NET in terms of the big .NET picture. We know you're anxious to dig into the fun stuff, so we'll do our best to keep this chapter as quick, fun, and rewarding as we can.

The Big .NET Picture

.NET is a software development and application execution environment that allows you to create, compile, test, deploy, and execute software that may be coded in a variety of different programming languages that adhere to a single set of Common Language Runtime files. In .NET's initial public release, Microsoft presents new versions of its most popular programming languages: Visual Basic and C++, which are now called Visual Basic .NET and MC++ (Managed C++). Although Microsoft has retired J++, they introduce two new languages: J# and C# (pronounced j-sharp and c-sharp respectively). In terms of their respective performance and power, all of these languages are very similar. In terms of the syntax they use, VB.NET is the only programming language that is not derived from the C Language. Despite the subtle differences between them and their individual compilers, the resulting compiled code is the same for every language. This insures completely seamless language interoperability on a common integrated platform that is supported by the .NET Framework's Class Library and Runtime. Microsoft bundles support for all of these new languages in its latest release of Visual Studio, now called Visual Studio.NET (VS.NET). Microsoft's entire product line of development packages has undergone significant changes to satisfy the requirements of this new framework. Of course, Microsoft would love it if you decided to buy Visual Studio .NET to develop your .NET applications, but .NET's open architecture is also an invitation to any programming language and development environment. In other words, the output of PASCAL's compiler will look no different than the output produced by C#, Eiffel, COBOL, Visual Basic .NET, and so on. As long as a programming language has a compiler that adheres to the .NET Framework's extremely strict set of rules to produce a common executable language, it is a welcome addition to the .NET family.

The .NET Framework

Currently, the .NET framework will run on the following operating systems: Windows 98, Windows ME, Windows 2000, and Windows XP. (We expect that this list of operating systems will eventually include third-party O/Ss, so we recommend that you check "http://msdn.microsoft.com/net/" to check for any new additions to that list.)

From a high-level view, the .NET Framework can be described as a little virtual operating system that runs on top of one of the operating systems we mentioned. A closer inspection would reveal that the framework is made up of two main components: the .NET Class Library and the Common Language Runtime (CLR).

Class Orientation

The .NET Class Library is a huge organized hierarchy of class objects, shown in Figure 1.1. These objects expose services that you can use to develop your own services. They include support for things like Windows Forms and Web Services, as well as objects for working with XML and data. To include these services in our applications, we navigate the hierarchy using traditional object-oriented programming principles. Navigating this hierarchy is a lot like you would navigate hierarchy of files and folders on your hard drive. For example, if you were referring me to a certain SQL driver on my system (assuming we have the same OS) you would use something like "c:\WINNT\System\Data\SQLClient\". A similar reference included in your code would look like "System.Data.SQLClient". The only difference is that the object-oriented code references separate each level of the hierarchy with a dot ".". These explicit references to groups of classes within the Framework's class libraries are also referred to as namespaces in .NET. You can think of namespaces as organizing classes just as folders organize files in a file system.

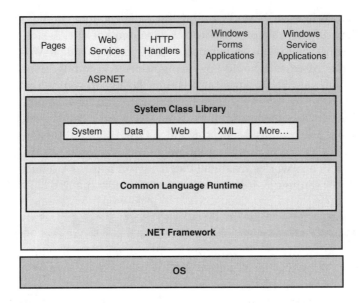

Figure 1.1: *The .NET Framework's Architecture.*

A *namespace* is a unique hierarchical reference to a specific class or group of similar classes. For example, the base classes that provide the services that support the runtime environment are found in the System namespace. This namespace includes services for things like I/O, security, data, and Web-related operations. To access these namespaces programmatically, your reference would look like System.Web or System.Data. The more specific a namespace is, the more specific its services will usually be. For example, if I wanted to connect to an SQL database, I could use the System.Data. SqlClient namespace.

We also use the benefits of a unique class reference so that two objects with the same name cannot clash. Imagine that you have an application that allows remote clients to call Web services in your Customers.Customer object. If that remote client has a local reference to its own version of an object named Customers.Customer, there will be some major problems for that remote client. Microsoft recommends that each developer create at least two unique namespace levels that become the root references for all their object creations. For example, a much better reference to my applica-tion's "Customer class" might look something like this:

```
"JoesGarage.GlennCook.SimpleCSharp.ASPWebServiceApp.Customers.Customer"
```

EXAMPLE

Runtime Hosts

The last component in the framework that at least deserves an honorable mention as a "main component" (especially in this book) is a .NET runtime host. A *runtime host* is an application that loads the .NET runtime into its process. ASP.NET is an example of an application that loads the runtime into its process for its Web-related services. Internet Explorer is another example of a runtime host allowing us to download and execute managed code within its processes. The last runtime host component included in the framework is shell executables. This piece is actually what calls the .NET runtime from your operating system when you want to start a .NET application. It will also transfer the control of the .NET application from your system to the runtime.

The Common Language Runtime: A New Interpretation of Older Technology

The Common Language Runtime has many similarities to the runtime environment that executes Java applications. You'll learn later on that there are just as many differences as there are similarities, but it provides a good frame of reference for learning about a managed code execution environment.

To understand how the runtime works, let's discuss it in terms of an imaginary Web Service application you have just finished coding within Visual Studio .NET. VS .NET will handle all the dirty details of what needs to be passed to the appropriate compiler for your code. In earlier versions of Visual Studio, each language had its own similar-looking IDE, but was a separate application. In VS .NET, you have one unified development environment that can call a number of different languages' compilers. Alternatively, you can pass these specific command-line arguments to the compiler on your own using the appropriate syntax at the command-line prompt. This will involve a bit more research and studying on your part, but if you insist on this approach, at least do yourself a favor and download an evaluation version of VS .NET. If nothing else, the evaluation version will help you learn what it will pass to the compiler along with your code. In order to compile a simple C# application, a command line call to the compiler might look like:

```
"c:/>csc.exe simpleCSharp.cs"
```

EXAMPLE

Each programming language has its own compiler. Every one of these compilers must adhere to a common set of strict rules found at the core of the CLR. These strict rules ensure that each language's compiler will produce the same type of compiled code. Even though your compiled .NET application will have the same extension as a traditional Win32-based executable (that is, EXE or DLL), the internal results of the files are completely different. A .NET executable is compiled into what could be described as an "executable package" that includes Microsoft's Intermediate Language (MSIL or

IL), metadata, an assembly manifest, and any additional assemblies or files the application makes reference to. In .NET, your application's executable is more commonly referred to as an assembly. An *assembly* is the compiled code that you will distribute to clients.

Before we discuss what happens to the assembly when a client launches the application, let's take a closer look at the internal components that make up a .NET assembly.

Intermediate Language and Metadata

Intermediate Language (IL) is .NET's version of compiled code. Whether you are compiling an ASP.NET DLL written in COBOL, or a Windows Forms EXE written in C#, the result is always this common self-describing intermediate language. IL is a simple text-based syntax that is complemented by a self-describing component called metadata. The combination of these two technologies gives .NET's managed runtime the ability to perform more operations in less time with less overhead.

The similarities between .NET and Java's managed runtime model will often draw comparisons with .NET's intermediate language and Java's byte code. This similarity comes from the benefits of a common compiled code that is capable of running on any machine that supports their respective runtime environment. In terms of their form and function, however, the two are completely different. .NET's compiled code (IL and metadata) offers some significant advantages over Java's integer-based byte code compilations.

.NET applications are Just-In-Time compiled a second time into native machine code. This is the same type of machine language code a 32-bit C++ executable would be compiled into. An assembly's descriptive text-based syntax allows the runtime the ability to intelligently compile an application into the most efficient set of native machine instructions for a given system. The .NET runtime also gives the developer compilation options to instruct the runtime to dynamically Just-In-Time (JIT) compile their application to machine language, or pre-compile everything to native machine code during installation. For example, if you want to avoid the overhead involved with JIT compiling, you can instruct the runtime to compile your application to native machine code during its initial set-up and installation process.

Java applications are compiled into an integer-based syntax that is never compiled into native machine code. Instead, the Java runtime uses a process that interprets its byte code compilations dynamically. Since an interpreter is essentially software that emulates a CPU, there is additional overhead in supporting this type of design.

In terms of performance differences, a recent benchmark comparison of the J2EE vs .NET (released by Microsoft while .NET was still in Beta) demonstrated that .NET greatly outperforms J2EE at almost every level while using only a fraction of the CPU's resources that J2EE required.

.NET precompiles its applications into native machine language with the help of an assembly's metadata. *Metadata* is XML that thoroughly describes the location and purpose of every object, property, argument, delegate, and method within a .NET application's assembly. Metadata eliminates the overhead associated with interpreting and managing the unknown. The runtime also uses metadata to validate the accuracy and purpose of each function to avoid errors, optimize memory management, and protect the user from malicious attacks.

Figure 1.2 shows the process of compiling an application into an assembly. While coded primarily in C#, you'll notice it includes references to files coded in many other languages.

.NET's compiled code also addresses something commonly referred to as "DLL Hell." In the past, developers would have to tweak and build multiple versions of their Win32 applications to create compatible executables for each category of popular system configurations. All it would take to destroy all your brilliant efforts is for another application to upgrade a shared system DLL to a newer version. .NET developers will not have to struggle with these issues any more, but .NET has costs associated with it that Win32 apps don't have. In other words, you should not expect your managed .NET applications to run as quickly as similar unmanaged Win32 applications. Microsoft's stance is that IL's self-describing code will eventually allow the runtime to compile native code so specific to an end user's system that it will easily be able to outperform Win32 applications. And of course, ASP.NET runs several times faster than classic ASP, so it is by no means slow.

The true inner beauty and power of every compiled .NET application is its Metadata. It is a "novel" solution that preserves the benefits of a managed code environment but uses new technology to overcome the performance losses associated with it. The idea is that the compiled code should read like a novel but has no room for interpretation, ambiguity, and assumptions: "Nothing but the facts, please." This enables the CLR to quickly compile (yes, there is a second compilation) and manage the safest and fastest execution environment possible.

Metadata is really nothing more than XML code that describes the entire contents of the assembly. When a user starts a .NET application, the runtime will access the assembly manifest, which is made up of metadata that

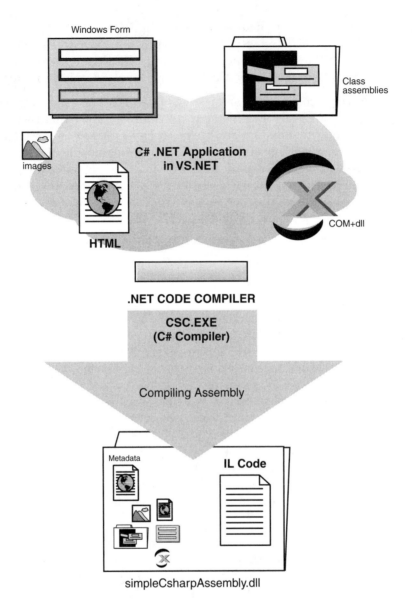

Figure 1.2: Compiling a .NET application into an assembly.

describes the specific contents of the package. It's like the table of contents for a .NET application. The manifest is also the runtime's main entry point for gathering and examining the data it needs to begin compiling the assembly into native machine language. You can also access this information via a disassembler included with the framework called ILDASM.EXE. This tool presents the high-level details of an assembly in a readable and organized hierarchy that describes the specific details of every object, method, argument, and property in your application. If you haven't done your homework, you might think this is Microsoft's consummate security blunder. Without digging into the specific details right now, suffice to say that this is not a blunder, and the intellectual integrity of an application targeted for the .NET Framework is no more or less vulnerable to hackers than an executable compiled for any other platform.

The JIT Compiler

Another critical component in the .NET Framework is the JIT (Just-In-Time) compiler (also known as "the JIT-ter"). This is the piece that actually compiles the contents of the assembly into machine language. It will not compile the entire assembly into memory all at once. Its initial responsibility is to examine the manifest to identify the critical pieces to compile and load to ensure that the application opens quickly. Beyond that point, the JIT compiler will only load the pieces of the application that it needs. The final product of this "just in time" approach is a runtime environment with more available memory space to process what is being used, faster. Microsoft believes that this approach will also guarantee that .NET applications will be able to outperform their much older, unmanaged, and occasionally delinquent cousin, the Win32 executable.

Let's take a look at components within the Common Language Runtime that prepare, compile, and manage a .NET application.

Summary

The .NET Framework is the infrastructure that supports an integrated development and execution platform that allows seamless interoperability between programs developed in a variety of languages. The framework is governed by a common yet strict set of standards, which are enforced by the Common Language Runtime (CLR). These rules are the foundation of .NET's multilanguage interoperability.

The output of a compiled .NET executable is called an assembly. An assembly is made up of MSIL code and metadata. This is the package that is delivered to the end user, which is compiled a second time into native machine language when the user starts the application. An assembly has a .DLL extension, but is different from a traditional Windows DLL.

Intermediate Language (IL) is an optimized compiled code developed by Microsoft that .NET's "jitter" (JIT) uses to compile into native machine code.

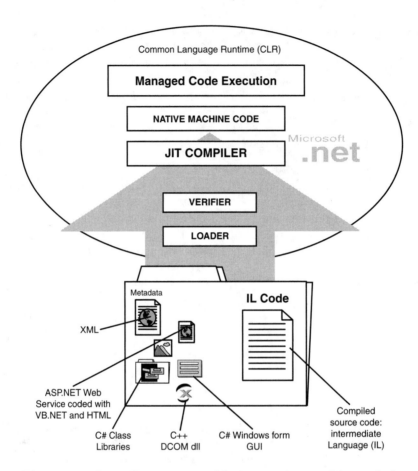

Figure 1.3: *Compiling an assembly into native machine code for execution within the Common Language Runtime.*

An assembly's intermediate language contains descriptive XML code that gives the CLR detailed information about the entire application. It gives the JIT compiler a virtual road map of your application so that the native code can provide the runtime with information about shortcuts during rush hour, the history of the area, unsafe areas to avoid, and when it should put out the garbage.

- The operating systems and servers that support the framework

- The compiled applications and Web services that will run within the framework

- The .NET Framework and its Common Language Runtime

- New services yet to be invented

- Nonproprietary communication protocols like XML and SOAP for exchanging data and services

What's Next?

In the next chapter, we will see how ASP.NET fits into the .NET architecture, what some of its most exciting features are, and how it differs from classic ASP. By the end of the chapter, if you're currently building web sites using ASP, you should be eager to make the jump to ASP.NET and start taking advantage of all of the benefits it has over ASP.

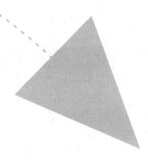

An Introduction To ASP.NET

Microsoft Active Server Pages (ASP) technology has evolved once more. This time, the changes Microsoft has made are so great that they have chosen not to make another point release of ASP (to 4.0), but have labeled this next generation of their Internet technology ASP.NET. ASP.NET (formerly *Next Generation Web Services* or *ASP+*) and the .NET framework will change the way developers build powerful Internet applications more than any prior evolution of ASP before it. Although entire books could be written about the .NET framework (and, as you read this, I'm sure they have been), we can only cover some of the major points about this new architecture before jumping into specific ASP.NET examples.

In this chapter you will

- Take a look at a brief history of Active Server Pages (ASP)

- Learn what ASP.NET is

- Compare the benefits ASP.NET with those of "Classic ASP"

Moving to .NET

What is .NET? .NET is Microsoft's new programming architecture, and is an effort to unify development so that true language independence can be achieved. Further, .NET is designed for the disconnected Internet programming model, rather than the traditional two-tier client/server model that Distributed Component Object Model (DCOM) and other earlier models supported. ASP.NET is just one piece of this new architecture, and of course is the focus of this book.

What does ASP.NET do for you, the developer? Well, let's look at a list of 15 cool new things about ASP.NET as compared to ASP 3.0. This comparison is not meant to be complete, because this is just an introduction to ASP.NET, but it should give you a good idea of why ASP.NET is far superior to its predecessor. So, in no particular order, here are some of the major improvements. Don't worry if there are some items listed that are unclear—we will cover each point in more detail before the end of the chapter.

- Compiled code, not interpreted
- Separation of code from content
- No more "DLL hell"
- Side-by-side installation
- Real debugging
- Real programming languages
- Real error handling
- Applications can be deployed with XCOPY or FTP
- Applications can be administered with XML-structured configuration files
- Event-based programming model
- Improved object model
- More integrated functions, such as form validation and integral form handling
- Web Services
- Great performance enhancements from features like page caching
- Better tools—Visual Studio .NET rules!

This chapter will provide a brief look at the background of ASP.NET and how it has evolved from ASP. I'll explain the key differences between ASP 3.0 and ASP.NET in an overview fashion, and issues such as migrating from "classic ASP" to ASP.NET will be covered in later chapters.

A Brief History of ASP

When Active Server Pages was first released in November of 1996, four years ago as this book is going to press, it provided an easy way to create dynamic Web pages. Although Common Gateway Interface (CGI) and Perl were very popular at the time, ASP quickly gained popularity for four reasons. These included ease of data access, ease of page design, Component Object Model (COM) interoperability, and a relatively flat learning curve for many programmers already familiar with Visual Basic.

For more information about the origins of ASP, originally code-named Denali, see http://msdn.microsoft.com/library/periodic/period96/Denali.htm.

First, if ASP had not been released with ActiveX Data Objects (ADO), it most likely would not have gained in popularity as quickly as it did. ADO replaced Remote Data Objects (RDO) and later Data Access Objects (DAO) as Microsoft's preferred method of accessing databases, and it provided a simple, straightforward object model.

Second, with the release of ASP 1.0 came the first Microsoft Visual Studio application suite, which includes Visual InterDev 1.0. This tool provided many features, especially for a 1.0 product, and took advantage of Microsoft's FrontPage Server Extensions (FPSE) to allow easy maintenance of Web sites without the need for a separate FTP client. Intellisense for COM and built-in ASP objects as well as a data access control made this a very popular editor despite its shortcomings, such as its Graphical User Interface (GUI) editor, which relied on an early version of FrontPage.

It is probably safe to say that if it were not for ASP, the third-party component market would not be the multimillion dollar per year industry that it is today. Certainly this was not the only factor, as third-party controls for Visual Basic predated the COM revolution, but in my opinion, ASP and COM have allowed some businesses to become very profitable by selling pre-packaged components for use on web servers. The ability to purchase off-the-shelf components and plug them into a Web site simply did not exist for all but the most skilled of programmers prior to the release of ASP 1.0. By bringing this capability to the masses, ASP opened up an entirely new market for component vendors, who continue to provide powerful off-the-shelf tools that are easily integrated into ASP applications.

The fourth feature of ASP that sparked its popularity was its use of VBScript as its default language. This allowed the many programmers who were already familiar with Visual Basic to quickly jump into ASP programming with minimal learning required. For the many programmers familiar with JavaScript, or the syntactically similar C, JScript was offered as well. In fact, Microsoft provided the ability to use other third-party languages as well, and it wasn't long before one could write ASP code in Perl.

As cool as it was, ASP 1.0 had some significant limitations. One major limitation for anyone working with COM components was that the Web server needed to be restarted whenever a Dynamic Link Library (DLL) needed to be updated (A COM object is stored as a .DLL file). Other security and performance issues were addressed, but the largest improvements from ASP 1.0 to 2.0 came in the form of Microsoft Transaction Server (MTS). ASP 2.0 shipped as part of Internet Information Server (IIS) 4.0 and MTS 1.0 shipped as part of the free Windows NT 4 Option Pack.

With IIS 4.0, Microsoft introduced the new Microsoft Management Console (MMC), which was used to administer both IIS 4.0 and MTS. MTS made life much easier for anyone developing or using COM components. It handled installation and uninstallation of the components, alleviating the need to restart the Web service (or often the server itself), and also removed a lot of the burden of handling transactions from the developer. In addition, it acted as an object broker, effectively caching object instances and brokering them out on request. This technique led to the current focus on "stateless" components because this was necessary for such object reuse to be effective. In addition, newer versions of ADO further enhanced developers' abilities to work with remote data, using new techniques like XML streams, among other things.

In February 2000, Microsoft released IIS 5.0 with Windows 2000. With IIS 5.0, ASP was in version 3.0, and MTS was replaced with COM+ services. COM+ essentially combined the functionality of MTS with message queuing services, and ASP gained some additional functionality, including a few more methods and intrinsic object properties. On the whole, the major differences between programming in ASP 2.0 and ASP 3.0 lay in the supporting services like COM+ more than in the language itself. Anyone who could write VBScript in ASP 1.0 with Visual InterDev 1.0 would still be perfectly at home using IIS 4.0 or IIS 5.0. This simply is not the case with ASP.NET.

Microsoft employees Mark Anders and Scott Guthrie began developing what would become ASP.NET in early January of 1998. At this time, ASP was just a year old, but some of its limitations were already quite evident.

For instance, the restriction to scripting languages and the lack of a component model for ASP made it difficult to develop good tools for it. The interspersing of code with output HyperText Markup Language (HTML) frequently resulted in problems when designers and developers worked together on the same project. ASP.NET was designed from the start to address the limitations of ASP and overcome them.

Mark and Scott chose to build ASP.NET, then called ASP+, on the Next Generation Web Services (NGWS) Runtime that was then in development. NGWS, which would become .NET, provided a rich set of programming libraries, and would soon include the new language C#, in which ASP.NET itself is written. At this time, ASP.NET has been in development for over three years, and Microsoft's focus with this product remains on these priorities:

- **Factored design.** ASP.NET is written as a set of modular components that can be replaced or extended as needed.

- **Scalability.** Great efforts were made to build a highly scalable model, especially with regard to maintaining state.

- **Availability.** ASP.NET has been designed to intelligently detect crashes, memory leaks, and deadlocks and to recover from these events gracefully.

- **Performance.** ASP.NET takes advantage of compiled languages and early binding to improve performance, and also features extensive caching support.

- **Tools integration.** Microsoft's goal is to make building a Web site as easy as building a form using Visual Basic. Visual Studio .NET is the first tool to provide this functionality, but the other vendors are sure to follow with their own toolsets.

Why ASP Developers Need This Book

If you have read the last couple of pages, you understand that the evolution of ASP has primarily involved changes in peripheral services, not the core ASP engine itself. ASP.NET, previously known as Next Generation Web Services, is a truly different creature than ASP, and will require you to rethink how you go about designing and building Internet applications. Why should you bother to learn this new way of doing things when you already build great applications using classic ASP? What are the benefits that make it worth it? Or, if you're just getting into web development, why should you choose ASP.NET instead of the more established Active Server Pages technology?

Benefits of ASP.NET over ASP

ASP.NET and the .NET Framework feature many advantages over classic ASP. ASP.NET outperforms ASP, and is more robust, secure, and scalable. It has better tools, allowing programmers to be more productive, and it will support many different languages, allowing developers to use whichever one they prefer. ASP.NET will also be easier to manage and deploy. Let's expand on our list of advantages of ASP.NET over ASP that were mentioned at the start of this chapter.

ASP.NET Is Compiled, not Interpreted

Compiled programs run faster than interpreted ones. Thus, ASP.NET, which is compiled, runs faster than classic ASP, which is interpreted. Each page is compiled the first time it is requested, and then the compiled code of the page is kept until that page is changed or the application is restarted. Optionally, files can be precompiled at deployment time, to reduce latency when pages are first accessed.

Separation of Code from Content

ASP.NET will allow true separation of code from presentation, which will allow graphic designers and programmers to work together with less frustration and time spent merging pages' looks with their functionality. This is done through the use of "code behind" pages, which are referenced using a page directive in the header of the page with the presentation code.

No More "DLL Hell"

Users and developers of COM components have come to refer to the problems with COM deployment as "DLL Hell." This means that installing or moving COM components often breaks dependent applications without warning. Otherwise stable applications are frequently broken when a new application updates an existing component. "DLL Hell" exists because the COM protocol requires that components do not change the interfaces they expose, and so any time a component's interface changes, it gets a new identifier that basically makes it a new version of the component. Programs that relied on one version of a component are frequently broken when they try to communicate with a newer version of that component. If you have ever installed a new program on your computer only to find that some of your other programs no longer work afterward, you have experienced "DLL Hell."

With ASP.NET, components don't have to be shared across the server, but can be placed with individual applications. Also, components are kept with the application, and the entire application can be moved using simple file copying. No registry changes or dealing with MTS/COM+ is necessary! This makes it very easy to maintain an ASP.NET application remotely, such as through a Web hosting provider. Of course, components *can* still be shared, but that decision is now left to the developer or administrator.

Side-by-Side Installation

If you're not sure you're ready to migrate your production applications to ASP.NET yet, don't worry. The new services and features can be installed and running in parallel with your existing classic ASP applications (on IIS 4 or 5). In fact, they can share the same folder structure—all that you need do to migrate each file (after you've made it utilize the new features of ASP.NET) is change the file extension from .asp to .aspx (and of course update your links to this file accordingly). You will literally be able to migrate your applications a page at a time.

Real Debugging

ASP.NET features easier debugging than did Classic ASP (which isn't saying much). One simple addition is a trace command that is only compiled into the running code when a compile flag is set. No need to build your own debugging code using if-then and Response.Write. Also, with Visual Studio .NET, you can step through your ASP.NET code, your include files and Web controls, and your .NET components, even if each of these uses a different programming language, without being on the server. It is *real* debugging, just as with any other Visual tool!

Real Programming Languages

Although ASP supports several scripting languages, ASP.NET (and in fact the .NET Framework) will support any language that can be compiled to its intermediate language (IL) format, which at the time of printing includes over 16 different languages, including Ada, APL, COBOL, C#, Eiffel, Haskell, Jscript, ML, Oberon, OZ, Pascal, Perl, Python, Scheme, Smalltalk, VB, and others. Similar to Java (don't tell anyone), ASP.NET languages are compiled to a standard format (the Intermediate Language, or IL) that the .NET architecture then compiles and executes with the Common Language Runtime (CLR). Note that there are quite a few differences between the implementation of .NET and Java, but they are beyond the scope of this book to cover. Microsoft .NET's language independence means that developers can use whatever programming language they feel most comfortable with and won't need to learn a new language to learn ASP.NET.

Real Error Handling

ASP.NET features better error handling, including the ability to send all programming errors to a single error handler page, transferring all of the page's attributes (like Request and other variables) as well. Having a central location to manage errors is a vast improvement over having to check for errors every few lines of VBScript and write a custom error handler for each case.

Further, Visual Basic.NET now supports the Try...Catch structure familiar to Java and JavaScript programmers. Although On Error Resume Next is still supported, it is not recommended and should be replaced with Try...Catch blocks, which offer greater flexibility and better cross language compatibility.

Directory-Based Deployment

Migrating an ASP application from one server to another is a daunting task. FrontPage extensions, COM components, and Web settings are all separate from the actual files in the directory to be moved. With ASP.NET, you can deploy your application, complete with server settings and components, using XCOPY or FTP. This makes backing up a site much easier, and eliminates a lot of the hassle involved with remote Web hosting.

Once, in the days of MS-DOS, programs were as easy to install, move, and uninstall as directories were to copy. Moving the files moved the program. With the advent of Windows and the notorious system registry, this simplicity was lost. Now, with .NET, we can once again install entire applications using nothing more than a file manager or FTP client.

File-Based Application Configuration

Administering the application can be done entirely via XML configuration files—no need for direct access to the server! Again, this makes remote maintenance much easier than with classic ASP. And because the configuration files use a standard XML format, you can expand them to include your own application-specific settings as well, and third-party administration tools can also be written to manage ASP.NET applications by using these files. The current beta of Visual Studio .NET does not offer a graphical means of maintaining these settings, but one is likely to be released in a later version of VS.NET.

Event-Based Programming Model

ASP pages are simple scripts that begin execution at the top of the file and continue line by line down the page until the script has completed. By contrast, ASP.NET pages feature an event-based programming model, which should be familiar to Visual Basic programmers. Page execution can now be viewed as a series of events and event handlers, such as a page loading or a button being clicked. This helps to eliminate much of the "spaghetti code" associated with ASP pages, making code easier to maintain and modify. This programming model also makes it much easier for powerful tools to be written to aid developers.

For example, to add some functionality to a button on a web page using Visual Studio .NET, the process mirrors that of VB6. First, you drag a button onto your page in Design View. Next, you double-click on the button, bringing up its "OnClick" handler. Finally, you add the code you want to execute to this method. Very straightforward, and minimal learning curve for anyone familiar with VB's environment.

Improved, Extensible Object Model

ASP.NET has an improved object model that will allow for improved development tools. Visual Basic Web Forms will provide to ASP.NET developers the drag-and-drop form-based interface familiar to users of Visual Basic. This makes building event-driven pages much simpler.

What's more, the .NET Framework includes an extensive list of classes available to the ASP.NET developer (in any .NET language). These classes cover a wide range of functions not included in any of the ASP 3.0 objects, such as easy browser file uploads, custom image manipulation, and advanced encryption functions. Although this functionality was only available through additional COM components in ASP 3.0, it is all available "out of the box" to the ASP.NET developer.

More Integrated Functions

Built-in form/state management means that you no longer need to explicitly access form variables using the Request object! All of this drudgery is now handled behind the scenes by ASP.NET. Simply adding runat="server" to the form and each form element is the only coding needed.

Form validation functions, which can be done either server-side only, or both client-side and server-side, are built into ASP.NET. ASP.NET ships with many of the commonly required validation functions, and of course allows developers to build their own custom validation controls as well. Support for regular expressions means that very powerful validation functions can be written relatively easily. We will cover validation controls in Chapter 7.

Web Services

ASP.NET includes support for Web services, which allow applications to work together across the Internet by either exposing or consuming (or both) methods and data from other sites. Web services use the standard Simple Object Access Protocol (SOAP) to call methods across the Internet. This technology will allow Application Service Providers to easily expose their services, and will enable developers to easily integrate these services into their applications. Further, because the SOAP standard protocol is used, different applications running on different operating systems in different countries could easily communicate with one another through Web services. We will look more closely at how ASP.NET uses Web services in Chapter 11, "ASP.NET and Web Services."

Performance Improvements

ASP.NET's performance is greatly improved over classic ASP. One major advantage ASP.NET has over Classic ASP is that it is compiled, not interpreted. ASP.NET supports page-level caching, which can be configured on a page-by-page basis. This is one of the biggest scalability features to come out of ASP.NET. In classic ASP, the only way to achieve this was with complicated session and application variable code. In ASP.NET, it's a line of code to tell a page how long its output should be cached before executing again. Consider a catalog page that lists available inventory to order, being hit by fifty users per minute. In classic ASP that would be fifty database hits per minute (at least). With ASP.NET and one line of code, that page could be cached for five minutes (or as little or as long as desired), dropping database load to one hit per five minutes for this page, and greatly improving performance for the other 249 requests made in that time span. Page fragments and objects can also be cached, and caching is just one of several ways in which ASP.NET has enhanced application performance. All told, you can expect ASP.NET's performance to be at least two to three times that of Classic ASP's, with potential for more with the use of caching.

Better Tools

Lastly, ASP.NET features improved developer tools. Visual InterDev is no more. In its place is Visual Studio .NET, now an integrated application that features Web forms, which are built by dragging controls onto the form much like in Visual Basic. Visual Studio .NET also includes support for developing VB.NET, C++, C#, and so forth. There are no longer separate tools for each Microsoft-supported language; VS.NET does it all. It features so many improvements and wizards that we will give an overview of it in Appendix E.

Summary

In this chapter, we've reviewed the history of Active Server Pages from its release as Denali to the most recent version, ASP.NET. The release of the .NET framework is a dramatic shift in programming methodology, and ASP developers will need to relearn Internet application development in order to take advantage of the many enhancements offered by ASP.NET. However, its many advantages make the effort involved in learning it well worth it. We examined a handful of the ways ASP.NET has been improved over classic ASP, and we will see more examples of these benefits in coming chapters.

What's Next

For most of us, whenever Microsoft releases "the next big thing," the big question for us (apart from "How many books do I need to read to learn this?") is "How do I migrate my existing applications to this new technology?" Chapter 3, "Migrating from ASP to ASP.NET," describes how you can get started with ASP.NET, and provides working examples of the most common ASP code functions, translated to ASP.NET.

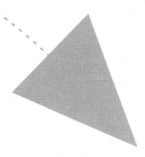

3

Migrating From ASP to ASP.NET

Most of you reading this chapter are wondering at this point how this book is going to help you learn ASP.NET while at the same time assisting you in migrating your existing ASP applications to the new .NET framework. Yes, Microsoft has come out with yet another methodology that requires you to relearn what you have learned and redesign your existing applications (if you want to take advantage of this new architecture's features). In Chapter 2, "An Introduction to ASP.NET," you learned **why** you want to go through all of this pain and trouble; now we're going to go over what's necessary to actually do it. Although the rest of the book is dedicated to new techniques and applications of ASP.NET, this chapter is devoted to helping you make the transition from ASP and COM architected solutions to an ASP.NET and Web services architecture.

In this chapter you will learn

- Where you can get ASP.NET and learn how to install it.

- Some of the basic differences between Classic ASP and ASP.NET.

- How to transform some common ASP tasks into their ASP.NET equivalents.

One of the important benefits of the .NET Framework is language independence. Similar to Java, all .NET languages are compiled into an intermediate language (IL) prior to their use by the Common Language Runtime (CLR) and ultimately the operating system. Although this intermediate language code is constant across platforms, the precompiled code can be in any language. At the time of publication, there is support for more than 20 languages, including Visual Basic, C++, C#, J#, JScript, and COBOL. For the purposes of this book, we will focus on the two languages which we expect will be most popular, C# (pronounced "see sharp") and VB.NET (VB7). C# is a new language that is very similar to C++, and has been under development for several years. In fact, the ASP.NET engine is written in C#, so you can be assured that it has a strong following in Redmond.

NOTE

You can learn more about the languages that can be used to develop .NET applications at:

http://msdn.microsoft.com/net/thirdparty/

Preparing to Use ASP.NET

ASP.NET is available from a variety of sources, including http://www.asp.net/, which is Microsoft ASP.NET's official home page, and on the Visual Studio .NET CDs. You can learn more about system requirements, licensing issues, and installation instructions at that URL. Note that to start using ASP.NET, all you need is the .NET runtime installed on your web server. With that, you can begin building ASP.NET pages using just a text editor.

Before installing the .NET framework on a production system, it is a good idea to back up all mission-critical files and applications. This advice applies to any installation, and of course your production servers should be periodically backed up anyway. Given that you are probably installing the .NET framework on your existing Web server, it's good to know that the .NET engine will not conflict with your existing IIS/ASP applications. You will be able to migrate from ASP to ASP.NET as quickly or gradually as you are comfortable with, down to a file-by-file level.

TIP

For more information about getting set up with ASP.NET, consider the following URLs:

http://msdn.microsoft.com/net/

http://msdn.microsoft.com/vstudio/

http://www.gotdotnet.com

http://msdn.microsoft.com/library/en-us/Dnaspp/html/aspnetmigrissues.asp

---

Basic Differences Between ASP and ASP.NET

Before we build our first ASP.NET page, let's go over some of the basic differences between ASP and ASP.NET, with regard to the file system and organization, and some architectural considerations.

Files

The first thing to note is that the file extension for an ASP.NET page is different from that of a Classic ASP page. Instead of using *.asp*, you use *.aspx* as your file extension. Similarly, in an ASP application you used the *global.asa* file to manage some of the application events, and in an ASP.NET application you will use the *global.asax* file. In addition to the global.asax file, an ASP.NET application also has a web.config file, which is used to set many application-specific configuration settings. Unlike the global.asax, web.config files are inherited by applications in subfolders. In fact, all .NET applications on a given server inherit from a base config file, machine.config, located in the operating system directory.

Table 3.1: Important ASP.NET File Types

Extension	Replaces ASP File	File Description
.asax	.asa	The global.asax file replaces the global.asa file and holds event handlers for the application, session, and page request events. The global.asax file is covered in Chapter 10, "ASP.NET Applications."
.ascx	None	ASP.NET User Controls must have the .ascx extension. User Controls are covered in Chapter 9, Using ASP.NET User Controls.
.asmx	None	ASP.NET Web Services use the .asmx extension. Chapter 11, "ASP.NET and Web Services," covers these files in detail.
.aspx	.asp	The default extension for ASP.NET pages, which take the place of ASP pages.
.config	None	Configuration files store application settings in XML format. The web.config file is the most commonly used configuration file. These files are described in Chapter 10, "ASP.NET Applications."
.cs	None	C# source files typically have the .cs extension.
.js	None	Jscript source files typically have the .js extension.
.vb	None	Visual Basic source files typically have the .vb extension.

Maintaining State Between ASP and ASP.NET

One thing to be aware of as you migrate your files from ASP to ASP.NET is that session state is not shared across the two architectures. That is, while you certainly can migrate to ASP.NET one page at a time, .aspx page and .asp pages cannot share the same session state. If your application relies heavily on session variables, this is something to consider. There are several ways to deal with this problem.

To maintain state between .asp and .aspx files, it is necessary to use an alternative to the built-in session object of either architecture. There are several possibilities, each with advantages and disadvantages, and because sessions have many known scalability issues in Classic ASP, it is likely that many sites will not make heavy use of them, and will not have a difficult time migrating to ASP.NET because of this. Instead of using session variables, you can use cookies, querystrings, or hidden form fields. Each of these techniques allows you to persist user information from page to page. For very small and non-sensitive data, it is sufficient to simply pass the actual data around. However, for more detailed or secure information, you should pass around a unique identifier that ties to a database that holds the actual data. Using any of these methods, you will be able to maintain application state between .asp and .aspx pages.

Language Differences

Another thing you will quickly run into as you convert your .asp pages to .aspx pages is the language difference. VBScript is no longer used; instead VB.NET (VB7) (or another .NET language) is used for ASP.NET development. JScript, although still supported, has undergone a great deal of revision in order to be compliant with .NET. This book will focus primarily on VB.NET and C# for its examples. Listings 3.1, 3.2, and 3.3 show a very simple page that uses code to display *Hello World* to the browser. You can see that there are some important language differences between the current ASP languages and the new ASP.NET languages.

Listing 3.1: Source code for HelloVB.asp.

```
<%@ Language=VBScript %>
<%Option Explicit%>
<html>
<head>
</head>
<body>
<%
Response.Write "Hello World"
%>
</body>
</html>
```

Listing 3.2: Source code for HelloVB.aspx.

```
<%@ Page Language="VB" %>
<html>
<head>
</head>
<body>
<%
Response.Write("Hello World")
%>
```

Listing 3.2: continued

```
</body>
</html>
```

Listing 3.3: Source code for HelloCS.aspx.

```
<%@ Page Language="C#"%>
<html>
<head>
</head>
<body>
<%
Response.Write("Hello World");
%>
</body>
</html>
```

Figure 3.1 is an example of what the output of one of these files would be. Displayed is HelloVB.aspx, but each of the files would produce the exact same output.

Figure 3.1: HelloVB.aspx.

NOTE

You can see these and every other example in this book by going to:

```
http://www.aspauthors.com/aspnetbyexample/ch03/
```

As you can see, there are some subtle differences in syntax between VBScript and VB.NET. We will see as we move on through the book that C# has its own unique syntax as well, which is very close to C/C++, JScript, or Java. However, because all languages in ASP.NET rely on the same .NET Framework of objects, the code for any given function often looks very similar regardless of the language in which it was written.

For a quick reference to the VB.NET language, refer to Appendix C. A similar reference to C# is found in Appendix D. For now, just remember one key difference between VB and VBScript, which is that methods now require parentheses, and will not compile without them. We'll see more differences as we continue, and answer some questions you may have about the new C# language.

Common ASP Tasks and Their ASP.NET Equivalents

To help ease your transition from Classic ASP to ASP.NET, let's take a look at some of the more common ASP applications and see how they would be done using ASP.NET. This section examines examples such as how to do a very simple user login screen, how to make a form post back to itself and persist its values, and how to display the contents of a recordset in a table. You will also look at a way to use Classic ASP page template `include` files in ASP.NET pages by using user controls.

Read a Form

One of the most common tasks performed by an ASP page is reading and working with output from HTML forms, using the `Request` object. In keeping with the theme of this chapter, we'll take a look at a very simple ASP page that takes form input and outputs it to the screen. We'll also demonstrate how to maintain state of form elements. Then we'll demonstrate how to do the same thing using ASP.NET, both in VB and C#. These simple examples will help prepare us for more advanced scenarios in this chapter and the rest of the book.

First, let's look at the ASP version of a form that collects some very simple information from the user, and when the Save button is clicked, returns a simple message and retains all of their selections in the form. This example makes use of textboxes, checkboxes, and select listboxes, and is shown in Figure 3.2.

For an ASP page to parse this form, it must do several things. First, it needs to determine whether or not the form has been submitted or not, so that it knows whether to display the special message. Second, it must assign the request variables to local variables to ensure optimum performance. Finally, it must use these local variables in displaying the form itself, in order to persist the values selected previously. All of this means that there is ASP code interspersed throughout our final product, as shown in Listing 3.4.

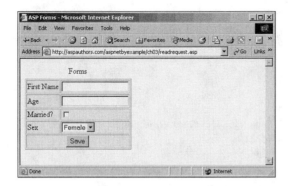

Figure 3.2: *Our sample HTML form.*

Listing 3.4: Source code for readrequest.asp.

```asp
<%Option Explicit%>
<%
Dim first_name
Dim age
Dim married_check
Dim married
Dim sex
Dim strOutput
Dim fSubmit

first_name  = Request.Form("first_name")
age = Request.Form("age")
married = Request.Form("married")
sex = Request.Form("sex")
If married <> "" Then
    married_check="checked"
    married = "married"
Else
    married_check = ""
    married = "single"
End If

'Check postback
fSubmit = Request("btnSubmit") = "Save"

If fSubmit Then
    strOutput = "Hello, " & first_name & ".  You are a " & age & " year old, "
 & married & " " & sex & "."
End If

%>
<!DOCTYPE HTML PUBLIC "-//W3C//DTD HTML 4.0 Transitional//EN"
```

Listing 3.4: continued

```
               "http://www.w3.org/TR/REC-html40/loose.dtd">
<html>
<head>
<title>ASP Forms</title>
</head>
<body>
<form action="<%=Request.Servervariables("URL")%>" method="post"
id="form1" name="form1">
<table border="1" bgcolor="#EEEEEE">
    <caption>Forms</caption>
    <tr>
        <td>First Name</td>
        <td><input type="text" name="first_name" value="<%=first_name%>"></td>
    </tr>
    <tr>
        <td>Age</td>
        <td><input type="text" name="age" value="<%=age%>"></td>
    </tr>
    <tr>
        <td>Married?</td>
        <td><input type="checkbox" name="married" <%=married_check%>></td>
    </tr>
    <tr>
        <td>Sex</td>
        <td><select name="sex">
            <% If sex="male" Then %>
                <option value="female">Female</option>
                <option selected value="male">Male</option>
            <% Else %>
                <option selected value="female">Female</option>
                <option value="male">Male</option>
            <% End If %>
            </select>
        </td>
    </tr>
    <tr>
        <td colspan="2" align="center">
            <input type="submit" name="btnSubmit" value="Save">
        </td>
    </tr>
</table>
</form>
<%=strOutput%>
</body>
</html>
```

There are, of course, many different techniques to do what this ASP page is doing. However, ASP is not the topic of this book, so we won't go into detail about other methods of persisting form values or why we chose the methods we did. Suffice to say that the preceding page works as expected.

Thankfully, in ASP.NET, we can separate out the form's presentation code from the programming code of the page. ASP.NET takes care of maintaining the state of the form elements for us as long as we declare our controls using `runat="server"`. As you will see, ASP.NET offers two different sets of controls for describing form elements: HTML controls and Web controls. The names are very similar, so it is easy to get these confused. HTML controls look just like standard HTML, but with the attribute of `runat="server"` added to them. For example, the following is an HTML control:

```
<input type="text" id="first_name" runat="server">
```

Web controls also require the use of `runat="server"`, but are an entirely new syntax from anything available in ASP prior to ASP.NET. These controls use a *tagprefix* of `asp`, followed by the name of the control. Tagprefixes provide a way to uniquely identify controls that might otherwise have the same name. In this case, our control name is TextBox, and our complete Web Control tag would look like this:

```
<asp:TextBox id="first_name" runat="server" />
```

The actual HTML output by both of these controls is nearly identical. The first outputs this HTML:

```
<input name="first_name" id="first_name" type="text" />
```

And the second produces this output:

```
<input name="first_name" type="text" id="first_name" />
```

And why, you may ask, are there two different ways to do the same thing? Well, the former method uses code that "looks" more like plain HTML. This makes it a good choice if you are working with a GUI HTML editor or with separate programmers and HTML designers. The second method allows for more programmatic control, and has more of a VB "feel" to its usage. The choice of which to use is largely a matter of taste; for the examples in this chapter we will use Web controls. Chapter 5, "HTML/ Web Controls," covers this topic in detail.

You will note that in the ASP.NET version of readrequest.asp, there is no programming code within the HTML section of the page. In fact, a powerful method of coding ASP.NET pages is through the use of a codebehind page, in which all of the programming code is kept in a separate file entirely, completely separating HTML layout and presentation logic from programming code. For clarity, we are presenting these examples as single files, but in later chapters some examples will use the codebehind style. Whether or not you choose to use codebehind pages is largely a question of style.

Neither one performs better than the other. If you are using Visual Studio. NET, however, the default method is to use codebehind files, and some of the features, like code completion, are not available for single-page ASP. NET pages. Listing 3.5 displays readrequestVB.aspx, the VB version of our ASP.NET page.

Listing 3.5: Source code for readrequestVB.aspx.

```
<%@ Page Language="VB" Trace="False" %>
<script runat="server">
Sub Page_Load(Src As Object, E As EventArgs)
    Dim strMarried As String
    If Not Page.IsPostBack Then
        'Build listbox -- this could be stored in a user control
        sex.Items.Add("Female")
        sex.Items.Add("Male")
    Else
        If married.Checked Then
            strMarried = "married"
        Else
            strMarried = "single"
        End If
        output.Text = "Hello, " & first_name.Text & ".  You are a " & age.Text
 & " year old, " & strMarried & " " & sex.SelectedItem.Text & "."
    End If
End Sub
</script>
<!DOCTYPE HTML PUBLIC "-//W3C//DTD HTML 4.0 Transitional//EN"
            "http://www.w3.org/TR/REC-html40/loose.dtd">
<html>
<head>
<title>ASP Forms</title>
</head>
<body>
<form runat="server" id="form1">
<table border="1" bgcolor="#EEEEEE">
    <caption>Forms</caption>
    <tr>
        <td>First Name</td>
        <td><asp:Textbox runat="server" id="first_name" />
        </td>
    </tr>
    <tr>
        <td>Age</td>
        <td><asp:Textbox runat="server" id="age" /></td>
    </tr>
    <tr>
```

Listing 3.5: continued

```
        <td>Married?</td>
        <td>
        <asp:CheckBox runat="server" id="married" />
        </td>
    </tr>
    <tr>
        <td>Sex</td>
        <td><asp:DropDownList runat="server" id="sex" /></td>
    </tr>
    <tr>
        <td colspan="2" align="center">
            <asp:Button runat="server" Text="Save" />
        </td>
    </tr>
</table>
</form>
<asp:Label runat="server" id="output" />
</body>
</html>
```

As you can see, our programming code in this page is limited to the Page_
Load method, which is the first method called on any ASP.NET page whenever it is loaded. Here, we check to see if the form was submitted by checking the Boolean property of the Page object, IsPostBack. If the page was not
submitted (that is, this is the first time it is being viewed), we use this
opportunity to build our list box for the Sex DropDownList. In a more complicated form, you might read a list of possible values from a database in
this portion of your code. If the form has been submitted (IsPostBack is
True), we simply set the value of the strMarried variable to an appropriate
string depending on whether or not the Married checkbox was selected, and
display our message as the value of the asp:Label control, output.

Because ASP.NET builds upon a common framework, the code segments
involved in different programming languages typically bear a strong resemblance to one another. For instance, Listing 3.6 lists the C# version of the
Page_Load method (the rest of the file remains the same).

Listing 3.6: Source code for readrequestCS.aspx.

```
<%@ Page Language="C#" Trace="False" %>
<script runat="server">
void Page_Load(Object Src, EventArgs E){
    String strMarried;
    if (!Page.IsPostBack){
        //Build listbox -- this could be stored in a user control
        sex.Items.Add("Female");
        sex.Items.Add("Male");
    } else {
        if (married.Checked)
```

Listing 3.6: continued

```
            strMarried = "married";
        else
            strMarried = "single";
        output.Text = "Hello, " + first_name.Text + ".  You are a " + age.Text
 + " year old, " + strMarried + " " + sex.SelectedItem.Text + ".";
    }
}
</script>
```

Line by line, this code is identical to the VB version except for minor syntactical variations. If you are a VB or VBScript programmer, you will find that C# is really not that difficult to pick up for this reason, especially if you have any C/C++/Java experience. All of the examples in this book are available in both VB and C#, although to make the most of the available space, only one or the other will be presented. In such cases, the other example will typically be available on the book's supporting Web site.

TIP

You can view this book's examples LIVE at

http://aspauthors.com/aspnetbyexample/

Validate a Form's Entries

Form validation is an important, but often neglected, part of many classic ASP applications. Typical ASP applications involve a mixture of client-side and server-side form validation techniques, and unfortunately this often results in poor validation. Also, because of the added complexity of using both client-side and server-side scripting, many developers simply don't bother with validation at all, resulting in a less satisfying user experience and frequently less data integrity. ASP.NET provides an entire suite of validation controls, which will be covered in detail in Chapter 8, "Using ASP.NET Validation Controls." Here we will demonstrate some simple form validation techniques, using classic ASP with client-side JavaScript, and ASP.NET. This example is not meant to give complete coverage to ASP.NET's validation controls; we'll only be looking at a few simple cases and building on the previous section's forms.

Our previous form included a few textboxes, a drop-down list, and a checkbox. It didn't have any validation code at all. First of all, we will update that example so that it uses client and server-side code to validate the following rules:

- First Name must be non-blank
- Age must be non-blank

- Age must be numeric and above zero

- Sex must be selected (we will make the default blank)

The client-side code required to accomplish these tasks takes the form of a `validate()` JavaScript method that is called whenever the user attempts to submit the form. This method uses a number of functions from a library I have developed over the years, the contents of which are beyond the scope of this book but which are available from the book's Web site. Their function should be fairly obvious from their usage in the `validate()` method. You can download the JavaScript file "script.js" at the book's Web site.

Note that you will never encounter the server-side validation if you are using a browser that supports JavaScript for client-side validation, because the client-side script will ensure that no bad data is ever passed to the server. However, it is good practice to always validate data server-side regardless of any client-side script, because some browsers do not support JavaScript, and because it is possible for a user to "spoof" your server by saving your form on their local machine, removing the validation code from it, and then submitting it to your server. For this reason, ASP.NET always does server-side validation when we use its validation controls, and only uses client-side validation with browsers that support it.

Listing 3.7 shows the new classic ASP page, readvalidrequest.asp, that incorporates the validation rules we have established.

Listing 3.7: Source code for readvalidrequest.asp.

```
<%Option Explicit%>
<%
Dim first_name
Dim age
Dim married_check
Dim married
Dim sex
Dim strOutput
Dim strError
Dim fSubmit

first_name    = Request.Form("first_name")
age        = Request.Form("age")
married        = Request.Form("married")
sex        = Request.Form("sex")
If married <> "" Then
    married_check="checked"
    married = "married"
Else
    married_check = ""
    married = "single"
```

Listing 3.7: continued

```
End If

'Check postback
fSubmit = Request("btnSubmit") = "Save"

If fSubmit Then
    If first_name = "" Then
        strError = strError & "You must enter a value for first name.<br>"
    End If
    If age = "" Then
        strError = strError & "You must enter a value for age.<br>"
    ElseIf Not isNumeric(age) Then
        strError = strError & _
"You must enter a positive numeric value for age.<br>"
    ElseIf age <= 0 Then
        strError = strError & _
"You must enter a positive numeric value for age.<br>"
    End If
    If sex = "" Then
        strError = strError & "You must select a value for sex.<br>"
    End If
    'Only show output if no errors
    If strError = "" Then
        strOutput = "Hello, " & first_name & ".  You are a " & age & " year
old, " & married & " " & sex & "."
    End If
End If

%>
<!DOCTYPE HTML PUBLIC "-//W3C//DTD HTML 4.0 Transitional//EN"
            "http://www.w3.org/TR/REC-html40/loose.dtd">
<html>
<head>
<title>ASP Forms</title>
<script type="text/javascript" src="script.js">
<!--
// displays only if script file not found
document.write ("JavaScript library not found.");
//-->
</script>
<script TYPE="text/javascript">
<!--
function validate(){
    with (document.form1){
        if (isBlank(first_name,"You must enter a value for first name.")){
            return false;
```

Listing 3.7: continued

```
        }
        if (isBlank(age,"You must enter a value for age.")){
            return false;
        }
    if (!isInteger(age.value,"You must enter a positive numeric value for
age.")){
            age.focus();
            return false;
        }
        if (!isSelected(sex,"You must select a value for sex.")){
            return false;
        }
    }
    return true;
}
//-->
</script>
</head>
<body>
<form action="<%=Request.Servervariables("URL")%>" method="post" id="form1"
    name="form1" onSubmit="return validate();">
<b><%=strError%></b>
<table border="1" bgcolor="#EEEEEE">
    <caption>Forms</caption>
    <tr>
        <td>First Name</td>
        <td><input type="text" name="first_name" value="<%=first_name%>"></td>
    </tr>
    <tr>
        <td>Age</td>
        <td><input type="text" name="age" value="<%=age%>"></td>
    </tr>
    <tr>
        <td>Married?</td>
        <td><input type="checkbox" name="married" <%=married_check%>></td>
    </tr>
    <tr>
        <td>Sex</td>
        <td><select name="sex">
                <option value="">
            <% If sex="male" Then %>
                <option value="female">Female</option>
                <option selected value="male">Male</option>
            <% ElseIf sex="female" Then %>
                <option selected value="female">Female</option>
                <option value="male">Male</option>
            <% Else %>
```

Listing 3.7: continued

```
                <option value="female">Female</option>
                <option value="male">Male</option>
            <% End If %>
            </select>
        </td>
    </tr>
    <tr>
        <td colspan="2" align="center">
            <input type="submit" name="btnSubmit" value="Save">
        </td>
    </tr>
</table>
</form>
<%=strOutput%>
</body>
</html>
```

Let's take a quick look at the validation we are doing in this code. We will just focus on the ASP server-side validation, because client-side JavaScript is beyond the scope of this book (and, you'll see in a moment, no longer required knowledge for client-side form validation because ASP.NET takes care of this for us). Our validation code is only done on a form submit, as demonstrated by the code snippet shown in Listing 3.8.

Listing 3.8: Source code for readvalidrequest.asp.

```
If fSubmit Then
    If first_name = "" Then
        strError = strError & "You must enter a value for first name.<br>"
    End If
    If age = "" Then
        strError = strError & "You must enter a value for age.<br>"
    ElseIf Not isNumeric(age) Then
        strError = strError & _
"You must enter a positive numeric value for age.<br>"
    ElseIf age <= 0 Then
        strError = strError & _
"You must enter a positive numeric value for age.<br>"
    End If
    If sex = "" Then
        strError = strError & "You must select a value for sex.<br>"
    End If
    'Only show output if no errors
    If strError = "" Then
        strOutput = "Hello, " & first_name & ".  You are a " & age & " year
old, " & married & " " & sex & "."
    End If
End If
```

As you can see, we check first_name, age, and sex to see if they are blank (""), and build an error string if they are. We also verify that age is numeric and positive, again setting appropriate error messages if we find its value to be invalid. Finally, we only output our message if there were no errors. In a more complex example, we might use this technique to limit database updates to valid values. On our HTML page, then, we display the error message as bold text, which remains unseen if no errors were encountered.

Now let's take a look at this same page in ASP.NET, using the built-in validation controls (which you will see in more detail in Chapter 8, "Using ASP.NET Validation Controls"). Listing 3.9 shows readvalidrequestVB.aspx, which uses three validation controls, the RequiredFieldValidator, RangeValidator, and ValidationSummary controls.

Listing 3.9: Source code for readvalidrequestVB.aspx.

```
<%@ Page Language="VB" Trace="False" %>
<script runat="server">
Sub Page_Load(Src As Object, E As EventArgs)
    Dim strMarried As String
    If Not Page.IsPostBack Then
        'Build listbox -- this could be stored in a user control
        sex.Items.Add("")
        sex.Items.Add("Female")
        sex.Items.Add("Male")
    Else
        If married.Checked Then
            strMarried = "married"
        Else
            strMarried = "single"
        End If
        output.Text = "Hello, " & first_name.Text & ".  You are a " & age.Text
 & " year old, " & strMarried & " " & sex.SelectedItem.Text & "."
    End If
End Sub
</script>
<!DOCTYPE HTML PUBLIC "-//W3C//DTD HTML 4.0 Transitional//EN"
            "http://www.w3.org/TR/REC-html40/loose.dtd">
<html>
<head>
<title>ASP Forms</title>
</head>
<body>
<form runat="server" id="form1">
<asp:ValidationSummary id="validSummary" runat="server"
    headerText="***Errors On Your Form***"
```

Listing 3.9: continued

```
    showSummary="True"
    displayMode="List" />
<table border="1" bgcolor="#EEEEEE">
    <caption>Forms</caption>
    <tr>
        <td>First Name</td>
        <td><asp:Textbox runat="server" id="first_name" />
            <asp:RequiredFieldValidator id="required_first_name" runat="server"
            controlToValidate="first_name"
            errorMessage="You must enter a value for first name."
            display="none" />
        </td>
    </tr>
    <tr>
        <td>Age</td>
        <td><asp:Textbox runat="server" id="age" />
            <asp:RequiredFieldValidator id="required_age" runat="server"
            controlToValidate="age"
            errorMessage="You must enter a value for age."
            display="none" />
            <asp:RangeValidator id="required_age_range" runat="server"
            controlToValidate="age"
            type="Integer"
            minimumValue="1"
            maximumValue="150"
            errorMessage="You must enter a positive number value for age."
            display="none" />
        </td>
    </tr>
    <tr>
        <td>Married?</td>
        <td>
        <asp:CheckBox runat="server" id="married" />
        </td>
    </tr>
    <tr>
        <td>Sex</td>
        <td><asp:DropDownList runat="server" id="sex" />
            <asp:RequiredFieldValidator id="required_sex" runat="server"
            controlToValidate="sex"
            errorMessage="You must select a value for sex."
            display="none" />
        </td>
    </tr>
    <tr>
```

Listing 3.9: continued

```
        <td colspan="2" align="center">
            <asp:Button runat="server" Text="Save" />
        </td>
    </tr>
</table>
</form>
<asp:Label runat="server" id="output" />
</body>
</html>
```

You can see that there is no difference in our VB code for this page versus readrequestVB.asp, except that we have added a blank entry to our Sex DropDownList in the Page_Load (because not much has changed, the C# code will not be displayed, but is available on the book's support Web site, at http://aspauthors.com/aspnetbyexample/). The real differences are in the HTML code, with the addition of a few more controls.

The first control we encounter as we move down the page is the ValidationSummary control. This control is used to display summarized results of validation, and mirrors the way in which our ASP page's server-side validation was displayed:

```
<asp:ValidationSummary id="validSummary" runat="server"
headerText="***Errors On Your Form***"
showSummary="True"
displayMode="List" />
```

This control is fairly intuitive to use. HeaderText is displayed as the header for the error listing. Setting showSummary to True ensures that it is displayed if errors are found. By default errors are listed in a bulleted list, but in this example we are listing them separated by <br> tags instead by using the displayMode of "List".

The next control we use is the RequiredFieldValidator:

```
<asp:RequiredFieldValidator id="required_first_name" runat="server"
controlToValidate="first_name"
errorMessage="You must enter a value for first name."
display="none" />
```

This is a very simple control, which merely ensures that the user enters something into a form field. The display property is used to determine how the control is displayed on the screen. In our case, because we are using the ValidationSummary control for display, our individual validation controls will all use a display of none.

Finally, to ensure that the age entered is a positive number, we use a RangeValidator:

```
        <asp:RangeValidator id="required_age_range" runat="server"
        controlToValidate="age"
```

```
            type="Integer"
            minimumValue="1"
            maximumValue="150"
            errorMessage="You must enter a positive number value for age."
            display="none" />
```

This requires three new properties to be set; `type`, `minimumValue`, and `maximumValue`. It ensures that the linked control (in our case, age) falls within the range specified by `minimumValue` and `maximumValue`, using the comparison technique listed in the `type` parameter. Note that it is not sufficient to provide only a `minimumValue` or a `maximumValue` for this control, so in enforcing our rule of positive numbers for age, we were forced to specify an upper limit as well. If I had really wanted to only specify a lower limit, I could have used a custom validation control for that purpose.

The Login Page

One of the more common features of interactive Web sites today is the login screen. Often this form will reside in the corner of a site's main page, or will appear whenever a secure page is requested and the user has not authenticated. The simplest way to restrict access to certain pages in Classic ASP is to use a login `include` file, and simply include the file on those pages that require authentication.

For this first example, we have two Classic ASP pages, a page that requires users to register before viewing it (secret.asp), and a login page that is implemented using an `include` file (login_simple.asp). This example happens to use cookies, but you could use any of the state management techniques discussed earlier just as easily. Remember, though, that if you use session variables, you won't be able to transfer state between ASP and ASP.NET pages.

NOTE

You can run these examples live on this book's support Web site, at

`http://aspauthors.com/aspnetbyexample/ch03/`

The source code for secret.asp shows this very simple page, the most important part of which is the second line, where it includes the login code (see Listing 3.10).

Listing 3.10: Source code for secret.asp.

```
<% OPTION EXPLICIT %>
<!-- #INCLUDE FILE="login_simple.asp" -->
<!DOCTYPE HTML PUBLIC "-//W3C//DTD HTML 4.0 Transitional//EN"
"http://www.w3.org/TR/REC-html40/loose.dtd">
<html>
```

Listing 3.10: continued

```
<head>
<title>Login Test</title>
</head>
<body>
<b>Top Secret Page</b><br>
<%=Request.Cookies("Username")%> Logged In!
</body>
</html>
```

As you can see, the page we want to protect simply uses an include statement to add the login functionality to the page. Because it uses an in-memory cookie, which lasts until the user's browser is closed, the login is only required the first time the user accesses this or any other protected page on this site.

The login include file, login_simple.asp, is really fairly simple, but because it contains three separate HTML pages within it, it is fairly long. Don't let that intimidate you; there are less than 30 actual lines of code! Listing 3.11 shows the complete file.

Listing 3.11: Source code for login_simple.asp.

```
<%

If Request.Cookies("ASPLogin") <> "True" Then
    Call Login()
End If

Sub Login ()
    Dim cmd
    Dim sql
    Dim connstring
    Dim fValidLogin

    fValidLogin = False
    connstring = "DSN=myDSN;UID=user;pwd=pass"

    If Request.Form("btnSubmit") <> "Submit Authorization" Then
    'Show login form
%>
<html>
<head>
<title>Login</title>
</head>

<body bgcolor="#FFFFFF" link="#010187" vlink="#010187" alink="#010187"
onLoad="document.Form1.frmUserID.focus();">
<center>
```

Listing 3.11: continued

```
(Note: You can test this form by using "user1" as the username and password)
<table border="2" cellpadding="6" width="80%">
<form action="<% = Request.ServerVariables("URL")%>?<%=Request.ServerVariables
 ("QUERY_STRING")%>" method="POST" Name="Form1">
<input type="hidden" name="frmLogin" value="true">
    <tr>
        <td align="right"><font size="2"
        face="Tahoma">User ID:</font></td>
        <td><input type="text" size="20"
        name="frmUserID" maxlength="10"></td>
    </tr>
    <tr>
        <td align="right"><font size="2"
        face="Tahoma">Password:</font></td>
        <td><input type="password"
        size="20" name="frmUserPass"></td>
    </tr>
    <tr>
        <td> </td>
        <td><input type="submit" name="btnSubmit"
        value="Submit Authorization"></td>
    </tr>
</form>
</table>
</center>
</body>
</html>
<%
        Response.End
    Else
        Set cmd = Server.CreateObject("ADODB.Command")
        With cmd
            .ActiveConnection = connstring
            .CommandText = "sp_AuthenticateUser"
            .CommandType = adCmdStoredProc
            'Add Parameters
            .Parameters.Append .CreateParameter("@UserID", adVarChar,
adParamInput, 20, Request.Form("frmUserID"))
            .Parameters.Append .CreateParameter("@Password", adVarChar,
adParamInput, 20, Request.Form("frmUserPass"))
            'Add Output Parameter
            .Parameters.Append .CreateParameter("@IsValid, adTinyInt,
adParamOutput, , 0)

            'Execute the function
            .Execute , , adExecuteNoRecords
```

Listing 3.11: continued

```
                If IsNull(.Parameters("@IsValid).Value) Then
                    fValidLogin = False
                Else
                    fValidLogin = CInt(.Parameters("@IsValid).Value) = 1
                End If
        End With
        Set cmd = Nothing
        If fValidLogin Then
            'Set Cookie
            Response.Cookies("ASPLogin") = "True"
            Response.Cookies("Username") = Request.Form("frmUserID")
        Else
        'Show Invalid Login screen.
%>
<html>
<head>
    <title>Login Failure</title>
</head>
<body bgcolor="#FFFFFF" link="#010187" vlink="#010187"
alink="#010187">
<center>
    <table border="2" cellpadding="6" width="80%">
        <tr>
            <td><center>
            <font size="2" face="Tahoma">UserID <%=request.form("frmUserID")%>
 and the password you provided
                is not a valid user/password combination. <br>
            <a href="<% = Request.ServerVariables("URL")%>"> Click here to
retry...</center></td>
        </tr>
    </table>
</center>
</body>
</html>
<%
            Response.End
        End If 'Check user exists
    End If
End Sub
%>
```

Now when you try to access secret.asp, you will first be presented with a simple login form (Figure 3.3). When you enter a valid username and password, though, you are authorized to see the actual page, which now knows who you are based on your login. The login include file calls a stored procedure, sp_AuthenticateUser, which checks the username and password against a database and returns an output parameter, @is_valid, which is either 1 if the user is valid or 0 otherwise. This stored procedure is shown in Listing 3.12.

Listing 3.12: Source code for sp_AuthenticateUser.

```
CREATE PROCEDURE dbo.sp_AuthenticateUser
  @UserID   varchar(20),
  @Password varchar(20) ,
  @IsValid int output
AS
   BEGIN
       if (select count(*) from aspuser
           where username= @UserID and password = @Password ) = 1
           set @IsValid = 1
       else
           set @IsValid = 0
       return
   END
```

The final result is a simple login page that prevents unauthorized users from seeing our secret page. Figure 3.3 demonstrates the login form and the secret page that is displayed when a valid login is provided.

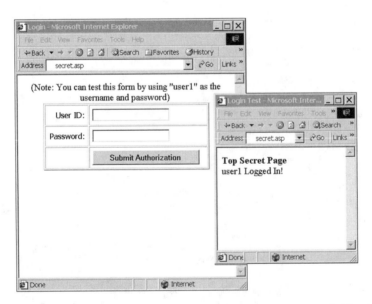

Figure 3.3: *Login screen and secret.asp after successful login.*

Now let's see how we would do this in ASP.NET. Although you can still use include files in ASP.NET, we're going to use a User control, which works much better than an ASP include file for several reasons. User controls can accept parameters, can be dynamically chosen at runtime, use their own variable scope, and can access any page-level variables. In effect, they have all of the advantages ASP includes with none of the disadvantages (like no runtime access and duplicate declarations if you include them twice).

Let's take a look at our secret page again, this time written in ASP.NET (secret.aspx, see Listing 3.13), and our login user control (login.ascx, see Listing 3.14). In this case, we have added a little more code to the .aspx page than we did to our .asp page, in order to control whether or not the .aspx page displays. By default, User controls are displayed along with the rest of the page, and because ASP.NET is event-driven, not interpreted top to bottom like an ASP page, it is more difficult to simply stop execution after the login form. So we use some code in the page load event to determine whether or not to display the login or the main page contents. This is not ideal, and we will look at another way to handle logins in ASP.NET next.

Listing 3.13: Source code for secret.aspx.

```
<%@ Page Language="C#" Debug="true" Trace="False" %>
<%@ Register TagPrefix="LoginModule" TagName="LoginModule" Src="login.ascx" %>
<script language="C#" runat=server>

protected void Page_Load(Object sender, EventArgs E) {
    // Get username to display
    if (Request.Cookies["UserName"] == null){
        display2.Text  = string.Empty;
        Login.Visible = true;
        main.Visible = false;
    } else {
        display2.Text = Request.Cookies["AspxUserName"].Value;
    }
}
</script>
<!DOCTYPE HTML PUBLIC "-//W3C//DTD HTML 4.0 Transitional//EN"
"http://www.w3.org/TR/REC-html40/loose.dtd">
<html>
<head>
<title>Login Test</title>
</head>
<body>
<form id="form1" runat="server">
<asp:Panel id="Login" MaintainState="true" visible="false"
    runat="server">
    <LoginModule:LoginModule runat="server"/>
</asp:Panel>
<span id="main" runat="server">
```

Listing 3.13: continued

```
<b>Top Secret Page</b><br>
<asp:Label id="display" runat="server" />
<asp:Label id="display2" runat="server" />  Logged In!
</span>
</form>
</body>
</html>
```

Listing 3.14: Source code for login.ascx.

```csharp
<%@ Import Namespace="System.Data.SqlClient" %>
<%@ Import Namespace="System.Data" %>

<script language="C#" runat=server>

    public String RedirectPage ="default.aspx";

    bool Authenticate(String user, String pass) {
            bool authenticated = false;
            try {
                        SqlConnection myConnection = new
            SqlConnection(ConfigurationSettings.AppSettings["connectionString"]);
                        SqlCommand myCommand = new SqlCommand
    ("sp_AuthenticateUser", myConnection);
                        myCommand.CommandType = CommandType.StoredProcedure ;

                    // Add Parameters
                    SqlParameter myUserId = new SqlParameter("@UserId",
    SqlDbType.VarChar, 20);
                    myUserId.Value =  user.Trim();
                    myCommand.Parameters.Add(myUserId);


                    SqlParameter myPassword = new
    SqlParameter("@Password",SqlDbType.VarChar, 15);
                    myPassword.Value = pass.Trim();
                    myCommand.Parameters.Add(myPassword);


                    SqlParameter IsValid = new
    SqlParameter("@IsValid",SqlDbType.Int);
                    IsValid.Direction = ParameterDirection.Output;
                    myCommand.Parameters.Add(IsValid);

                    // Execute the Query
                    myConnection.Open();
                    myCommand.ExecuteNonQuery();
                    myConnection.Close();
```

Listing 3.13: continued

```
                        if ( ((int)IsValid.Value) == 1)
                            authenticated =true;

                }
                catch(Exception e) {
                        Response.Write("Auth Exception: " + e.ToString());
                }

                return authenticated;
        }


    private void SubmitBtn_Click(Object sender, EventArgs e) {
        if (Authenticate(UserName.Text, Password.Value)) {
                        System.Web.Security.FormsAuthentication.SetAuthCookie
                        ➥(UserName.Text, true);
                        Response.Cookies["AspxUserName"].Value = UserName.Text;
                        Response.Redirect("secret.aspx");
        }

        else {
            ErrorMsg.Visible = true;
            //Response.Redirect(RedirectPage);
        }
    }

</script>
<!--BEGIN LOGIN MODULE-->
<table border="2" cellpadding="6" width="80%">
<input type="hidden" name="frmLogin" value="true">
    <tr>
        <td align="right"><font size="2"
        face="Tahoma">User ID:</font></td>
        <td><asp:textbox id="UserName" size="14" runat="server" /></td>
    </tr>
    <tr>
        <td align="right"><font size="2"
        face="Tahoma">Password:</font></td>
        <td><input id="Password" type="password" size="14" runat="server"></td>
    </tr>
    <tr>
        <td> </td>
        <td><input type="submit"  value="     Sign In     "
➥ onServerClick="SubmitBtn_Click" runat=server /></td>
    </tr>
    <tr>
        <td colspan=2 align=center>
            <span id="ErrorMsg" style="color:black;font:8pt verdana, arial"
```

Listing 3.14: continued
```
➥ Visible=false runat=server>
              <b>Invalid Account Name or Password!</b>
          </span>
       </td>
    </tr>
</table>
<!--END LOGIN MODULE-->
```

The login.ascx file uses the same `sp_AuthenticateUser` stored procedure as the login_simple.asp `include` file, and sets a cookie if the user is valid. The secret.aspx file then checks to see if this cookie has been provided, and displays the secret contents if it has. The login.ascx file also accepts a parameter, `RedirectPage`, which sets the location to redirect users to if their login fails.

Although the function of this ASP.NET login page is very similar to the ASP one, its implementation is not nearly as elegant. With the ASP `include` file, all that was required was to add one line to a page, the `include` statement, to protect it. With our ASP.NET solution, we need to add quite a bit more code to each page we want to protect. There has to be a better way!

In ASP.NET, the preferred way to configure security is through the web.config configuration file. In this file, you can specify all pages in the application that require a user login, specify how authentication is to be performed, and where to direct users who need authenticated. This makes it very easy to control access to your entire application through a single interface, instead of having to open many individual pages to make them require authentication. Using this technique, along with other application-level configuration settings, is covered in Chapter 10, "ASP.NET Applications."

View Results of Database Query

The last example we are going to look at in this chapter is how to view the results of a database query. Once more, we'll examine a simple ASP page that accomplishes this task, and then we will look at an ASP.NET page that does the same thing, using both VB and C#. For this example, we are going to produce a table that lists country names and their abbreviations. The source of the data is a table in a SQL server database, t_country, which has country_name and abbreviation columns.

Listing 3.15 shows countries.asp, a simple Web page that displays the results of a query against the t_country table.

Listing 3.15: Source code for countries.asp.

```
<%Option Explicit%>
<%
Dim strSql
Dim objRs
Dim objConn
Dim I

Set objRs = Server.CreateObject("ADODB.Recordset")
Set objConn = Server.CreateObject("ADODB.Connection")

%>
<!DOCTYPE HTML PUBLIC "-//W3C//DTD HTML 4.0 Transitional//EN"
            "http://www.w3.org/TR/REC-html40/loose.dtd">
<html>
<head>
<title>Countries</title>
</head>
<body>
<table cellspacing="0" cellpadding="1" rules="all" bordercolor="Black"
border="1" style="background-color:#EEEEEE;border-color:Black;font-family:
Verdana;font-size:8pt;width:700px;border-collapse:collapse;">
<%
strSql = "SELECT country_name as 'Country Name', abbreviation as 'Abbreviation' " & _
        " FROM t_country ORDER BY country_name"
objConn.Open Application("aspauthors_ConnectionString")
objRs.Open strSql, objConn
If Not objRs.EOF Then
    'Header
    Response.Write "<tr bgcolor=""#CCCCCC"">"
    For I = 0 To objRs.Fields.Count - 1
        Response.Write "<th>" & objRs.Fields(I).Name & "</th>"
    Next
    Response.Write "</tr>"
End If
While Not objRs.EOF
    Response.Write "<tr>"
    For I = 0 To objRs.Fields.Count - 1
        Response.Write "<td>" & objRs.Fields(I).Value & "</td>"
    Next
    Response.Write "</tr>"
    objRs.MoveNext
End
```

Listing 3.15: continued

```
objRs.Close
objConn.Close
Set objRs = Nothing
Set objConn = Nothing
%>
</table>
</body>
</html>
```

This is pretty basic ASP code. For this example, I chose to use a For loop to iterate through the different fields in order to display the header values and data. In this way, I could reuse all of the code used to output the table rows regardless of the query used to generate the ouput. The results of this query are displayed in Figure 3.4.

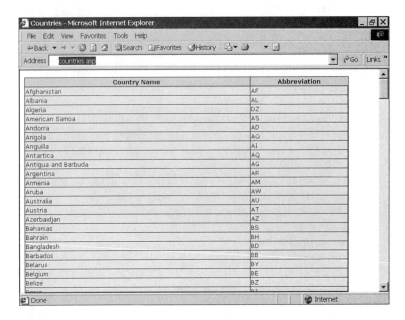

Figure 3.4: *Countries.asp.*

To accomplish the same thing using ASP.NET, we will take advantage of the DataGrid control. You will learn more about the DataGrid control in the next few chapters, but it is very useful for displaying (and modifying) data in HTML tables. Listing 3.16 displays countriesVB.aspx, and Listing 3.17 displays the script portion of countriesCS.aspx, the C# version of our ASP.NET page.

Listing 3.16: Source code for countriesVB.aspx.

```
<%@ Page Language="VB" %>
<%@ Import Namespace="System.Data" %>
```

Listing 3.16: continued

```
<%@ Import Namespace="System.Data.SqlClient" %>
<script language="VB" runat="server">
    Sub Page_Load(Src As Object, E As EventArgs)

        Dim MyConnection As SqlConnection
        Dim MyCommand As SqlCommand

            myConnection = new
➥ SqlConnection(ConfigurationSettings.AppSettings("connectionString"))
            myCommand = new SqlCommand("SELECT country_name as 'Country Name',
➥ " & _
                    "abbreviation as 'Abbreviation' FROM t_country " & _
                    "ORDER BY country_name", myConnection)

            myCommand.Connection.Open()
        MyDataGrid.DataSource=myCommand.ExecuteReader(CommandBehavior.
            ➥ CloseConnection)
        MyDataGrid.DataBind()
    End Sub
</script> <!DOCTYPE HTML PUBLIC "-//W3C//DTD HTML 4.0 Transitional//EN"
            "http://www.w3.org/TR/REC-html40/loose.dtd">
<html>
<head>
<title>Countries</title>
</head>
<body>
  <ASP:DataGrid id="MyDataGrid" runat="server"
    Width="700"
    BackColor="#eeeeee"
    BorderColor="black"
    ShowFooter="false"
    CellPadding="1"
    CellSpacing="0"
    Font-Name="Verdana"
    Font-Size="8pt"
    HeaderStyle-BackColor="#cccccc"
    MaintainState="false"
  />
</body>
</html>
```

Listing 3.17: Source code for countriesCS.aspx.

```
<%@ Page Language="C#" %>
<%@ Import Namespace="System.Data" %>
<%@ Import Namespace="System.Data.SqlClient" %>
<script language="C#" runat="server">
    protected void Page_Load(Object Src, EventArgs E)
    {
```

Listing 3.17: continued

```
                SqlConnection myConnection = new
➥ SqlConnection(ConfigurationSettings.AppSettings["connectionString"]);
                SqlCommand myCommand =
                    new SqlCommand("SELECT country_name as 'Country Name', " +
                    "abbreviation as 'Abbreviation' FROM t_country " +
                    "ORDER BY country_name", myConnection);

                myCommand.Connection.Open();
            MyDataGrid.DataSource=myCommand.ExecuteReader(CommandBehavior.
            ➥ CloseConnection);
            MyDataGrid.DataBind();
    }
</script>
```

In both of these ASP.NET examples, we see that the code involved to produce the same output as the ASP code is less, and there is no script interlaced with our HTML. This provides a much more object oriented, event driven programming experience than the serial processing of ASP scripts. These examples take advantage of imported libraries, SQL data objects, datasets, and datagrids. All of these concepts will be discussed further in the rest of the book, and are presented here as a primer.

Summary

In this chapter, we've looked at a lot of examples of ASP code and their ASP.NET counterparts. This should provide you with a good start to get your feet wet with ASP.NET and provide some examples you can use as a basis for your application migration to ASP.NET. If you have any ASP files that bear a resemblance to the examples here, you should be able to quickly use these examples to produce ASP.NET equivalents of your ASP scripts.

What's Next?

In Chapter 4, we will examine data access in ASP.NET. Those of you familiar with ADO should find the transition to ADO.NET to be relatively painless. ADO.NET provides some great new features over ADO, perhaps chief among them being the new Dataset object, which replaces the recordset as the primary ADO object. As you'll see, Datasets allow you to describe very detailed data spanning multiple tables, and even let you describe the relationships between the different tables within the Dataset. Because data access is one of the most important aspects of building dynamic Internet applications, we have chosen to tackle ADO.NET at this early stage of the book, so that future chapters can build on its usage and provide more useful examples.

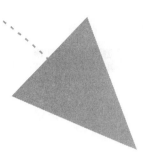

The New ADO—ADO.NET

Under .NET, data access has undergone a revolution. For many good reasons, the underlying premise of data access has shifted from connected access to disconnected access. In this chapter, you will learn

- Why ADO had to be replaced with ADO.NET

- The ADO.NET object model

- How to connect, retrieve, and update the database using ADO.NET

- How to use the ASP.NET data controls that make it easy to render data on a Web page

- How to use the XML support built into ADO.NET

ADO vs. ADO.NET

The History of Microsoft Data Access

You guessed it—Microsoft has changed the data access object model again. Before we jump right into the "how" of ADO.NET, we should spend a moment on the "why."

A long, long time ago (say four years), there were several object models for accessing data. If you wanted to talk to Access, you used Data Access Objects (DAO). Through DAO, you could take advantage of many Access-specific features. For example, you could create, repair, and compact databases. You could attach tables. You could create QueryDefs. For talking to Access, DAO was great, but Access wasn't the only database you ever wanted to talk to. What about Oracle? What about SQL Server?

The solution was Remote Data Objects (RDO). RDO was essentially for everything other than Access. RDO would let you talk to any Open Database Connectivity (ODBC) data source, so through it, you could access SQL, Oracle, Informix, Sybase, and others. You could execute stored procedures. You could even create something as exotic as a "disconnected recordset."

See any problems? All you want to do is talk to the database, and for what is logically the same operation, you have to use two different APIs. And going from DAO and Access to RDO and SQL was a significant porting operation. Even DAO and RDO weren't enough for everything. There were nontraditional data stores that had their own API. For example, Index Server and Exchange have custom APIs to access their data.

Along came ADO and OLEDB. During 1998, ADO really started to take off with Microsoft's marketing of "Universal Data Access." Finally, only one API existed for talking to any data source. At least, that was the claim. ADO was supposed to combine the best of DAO and RDO. It didn't really. With ADO, you lost the ability to compact your Access database. And, in many instances, it wasn't as fast as RDO. But, ADO did have some useful features. You could create hierarchical recordsets. It did let you access more types of data. You didn't have to go through ODBC because there were "native providers" for most databases.

But ADO had one fatal flaw. It was built around the concept of connected-ness. ADO assumed that you would want to connect to the data source, and stay connected while you retrieved data and performed operations on it. You could create a disconnected recordset, but it wasn't the default. The world of development, on the other hand, was moving in a different direction. With n-tier architectures, the demand was for disconnected data. XML was going through a technological big bang. Microsoft.NET had a different vision of the world, and ADO just didn't fit. ADO.NET was born.

ADO.NET is all about disconnected access. In general, you connect to the database only for the instant when you are retrieving or updating. Otherwise, the connection is closed. This is the default. When you retrieve the data, it is typically stored in something known as a "DataSet". You can think of the DataSet as a recordset on steroids. For starters, a single DataSet can store the results of many SQL queries. For example, you could retrieve all the authors, and store the results in a DataSet. You could then retrieve all the publishers, and store the results in the same DataSet. With another line of code, you can tell the DataSet that the authors and publishers are related on the PubId column (see Figure 4.1). In other words, the DataSet can act like a limited in-memory database, with a full understanding of the relationship between tables.

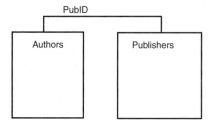

Figure 4.1: Multiple tables in a DataSet.

And again, this in-memory database is designed to not require an active connection to the actual database.

There's another fundamental difference between ADO and ADO.NET. With ADO, the Recordset was all-powerful. It not only allowed access to the data, but it provided the facilities to filter and sort the data. The Recordset, in other words, controlled the data and how you viewed it. ADO.NET divides this functionality between two objects. The DataSet is just concerned with storing the data. For your actual view of the data, which includes filtering and sorting, you use a DataView object.

As stated earlier, the DataSet keeps an in-memory copy of the data returned by a select statement. Often, this is exactly what you want. However, for very large DataSets, this isn't practical. For example, what if you wanted to do some massive import/export operations on your database? You're certainly not going to load the entire database into memory. There's an object for just such scenarios. It's called the DataReader.

The DataReader serves the same purpose as an ADO forward-only, read-only recordset. The DataReader allows you to iterate through a set of rows, one at a time. Also, for many scenarios, iterating through the result set a single time is all the functionality you need. For example, think of the times you've looped through a RecordSet to generate an HTML drop-down list. A DataReader provides all the functionality you need for this type of operation.

ADO vs. ADO.NET Object Model

Tables 4.1 and 4.2 compare the objects in ADO with the new objects in ADO.NET.

Table 4.1: ADO Objects

Object	Description
Connection	Allows your code to connect to a data source. Through the connection, you can issue commands that update the database, or return records.
Command	Used to send commands to the database. The command object was specifically useful for calling stored procedures because it contained a `Parameters` collection that you could use to access the input and output parameters of a stored procedure.
Recordset	Stores the results of a `select` statement. By default, the recordset was read-only, and used a server-side cursor. You could create server- or client-side cursors, as well as specify a number of locking options.

ADO was referred to as a *flat object model*, meaning that a lot of duplicate functionality was available through different objects. The connection object would connect to the database, but you could also issue commands through it directly. The recordset was used to store results, but it could maintain its own internal connection, and issue database commands. Although this could be convenient, in practice, it resulted in confusion and complexity.

In ADO.NET, they didn't try to make every object do everything (see Table 4.2). A connection is just a connection. You can't issue commands through it like you could in ADO. A command is only for issuing commands. A `DataSet` is only for storing data. With an ADO recordset, you got a lot of different and inconsistent behavior depending on the underlying database. With the `DataSet`, you get exactly the same behavior across all databases because it has no knowledge of the underlying database.

Table 4.2: ADO.NET Objects

Object	Description
DBConnection, SqlConnection, ADOConnection	Used to establish a connection to the database
DBCommand, SqlCommand, ADOCommand	Used to send INSERT, UPDATE, SELECT, and DELETE statements to the database

Table 4.2: continued

Object	Description
DataSet	Stores the results of one or more SELECT statements
DataView	Used to filter and sort a DataSet
DBDataReader, SQLDataReader, ADODataReader	Used to iterate through a set of records

Let's take a look at these objects in action.

Connecting to the Database

You can start working with ADO.NET by creating a new .NET project. First, launch Visual Studio.NET. Then, select "New Project" on the start screen. Choose "Visual C# Projects" for the project type, and "ASP.NET Web Application" for the template. Name the project "ado_net_by_example", and click "Ok". At this point, Visual Studio will create the initial project structure. Select the Project, Add Web Form menu command, and name the web form SqlCommand.aspx. Add a Label control to the Web Form by double-clicking the Label icon in the toolbox. In the Solution Explorer, right-click on SqlCommand.aspx, and select "View Code". You are now in the position to start writing ADO.NET code.

The first step in working with the database is establishing a connection. Add the code in Listing 4.1 to the Page_Load method.

Listing 4.1: Connecting to a SQL database.

```
//
// Connect to the database
//
SqlConnection cn = new SqlConnection(
    "server=localhost;" +
    "database=pubs;" +
    "uid=sa;" +
    "password=");

cn.Open();
```

As you can see, the constructor to the connection object takes a connection string as an argument. This connection string contains all the information needed to connect to a specific database. In this case, the connection string specifies the network name of the database server, the actual database on that server, and the authentication information. A connection to the database is actually established when the open method is called.

You should also note the data type of the connection object. Here, we are using something called a "SqlConnection". This object is specific for talking to SQL Server databases. The other connection object available is the

OleDbConnection object, which is built on top of the legacy ActiveX Data Objects.

This concept of having database-specific connection objects falls under the Microsoft term "Managed Provider."

ADO.NET does away with the "one size fits all" approach. Instead, it is preferable to create an instance of a connection object that is specific to the database that you want to connect to. The database-specific managed providers allow you to take advantage of functionality that is specific to a database. Table 4.3 lists some of the SQL specific properties of the SqlConnection class.

Table 4.3: **SqlConnection** *Properties and Methods—Specific to* **SqlConnection**

Properties/Methods	Description
ServerVersion	Gets the version number of the SQL Server that you are connected to
IsolationLevel	The SQL Server transaction isolation level
SaveTransaction	Saves a point in the transaction that can be rolled back to

The other advantage of database-specific providers is performance. If you go through ODBC, or OLE-DB, you are going through some generic middleware that attempts to make all databases look the same. This saves you from having completely different APIs for all the databases, but at the expense of performance. If, on the other hand, you use the SqlConnection object to talk to SQL Server, it will talk to SQL Server in a direct, efficient way, without any middleware layer. For this reason, you should always use a database-specific provider when possible rather than the generic OleDb provider.

Retrieving Data

Now that you've seen how to connect to the database, it's time to start issuing commands. The easiest way to send commands to the database is with the SqlCommand object.

Using the SqlCommand Object

The SqlCommand object contains all the functionality that you will need to issue Select, Insert, Update, and Delete statements. The SqlCommand object can return a DataReader, giving you the ability to iterate through the result set return from a Select. Finally, a SqlCommand allows you to call stored procedures, specifying the input and output arguments, and providing access to the return value.

EXECUTING SQL STATEMENTS

Listing 4.2 shows the `SqlCommand` object in action.

Listing 4.2: Retrieving data using the `SqlCommand`.

```
//
// Connect to the database
//
SqlConnection cn = new SqlConnection(
    "server=localhost;" +
    "database=pubs;" +
    "uid=sa;" +
    "password=");

cn.Open();

//
// Create a SqlCommand
//
System.Data.SqlClient.SqlCommand cmd = new
    System.Data.SqlClient.SqlCommand();
cmd.Connection = cn;
cmd.CommandText = "select * from authors";

//
// Execute the Command
//
SqlDataReader dr;
dr = cmd.ExecuteReader();

//
// Loop through the results
//
while (dr.Read())
{
    Label1.Text += dr["au_lname"] +
        ", " + dr["au_fname"] + "<br>";
}
```

Before this code will compile, you also need to add a "using" directive that references the System.Data.SqlClient namespace to the top of the file as shown in Listing 4.3.

Listing 4.3: Using Directive

```
namespace ado_net_by_example
{
    using System;
```

Listing 4.3: continued

```
using System.Collections;
using System.ComponentModel;
using System.Data;
using System.Drawing;
using System.Web;
using System.Web.SessionState;
using System.Web.UI;
using System.Web.UI.WebControls;
using System.Web.UI.HtmlControls;
using System.Data.SqlClient;
```

In this example, we use the `SqlCommand` object to retrieve data from the database. We do this by setting the `Connection` property of the command object so that it knows what database we want to talk to. The `CommandText` contains the SQL statement that we want to execute.

The results of the command will be stored in a `DataReader` object when the execute method is invoked. We'll take a closer look at the `DataReader` later. To test this code, right-click on SQLCommand.aspx in the Solution Explorer, and select "Set as Start Page". Then, press CTRL-F5 to start the application. You should see Internet Explorer launch, and the names of the authors listed.

The `DataReader` Object

The `DataRepeater` is populated when the `Execute` method of the `SqlCommand` object is called. The data repeater lets you scroll through a result set, one record at a time.

To scroll through the result set, you call the `Read` method. This method must be called once, prior to accessing the first record. `Read` will return false when you have reached the last record. A common problem with traditional ADO was that you could forget to call `MoveNext`, resulting in your code entering an infinite loop. As we can see, this is an impossibility with ADO.NET and the `DataReader`.

To access the columns of the result set, you simply index the `DataReader` with the column name:

```
LastName = dr["LastName"];
```

The `DataReader` is really optimized for batch-type operations on a large result set. The `DataReader` contacts the database whenever you request the next record, so that only one record is stored in memory at a time.

CALLING STORED PROCEDURES

In addition to executing ad-hoc queries, we can also execute stored procedures. In Visual Studio.NET, select the Project, Add Web Form, menu command. Name the new web form "StoredProc.aspx". Add a label control to the page by double-clicking the Label icon in the toolbox.

In the solution explorer, right-click on "StoredProc.aspx", and select "View Code". When the code window opens, add the following line to the list of "using" directives at the top of the file:

```
using System.Data.SqlClient;
```

Add the code shown in Listing 4.4 to the Page_Load method to call a stored procedure with input and output parameters.

Listing 4.4: Calling stored procedures with the SqlCommand object.

```
// Connect to the Database
SqlConnection cn = new SqlConnection(
    "server=localhost;" +
    "database=pubs;" +
    "uid=sa;" +
    "password=");

cn.Open();

// Create a command object
System.Data.SqlClient.SqlCommand cmd =
    new System.Data.SqlClient.SqlCommand();
cmd.Connection = cn;

// Set CommandText to the name of the
// stored procedure
cmd.CommandText = "AuthorCount";

// Indicate that we're calling a stored proc
cmd.CommandType = CommandType.StoredProcedure;

// Add parameters to the command object that
// mirror the actual parameters of the stored
// procedure
SqlParameter TempParam;
TempParam = new SqlParameter(
    "@state",SqlDbType.VarChar,2);
// For input paramteres, supply a value
TempParam.Value = "CA";
cmd.Parameters.Add(TempParam);
```

Listing 4.4: continued

```
TempParam = new SqlParameter(
    "@count", SqlDbType.Int);
// For output parameters, specify the direction.
// If we don't specify a direction, it will default
// to input.
TempParam.Direction = ParameterDirection.Output;
cmd.Parameters.Add(TempParam);

// Execute the proc
cmd.ExecuteNonQuery();

// Retrieve the data from the output parameter
// and display it on the page.
Label1.Text = cmd.Parameters["@count"].Value.ToString();
SqlParameterSqlParameterSqlParameter
```

The procedure for calling a stored procedure is similar to executing an ad-hoc query. We still have to set the `Connection` object to the `SqlConnection`. The `CommandText` property is set to the name of the stored procedure we want to execute.

This stored procedure has two parameters. An input parameter that takes a two-character state code, and an output parameter that will contain the number of authors from that state. To access these parameters, we have to manually add them to the `Parameters` collection of the `SqlCommand` object.

To add the parameters, we create a variable called `TempParam` that is of the type `SqlParameterSqlParameter`. When we create an instance of this variable, we can pass arguments to the constructor to specify the name of the parameter, its data type, and optionally its size (for parameters that are a character type).

For input parameters, we also need to specify a value, which we do through the value property of the `SqlParameter` object. After the parameter is created, we add it to the `Parameters` collection of the `SqlCommand` object.

For output parameters, we follow the same steps, with several exceptions. We need to specify that this is an output parameter by setting the `Direction` property of the `SqlParameter` object to `Output`. Also, for output parameters, we don't specify a value because the value will be calculated by the stored procedure.

After the parameters are added, we execute the command. Because this stored procedure doesn't return any records, we execute the command with a call to `ExecuteNonQuery`.

After the command executes, the results are waiting for us in the output parameter named @count. We retrieve this value with the following line of code:

```
Label1.Text = cmd.Parameters["@count"].Value.ToString();
```

Remember, cmd.Parameters is the collection of parameters for the stored procedure. @count is the name of the output parameter. .Value says that we want the value for this parameter (versus its size, or direction). The Value property returns an object. To convert it into something that we can display in a label, we use the ToString method. This method is available with most objects.

To test this page, you will first need to add the AuthorCount stored procedure to the pubs database. To add this procedure, open the Server Explorer in Visual Studio.NET. In the Server Explorer, drill down through the server name, and expand Sql Servers. Expand your server name, then expand the Pubs database. Right-click on "Stored Procedures", and select "New Stored Procedure". In the stored procedure editor, add the code shown in Listing 4.5.

Listing 4.5: AuthorCount Stored Procedure.

```
        CREATE PROC AuthorCount(
        @state varchar(2),
        @count int output
)
AS
        Select @count=count(*) from authors
        where state=@state
```

Finally, in the Solution Explorer, right-click on "StoredProc.aspx", and select "Set as Start Page". Press CTRL-F5 to start the application. You should see Internet Explorer launch, and display a page indicating that there are 15 authors in California.

The DataReader is great for dealing with large result sets, but if you aren't returning a huge number of rows, the DataSet offers many advantages.

The SqlDataAdapter Object

The SqlDataAdapter acts as a bridge between the SqlConnection and the DataSet. The SqlConnection provides access to the underlying database. The DataSet holds the actual data. The SqlDataAdapter moves data between the DataSet and the database, through the SqlConnection. To start working with the SqlDataAdapter, add a new page to the project called SqlDA1.aspx. Add a DataGrid to this page from the toolbox. Switch to the code view, and add the code shown in Listing 4.6.

Listing 4.6: Using the `SqlDataAdapter` to populate a `DataSet`.

```
SqlConnection cn = new SqlConnection(
    "server=localhost;" +
    "database=pubs;" +
    "uid=sa;" +
    "password=");

SqlDataAdapter cmd = new SqlDataAdapter(
    "select * from authors",cn);

DataSet ds = new DataSet();

cmd.Fill(ds,"authors");
DataGrid1.DataSource = ds.Tables["authors"];

DataGrid1.DataBind();
```

Regardless of the database operation, we still need a connection object. As you can tell, we use exactly the same connection for a `SqlDataAdapter` as we used previously for the `SQLDataReader`.

Next, we create an instance of the `SqlDataAdapter` object. The constructor for this object takes a SQL statement, and a reference to the `SqlConnection`, as arguments. It's important to note that with the `SqlDataAdapter`, we don't have to explicitly open the connection to the database. The `SqlDataReader` works in a "connected" mode, meaning that you need to keep a connection to the database open while you're accessing the data. The `SqlDataAdapter` works in a "disconnected" mode, meaning that when you execute the command, it will connect to the database, issue the SQL statement, get the results, and then disconnect. You don't maintain a connection while you're working with the actual data.

Next we see that we create an instance of the `DataSet` object. There are a few things to pay attention to here also. You'll notice that the objects we've been using so far have all been prefixed with "Sql". For example, "SqlConnection," "SqlDataAdapter," and "SqlDataReader". Why aren't we creating an instance of "SqlDataSet"? Is this just a typo? Absolutely not. All the objects that begin with "Sql" are specific to SQL Server. "OleDbConnection" may work differently, and have different properties and methods. The `DataSet`, however, is just a place to put and modify the data. It doesn't care where the data comes from, and it never talks directly to the underlying database. In other words, the `DataSet` is completely generic, and provides exactly the same functionality regardless of the underlying data source.

To actually populate the `DataSet`, we call the `FillDataSet` method of the `SqlDataAdapter` object. We pass the `DataSet` as an argument, as well as a text name for this result set. Here, we're calling the result set "authors," but we could use any string we want.

"Why name the result set?" you ask.

A `DataSet` is fundamentally different from any object you've ever worked with. You can store multiple result sets in a single `DataSet`. For example:

```
cmdAuthors.FillDataSet(ds,"authors");
cmdPubs.FillDataSet(ds,"pubs");
```

You can even tell the `DataSet` that the two result sets are related on a particular column (`pubId`, for example). Later, when you want to display data from a particular result set, you need a way to identify which one. Hence the need for naming the result set when you populate the `DataSet`.

Finally, we want to display the results somewhere. ASP.NET makes it so simple to display data from a database. We simply bind the `DataSource` property of a `DataGrid` to the table in the `DataSet` that stores a particular set of records. Listings 4.7 and 4.8 illustrate the complete listing, as well as the output.

Listing 4.7: Displaying data using the `SqlDataAdapter`—SqlDA1.aspx.

```
<%@ Page language="c#" Codebehind="SqlDA1.aspx.cs" AutoEventWireup="false"
➥ Inherits="ado_net_by_example.SqlDA1" %>
<!DOCTYPE HTML PUBLIC "-//W3C//DTD HTML 4.0 Transitional//EN" >
<HTML>
    <HEAD>
        <meta name="GENERATOR" Content="Microsoft Visual Studio 7.0">
        <meta name="CODE_LANGUAGE" Content="C#">
        <meta name="vs_defaultClientScript" content="JavaScript (ECMAScript)">
        <meta name="vs_targetSchema"
         content="http://schemas.microsoft.com/intellisense/ie3-2nav3-0">
    </HEAD>
    <body MS_POSITIONING="FlowLayout">
        <form id="SqlDA1" method="post" runat="server">
            <H1>
                Authors
            </H1>
            <P>
                <asp:DataGrid id="DataGrid1" runat="server"></asp:DataGrid>
            </P>
        </form>
    </body>
</HTML>
```

Listing 4.8: Displaying data using the SqlDataAdapter—SqlDA1.aspx.cs.

```
using System;
using System.Collections;
using System.ComponentModel;
using System.Data;
using System.Drawing;
using System.Web;
using System.Web.SessionState;
using System.Web.UI;
using System.Web.UI.WebControls;
using System.Web.UI.HtmlControls;
using System.Data.SqlClient;

namespace ado_net_by_example
{
    /// <summary>
    /// Summary description for SqlDA1.
    /// </summary>
    public class SqlDA1 : System.Web.UI.Page
    {
        protected System.Web.UI.WebControls.DataGrid DataGrid1;

        public SqlDA1()
        {
            Page.Init += new System.EventHandler(Page_Init);
        }

        private void Page_Load(object sender, System.EventArgs e)
        {
            SqlConnection cn = new SqlConnection(
                "server=localhost;" +
                "database=pubs;" +
                "uid=sa;" +
                "password=");

            SqlDataAdapter cmd = new SqlDataAdapter(
                "select * from authors",cn);

            DataSet ds = new DataSet();

            cmd.Fill(ds,"authors");
            DataGrid1.DataSource = ds.Tables["authors"];
            DataGrid1.DataBind();
        }
```

Listing 4.8: continued

```
    private void Page_Init(object sender, EventArgs e)
    {
        //
        // CODEGEN: This call is required by the ASP.NET Web Form Designer.
        //
        InitializeComponent();
    }

    #region Web Form Designer generated code
    /// <summary>
    /// Required method for Designer support - do not modify
    /// the contents of this method with the code editor.
    /// </summary>
    private void InitializeComponent()
    {
        this.Load += new System.EventHandler(this.Page_Load);

    }
    #endregion
    }
}
```

The DataSet Object

Populating a DataSet is just the beginning. As you'll see, the DataSet offers a substantial amount of functionality.

DATA BINDING

The concept of having a server control populate itself with data from a DataSet is known as "data binding." Actually, under .NET, data binding is a very powerful feature. Controls can bind to DataSets, DataReaders, arrays, variables, functions, or just about anything.

SORTING

Through the DataView, you can re-sort the contents of the DataSet, without accessing the database. In this scenario, we'll let the user choose what column they want to sort the results set on. To avoid doing a trip back to the database, we'll cache the DataSet for five minutes. First, let's factor out the code that retrieves and caches the authors from the database (see Listing 4.9).

Listing 4.9: Caching a `DataSet`.

```
protected DataSet LoadAuthors()
{
    DataSet ds;
    if (Cache["authors"] == null)
    {
        SqlConnection cn = new SqlConnection(
            "server=localhost;" +
            "database=pubs;" +
            "uid=sa;" +
            "password=");

        SqlDataAdapter cmd = new SqlDataAdapter(
            "select * from authors",cn);

        ds = new DataSet();

        cmd.Fill(ds,"authors");
        Cache.Insert("authors",ds,
            null,
            System.Web.Caching.Cache.NoAbsoluteExpiration,
            TimeSpan.FromMinutes(5));
    }
    else
    {
        ds = (DataSet)Cache["authors"];
    }
    return ds;
}
```

The code is similar to the preceding example, with several exceptions. We check to see if the `DataSet` is already cached. If the `DataSet` is not cached, we connect to the database and populate it as before. We then cache the `DataSet` for five minutes with the call to `Cache.Insert`. Here, we're using something called a "sliding expiration," which means that if this cache item doesn't get hit for five minutes, it gets trashed. The other option is an absolute expiration, which will throw the cache object away in X amount of time, no matter what.

This simplifies the `Page_Load` procedure to Listing 4.10.

Listing 4.10: SqlDataAdapter.cs—`Page_Load`.

```
protected void Page_Load(object sender, EventArgs e)
{
    if (!IsPostBack)
    {
```

Listing 4.10: continued

```
        DataSet ds = LoadAuthors();

        DataGrid1.DataSource = ds.Tables["authors"];
        DataGrid1.DataBind();
    }
}
```

Initially, we'll let the user choose the column to sort on by clicking on a button. Listing 4.11 shows how the buttons are added to the page.

Listing 4.11: SqlDA.aspx.

```
<%@ Page language="c#"
    Codebehind="SqlDataAdapter.cs"
    AutoEventWireup="false"
    Inherits="ado_net_by_example.SqlDataAdapter" %>
<html><head>
    <meta name="GENERATOR" Content="Microsoft Visual Studio 7.0">
    <meta name="CODE_LANGUAGE" Content="C#"></head>
<body>

<form method="post" runat="server">
    <h1>Authors:</h1>
    <asp:Button id=cmdLastName runat="server" Text="Last Name"/>
    <asp:Button id=cmdFirstName runat="server" Text="First Name"/>

    <p> </p>
    <asp:DataGrid id=DataGrid1 runat="server"/>
</form>
</body></html>
```

Finally, we'll add code in the code-behind page to handle the click events for these buttons (see Listing 4.12).

Listing 4.12: SqlDataAdapter.cs: Click Events.

```
protected void cmdFirstName_Click (object sender, System.EventArgs e)
{
    DataSet ds = LoadAuthors();
    DataView dv = ds.Tables["authors"].DefaultView;
    dv.Sort = "au_fname";
    DataGrid1.DataSource = dv;
    DataGrid1.DataBind();
}

protected void cmdLastName_Click (object sender, System.EventArgs e)
{
    DataSet ds = LoadAuthors();
    DataView dv = ds.Tables["authors"].DefaultView;
    dv.Sort = "au_lname";
```

Listing 4.12: continued

```
    DataGrid1.DataSource = dv;
    DataGrid1.DataBind();
}
```

When you re-compile and display the results in the browser, you should see output similar to Figure 4.2.

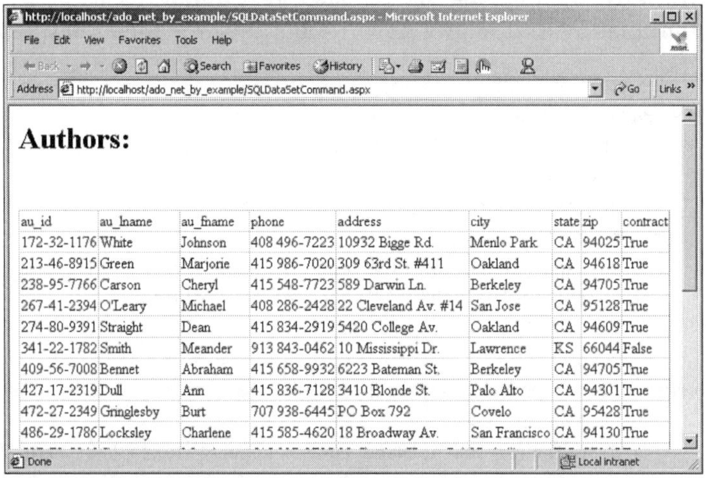

Figure 4.2: *Displaying data from the database.*

The first time the user views the page, the Page_Load event calls LoadAuthors. LoadAuthors determines that the author information doesn't exist in the cache, and so it connects to the database, populates a DataSet, and inserts it into the cache. It also populates a DataGrid so that the author information shows up on the page. When the user clicks the "First Name" or "Last Name" button, we end up in the appropriate click event. The click event also calls LoadAuthors, but this time the DataSet does exist in the cache. The DataSet is retrieved from the cache, and we set a reference to its DefaultView. By modifying the Sort property of this DataView, we change the way that the information will be rendered by the DataGrid. We haven't actually changed the DataSet, just the way we view its data.

FILTERING

Filtering data is equally simple. First, we'll add a drop-down list to our form so that the user can filter authors by state (see Listing 4.13).

Listing 4.13: Adding a drop-down list.

```
<%@ Page language="c#"
    Codebehind="SqlDataAdapter.cs"
```

Listing 4.13: continued

```
    AutoEventWireup="false"
    Inherits="ado_net_by_example.SqlDataAdapter" %>
<html><head>
    <meta name="GENERATOR" Content="Microsoft Visual Studio 7.0">
    <meta name="CODE_LANGUAGE" Content="C#"></head>
<body>

<form method="post" runat="server">
    <h1>Authors:</h1>
    <asp:Button id=cmdLastName runat="server" Text="Last Name"/>
    <asp:Button id=cmdFirstName runat="server" Text="First Name"/>
    State :
    <asp:dropdownlist id=lstState runat=server autopostback=True>
        <asp:listitem>All</asp:listitem>
        <asp:listitem>CA</asp:listitem>
        <asp:listitem>KS</asp:listitem>
        <asp:listitem>UT</asp:listitem>
    </asp:dropdownlist>

    <p> </p>
    <asp:DataGrid id=DataGrid1 runat="server"/>
</form>
</body></html>
```

Then we'll write code for the `SelectedIndex` event. Because the drop-down
has "autopostback" set to true, this server-side event will automatically fire
whenever the user changes the selection in the drop-down. Listing 4.17
shows the code for the event procedure.

Listing 4.14: `lstState_SelectedIndex` event.

```
protected void lstState_SelectedIndex (object sender, System.EventArgs e)
{
    DataSet ds = LoadAuthors();
    DataView dv = ds.Tables["authors"].DefaultView;
    String State = lstState.SelectedItem.ToString().ToUpper();
    if (State != "ALL")
    {
        dv.RowFilter = "State = '" + State + "'";
    }
    else
    {
        dv.RowFilter = "";
    }
    DataGrid1.DataSource = dv;
    DataGrid1.DataBind();
}
```

As you can see, filtering is very similar to sorting. Again, we call
`LoadAuthors` to retrieve the `DataSet`. It may come from the database, or the

cache. When we have the `DataSet`, we filter it by changing the `RowFilter` property of its `DefaultView`. To specify a filter, we use the syntax of a SQL `WHERE` clause. For example:

```
dv.RowFilter = "State = 'CA'"
```

In this case, the state is specified by the `SelectedItem` property of the drop-down list. If the user selects "All" from the drop-down, we don't want to do any filtering. We indicate no filtering by setting the `RowFilter` property to "", an empty string.

Listings 4.15 and 4.16 show the complete listing, with output.

Listing 4.15: Sorting and filtering with ADO.NET—SqlDataAdapter.aspx.

```
<%@ Page language="c#"
    Codebehind="SqlDataAdapter.cs"
    AutoEventWireup="false"
    Inherits="ado_net_by_example.SqlDataAdapter" %>
<html><head>
    <meta name="GENERATOR" Content="Microsoft Visual Studio 7.0">
    <meta name="CODE_LANGUAGE" Content="C#"></head>
<body>

<form method="post" runat="server">
    <h1>Authors:</h1>
    <asp:Button id=cmdLastName runat="server" Text="Last Name"/>
    <asp:Button id=cmdFirstName runat="server" Text="First Name"/>
    State :
    <asp:dropdownlist id=lstState runat=server autopostback=True>
        <asp:listitem>All</asp:listitem>
        <asp:listitem>CA</asp:listitem>
        <asp:listitem>KS</asp:listitem>
        <asp:listitem>UT</asp:listitem>
    </asp:dropdownlist>

    <p> </p>
    <asp:DataGrid id=DataGrid1 runat="server"/>
</form>
</body></html>
```

Listing 4.16: Sorting and filtering with ADO.NET—SqlDataAdapter.cs.

```
namespace ado_net_by_example
{
    using System;
    using System.Collections;
    using System.ComponentModel;
    using System.Data;
    using System.Data.SqlClient;
```

Listing 4.16: continued

```
using System.Drawing;
using System.Web;
using System.Web.SessionState;
using System.Web.UI;
using System.Web.UI.WebControls;
using System.Web.UI.HtmlControls;

/// <summary>
///     Summary description for SqlDA.
/// </summary>
public class SqlDA : System.Web.UI.Page
{
    protected System.Web.UI.WebControls.DataGrid DataGrid1;
    protected System.Web.UI.WebControls.DropDownList lstState;
    protected System.Web.UI.WebControls.Button cmdFirstName;
    protected System.Web.UI.WebControls.Button cmdLastName;

    public SqlDA()
    {
        Page.Init += new System.EventHandler(Page_Init);
    }

    protected void Page_Load(object sender, EventArgs e)
    {
        if (!IsPostBack)
        {
            DataSet ds = LoadAuthors();
            DataGrid1.DataSource = ds.Tables["authors"].DefaultView;
            DataGrid1.DataBind();
        }
    }

    protected DataSet LoadAuthors()
    {
        DataSet ds;
        if (Cache["authors"] == null)
        {
            SqlConnection cn = new SqlConnection(
                "server=localhost;" +
                "database=pubs;" +
                "uid=sa;" +
                "password=");

            SqlDataAdapter cmd = new SqlDataAdapter(
                "select * from authors",cn);
```

Listing 4.16: continued

```
            ds = new DataSet();

            cmd.Fill(ds,"authors");
            Cache.Insert("authors",ds,
                null,
                System.Web.Caching.Cache.NoAbsoluteExpiration,
                TimeSpan.FromMinutes(5));
        }
        else
        {
            ds = (DataSet)Cache["authors"];
        }
        return ds;
    }

    protected void Page_Init(object sender, EventArgs e)
    {
        //
        // CODEGEN: This call is required by the ASP+ Windows Form
        // Designer.
        //
        InitializeComponent();
    }

    /// <summary>
    ///     Required method for Designer support - do not modify
    ///     the contents of this method with the code editor.
    /// </summary>
    private void InitializeComponent()
    {
        cmdFirstName.Click +=
            new System.EventHandler (this.cmdFirstName_Click);
        cmdLastName.Click +=
            new System.EventHandler (this.cmdLastName_Click);
        lstState.SelectedIndexChanged +=
            new System.EventHandler (this.lstState_SelectedIndex);
        this.Load += new System.EventHandler (this.Page_Load);
    }

    protected void lstState_SelectedIndex (object sender,
        System.EventArgs e)
    {
        DataSet ds = LoadAuthors();
        DataView dv = ds.Tables["authors"].DefaultView;
        String State = lstState.SelectedItem.ToString().ToUpper();
```

Listing 4.16: continued

```
            if (State != "ALL")
            {
                dv.RowFilter = "State = '" + State + "'";
            }
            else
            {
                dv.RowFilter = "";
            }
            DataGrid1.DataSource = dv;
            DataGrid1.DataBind();
        }

        protected void cmdFirstName_Click (object sender, System.EventArgs e)
        {
            DataSet ds = LoadAuthors();
            DataView dv = ds.Tables["authors"].DefaultView;
            dv.Sort = "au_fname";
            DataGrid1.DataSource = dv;
            DataGrid1.DataBind();
        }

        protected void cmdLastName_Click (object sender, System.EventArgs e)
        {
            DataSet ds = LoadAuthors();
            DataView dv = ds.Tables["authors"].DefaultView;
            dv.Sort = "au_lname";
            DataGrid1.DataSource = dv;
            DataGrid1.DataBind();
        }
    }
}
```

When you compile the page, and display the results in the browser, you should see output similar to Figure 4.3.

Data Controls

We've seen that ADO.NET offers a lot of functionality, but ADO.NET becomes much more when combined with the data-aware server controls.

The DataGrid Control

The workhorse of these controls is the DataGrid. As we've seen in previous examples, this control makes it simple to display data from the database. The simplest way to add a DataGrid is as follows:

```
<asp:DataGrid id=DataGrid1 runat="server" />
```

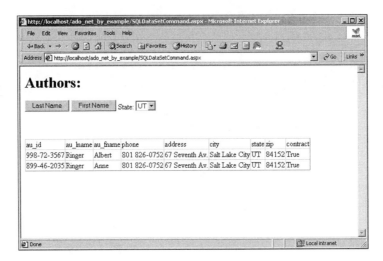

Figure 4.3: *Sorting and filtering data.*

The ID property gives us something we can write code against. By saying
`runat=server`, we can handle server-side events, and change the properties
of this control with code.

DataGrid APPEARANCE

Right out of the box, the `DataGrid` gives you a lot of control over how it
looks (see Listing 4.17).

Listing 4.17: Controlling the appearance of the `DataGrid`.

```
<asp:DataGrid id="DataGrid1" runat="server" BorderStyle="None"
    GridLines="Vertical" BorderWidth="1px" BorderColor="#999999"
    BackColor="White" CellPadding="3">

    <FooterStyle ForeColor="Black" BackColor="#CCCCCC"></FooterStyle>
    <HeaderStyle Font-Bold="True" ForeColor="White" BackColor="#000084">
    </HeaderStyle>
    <PagerStyle HorizontalAlign="Center" ForeColor="Black" BackColor="#999999"
        Mode="NumericPages"></PagerStyle>
    <SelectedItemStyle Font-Bold="True" ForeColor="White" BackColor="#008A8C">
    </SelectedItemStyle>
    <AlternatingItemStyle BackColor="#DCDCDC"></AlternatingItemStyle>
    <ItemStyle ForeColor="Black" BackColor="#EEEEEE"></ItemStyle>
</asp:DataGrid>
```

We can use the `HeaderStyle` property to indicate the color, font, and other
appearance features of the header row on the resulting table. `ItemStyle`
and `AlternatingItemStyle` control the appearance of the odd and even lines.

Custom Column Headings

So far, the DataGrid has simply output all the information from the DataSet. The column names from the database became the column headings in the grid. We can take more control over the output by specifying the columns that we want displayed (see Listing 4.18).

Listing 4.18: Custom column headings.

```
<asp:DataGrid id="DataGrid1" runat="server" BorderStyle="None"
    GridLines="Vertical" BorderWidth="1px" BorderColor="#999999"
    BackColor="White" CellPadding="3" '
    AutoGenerateColumns="False">

    <FooterStyle ForeColor="Black" BackColor="#CCCCCC"></FooterStyle>
    <HeaderStyle Font-Bold="True" ForeColor="White" BackColor="#000084">
    </HeaderStyle>
    <PagerStyle HorizontalAlign="Center" ForeColor="Black" BackColor="#999999"
        Mode="NumericPages"></PagerStyle>
    <SelectedItemStyle Font-Bold="True" ForeColor="White"
➡ BackColor="#008A8C"></SelectedItemStyle>
    <AlternatingItemStyle BackColor="#DCDCDC"></AlternatingItemStyle>
    <ItemStyle ForeColor="Black" BackColor="#EEEEEE"></ItemStyle>
    <Columns>
        <asp:BoundColumn DataField="au_lname" HeaderText="Last Name">
        </asp:BoundColumn>
        <asp:BoundColumn DataField="au_fname" HeaderText="First Name">
        </asp:BoundColumn>
        <asp:BoundColumn DataField="state" HeaderText="State">
        </asp:BoundColumn>
    </Columns>
</asp:DataGrid>
```

By setting the AutoGenerateColumns property of the DataGrid to false, we're saying that we are going to control which columns appear. We do this by accessing the Column property, and listing the data-bound columns. The DataField property specifies the column name from the database, and the Header Text defines the name of the column as it appears to the user.

This appears as shown in Figure 4.5.

Previously, we sorted the DataGrid by adding buttons to the page, but the DataGrid was built with sorting in mind. If you set the AllowSorting property to true, the column heading become hyperlinks. With a few lines of code, we can sort the column when the user clicks on the column heading. First, we set the AllowSorting property to true:

Figure 4.4: *Displaying data using the* `DataGrid`*.*

```
<asp:DataGrid id=DataGrid1 runat="server" ForeColor="Black"
    AutoGenerateColumns=False
    AllowSorting=True>
```

We also need to modify our custom columns to specify the sort field as shown in Listing 4.19:

Listing 4.19 : Adding the SortExpression

```
<Columns>
    <asp:BoundColumn DataField="au_lname" HeaderText="Last Name"
        SortExpression="au_lname"></asp:BoundColumn>
    <asp:BoundColumn DataField="au_fname" HeaderText="First Name"
        SortExpression="au_fname"></asp:BoundColumn>
    <asp:BoundColumn DataField="state" HeaderText="State"
        SortExpression="state"></asp:BoundColumn>
</Columns>
```

Then, we write code for the `SortCommand` event of the `DataGrid` as shown in Listing 4.20.

Listing 4.20: The SortCommand Event

```
protected void DataGrid1_SortCommand (object source,
    System.Web.UI.WebControls.DataGridSortCommandEventArgs e)
{
    DataSet ds = LoadAuthors();
    DataView dv = ds.Tables["authors"].DefaultView;
    dv.Sort = e.SortExpression.ToString();
    DataGrid1.DataSource = dv;
    DataGrid1.DataBind();
}
```

When the user clicks on a column heading, the SortCommand event fires. This event gets a DataGridSortCommandEventArgs argument that contains the name of the sort field for the column that the user clicked on. With this, we can set the Sort property of the DefaultView. We rebind the DataGrid, and the results are now resorted.

To work with sorting yourself, create a new page called DataGrid.aspx. Place the code from Listing 4.21 in the DataGrid.aspx file. Place the code from Listing 4.22 in the DataGrid.aspx.cs file.

Listing 4.21: Custom columns with sorting—DataGrid.aspx.

```
<%@ Page language="c#" Codebehind="DataGrid.cs" AutoEventWireup="false"
    Inherits="ado_net_by_example.DataGrid" %>
<HTML>
    <HEAD>
        <meta name="GENERATOR" Content="Microsoft Visual Studio 7.0">
        <meta name="CODE_LANGUAGE" Content="C#">
    </HEAD>
    <body>
        <form method="post" runat="server">
            <asp:DataGrid id="DataGrid1" runat="server" BorderStyle="None"
                GridLines="Vertical" BorderWidth="1px" BorderColor="#999999"
                BackColor="White" CellPadding="3" AutoGenerateColumns="False"
                AllowSorting="true">
                <FooterStyle ForeColor="Black" BackColor="#CCCCCC">
                </FooterStyle>
                <HeaderStyle Font-Bold="True" ForeColor="White"
                BackColor="#000084"></HeaderStyle>
                <PagerStyle HorizontalAlign="Center" ForeColor="Black"
                BackColor="#999999" Mode="NumericPages"></PagerStyle>
                <SelectedItemStyle Font-Bold="True" ForeColor="White"
                BackColor="#008A8C"></SelectedItemStyle>
                <AlternatingItemStyle BackColor="#DCDCDC">
                </AlternatingItemStyle>
                <ItemStyle ForeColor="Black" BackColor="#EEEEEE"></ItemStyle>
                <Columns>
                    <asp:BoundColumn DataField="au_lname"
                    HeaderText="Last Name" SortExpression="au_lname">
                    </asp:BoundColumn>
                    <asp:BoundColumn DataField="au_fname"
                    HeaderText="First Name" SortExpression="au_fname">
                    </asp:BoundColumn>
                    <asp:BoundColumn DataField="state" HeaderText="State"
                    SortExpression="state"></asp:BoundColumn>
                </Columns>
            </asp:DataGrid>
        </asp:DataGrid>
```

Listing 4.21: continued

```
        </form>
    </body>
</HTML>
```

Listing 4.22: Custom columns with sorting—DataGrid.aspx.cs.

```
namespace ado_net_by_example
{
    using System;
    using System.Collections;
    using System.ComponentModel;
    using System.Data;
    using System.Data.SqlClient;
    using System.Drawing;
    using System.Web;
    using System.Web.SessionState;
    using System.Web.UI;
    using System.Web.UI.WebControls;
    using System.Web.UI.HtmlControls;

    /// <summary>
    ///     Summary description for DataGrid.
    /// </summary>
    public class DataGrid : System.Web.UI.Page
    {
        protected System.Web.UI.WebControls.DataGrid DataGrid1;

    public DataGrid()
    {
        Page.Init += new System.EventHandler(Page_Init);
    }

        protected void Page_Load(object sender, EventArgs e)
        {
            if (!IsPostBack)
            {
                DataSet ds = LoadAuthors();
                DataGrid1.DataSource = ds.Tables["authors"].DefaultView;
                DataGrid1.DataBind();
            }
        }

        protected DataSet LoadAuthors()
        {
            DataSet ds;
```

Listing 4.22: continued

```csharp
            if (Cache["authors"] == null)
            {
                SqlConnection cn = new SqlConnection(
                    "server=localhost;" +
                    "database=pubs;" +
                    "uid=sa;" +
                    "password=");

                SqlDataAdapter cmd = new SqlDataAdapter(
                    "select * from authors",cn);

                ds = new DataSet();

                cmd.Fill(ds,"authors");
                Cache.Insert("authors",ds,
                    null,
                    System.Web.Caching.Cache.NoAbsoluteExpiration,
                    TimeSpan.FromMinutes(5));
            }
            else
            {
                ds = (DataSet)Cache["authors"];
            }
            return ds;
        }

        protected void Page_Init(object sender, EventArgs e)
        {
            //
            // CODEGEN: This call is required by the ASP+ Windows Form
            // Designer.
            //
            InitializeComponent();
        }

        /// <summary>
        ///     Required method for Designer support - do not modify
        ///     the contents of this method with the code editor.
        /// </summary>
        private void InitializeComponent()
        {
            this.DataGrid1.SortCommand += new
                System.Web.UI.WebControls.DataGridSortCommandEventHandler(
                    this.DataGrid1_SortCommand);
            this.Load += new System.EventHandler(this.Page_Load);
```

Listing 4.22: continued

```
    }

    protected void DataGrid1_SortCommand (object source,
        System.Web.UI.WebControls.DataGridSortCommandEventArgs e)
    {
        DataSet ds = LoadAuthors();
        DataView dv = ds.Tables["authors"].DefaultView;
        dv.Sort = e.SortExpression.ToString();
        DataGrid1.DataSource = dv;
        DataGrid1.DataBind();
    }
  }
}
```

The Repeater Control

The DataGrid is great for rendering data as an HTML table, but sometimes, that's not the look we're going for. To have even more control over the output, we can use the Repeater control. This is known as a "look-less" control, meaning, not only can we take control over the display, we have to take control because this particular object has no default appearance at all. Instead, we're going to specify the look of the header, footer, and each item with a series of templates. To begin, add a new Web Form to the project named "Repeater". Switch to HTML view, and add the code in Listing 4.23 to the Form tag.

Listing 4.23: The Repeater control.

```
<asp:Repeater id=Repeater1 runat="server">
    <HeaderTemplate>
        <h1>Authors</h1>
    </HeaderTemplate>

    <ItemTemplate>
        <table>
            <tr>
                <td>First Name : </td>
                <td><%# DataBinder.Eval(Container.DataItem, "au_fname") %></td>
            </tr>
            <tr>
                <td>Last Name : </td>
                <td><%# DataBinder.Eval(Container.DataItem, "au_lname") %></td>
            </tr>
            <tr>
```

Listing 4.23: continued

```
                <td>State : </td>
                <td><%# DataBinder.Eval(Container.DataItem, "state") %></td>
            </tr>
        </table>
    </ItemTemplate>

    <SeparatorTemplate>
        <hr>
    </SeparatorTemplate>

</asp:Repeater>
```

The contents of the HeaderTemplate will get output first. Then, the ItemTemplate gets displayed for each row from the data source. To output the value of a particular column, use the following syntax:

```
<%# DataBinder.Eval(Container.DataItem, "au_lname") %>
```

The "<%# ... %>" is the data-binding syntax for ASP.NET. Between these brackets, you can call a function, output the value of a variable, or get your data from any other source. Each time the ItemTemplate gets hit, the Container.DataItem will contain the next row of data from the data source. To simplify getting a value from this row, we use the Eval method of the DataBinder class, passing Container.DataItem, and the name of the column whose value we want. Finally, the contents of the separator template will be output between each DataItem.

Check out Listings 4.24 and 4.25, and Figure 4.5 for the complete listing and output.

Listing 4.24: Using the DataRepeater—RepeaterControl.aspx.

```
<%@ Page language="c#" Codebehind="RepeaterControl.cs" AutoEventWireup="false"
    Inherits="ado_net_by_example.RepeaterControl" %>
<html>
<head>
    <meta name="GENERATOR" Content="Microsoft Visual Studio 7.0">
    <meta name="CODE_LANGUAGE" Content="C#">
</head>
<body>

<form method="post" runat="server">
    <asp:Repeater id=Repeater1 runat="server">
        <HeaderTemplate>
            <h1>Authors</h1>
        </HeaderTemplate>
```

Listing 4.24: continued

```
    <ItemTemplate>
        <table>
            <tr>
                <td>First Name : </td>
                <td><%# DataBinder.Eval(Container.DataItem, "au_fname") %>
                </td>
            </tr>
            <tr>
                <td>Last Name : </td>
                <td><%# DataBinder.Eval(Container.DataItem, "au_lname") %>
                </td>
            </tr>
            <tr>
                <td>State : </td>
                <td><%# DataBinder.Eval(Container.DataItem, "state") %>
                </td>
            </tr>
        </table>
    </ItemTemplate>

    <SeparatorTemplate>
        <hr>
    </SeparatorTemplate>

    </asp:Repeater>

</form>

</body>
</html>
```

Listing 4.25: Using the `DataRepeater`—`RepeaterControl.cs`.

```
namespace ado_net_by_example
{
    using System;
    using System.Collections;
    using System.ComponentModel;
    using System.Data;
    using System.Data.SqlClient;
    using System.Drawing;
    using System.Web;
    using System.Web.SessionState;
    using System.Web.UI;
    using System.Web.UI.WebControls;
    using System.Web.UI.HtmlControls;
```

Listing 4.25: continued

```
/// <summary>
///     Summary description for RepeaterControl.
/// </summary>
public class RepeaterControl : System.Web.UI.Page
{
    protected System.Web.UI.WebControls.Repeater Repeater1;

public RepeaterControl()
{
    Page.Init += new System.EventHandler(Page_Init);
    }

    protected void Page_Load(object sender, EventArgs e)
    {
        if (!IsPostBack)
        {
            DataSet ds = LoadAuthors();
            Repeater1.DataSource = ds.Tables["authors"];
            Repeater1.DataBind();
        }
    }

    protected DataSet LoadAuthors()
    {
        DataSet ds;
        if (Cache["authors"] == null)
        {
            SqlConnection cn = new SqlConnection(
                "server-localhost;" +
                "database=pubs;" +
                "uid=sa;" +
                "password=");

            SqlDataAdapter cmd = new SqlDataAdapter(
                "select * from authors",cn);

            ds = new DataSet();

            cmd.Fill(ds,"authors");
            Cache.Insert("authors",ds,
                null,
                System.Web.Caching.Cache.NoAbsoluteExpiration,
                TimeSpan.FromMinutes(5));
        }
```

Listing 4.25: continued

```
        else
        {
            ds = (DataSet)Cache["authors"];
        }
        return ds;
    }

    protected void Page_Init(object sender, EventArgs e)
    {
        //
        // CODEGEN: This call is required by the ASP+ Windows Form
        // Designer.
        //
        InitializeComponent();
    }

    /// <summary>
    ///     Required method for Designer support - do not modify
    ///     the contents of this method with the code editor.
    /// </summary>
    private void InitializeComponent()
    {
        this.Load += new System.EventHandler (this.Page_Load);
    }
  }
}
```

Figure 4.5: *Displaying data using the* Repeater *control.*

The DataList Control

The last data control that we're going to look at is the DataList control. This control offers "directional rendering," which means that you can output each item in rows and columns. We'll simply replace the Repeater with the DataList, and set its RepeatDirection to Horizontal or Vertical. We then specify the number of columns in the output by specifying a value for RepeatColumns:

```
<asp:datalist id=DataList1 runat="server"
    repeatdirection="Vertical"
    repeatcolumns="2">
```

Here's the complete output in Listings 4.26 and 4.27. You can see the output in Figure 4.6.

Listing 4.26: Using the DataList—DataListControl.aspx.

```
<%@ Page language="c#" Codebehind="DataListControl.cs" AutoEventWireup="false"
    Inherits="ado_net_by_example.DataListControl" %>
<html>
    <head>
        <meta name="GENERATOR" Content="Microsoft Visual Studio 7.0">
        <meta name="CODE_LANGUAGE" Content="C#">
    </head>
    <body>
        <form method="post" runat="server">
            <asp:datalist id="DataList1" runat="server"
                repeatdirection="Vertical" repeatcolumns="2">
                <HeaderTemplate>
                    <h1>
                        Authors
                    </h1>
                </HeaderTemplate>
                <ItemTemplate>
                    <table>
                        <tr>
                            <td>
                                First Name :
                            </td>
                            <td>
                                <%# DataBinder.Eval(
                                    Container.DataItem, "au_fname") %>
                            </td>
                        </tr>
                        <tr>
                            <td>
                                Last Name :
                            </td>
```

Listing 4.26: continued

```
                              <td>
                                  <%# DataBinder.Eval(
                                      Container.DataItem, "au_lname") %>
                              </td>
                          </tr>
                          <tr>
                              <td>
                                  State :
                              </td>
                              <td>
                                  <%# DataBinder.Eval(
                                      Container.DataItem, "state") %>
                              </td>
                          </tr>
                      </table>
                  </ItemTemplate>
              </asp:datalist>
          </form>
      </body>
</html>
```

Listing 4.27: Using the `DataList`—DataListControl.cs.

```csharp
namespace ado_net_by_example
{
    using System;
    using System.Collections;
    using System.ComponentModel;
    using System.Data;
    using System.Data.SqlClient;
    using System.Drawing;
    using System.Web;
    using System.Web.SessionState;
    using System.Web.UI;
    using System.Web.UI.WebControls;
    using System.Web.UI.HtmlControls;

    /// <summary>
    ///     Summary description for DataListControl.
    /// </summary>
    public class DataListControl : System.Web.UI.Page
    {
        protected System.Web.UI.WebControls.DataList DataList1;

        public DataListControl()
        {
```

Listing 4.27: continued

```
        Page.Init += new System.EventHandler(Page_Init);
    }

    protected void Page_Load(object sender, EventArgs e)
    {
        if (!IsPostBack)
        {
            DataSet ds = LoadAuthors();
            DataList1.DataSource = ds.Tables["authors"].DefaultView;
            DataList1.DataBind();
        }
    }

    protected DataSet LoadAuthors()
    {
        DataSet ds;
        if (Cache["authors"] == null)
        {
            SqlConnection cn = new SqlConnection(
                "server=localhost;" +
                "database=pubs;" +
                "uid=sa;" +
                "password=");

            SqlDataAdapter cmd = new SqlDataAdapter(
                "select * from authors order by au_lname",cn);

            ds = new DataSet();

            cmd.Fill(ds,"authors");
            Cache.Insert("authors",ds,
                null,
                System.Web.Caching.Cache.NoAbsoluteExpiration,
                TimeSpan.FromMinutes(5));
        }
        else
        {
            ds = (DataSet)Cache["authors"];
        }
        return ds;
    }

    protected void Page_Init(object sender, EventArgs e)
    {
        //
        // CODEGEN: This call is required by the ASP+ Windows Form
```

Listing 4.27: continued

```
            // Designer.
            //
            InitializeComponent();
        }


        /// <summary>
        ///    Required method for Designer support - do not modify
        ///    the contents of this method with the code editor.
        /// </summary>
        private void InitializeComponent()
        {
            this.Load += new System.EventHandler (this.Page_Load);
        }
    }
}
```

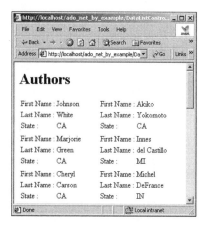

Figure 4.6: Displaying data using the DataList.

As you can see, directional rendering is very simple with the DataList. For those of you who've had to hand-code these kinds of pages in the past with ASP, I'm sure you can appreciate the elegance of this control.

Working with XML

Microsoft has recognized that XML "is the future." XML is becoming a substrate upon which all kinds of solutions are built. It's a great technology for business-to-business (B2B) and application-to-application (A2A) communication. It's useful for persisting data and "Save As" scenarios. It's even being used for platform and language-independent remote procedure calls (see the chapter on Web Services). But, at its core, XML is just text (see Listing 4.28).

Listing 4.28: A customer as XML.

```
<?xml version="1.0" encoding="utf-8" ?>
<Customer>
    <Name>
        <First>Scott</First>
        <Last>Swigart</Last>
    </Name>
    <Street>2222 NE Somewhere</Street>
    <City>Portland</City>
    <State>OR</State>
    <ZIP>97211</ZIP>
    <Web>http://www.3leafsolutions.com</Web>
</Customer>
```

Generating XML

The beauty of XML is that you can use it to represent any data, no matter how complex. XML has been used to describe molecules, financial transactions, mathematical equations, vector graphics, purchase orders, Shakespeare's plays, and more. With XML, you are completely free to make up whatever tags you want, and place them in whatever hierarchy you want.

A common use for XML is exporting data from a database so that it can be used on any platform, from any language (see Listings 4.29 and 4.30). Again, ASP.NET makes this simple. You can see the output of this page in Figure 4.7.

Listing 4.29: Outputting data as XML—ExportXML.aspx.

```
<%@ Page language="c#"
    Codebehind="ExportXML.cs"
    AutoEventWireup="false"
    Inherits="ado_net_by_example.ExportXML" %>
```

Listing 4.30: Outputting data as XML—ExportXML.cs.

```
namespace ado_net_by_example
{
    using System;
    using System.Collections;
    using System.ComponentModel;
    using System.Data;
    using System.Data.SqlClient;
    using System.Drawing;
    using System.Web;
```

Listing 4.30: continued

```csharp
using System.Web.SessionState;
using System.Web.UI;
using System.Web.UI.WebControls;
using System.Web.UI.HtmlControls;
using System.Xml;
using System.IO;

/// <summary>
///     Summary description for ExportXML.
/// </summary>
public class ExportXML : System.Web.UI.Page
{

public ExportXML()
{
    Page.Init += new System.EventHandler(Page_Init);
    }

    protected void Page_Load(object sender, EventArgs e)
    {
        if (!IsPostBack)
        {
            SqlConnection cn = new SqlConnection(
                "server=localhost;" +
                "database=pubs;" +
                "uid=sa;" +
                "password=");

            SqlDataAdapter cmd = new SqlDataAdapter(
                "select * from authors order by au_lname",cn);

            DataSet ds = new DataSet();

            cmd.Fill(ds,"authors");

            Response.ContentType="text/xml";
            StringWriter s = new StringWriter();
            ds.WriteXml(s);
            Response.Write (s.ToString());
        }
    }

    protected void Page_Init(object sender, EventArgs e)
    {
        //
```

Listing 4.30: continued

```
            // CODEGEN: This call is required by the ASP+ Windows Form Designer.
            //
            InitializeComponent();
        }


        /// <summary>
        ///     Required method for Designer support - do not modify
        ///     the contents of this method with the code editor.
        /// </summary>
        private void InitializeComponent()
        {
            this.Load += new System.EventHandler (this.Page_Load);
        }
    }
}
```

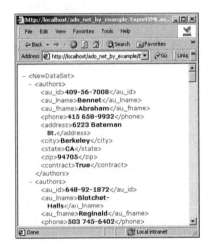

Figure 4.7: *Converting data to XML.*

As you can see, the DataSet contains a method called WriteXml that takes a
Stream as an argument. This way, we can easily write XML out to a text
file, or store it in a string. In our case, we simply output the string with
Response.Write, and now we've exposed data from our database to the
Internet as XML.

If we want to generate a Schema to go with our XML data, it's also very
simple:

```
Response.ContentType="text/xml";
StringWriter s = new StringWriter();
ds.WriteXmlSchema(s);
Response.Write (s.ToString());
```

This outputs to the following:

```xsd
<xsd:schema id="NewDataSet" targetNamespace="" xmlns=""
    xmlns:xsd="http://www.w3.org/2001/XMLSchema"
    xmlns:msdata="urn:schemas-microsoft-com:xml-msdata">
<xsd:element name="NewDataSet" msdata:IsDataSet="true">
  <xsd:complexType>
    <xsd:choice maxOccurs="unbounded">
      <xsd:element name="authors">
        <xsd:complexType>
          <xsd:sequence>
            <xsd:element name="au_id" type="xsd:string" minOccurs="0" />
            <xsd:element name="au_lname" type="xsd:string" minOccurs="0" />
            <xsd:element name="au_fname" type="xsd:string" minOccurs="0" />
            <xsd:element name="phone" type="xsd:string" minOccurs="0" />
            <xsd:element name="address" type="xsd:string" minOccurs="0" />
            <xsd:element name="city" type="xsd:string" minOccurs="0" />
            <xsd:element name="state" type="xsd:string" minOccurs="0" />
            <xsd:element name="zip" type="xsd:string" minOccurs="0" />
            <xsd:element name="contract" type="xsd:boolean" minOccurs="0" />
          </xsd:sequence>
        </xsd:complexType>
      </xsd:element>
    </xsd:choice>
  </xsd:complexType>
</xsd:element>
</xsd:schema>
```

If you've done much work with XML, you may notice that this schema looks a little different than what you're used to. The Microsoft XML Parser (MSXML) supported a schema specification called "XML Data Reduced (XDR)," which was essentially Microsoft-specific. In the meantime, the W3C has been working on an industry-standard schema recommendation. I'm happy to report that .NET supports the W3C recommendation. What's even better is that a DataSet can generate this schema document for you just by calling its WriteXmlSchema method.

Consuming XML

Fortunately, XML isn't a one-way trip for a DataSet. A DataSet can populate itself just as easily from an XML document (see Listing 4.31).

Listing 4.31: Populating a DataSet from XML.

```
DataSet ds = new DataSet();
ds.ReadXmlSchema(Server.MapPath("AuthorSchema.xsd"));
ds.ReadXml(Server.MapPath("Authors.xml"));

DataGrid1.DataSource = ds.Tables["authors"].DefaultView;
DataGrid1.DataBind();
```

To populate a DataSet, we just create an instance of a DataSet object. If we have a schema, we load it first by calling the ReadXmlSchema method of the DataSet. This needs a physical path to the file, so we use Server.MapPath to convert the relative path to the physical path.

After we've read in the schema, the DataSet knows the columns, and the data types of the columns. We can now load in the actual data with a call to ReadXml. That's it! Our DataSet is populated, and we can bind a DataGrid to it as before.

Summary

In this module, you've learned that the object model for ADO.NET is fundamentally different from ADO. Rather than assuming a constant connection to the database, you're working in a disconnected environment. ADO.NET also makes a distinction between the data, and our view of the data, with the DataSet and DataView.

ADO.NET supports "managed providers," which will allow you to access the database as efficiently as possible, but still maintain consistency through inheritance.

If you are accessing large result sets, you should use the DataReader to avoid storing the entire result set in memory. If we're working with smaller result sets, we should use the DataSet because the data is returned in one chunk, and the DataSet offers more functionality. For example, the DataSet allows sorting and filtering, and the DataSet knows how to serialize to XML. When combined with caching, this results in a great experience for the user, and a light load on the database.

When displaying data, you have a choice between several controls. The DataGrid renders each row from the database as a row of an HTML table. The Repeater doesn't have any default output, giving you maximum flexibility with the rendering through templates. With the DataList, each row from the database is rendered as a cell of a table, allowing "directional rendering."

Finally, .NET is built with XML in mind. The DataSet has native support for importing and exporting XML data.

What's Next?

In Chapter 5, we explore how to use HtmlControls and WebControls, how they differ from one another, and under what circumstances you will want to use each type of control.

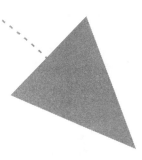

HTML/Web Controls

The simplest server controls provided by the ASP.NET Framework are the HtmlControls and WebControls. These two classes of controls simply render standard HTML tags, and provide two different means of programmatically accessing HTML display logic. HtmlControls and WebControls overlap somewhat, in that almost any HTML tag can be rendered as either an HtmlControl or a WebControl. In this chapter we will explore how to use these controls, how they differ from one another, and under what circumstances it would be appropriate to use one or the other type of control.

In this chapter, you will

- Learn what ASP.NET server controls are.

- Learn the differences between HtmlControls and WebControls, and when to use each.

What Are Server Controls, Anyway?

Before we get into the subtleties of HtmlControls and WebControls, we should really explain what a *server control* is. All server controls inherit from the `System.Web.UI.Control` class in the .NET Framework. As such, they share a common set of methods and properties that describe how all controls behave. In fact, all of the controls described in the next several chapters share a common heritage: They all inherit from the `System.Web.UI.Control` class.

For those of you who have never developed with Visual Basic or a similar application, the concept of controls might be new to you. Basically, a control is a programmatic object that is rendered as a part of the user interface (UI). With the right development application, such as Visual Studio .NET, you can create Web pages using controls simply by dragging and dropping controls from a toolbox onto the page. Further, you can modify all of the properties of a control programmatically, so for instance, if you need to set the value of a text box, you can do it from anywhere in your code, rather than having to add ASP script within the HTML of the <input> tag. There are many advantages to this, including the ability to keep all programming logic separate from HTML code, which allows greater reuse and makes it easier for teams of developers and graphic designers to work together.

The simplest controls provided with ASP.NET are the HtmlControls and WebControls described in this chapter. These controls, for the most part, simply render HTML with minimal bells and whistles. The more advanced server controls will be covered in later chapters, as will building your own custom controls.

NOTE

All of the samples in this chapter will be in C#. The VB.NET versions of the samples can be viewed at http://aspauthors.com/aspnetbyexample/ch05/.

Why Two Kinds of Controls?

Because HtmlControls and WebControls can both render the same standard HTML tags (for instance, a <form> </form> tag), why were both included in ASP.NET? There are several reasons. As we shall see, there are many cases in which either an Html or a Web Control will perform equally well on a page (or WebForm, as ASP.NET pages are often called). The chief differences between the two kinds of controls lie in their syntax and object model. The HtmlControl controls are designed to map as closely as possible to actual HTML tags, generally on a one-to-one basis. This means that, for instance, there are separate HtmlControls for text boxes (<input type=text>) and textareas (<textarea></textarea>).

WebControls, on the other hand, use a more consistent object model that groups like controls together and differentiates between them using properties (for instance, because the only difference between an <input type=text> and a <textarea> tag is that a textarea allows multiple lines of input, the TextBox WebControl includes a property TextMode that can be set to MultiLine).

The WebControls tend to have more features and a more intuitive object model than the HtmlControls. However, the beauty of HtmlControls is that they can be created directly from existing HTML tags simply by adding the runat="server" attribute. This makes it very easy to update existing HTML and to allow Web page design software to edit ASP.NET pages without choking on the custom syntax required for WebControls.

When Should I Use Each Kind of Control?

Generally, WebControls are more feature-rich and have a more consistent object model than the HtmlControls. However, if you are more familiar with HTML tags than with VB controls, you might find the HtmlControls easier to work with. If you need to programmatically alter the value of an HTML tag that doesn't have a corresponding WebControl, such as the <title> of a page, using an HtmlControl would be the easiest way to go. Also, if you need to work with graphic page designers who are using tools that understand HTML tags but not ASP.NET controls, you might find it easier to work with HtmlControls.

HtmlControls

The HtmlControls all inherit from System.Web.UI.HtmlControls.HtmlControl, and are the most basic server controls in the Framework. Any HTML tag can be made into an HtmlControl simply by adding runat="server" to it. There are about a dozen HtmlControls that have specific behavior, and thus have their own subclassed classes to describe them. Any other control is created as an HtmlGenericControl class. Figure 5.1 demonstrates the class hierarchy for the HtmlControls.

HtmlControl Properties and Methods

Because all HtmlControls inherit from the System.Web.UI.HtmlControls.HtmlControl class, its properties and methods are available to all HtmlControls, described in Table 5.1. The next sections introduce a few of the more commonly used attributes of this class.

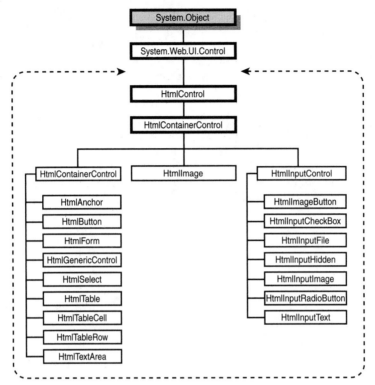

System.Web.UI.HtmlControls Namespace

Figure 5.1: *HtmlControls class hierarchy.*

Table 5.1: Summary of **HtmlControl** Properties and Methods

Name	Inherited	Item	Description
Attributes : AttributeCollection		Property	Returns a collection of name-value pairs that map to attributes of the HTML tag. Used for custom attributes that are not valid HTML and HTML attributes not exposed by a control's properties.
ClientID : String	Yes	Property	Returns the server control identifier created by ASP.NET.

Table 5.1: continued

Name	Inherited	Item	Description
Controls : ControlCollection	Yes	Property	Returns a collection of the child controls of the current control.
Disabled : Boolean		Property	Sets or returns whether or not the HtmlControl is disabled. Defaults to false.
EnableViewState : Boolean	Yes	Property	Sets or returns whether or not the HtmlControl should retain its value between page postbacks. Defaults to true.
ID : String	Yes	Property	The programmatic identifier of the control. Can be set with id= in the control's declaration.
Style : CssStyleCollection		Property	Returns a CssStyleCollection that holds CSS style properties for the HtmlControl.
TagName : String		Property	Returns the name of the HTML element that was used to create this HtmlControl, such as "b" or "form".
Visible : Boolean	Yes	Property	Returns or sets whether or not the control should be displayed when the page is rendered. Defaults to true.
DataBind : Void	Yes	Method	Binds a datasource to the control and its child controls.
FindControl : Control	Yes	Method	Searches the current naming container for a control with the ID provided, and returns that control if found.
HasControls : Boolean	Yes	Method	Returns true if the HtmlControl contains any child controls, otherwise returns false.

The properties and methods marked "Yes" in the Inherited column are properties and methods of HtmlControl that it inherits from the System.Web.UI.Control class. These properties and methods are a part of every control, whether it is an HtmlControl, a WebControl, or a custom control that you write yourself (custom controls are covered in Chapter 12, Custom ASP.NET Controls).

HtmlContainerControl Properties

As we saw in Figure 5.1, many HtmlControls inherit from another base class, HtmlContainerControl (which in turn inherits from HtmlControl). These controls represent HTML elements that are made up of both starting and ending tags, with content in between, such as `<table>...</table>` or `<a>...</a>`. As such, they are said to contain additional HTML, and to access their contents, they expose two properties as described in Table 5.2.

Table 5.2: **HtmlContainerControl** *Properties*

Property	Description
InnerHtml : String	Gets or sets all of the content found between the opening and closing tags of the HtmlControl.
InnerText : String	Gets or sets the text between the opening and closing tags of the HtmlControl. Automatically encodes special characters (such as "<" or ">") so that they are displayed on the page as typed (for example, "<" or ">"). If you need to add HTML content, use the InnerHtml property.

An HtmlControl Example

The easiest way to get a quick handle on how HtmlControls work is through an example. In one page, we will use every HtmlControl. To demonstrate how the controls are created by ASP.NET based on these HTML tags, we will use an ASP.NET feature called Tracing, which will be covered in more detail in Chapter 13, "Debugging ASP.NET Overview." As part of the Trace output, you can see the Control Tree, which describes all of the controls created on the page, and how they are nested within one another. Figure 5.2 shows the output of the page, without the trace.

As you can see, this sample page makes use of many different HTML elements, such as images, links, buttons, radio buttons, check boxes, and drop-down lists. All of these HTML elements have corresponding HtmlControls, as Figure 5.3 demonstrates.

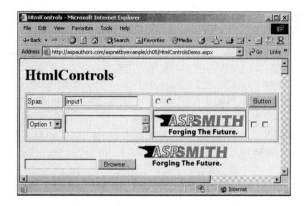

Figure 5.2: *HtmlControls demo page.*

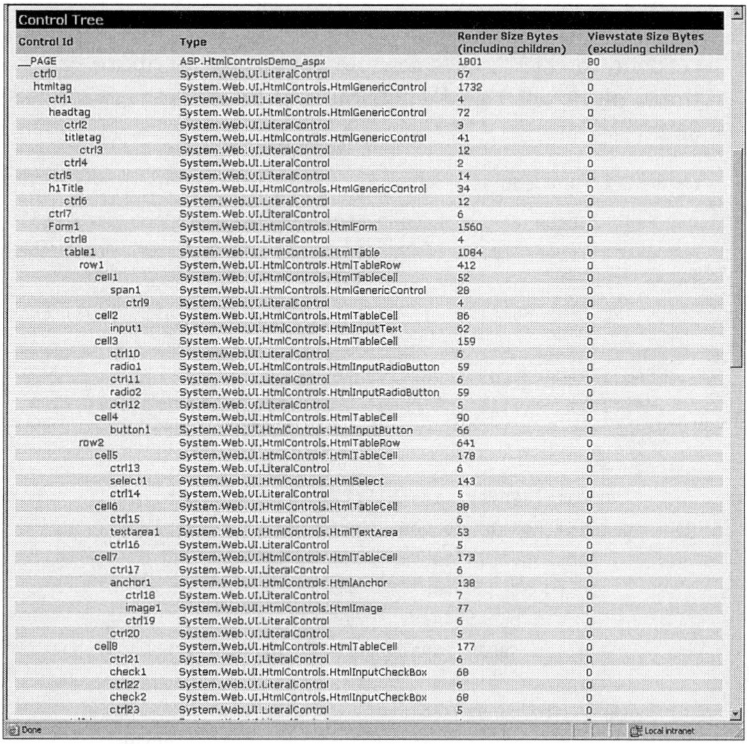

Control Tree

Control Id	Type	Render Size Bytes (including children)	Viewstate Size Bytes (excluding children)
__PAGE	ASP.HtmlControlsDemo_aspx	1801	80
ctrl0	System.Web.UI.LiteralControl	67	0
htmltag	System.Web.UI.HtmlControls.HtmlGenericControl	1732	0
ctrl1	System.Web.UI.LiteralControl	4	0
headtag	System.Web.UI.HtmlControls.HtmlGenericControl	72	0
ctrl2	System.Web.UI.LiteralControl	3	0
titletag	System.Web.UI.HtmlControls.HtmlGenericControl	41	0
ctrl3	System.Web.UI.LiteralControl	12	0
ctrl4	System.Web.UI.LiteralControl	2	0
ctrl5	System.Web.UI.LiteralControl	14	0
h1Title	System.Web.UI.HtmlControls.HtmlGenericControl	34	0
ctrl6	System.Web.UI.LiteralControl	12	0
ctrl7	System.Web.UI.LiteralControl	6	0
Form1	System.Web.UI.HtmlControls.HtmlForm	1560	0
ctrl8	System.Web.UI.LiteralControl	4	0
table1	System.Web.UI.HtmlControls.HtmlTable	1084	0
row1	System.Web.UI.HtmlControls.HtmlTableRow	412	0
cell1	System.Web.UI.HtmlControls.HtmlTableCell	52	0
span1	System.Web.UI.HtmlControls.HtmlGenericControl	28	0
ctrl9	System.Web.UI.LiteralControl	4	0
cell2	System.Web.UI.HtmlControls.HtmlTableCell	86	0
input1	System.Web.UI.HtmlControls.HtmlInputText	62	0
cell3	System.Web.UI.HtmlControls.HtmlTableCell	159	0
ctrl10	System.Web.UI.LiteralControl	6	0
radio1	System.Web.UI.HtmlControls.HtmlInputRadioButton	59	0
ctrl11	System.Web.UI.LiteralControl	6	0
radio2	System.Web.UI.HtmlControls.HtmlInputRadioButton	59	0
ctrl12	System.Web.UI.LiteralControl	5	0
cell4	System.Web.UI.HtmlControls.HtmlTableCell	90	0
button1	System.Web.UI.HtmlControls.HtmlInputButton	66	0
row2	System.Web.UI.HtmlControls.HtmlTableRow	641	0
cell5	System.Web.UI.HtmlControls.HtmlTableCell	178	0
ctrl13	System.Web.UI.LiteralControl	6	0
select1	System.Web.UI.HtmlControls.HtmlSelect	143	0
ctrl14	System.Web.UI.LiteralControl	5	0
cell6	System.Web.UI.HtmlControls.HtmlTableCell	88	0
ctrl15	System.Web.UI.LiteralControl	6	0
textarea1	System.Web.UI.HtmlControls.HtmlTextArea	53	0
ctrl16	System.Web.UI.LiteralControl	5	0
cell7	System.Web.UI.HtmlControls.HtmlTableCell	173	0
ctrl17	System.Web.UI.LiteralControl	6	0
anchor1	System.Web.UI.HtmlControls.HtmlAnchor	138	0
ctrl18	System.Web.UI.LiteralControl	7	0
image1	System.Web.UI.HtmlControls.HtmlImage	77	0
ctrl19	System.Web.UI.LiteralControl	6	0
ctrl20	System.Web.UI.LiteralControl	5	0
cell8	System.Web.UI.HtmlControls.HtmlTableCell	177	0
ctrl21	System.Web.UI.LiteralControl	6	0
check1	System.Web.UI.HtmlControls.HtmlInputCheckBox	68	0
ctrl22	System.Web.UI.LiteralControl	6	0
check2	System.Web.UI.HtmlControls.HtmlInputCheckBox	68	0
ctrl23	System.Web.UI.LiteralControl	5	0

Figure 5.3: *HtmlControls demo page Control Tree.*

Examining the Control Tree in the trace output, we see that the first HtmlControl on the page has the ID of `htmltag`, and is an `HtmlGenericControl`. There are several of these generic controls, including ***`headtag`***, ***`titletag`***, and ***`H1Title`***, which are simply HTML tags with `runat="server"` added to them, but which don't have any special object behavior. Because there are dozens of legal elements defined in the HTML specification, but many whose behavior is not particularly different from many other tags, the HtmlGenericControl provides the programmatic interface to all of these tags. The HtmlGenericControl only exposes one property in addition to the ones described in the HtmlControl and HtmlContainerControl classes, and that is the TagName property. TagName is a String that can be used to get or set the name of the element that the HtmlGenericControl represents. For instance, the TagName of the tag <a href='foo'> is 'a'.

Also note the many LiteralControl controls on the page. These are placed between any HtmlControls that could have additional HTML content between them (which is between almost every control). Note that because there is no valid HTML that can be placed between a <tr> tag and its child <td> tags, there are no LiteralControls wrapping these tags.

Looking at Listing 5.1, you will notice that the HtmlGenericControls all correspond to HTML tags that have had the attribute runat="server" added to them, along with an ID attribute. If no ID is specified, ASP.NET will assign one.

EXAMPLE

Listing 5.1: HtmlControlsDemo.aspx.

```
<%@ Page language="c#" Codebehind="HtmlControlsDemo.aspx.cs"
AutoEventWireup="false" Inherits="Html_Web_Controls.HtmlControlsDemo"
Trace="True"%>
<!DOCTYPE HTML PUBLIC "-//W3C//DTD HTML 4.0 Transitional//EN" >
<HTML runat="server" id="htmltag">
  <HEAD id="headtag" runat="server">
    <title id="titletag" runat="server">HtmlControls</title>
</HEAD>
  <body >
    <h1 runat="server" id="h1Title">HtmlControls</h1>
    <form id="Form1" method="post" runat="server">
        <table runat="server" id="table1">
        <tr runat="server" id="row1">
            <td runat="server" id="cell1">
                <span runat="server" id="span1">Span</span>
            </td>
            <td runat="server" id="cell2">
                    <input id="input1" runat="server"
                        value="input1">
            </td>
            <td runat="server" id="cell3">
                <input id="radio1" runat="server"
                    type="radio" value="Choice 1" >
                <input id="radio2" runat="server"
```

Listing 5.1: continued

```
                        type="radio" value="Choice 2" >
            </td>
            <td runat="server" id="cell4"><input type="button"
            runat="server" id="button1" value="Button" ></td>
        </tr>
        <tr runat="server" id="row2">
            <td runat="server" id="cell5">
                <select runat="server" id="select1">
                    <option >Option 1</option>
                    <option >Option 2</option>
                </select>
            </td>
            <td runat="server" id="cell6">
                <textarea runat="server" id="textarea1"></textarea>
            </td>
            <td runat="server" id="cell7">
                <a runat="server" id="anchor1"
                    href="http://aspsmith.com/">
                    <img
                    src="http://aspsmith.com/images/aspsmith_logo_197x53.gif"
                        runat="server" id="image1" >
                </a>
            </td>
            <td runat="server" id="cell8">
                <input type="checkbox" runat="server"
                    id="check1" value="choice 1" name="check1">
                <input type="checkbox" runat="server"
                    id="check2" value="choice 2" name="check2">
            </td>
        </tr>
        </table>
        <input type="hidden" runat="server" id="hidden1">
        <input type="file" runat="server" id="file1" >
        <input type="image" runat="server" id="imagebutton1"
        alt="Input type=image"
        src="http://aspsmith.com/images/aspsmith_logo_197x53.gif">
    </form>

  </body>
</HTML>
```

HtmlForm Properties

Looking once more at Figure 5.3, we see that the first nongeneric HtmlControl on the page is Form1. Form1 is an HTML form tag, and is represented by the HtmlForm class, which has several properties specific to it, described in Table 5.3.

Table 5.3: `HtmlForm` *Properties*

Property	Description
`Enctype : String`	Gets or sets the encoding type. The default is `application/x-www-form-urlencoded`. File upload forms should use `multipart/form-data`.
`Method : String`	Gets or sets a value that indicates how the browser posts form data. The two most common methods are `GET` and `POST`. The default is `POST`.
`Name : String`	Gets or sets the identifier name of the control. Identical to the `UniqueID` property.
`Target : String`	Gets or sets the value that represents the frame or window where the form's output should be sent. Not required for typical postback operations.

It is interesting to note that the `HtmlForm` control does not have an `Action` property, which is a valid attribute of the `<form>` tag in HTML. The `Action` attribute specifies a URL to which the form should be posted. ASP.NET's event model is designed around the concept of pages that post back to themselves, and so if a page needs to submit data to another page, it should simply use an HTML form tag and no server controls. In most situations, multiple pages are not needed, and a single page using postbacks and redirects will work.

Table Control Properties

Continuing with our walkthrough of Figure 5.3, the next controls we encounter after `Form1` are `table1`, `row1`, and `cell1`. These controls are instances of `HtmlTable`, `HtmlmTableRow`, and `HtmlTableCell` classes, respectively. These controls are, not surprisingly, used to represent HTML table structures. As such, they expose a number of properties that are useful in formatting these tables, and basically map directly to HTML attributes (see Table 5.4).

Table 5.4: Table Control Properties

Class	Properties (String unless noted)
`HtmlTable`	Align, BgColor, Border : Int32, BorderColor, CellPadding : Int32, CellSpacing : Int32, Height, Rows : HtmlTableRowsCollection, Width
`HtmlTableRow`	Align, BgColor, Border, BorderColor, Cells: HtmlTableCellCollection, Height, Valign
`HtmlTableCell`	Align, BgColor, Border, BorderColor, ColSpan : Int32, Height, NoWrap : Boolean, RowSpan : Int32, VAlign, Width

Using these properties, it is very easy to programmatically alter the formatting of tables and their contents. For instance, adding these lines to the Page_Load event of the HtmlControlsDemo.aspx.cs page (the codebehind page for HtmlControlsDemo.aspx), which is executed whenever the page is loaded

EXAMPLE

```
private void Page_Load(object sender, System.EventArgs e)
{
    // Put user code to initialize the page here
    table1.Border = 2;
    row1.BorderColor = "red";
    cell1.BorderColor = "blue";
}
```

results in this HTML output:

OUTPUT

```
<table id="table1" border="2">
<tr id="row1" bordercolor="red">
<td id="cell1" bordercolor="blue">
...
```

HtmlInputControl Properties

Continuing on with the sample page, the next new controls we encounter are input1, an HtmlInputText control, radio1 and radio2, a pair of HtmlInputRadioButton controls, and button1, an HtmlInputButton. All of these controls inherit from the HtmlInputControl base class, which exposes the three properties described in Table 5.5, in addition to those of its parent, HtmlControl.

Table 5.5: **HtmlInputControl** *Properties*

Property	Description
Name : String	Same as for HtmlForm.
Type : String	Gets the type of the control. Possible values include button, checkbox, file, hidden, image, password, radio, reset, submit, and text.
Value : String	Gets or sets the contents of the control.

The HtmlInputText control simply displays a text box, and exposes integer properties of MaxLength and Size that map directly to the HTML attributes of the same name. The HtmlInputRadioButton control renders to a radio button, and includes a Boolean property Checked that can be read or set. In addition, the HtmlInputText and HtmlInputRadioButton controls both have an event, ServerChange, that is raised whenever the value of the control changes. When this event occurs, if there is a corresponding event handler function set up in the ASP.NET page, that function will be executed in response to the event. This is what allows ASP.NET to use an event-driven programming model, as opposed to the more procedural programming model of ASP.

The HtmlInputButton control maps to an HTML button, and has one new property, CausesValidation, which is Boolean. This property defaults to true, and determines whether or not clicking on this button should cause validation controls to be activated. We will cover validation controls in

Chapter 8, "Using ASP.NET Validation Controls." The HtmlInputButton also raises an event, ServerClick, which occurs when the button is clicked.

HtmlSelect Properties

Moving to row two of our sample page, we find controls for HtmlSelect, HtmlTextArea, HtmlAnchor, HtmlImage, and HtmlInputCheckBox. Of these, the HtmlSelect control is the most complicated, primarily because it can be populated automatically from a data source using data binding. It exposes the properties described in Table 5.6.

Table 5.6: HtmlSelect Properties

Property	Description
DataSource : Object	Gets or sets the object to be used as the data source for this control.
DataTextField : String	Gets or sets the name of the field in the data source that will provide the text for each option in the list.
DataValueField : String	Gets or sets the name of the field in the data source that will provide the value for each option in the list.
InnerHtml : String	Same as for HtmlContainer.
InnerText : String	Same as for HtmlContainer.
Items : ListItemCollection	A collection of ListItems that make up the options in the selection list.
Multiple : Boolean	Gets or sets a value indicating whether multiple values in the selection list can be selected. Defaults to false.
Name : String	Same as for HtmlForm.
SelectedIndex : Int32	Gets or sets the zero-based index of the selected list item.
SelectedIndices : Int32 Array	Gets or sets an array of integers, each of which represents a selected item in the option list.
Size : Int32	Gets or sets a value corresponding to the number of options to list on a page at a time. Defaults to 1.
Value : String	Gets or sets value of the currently selected item.

We'll look at some different ways of populating select lists later in this chapter. For this example, you can see that we simply added <option> tags just as we normally would on an HTML page. In addition to the properties listed in Table 5.6, the HtmlSelect control also has one event, ServerChange, which is fired whenever the selected item of the list changes.

HtmlTextArea Properties

The HtmlTextArea control, textarea1, is the next one we see in our example, and Table 5.7 describes the properties unique to it.

Table 5.7: **HtmlTextArea** *Properties*

Property	Description
Cols : Int32	Gets or sets the number of columns the control should have. Maps directly to HTML attribute.
Name : String	Same as for HtmlForm.
Rows : Int32	Gets or sets the number of rows the control should have. Maps directly to HTML attribute.
Value : String	Gets or sets the value of the contents of the textarea box.

HtmlAnchor Properties

The Anchor tag is probably one of the most commonly used HTML tags, and it exposes several properties unique to the HtmlAnchor control, as described in Table 5.8.

Table 5.8: **HtmlAnchor** *Properties*

Property	Description
Href : String	Gets or sets the URL target of the link.
Name : String	Same as for HtmlForm.
Target : String	Same as for HtmlForm.
Title : String	Provides a tool tip for the link on the page.

Again, these properties pretty much just map to HTML attributes. The Anchor tag also supports one event, ServerClick, which is fired whenever a user clicks on the link.

HtmlImage Properties

The HtmlImage control maps to the HTML <img> tag, and has the properties described in Table 5.9.

Table 5.9: **HtmlImage** *Properties*

Property	Description
Align : String	Gets or sets the alignment of the image relative to other elements on the page. Valid values include left, center, right, top, middle, and bottom.
Alt : String	Gets or sets the caption displayed if the image is unavailable or the user moves their mouse over the image.
Border : Int32	Gets or sets the width, in pixels, of the image's border.
Height : Int32	Gets or sets the height of the image, in pixels.
Src : String	Gets or sets the URL of the image file to be displayed by this control.
Width : Int32	Gets or sets the width of the image, in pixels.

All of the HtmlImage properties map directly to HTML attributes. The last HtmlControl we see in this row of the table is the HtmlInputCheckBox. The HtmlInputCheckBox supports one new property, Checked, which is a Boolean value representing whether or not the control is checked. It also supports one event, ServerChange, which is fired whenever the value of the control changes.

Finally, there are three last HtmlControls on the page that we haven't yet covered. They are shown at the bottom of the Control Tree in the trace output, and appear under the table on the page. They are all HtmlInputControls. These last controls include the HtmlInputHidden, HtmlInputFile, and HtmlInputImage controls.

The HtmlInputHidden control is one of the more useful HtmlControls, because you can use it easily to persist values from page to page with the same techniques employed by most classic ASP applications. However, you should avoid using custom hidden form fields to persist values, because ASP.NET offers several other methods that are usually better. You might store the data as a cookie, or in ViewState, or even in the cache, instead of storing it in its own hidden form field. Consider these alternatives when you are architecting your solutions. The HtmlInputHidden control is very simple, and aside from the properties of the HtmlInputControl, it handles a ServerChange event that is fired whenever its value is changed.

HtmlInputFile Properties

For file uploading, the HtmlInputFile control should be used. It exposes several properties unique to the file uploading process, which are detailed in Table 5.10.

Table 5.10: HtmlInputFile *Properties*

Property	Description
Accept : String	Gets or sets a comma-separated list of MIME types that the control will accept as uploads.
MaxLength : Int32	Gets or sets the maximum size of the file to be uploaded, in bytes.
PostedFile : HttpPostedFile	Provides access to the file that was uploaded to the control.
Size : Int32	Gets or sets the width of the text box where the file path is entered.

Uploading files was something difficult to manage in classic ASP, requiring a custom component or at the very least some very complicated script code. File uploading with ASP.NET is just as easy as posting any other data to a form—just one of the many benefits of ASP.NET.

HtmlInputImage Properties

The last HtmlControl on the page is an HtmlInputImage control (imagebutton1). HtmlInputImage controls combine the functions of the HtmlImage and the HtmlInputButton controls, and have the following properties:

`HtmlInputImage` controls combine the functions of the `HtmlImage` (with the properties `Align : String, Alt : String, Border : Int32,` and `Src : String` properties) and the `HtmlInputButton` controls (with the `CausesValidation : Boolean` property).

That's it; we've looked at every HtmlControl that ships with ASP.NET now, at least briefly. As you've seen, using these controls is very easy, so we're not going to waste time going into any greater depth with these examples. Next we'll take a look at WebControls, which are somewhat more powerful than HtmlControls and are what we will use for the most part throughout the rest of the book in our examples.

WebControls

WebControls are all derived from `System.Web.UI.WebControls.WebControl`, which itself derives from the `Control` class. The hierarchy of WebControls thus looks very similar to the HtmlControl class hierarchy from Figure 5.1. Figure 5.4 shows the WebControl class hierarchy.

For this chapter, we'll be looking at the controls on the left side of Figure 5.4. Most of the more complex controls are covered in the next few chapters.

`WebControl` Properties

To begin, though, we should take a look at the `WebControl` class itself, because all of its properties and methods are built into every WebControl. The most commonly used properties of the `WebControl` class are detailed in Table 5.11.

Table 5.11: **WebControl** *Properties*

Property	Description
`AccessKey : String`	Gets or sets a keyboard key to be used as a shortcut for setting focus to this control.
`Attributes : AttributeCollection`	Same as for HtmlControl.
`BackColor : Color`	Gets or sets the background color of the control. Defaults to `Empty`.
`BorderColor : Color`	Gets or sets the border color of the control. Defaults to `Empty`.
`BorderStyle : BorderStyle`	Gets or sets the border style of the control. Defaults to `NotSet`.
`BorderWidth : Unit`	Gets or sets the border width of the control. Defaults to `Empty`.
`CssClass : String`	Gets or sets the CSS class for the control. Defaults to `Empty`.
`Enabled : Boolean`	Gets or sets a value indicating whether the control is enabled. Defaults to true.
`Font : FontInfo`	Gets font information from the control.
`ForeColor : Color`	Gets or sets the foreground color of the control. Typically used for the text of the control. Defaults to `Empty`.

Table 5.11: continued

Property	Description
Height : Unit	Gets or sets the height of the control. Defaults to Empty.
Style : CssStyleCollection	Same as for HtmlControl.
TabIndex : Int16	Gets or sets the tab index of the control. Used to determine the tab order on the page. Defaults to 0.
ToolTip : String	Gets or sets the tool tip value for the control. Defaults to Empty.
Width : Unit	Gets or sets the width of the control. Defaults to Empty.

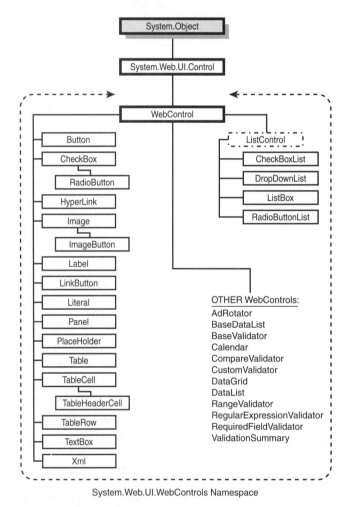

System.Web.UI.WebControls Namespace

Figure 5.4: WebControls class hierarchy.

At first glance, you can easily see that the WebControl base class has a lot more properties than the HtmlControl base class. In addition to those properties listed here, WebControls also share all of the properties and methods of the System.Web.UI.Control class, such as the ones in italics in the description of the HtmlControl class at the start of this chapter. Furthermore, notice that almost all of the properties are strongly typed to custom datatypes. Instead of using a string for colors and an integer for pixel lengths like many of the HtmlControls do, the WebControl class uses a Color class and a Unit class to allow for strongly typed property setting. This makes for code that is easier to read and debug at compile time as opposed to runtime.

As with the HtmlControls, it is fairly simple to create a single ASP.NET page that demonstrates the use of every WebControl we will be covering in this chapter. Figure 5.5 shows what this page looks like in a browser.

As with the HtmlControls section, we'll go ahead and look at the complete source code for our demo page before we go through each control as it appears on the page. Listing 5.2 shows the source for our example.

EXAMPLE

Listing 5.2: WebControlsDemo.aspx.

```
<%@ Page language="c#" Codebehind="WebControlsDemo.aspx.cs"
Src="WebControlsDemo.aspx.cs" AutoEventWireup="false"
Inherits="ASPAuthors.aspnetbyexample.ch05.WebControlsDemo" %>
<!DOCTYPE HTML PUBLIC "-//W3C//DTD HTML 4.0 Transitional//EN" >
<HTML>
  <HEAD>
        <title>WebControls</title>
</HEAD>
    <body>
        <h1>
            WebControls
        </h1>
        <form id="WebControls" method="post" runat="server">
            <table>
                <tr>
                    <td>
                        Button
                    </td>
                    <td>
                        <asp:Button runat="server" id=Button1></asp:Button>
                    </td>
                </tr>
                <tr>
                    <td>
                        Checkbox
                    </td>
                    <td>
                        <asp:CheckBox runat="server"
                        id=CheckBox1></asp:CheckBox>
                    </td>
                </tr>
                <tr>
```

```
            <td>
                RadioButton
            </td>
            <td>
                <asp:RadioButton runat="server" id="RadioButton1"
                GroupName="Group"></asp:RadioButton>
                <asp:RadioButton runat="server" id="RadioButton2"
                GroupName="Group"></asp:RadioButton>
            </td>
        </tr>
        <tr>
            <td>
                HyperLink
            </td>
            <td>
                <asp:HyperLink runat="server"
                id=HyperLink1></asp:HyperLink>
            </td>
        </tr>
        <tr>
            <td>
                Image
            </td>
            <td>
                <asp:Image runat="server" id=Image1></asp:Image>
            </td>
        </tr>
        <tr>
            <td>
                ImageButton
            </td>
            <td>
                <asp:ImageButton runat="server"
                id=ImageButton1></asp:ImageButton>
            </td>
        </tr>
        <tr>
            <td>
                Label
            </td>
            <td>
                <asp:Label runat="server" id=Label1></asp:Label>
            </td>
        </tr>
        <tr>
            <td>
                LinkButton
            </td>
            <td>
                <asp:LinkButton runat="server"
                id=LinkButton1></asp:LinkButton>
            </td>
        </tr>
        <tr>
            <td>
                Literal
            </td>
            <td>
                <asp:Literal runat="server"
```

```
➥id=Literal1></asp:Literal>
                    </td>
                </tr>
                <tr>
                    <td>
                        Panel
                    </td>
                    <td>
                        <asp:Panel runat="server" id=Panel1></asp:Panel>
                    </td>
                </tr>
                <tr>
                    <td>
                        PlaceHolder
                    </td>
                    <td>
                        <asp:PlaceHolder runat="server"
                        id=PlaceHolder1></asp:PlaceHolder>
                    </td>
                </tr>
                <tr>
                    <td>
                        Table, Row, Cell
                    </td>
                    <td>
                        <asp:Table runat="server" id=Table1>
<asp:TableRow id="TableRow1" runat="server">
<asp:TableCell id="TableCell1" runat="server"></asp:TableCell></asp:TableRow>
                        </asp:Table>
                    </td>
                </tr>
                <tr>
                    <td>
                        TextBox
                    </td>
                    <td>
                        <asp:TextBox runat="server"
➥id=TextBox1></asp:TextBox>
                    </td>
                </tr>
                <tr>
                    <td>
                        XML
                    </td>
                    <td>
                        <asp:Xml runat="server" id=Xml1></asp:Xml>
                    </td>
                </tr>
            </table>
        </form>
    </body>
</HTML>
```

Some of the values in this example are set in the codebehind; the complete source is available on the book's Web site at http://aspauthors.com/ aspnetbyexample/ch05/.

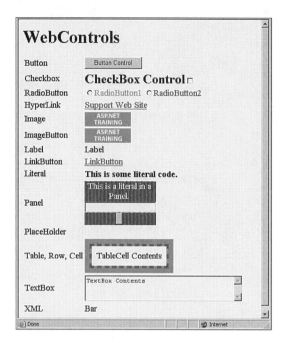

Figure 5.5: *WebControlsDemo.aspx.*

Button

The Button WebControl is used to render any HTML button, and supports Click or custom Command events. Its properties are described in Table 5.12.

Table 5.12: Button Properties

Property	Description
CausesValidation : Boolean	Gets or sets a value that determines whether clicking this control causes ValidationControls to execute their behavior. Defaults to true.
CommandArgument : String	Gets or sets an optional parameter that would be passed to the Command event. Should be used in conjunction with the CommandName property. Defaults to Empty.
CommandName : String	Gets or sets the command name associated with the control. Defaults to Empty.
Text : String	Gets or sets the text displayed in the control.

For our example, the only one of these properties we used was the Text property, which we set to "Button Control" using code. The CausesValidation property is a good one to remember because any page that has multiple buttons, only some of which are used to submit values, should have the other buttons' CausesValidation property set to false.

In addition to these properties, the Button control supports two events: Click and Command. The Click event is fired whenever the button is clicked. The Command event is fired if there is a CommandName specified, in which case the name specified in CommandName determines the signature of the event handler that is expected. Using CommandName and CommandArgument, you can specify a particular command to execute, such as a sort, and specify a single argument for that command, such as ascending.

CheckBox

The CheckBox control exposes the properties described in Table 5.13.

Table 5.13: **CheckBox** *Properties*

Property	Description
AutoPostBack : Boolean	Gets or sets a value that determines whether a change to this control should result in an automatic form postback. Defaults to false.
Checked : Boolean	Gets or sets whether or not the control is checked. Defaults to false.
Text : String	Gets or sets the text label associated with the control. Defaults to Empty.
TextAlign : TextAlign	Gets or sets the alignment of the text label (that is, which side of the control the text appears on). The default is Right.

In our example, we have set the AutoPostBack value of CheckBox to true, so checking or unchecking the box results in the form posting immediately. The CheckBox control also supports one event, CheckedChanged, which is fired on any postback where the value of the check box has changed. The use of this control is also covered in the example from Listing 5.2.

RadioButton

The RadioButton control is a subclass of the CheckBox control, so it includes all of that control's behavior. In addition, it has the GroupName : String property, which gets or sets the name of the group to which the radio button belongs. Only one RadioButton in a group can be set at a time. Defaults to Empty.

To demonstrate the use of the GroupName property, the example uses two radio buttons with the same group name. Thus, only one or the other of the two buttons can be selected at a time, which is how one typically uses the radiobutton control.

HyperLink

The HyperLink control simply renders a link on a page, which can be either text or an image. Table 5.14 describes the HyperLink properties.

Table 5.14: **HyperLink** *Properties*

Property	Description
ImageUrl : String	Gets or sets the URL for the image to be used by this link. If set, the Text property is used for the ALT text of the image. Defaults to Empty.
NavigateUrl : String	Gets or sets the URL to which the hyperlink should link. Defaults to Empty.
Target : String	Gets or sets the frame or window that should load the page linked to by NavigateUrl. Defaults to Empty.
Text : String	Gets or sets the text caption for the link. Defaults to Empty.

HyperLinks are fairly simple controls, and do not support any events.

Image

The Image WebControl renders an image on a page. Table 5.15 describes the Image properties.

Table 5.15: **Image** *Properties*

Property	Description
AlternateText : String	Gets or sets the alternate text that is displayed in place of the image when the image is unavailable, or as a ToolTip.
Enabled : Boolean	This property doesn't appear to be implemented in ASP.NET Beta 2.
Font : FontInfo	Gets or sets the font properties of the alternate text. This property has no effect in Internet Explorer.
ImageAlign : ImageAlign	Gets or sets the alignment of the Image in relation to other page elements. Defaults to NotSet. Allowable values include NotSet, Left, Right, Baseline, Top, Middle, Bottom, AbsBottom, AbsMiddle, and TextTop.
ImageUrl : String	Gets or sets the location of an image to display in the control.

The Image control does not support any events. As with all WebControls, the Image control has properties for height and width that can be used to control the size of the image to be rendered.

ImageButton

The ImageButton WebControl inherits from the Image WebControl, and thus has all of its properties. In addition, the ImageButton has several additional properties and events that make it behave like a Button. It includes the following properties: CausesValidation : Boolean, CommandArgument : String, and CommandName : String, which function in the same way as the Button properties of the same name.

In addition, the ImageButton supports the Click and Command events, which behave just like the corresponding events for the Button WebControl.

Label

The Label is a very simple WebControl that simply renders text on a page. Label has the Text : String property, which gets or sets the value that is rendered by the Label.

Note that the Label control always renders its Text property within a <span> tag. If you want to only output specific text to the browser with no extra tags, you should use the Literal WebControl.

LinkButton

The LinkButton is another variant of the Button control, which renders on the page as a hyperlink. Table 5.16 shows its properties.

Table 5.16: **LinkButton** *Properties*

Property	Description
CausesValidation : Boolean	Same as for Button.
CommandArgument : String	Same as for Button.
CommandName : String	Same as for Button.
Text : String	Gets or sets the value that is rendered on the page as the hyperlink.

The LinkButton also supports the Click and Command events, which behave just like the corresponding events for the Button WebControl.

Literal

The Literal control is the simplest of all the WebControls. It has the Text : String property and simply gets or sets the text to be output to the browser, outputting the contents of that property to the page when it is rendered.

You'll want to use the Literal control instead of a Label whenever you need complete control over the HTML you will output, such as if you are setting the content of a <title> tag. For instance:

```
<title><asp:Literal runat="server" id="litTitle"/></title>
```

Panel

The Panel WebControl acts as a container for other controls, which lets you adjust the style and visibility of many controls at once. This can be useful if you want to create a single ASP.NET page that has several pages of content, like a "wizard" application. Table 5.17 describes the properties of the Panel control.

Table 5.17: **Panel** *Properties*

Property	Description
BackImageUrl : String	Gets or sets the URL for the background image of the control. Defaults to Empty.
HorizontalAlign : HorizontalAlign	Gets or sets the horizontal alignment of the controls in the Panel. Defaults to NotSet.
Wrap : Boolean	Gets or sets a value determining whether controls in the Panel should wrap. Defaults to true.

Panels do not support any additional events. One of the WebControl properties that is most commonly used with the Panel control is the Visible property. By positioning several Panels over the tops of one another, you can create a single page that acts like a wizard control by having tabs that make one Panel invisible and another visible. This is just one of the more common uses for the Panel control.

PlaceHolder

The PlaceHolder control simply provides a bookmark to a point in a page. It is used to allow you to programmatically insert controls at a specific point on an ASP.NET page. Because it doesn't render any UI itself, or have any purpose other than to provide a placeholder, the PlaceHolder control has no other properties or methods.

Table, TableRow, and TableCell

The Table, TableRow, and TableCell controls are very similar to the HtmlControls that serve the same purpose. You can use them to programmatically build HTML tables. Table 5.18 describes the Table WebControl properties.

Table 5.18: **Table** *Properties*

Property	Description
BackImageUrl : String	Gets or sets the URL of the image to display as the background for the table. Defaults to Empty.
CellPadding : Int32	Gets or sets the distance in pixels between the border and the contents of any cell in the table. Defaults to –1 (not set).
CellSpacing : Int32	Gets or sets the distance in pixels between table cells. Defaults to –1 (not set).
GridLines : GridLines	Gets or sets a value determining how the gridlines of the table are displayed. Options for the GridLines Enum currently include Both, None, Horizontal, or Vertical.

Table 5.18: continued

Property	Description
HorizontalAlign : HorizontalAlign	Gets or sets a value determining how the table is aligned within the page. Possible values include Center, Justify, Left, NotSet, and Right.
Rows : TableRowCollection	Gets a reference to the collection of Row objects in the table.

Within a table, there are typically one or more TableRow controls, and these are accessed via the Rows collection. Table 5.19 describes the properties of each TableRow.

Table 5.19: **TableRow** *Properties*

Property	Description
Cells : TableCellCollection	Gets a collection of TableCell objects that represent the cells of this row in the Table control.
HorizontalAlign : HorizontalAlign	Gets or sets the horizontal alignment to be used by the contents of the row.
VerticalAlign : VerticalAlign	Gets or sets the vertical alignment to be used by the contents of the row.

Finally, Table 5.20 describes the properties of the TableCell control.

Table 5.20: **TableCell** *Properties*

Properties	Description
ColumnSpan : Int32	Gets or sets a value determining how many columns the cell should span. Corresponds to the ColSpan HTML attribute. Defaults to 1.
HorizontalAlign : HorizontalAlign	Gets or sets the horizontal alignment to be used by the contents of the cell.
RowSpan : Int32	Gets or sets a value determining how many rows the cell should span. Corresponds to the RowSpan HTML attribute. Defaults to 1.
Text : String	Gets or sets the text contents of the cell. Defaults to Empty.
VerticalAlign : VerticalAlign	Gets or sets the vertical alignment to be used by the contents of the cell.
Wrap : Boolean	Gets or sets a value that determines whether the contents of the cell should wrap. Defaults to true.

TextBox

The TextBox WebControl is one of the most commonly used WebForm controls for gathering user input. In addition, this one control can be configured to display as a password control, a regular text input control, or a multiline textarea control. Table 5.21 describes its properties.

Table 5.21: **TextBox** *Properties*

Property	Description
AutoPostBack : Boolean	Gets or sets a value that determines if the control does an automatic postback whenever a user changes its contents. Defaults to false.
Columns : Int32	Gets or sets the width of the text box in characters. Defaults to 0.
MaxLength : Int32	Gets or sets the maximum number of characters the text box can hold. Defaults to 0 (unlimited).
ReadOnly : Boolean	Gets or sets a value determining if the contents of the TextBox can be changed. Defaults to false.
Rows : Int32	Gets or sets the height of the TextBox in rows. Defaults to 0. Only applies to MultiLine TextMode.
Text : String	Gets or sets the contents of the TextBox. Defaults to Empty.
TextMode : TextBoxMode	Gets or sets the behavior of the TextBox. Can be either MultiLine, Password, or SingleLine. Defaults to SingleLine.
Wrap : Boolean	Gets or sets a value indicating whether the text content wraps within the text box. Defaults to true.

The TextBox control also includes one event, TextChanged, which is fired whenever the user changes the content of the TextBox and posts back the page.

This brings us to our last WebControl (finally!), the Xml WebControl.

Xml

The Xml WebControl is a bit more advanced than the other controls and allows you to display and transform XML documents on your ASP.NET page. Complete coverage of this control is beyond the scope of this book; however, its properties are described in Table 5.22 for completeness's sake.

Table 5.22: **Xml** *Properties*

Property	Description
Document : XmlDocument	Gets or sets the XmlDocument to display on the page.
DocumentContent : String	Gets or sets a string that contains the XML document to display in the control.
DocumentSource : String	Gets or sets the URL to an XML document to display in the control.
Transform : XslTransform	Gets or sets the XslTransform object that transforms the XML document before it is output.

Table 5.22: continued

Property	Description
TransformArgumentList : XsltArgumentList	Gets a collection of arguments used in the transformation process.
TransformSource : String	Gets or sets the URL to the XSLT document to use to format the XML document before it is output.

For outputting XML data to the client that you want to build programmatically, the Xml WebControl is the way to go.

Populating ListBoxes

One of the most common tasks you will encounter with using WebControls is populating their values from a data source. DropDownList, in particular, is one of the controls that most commonly needs to be populated from a data source of some kind. To wrap up this chapter, we're going to cover three different ways of populating DropDownList controls using ASP.NET. This example uses WebControls, but you could easily convert to using HtmlControls using the same syntax. The complete source code for the ASP page and codebehind is in Listings 5.3 and 5.4.

EXAMPLE

Listing 5.3: Populating drop-down lists (DropDownList.aspx).

```
<%@ Page language="c#" Codebehind="DropDownList.aspx.cs"
AutoEventWireup="false"
Inherits="ASPAuthors.aspnetbyexample.ch05.DropDownList"
Src="DropDownList.aspx.cs" %>
<!DOCTYPE HTML PUBLIC "-//W3C//DTD HTML 4.0 Transitional//EN" >
<html>
<head>
    <title>Populating DropDownLists</title>
</head>
  <body>
    <form id="DropDownList" method="post" runat="server">
    Declarative:
    <asp:DropDownList id="DropDownList1" runat="server">
        <asp:ListItem>One</asp:ListItem>
        <asp:ListItem>Two</asp:ListItem>
    </asp:DropDownList>
    <br>
    Programmatic Adding:
    <asp:DropDownList id="Dropdownlist2" runat="server"></asp:DropDownList>
    <br>
    Programmatic DataBinding:
    <asp:DropDownList id="Dropdownlist3" runat="server"></asp:DropDownList>
      </form>
  </body>
</html>
```

Listing 5.4: Populating drop-down lists (DropDownList.aspx.cs).

```
private void Page_Load(object sender, System.EventArgs e)
{
    if(!Page.IsPostBack)
    {
        // Programmatic Adding
        Dropdownlist2.Items.Add("One");
        Dropdownlist2.Items.Add(new ListItem("Two","2"));
        Dropdownlist2.Items.Insert(0,""); // Add a blank item to the top

        // Create a data source
        ArrayList AL = new ArrayList();
        AL.Add("One");
        AL.Add("Two");

        // Set values using databinding
        Dropdownlist3.DataSource = AL;
        Dropdownlist3.DataBind();

        // Set selected item to "Two"
        Dropdownlist3.Items.FindByText("Two").Selected = true;
    }
}
```

The result of this page is shown in Figure 5.6. Notice that the third control has "Two" as its selected item, because we set that in our last line of code in Listing 5.4.

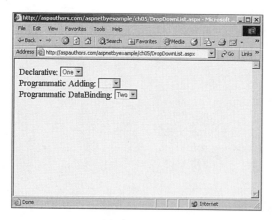

Figure 5.6: *Several* ListBox *controls.*

This example shows three ways to add controls to a list control, in this case a DropDownList WebControl. These three techniques include declaratively adding items, programmatically adding items using the Items collection of the control, or databinding the control to a data source.

Declarative

The simplest way to populate a list control is to add `ListItem` tags (`<asp:ListItem>foo</asp:/ListItem>`) to the control itself on the web page. By using the properties of the `ListItem` (`Value`, `Text`, and `Selected`), you can also set the value as well as the text of the list item, or whether it is selected, just as you can do with HTML Option tags.

Programmatic with Items Collection

The second easiest way to build up a list of items in a `DropDownList` or `ListBox` control is to use the Items collection's `Add` or `Insert` method. The `Add` method takes either a string value or a `ListItem` object, both of which are shown in the example. Likewise, the `Insert` method accepts an integer index value (where 0 is the first item in the list) where the item should be inserted, and either a string value or a `ListItem` object for the item to add to the list. You can also use the `Items` collection to locate an item in the list and make it `Selected` (or not), using the `FindByText` or `FindByValue` methods of the Items collection.

Programmatic with Databinding

The most advanced way to populate a list of items (but also the easiest if you have a component returning a dataset or datareader) is to simply bind the `DropDownList` to a datasource using databinding. We looked at databinding some last chapter, and we will see more of it in the next chapter. In our example, we created an `ArrayList` simply to use as our data source. If you bind to an actual database, you might want to also set the `DataTextField` and `DataValueField` to the fields in the data source that correspond to what you want displayed (for example, an ID column and the corresponding text associated with that ID).

Summary

HtmlControls and WebControls provide two different ways for developers to create and programmatically manipulate the HTML tags that form the presentation of Internet applications. Using these controls is very similar to using controls in Visual Basic, and it will be fairly easy for developer tools vendors to create drag-and-drop editors supporting these controls, as Visual Studio .NET already does. Developers can generally choose whether to use HtmlControls or WebControls as a matter of taste, although there are certain conditions that particularly favor one implementation or the other.

What's Next?

In the next chapter, we'll see how to use ASP.NET's List Controls, including the DataList and DataGrid. Using databinding and list controls, it is very easy to create data-driven web forms using very little code.

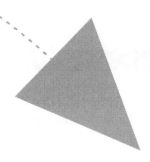

Using ASP.NET List Controls

As you've discovered in previous chapters, one of the greatest advantages of ASP.NET is the separation of your business logic from presentation markup. Perhaps no other set of controls illustrates this better than the ASP.NET list controls: DropDownList, ListBox, CheckBoxList, and RadioButtonList. The purpose of this chapter is to give you an overview of these four controls and get you started using them in your ASP.NET applications.

In this chapter you will learn:

- What the properties, methods, and events of ASP.NET list controls are
- How to databind both the items collection and the selection property of each control
- How to change the layout and display of these controlss

NOTE

The purpose of this book is to get you up and running quickly with ASP.NET by providing an example-driven discussion of the platform. Therefore, this book cannot adequately cover some of the advanced Object-Oriented Programming (OOP) principles upon which the entire .NET platform was built. Although you don't have to be an OOP expert to start building real-world applications with ASP.NET, I encourage you to explore some of the new OOP features of VB.NET and C# on your own by consulting the other resources listed in this book. If you have extensive experience with other OOP languages such as C++ or Java, you should already be up to speed on these concepts.

The `ListControl` Class

All ASP.NET list controls inherit from `ListControl` in the `System.Web.UI.WebControls` namespace. *Inheritance* is the foundation of OOP design and is the means by which one class acquires all the behavior and attributes of its parent class. The new class indicates only how it is different from its parent by overriding or adding to the properties, methods, and events of the parent class. Table 6.1 shows a summary of the properties, methods, and events of the `ListControl` class. Each of the four controls discussed in this chapter shares these common attributes, so please take a moment to review them before the first example.

Table 6.1: Properties, Methods, and Events of the `ListControl` Class

Name	Item	Description
AutoPostBack	Property	Gets or sets whether the control automatically posts back to the server when the list selection is changed
ClearSelection	Method	Clears the current list selection
DataSource	Property	Gets or sets the data source that populates the items in the list control
DataTextField	Property	Gets or sets the data source field that provides the text for items in the list
DataValueField	Property	Gets or sets the data source field that provides the value for items in the list
Items	Property	Gets the collections of items in the list
SelectedIndex	Property	Gets the ordinal for the first selected item in the list
SelectedIndexChanged	Event	Raised on the server whenever the list selection is changed
SelectedItem	Property	Gets the first selected item in the list

Because `ListControl` is an *abstract* base class and therefore cannot be instantiated, we must work with the derived list controls to provide examples of the attributes listed in Table 6.1. We'll cover each of these common properties, methods, and events when we introduce each of the four list controls in this chapter. Just keep in mind that items in Table 6.1 may be discussed in the context of an individual control, but they are common to all the list controls in this chapter. When we introduce each control, attributes unique to that control will be so noted.

Because the `DropDownList` control is perhaps the most straightforward and no doubt will be the most commonly used in your ASP.NET applications, let's take a look at it first.

Working with `DropDownList`

You can add a `DropDownList` control to the form in the same way as the intrinsic controls covered in the previous chapter, as shown in Listing 6.1.

Listing 6.1: Declaring the `DropDownList` control.

```
<asp:DropDownList id="StatusList" runat="server">
    <asp:ListItem value="100">Pending</asp:ListItem>
    <asp:ListItem value="200" Selected="True">In Transit</asp:ListItem>
</asp:DropDownList>
```

As this code snippet illustrates, you simply add a `DropDownList` tag using the `ASP:` namespace, as you do for all Web controls. You then set the `id` property and set `runat="server"` so that you can reference the control programmatically. Next, you need to add some options to the list control. You do this by adding `ListItem` tags inside the list control. In the preceding example, we set the values of the list items by setting the `value` property. We have also set the second list item as the initially selected item in the control by setting its `Selected` property to `True`. We set the text to be displayed by each list item with the text between the opening and closing tags of the list item. You could also explicitly set the `Text` property in this fashion:

```
<asp:ListItem value="100" Text="Pending" />
```

Please note that this declaration does not require a closing tag, so you can use the XML shorthand method by including a forward slash in the opening `<asp:ListItem>` tag.

Getting the `SelectedItem`

In the example shown in Listing 6.2, we allow the user to update the status of an order and display the status code below the selection when the button is clicked.

EXAMPLE

Listing 6.2: Using the `SelectedItem` property of the `DropDownList` control (06ddl01.aspx).

```
<%@ Page language="vb" autoeventwireup="false" codebehind=""%>
<html>
<head>
<title>Chapter 6: ASP.NET List Controls</title>
<script language="VB" runat="server">
    Sub UpdateButton_Click(sender As Object, e As EventArgs)
        StatusLabel.Text = StatusLabel.Text & _
            StatusLabel.Text = "Order status at " & FormatDateTime(Now(), 3) _
            & StatusList.SelectedItem.Value & "<br>"
    End Sub
</script>
</head>
```

Listing 6.2: continued

```
<body>
    <form runat="server">
        <h3>Using DropDownList</h3>
        Please update the order status:
        <asp:DropDownList id="StatusList" runat="server">
            <asp:ListItem value="100">Pending</asp:ListItem>
            <asp:ListItem value="200">In Transit</asp:ListItem>
            <asp:ListItem value="300">Delivered</asp:ListItem>
            <asp:ListItem value="400">Backorder</asp:ListItem>
            <asp:ListItem value="500">Cancelled</asp:ListItem>
        </asp:DropDownList>
        <asp:button
            text="Update"
            OnClick="UpdateButton_Click"
            runat="server"
            ID="UpdateButton"/>
        <p>
        <asp:Label id="StatusLabel" runat="server"/>
        </p>
    </form>
</body>
</html>
```

The output for Listing 6.2 is shown in Figure 6.1.

OUTPUT

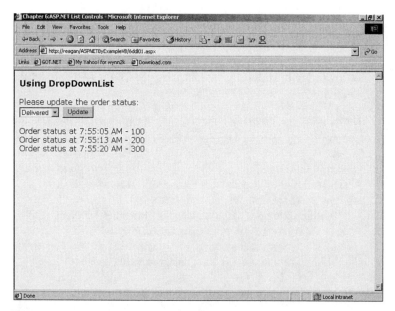

Figure 6.1: *The numeric status code corresponds to the chosen list item.*

Using the `SelectedIndexChanged` Event

Note that in the previous example, we logged the time and the status every time the Update button is clicked. Although we are only printing the output to the screen in this basic example, we could easily update a database or some other data source. If instead you wanted to log only status changes, you simply respond to the `SelectedIndexChanged` event by setting up the event handler as shown in Listing 6.3.

Listing 6.3: Declaring the event handler for the `SelectedIndexChanged` event.

```
Sub StatusList_SelectedIndexChanged(sender As Object, e As EventArgs)
    StatusLabel.Text = StatusLabel.Text & _
        StatusLabel.Text = "Order status at " & FormatDateTime(Now(), 3) _
        & StatusList.SelectedItem.Value & "<br>"
End Sub
```

Next, we need to specify the event handler by setting the `onSelectedIndexChanged` attribute for the DropDownList tag:

```
<asp:DropDownList
id="StatusList"
runat="server"
onSelectedIndexChanged="StatusList_SelectedIndexChanged">
```

So now the full example looks like Listing 6.4.

EXAMPLE

Listing 6.4: Handling the `SelectedIndexChanged` event of the `DropDownList` control (06ddl02.aspx).

```
<%@ Page language="vb" autoeventwireup="false" codebehind=""%>
<html>
<head>
<script language="VB" runat="server">
   <h3>Using DropDownList</h3>
   Please update the order status:
   Sub StatusList_SelectedIndexChanged(sender As Object, e As EventArgs)
       StatusLabel.Text = StatusLabel.Text &
           StatusLabel.Text = "Order status at " & FormatDateTime(Now(), 3)
           & StatusList.SelectedItem.Value & "<br>"
   End Sub
</script>
</head>
<body>
    <form runat="server">
        <asp:DropDownList id="StatusList" runat="server"
            onSelectedIndexChanged="StatusList_SelectedIndexChanged">
            <asp:ListItem value="100">Pending</asp:ListItem>
            <asp:ListItem value="200">In Transit</asp:ListItem>
            <asp:ListItem value="300">Delivered</asp:ListItem>
            <asp:ListItem value="400">Backorder</asp:ListItem>
```

Listing 6.4: continued

```
            <asp:ListItem value="500">Cancelled</asp:ListItem>
        </asp:DropDownList>
        <asp:button text="Update" runat="server" ID="UpdateButton"/>
        <p>
        <asp:Label id="StatusLabel" runat="server"/>
        </p>
    </form>
</body>
</html>
```

AutoPostBack: When You Just Can't Wait

In the preceding example, although the list now fires the
SelectedIndexChanged event only when the list selection changes, the event
also does not get handled until the user performs an explicit post-back to
the server by clicking the Update button. You can automatically perform
this post-back simply by setting the autopostback property to True:

```
<asp:DropDownList id="StatusList" runat="server"
        onSelectedIndexChanged="StatusList_SelectedIndexChanged"
        autopostback="True">
```

Go ahead and try the example again and notice how the form performs the
post-back only when the value is changed, not just when the list control is
clicked.

Using ListBox

Now that you've seen how to read list control selection values, let's take a
look at some of the other list control characteristics. For the next set of
examples, we'll keep it interesting by introducing the ListBox control. This
control is a close relative of the DropDownList control. In fact, both controls
are rendered with the HTML <SELECT> tag. The DropDownList control displays only one item at a time and provides a drop-down list to view all
items. However, the ListBox control displays a set number of items and provides scroll bars to view the rest of the choices. We add a ListBox to the
form as shown in Listing 6.5.

Listing 6.5: Declaring the ListBox control.

```
<asp:ListBox id="UserList" runat="server" Rows="4">
    <asp:ListItem>Paula</asp:ListItem>
    <asp:ListItem>Chris</asp:ListItem>
    <asp:ListItem Selected="True">Eric</asp:ListItem>
    <asp:ListItem>Wynn</asp:ListItem>
</asp:ListBox>
```

This ListBox will display a list of users to choose from. The Rows property
determines how many items in the list will be displayed. If the control

contains more items than this value, scrollbars will be displayed to scroll the list. Much in the same way we did for the DropDownList control, we've set the third list item in the control to be the default selection.

Using SelectedIndex

Listing 6.6 shows you how to use the SelectedIndex method of one ListBox control to set the selection for another ListBox control. Figure 6.2 shows you the output of this listing.

EXAMPLE

Listing 6.6: Using the SelectedItem property of the ListBox control (06lstb01.aspx).

```
<%@ Page language="vb" autoeventwireup="false" codebehind=""%>
<html>
<head>
<script language="VB" runat="server" ID=Script1>
    Sub UpdateButton_Click(sender As Object, e As EventArgs)
        GroupList.SelectedIndex = UserList.SelectedIndex
    End Sub
</script>
</head>
<body>
<form runat="server" ID=Form1>
        <h3>Using ListBox</h3>
        Please update the order status:
    <TABLE WIDTH="300" BORDER="0" CELLSPACING="1" CELLPADDING="1">
        <TR>
            <TD NOWRAP>Users:</TD>
            <TD NOWRAP></TD>
            <TD NOWRAP></TD>
        </TR>
        <TR>
            <TD NOWRAP>
                <asp:ListBox id="UserList" runat="server" Rows="4">
                    <asp:ListItem>Paula</asp:ListItem>
                    <asp:ListItem>Chris</asp:ListItem>
                    <asp:ListItem selected="True">Eric</asp:ListItem>
                    <asp:ListItem>Wynn</asp:ListItem>
                </asp:ListBox>
            </TD>
            <TD NOWRAP>
                <asp:button text="Update ->" runat="server"
                  ID="UpdateButton" onclick="UpdateButton_Click"/>
            </TD>
            <TD NOWRAP>
                <asp:ListBox id="GroupList" runat="server" Rows="4">
                    <asp:ListItem>Paula</asp:ListItem>
                    <asp:ListItem>Chris</asp:ListItem>
                    <asp:ListItem>Eric</asp:ListItem>
```

Listing 6.6: continued

```
                        <asp:ListItem>Wynn</asp:ListItem>
                    </asp:ListBox>
                </TD>
            </TR>
        </TABLE>
</form>
</body>
</html>
```

OUTPUT

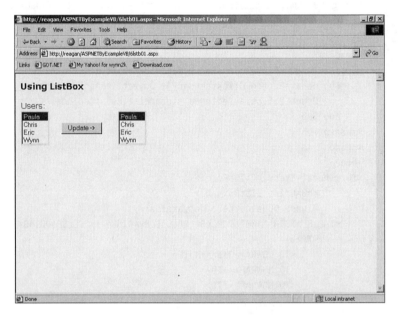

Figure 6.2: *The selection of the second list control is updated based on the first list control.*

Note how in the event handler, we merely set the SelectedIndex property of the second control equal to the same property on the first control, and voilà! The selection of the second list control changes.

Selecting Multiple Items with SelectionMode

You probably noticed that in the ListBox example, you could only select one list item at a time. This is because the ListBox control has a SelectionMode property that determines how many list items can be selected at one time. This property defaults to Single, so in order to allow multiple selections, simply set the SelectionMode property to Multiple, like this:

```
<asp:ListBox id="GroupList" runat="server" Rows="4" SelectionMode="Multiple">
```

After making this change, run your form again. You will notice that, although you may select multiple users from the list control, only the first selection is copied over to the second list. This is because the `SelectedIndex` property returns only the index for the first item in the selection. To work with multiple selections, you must work with a new property—the `Items` collection.

Working with the `Items` Collection

The `Items` collection is a special property of type `ListItemCollection` in the `System.Web.UI.WebControls` namespace and is shared by all ASP.NET list controls. This class does the grunt work in managing the list items for each list control. Table 6.2 shows a summary of the properties and methods for the `ListItemCollection` class. Please take a moment to review them before we move on with an example of manipulating the items in a list control programmatically.

Table 6.2: Summary of the Properties and Methods of the **`ListItemCollection`** *Class*

Name	Item	Description
Add	Method	Overloaded. Adds a new item to the collection by supplying either a `ListItem` object or string value
All	Property	Gets an array of type `ListItem` of all items in the list
Clear	Method	Removes all items from the list
Contains	Method	Indicates whether or not the supplied item is in the list
Count	Property	Gets the number of items in the list
IndexOf	Method	Gets the ordinal for the specified item in the list
Insert	Method	Overloaded. Inserts an item into the list at the given index location based on the supplied `ListItem` object or string value
Item	Method	Gets the item referenced by the given index
Remove	Method	Overloaded. Removes the item in the list matching the specified `ListItem` or string value
RemoveAt	Method	Removes the item in the list matching the specified index

TIP

Unless you've gotten an in-depth look at the .NET languages already, you may be wondering about certain methods in Table 6.2. With the language enhancements of VB.NET and the introduction of C#, .NET developers can now take advantage of *overloaded* methods. These methods share the same name and return types, but have different *signatures* or number and types of arguments. This feature allows for cleaner and more flexible code.

Now that you've taken a peek at the `Items` collection, let's extend the previous example. Because we've already established that we can't use the

`SelectedIndex` property to retrieve multiple selections, let's tackle the problem from a different angle. Listing 6.7 shows the modified event handler to handle multiple selections in the list box.

Listing 6.7: Using the `Items` collection to handle multiple selections in a `ListBox` control.

```
Sub UpdateButton_Click(sender As Object, e As EventArgs)
    Dim UserItem as ListItem
    GroupList.ClearSelection()
    For Each UserItem in UserList.Items
        If UserItem.Selected = True Then
            GroupList.Items.Item(UserList.Items.IndexOf(UserItem)).Selected
 = True
        End If
    Next
End Sub
```

We've introduced several new methods here, so let's walk through the listing. The first call we make is to the `ClearSelection` method of the second list control to unselect any currently selected items. Then we simply loop through the `Items` collection of the first list control and test each item's `Selected` property. If the current item is selected, we need to select the corresponding item in the second list control. To do this, we first have to determine the ordinal for the current `ListItem` in the loop. We find this value by passing the current item, `UserItem`, to the `IndexOf` method of the `Items` collection of the first list control. We can then pass the return value of this method to the `Item` method of the `Items` property of the second list control to get a reference to the `ListItem` we're currently after. We then set its `Selected` property to `True` and proceed to the next item in the list. Because the `Item` method is the indexer for the collection, you may optionally use this syntax to reference a member of the `Items` collection:

```
GroupList.Items(index)
```

Note that we omitted the `Item` method and passed the ordinal value to the `Items` collection directly. Either syntax is acceptable, but the first approach is more descriptive.

Adding Items with the `Add` Method

So far, you've seen how easy it is to manipulate list controls with ASP.NET, but the platform's true power for developers is the new ability to add and remove list items programmatically. Listing 6.8 outlines how easy it is to add items to a list control, and Figure 6.3 shows the output.

EXAMPLE

Listing 6.8: Using the `Add` method to add items to the `CheckBoxList` control (6chklst01.aspx).

```
<%@ Page language="vb" autoeventwireup="false" codebehind=""%>
<html>
```

Listing 6.8: continued

```
<head>
<script language="VB" runat="server" ID=Script1>
    Sub AddButton_Click(sender As Object, e As EventArgs)
        ItemList.Items.Add(ItemText.Text)
    End Sub
</script>
</head>
<body>
<form runat="server">
    <h3>Adding items with the Add method</h3>
    Item text: <br>
    <asp:textbox id="ItemText" runat="Server" />
    <asp:button text="Add" runat="server"
        ID="AddButton" onclick="AddButton_Click"/>
    <br>
    <asp:checkboxlist id="ItemList" runat="server"/>
</form>
</body>
</html>
```

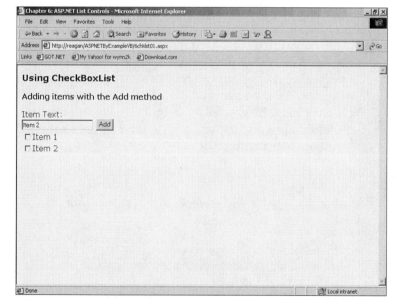

Figure 6.3: *The output from the code in Listing 6.8.*

In this example, we introduce another type of list control, the CheckBoxList control. You generally use this control when you need to present the user with options for a multiple-choice question when more than one answer is allowed. If your scenario requires only one item to be selected, you should use the RadioButtonList introduced later in this chapter.

In this example, simply enter some text in the text box and click the Add button to add a new item to the list. However, you might have noticed that nothing prevents us from adding duplicates. Most of the time, we would not want duplicate items in the list, so to prevent this, we use the Contains method of the Items collection, as shown in Listing 6.9.

Listing 6.9: Preventing duplicates when adding items to the ListBox control.

```
Dim NewItem = New ListItem(ItemText.Text)
If Not ItemList.Items.Contains(NewItem) Then
    ItemList.Items.Add(ItemText.Text)
End If
```

The Contains method expects an argument of type ListItem, so we create our own item named NewItem from the supplied text. We then simply pass the item to the Contains method of the Items collection, which tells us if the item already is in the list. If the item is not in the list, we proceed to add the item as in the previous example.

POPULATING LIST CONTROLS BASED ON USER SELECTION

Now that you have a handle on adding items to the list, let's consider a more real-world example. In designing Web-based applications, the need often arises to populate one list based on the selection of another list. You probably already have a good idea how to do this, so let's walk through an example. We're going to populate a list of vehicle models based on the vehicle make the user selects. Normally we would get the data for this kind of information from an external data source, such as a database or XML file. We'll hard-code the entries for now, as shown in Listing 6.10, and we'll discuss databinding list options a little later in the chapter. Figure 6.4 shows the output from Listing 6.10.

EXAMPLE

Listing 6.10: Using the Items collection to handle multiple selections in a ListBox control (6radlst01.aspx).

```
<%@ Page language="vb" autoeventwireup="false" codebehind=""%>
<html>
<head>
<script language="VB" runat="server">
    Sub MakesList_SelectedIndexChanged(sender As Object, e As EventArgs)
        ModelsList.Items.Clear()
        Select Case MakesList.SelectedItem.Value
            Case "GMC"
                ModelsList.Items.Add("Sierra")
                ModelsList.Items.Add("Yukon")
```

Listing 6.10: continued

```
                ModelsList.Items.Add("Yukon XL")
                ModelsList.Items.Add("Sonoma")
            Case "Chevrolet"
                ModelsList.Items.Add("Silverado")
                ModelsList.Items.Add("Tahoe")
                ModelsList.Items.Add("Suburban")
                ModelsList.Items.Add("S-15")
                ModelsList.Items.Add("Monte Carlo")
            Case "Pontiac"
                ModelsList.Items.Add("Grand AM")
                ModelsList.Items.Add("Grand Prix")
                ModelsList.Items.Add("Bonnevile")
        End Select
End Sub
</script>
</head>
<body>
<form runat="server">
<h3>Adding list items based upon user selection</h3>
<TABLE WIDTH="300" BORDER="0" CELLSPACING="1" CELLPADDING="1">
    <TR>
        <TD NOWRAP>Makes:</TD>
        <TD NOWRAP>Models:</TD>
    </TR>
    <TR>
        <TD NOWRAP valign="top">
            <asp:radiobuttonlist id="MakesList" runat="server"
                onselectedindexchanged="MakesList_SelectedIndexChanged"
                autopostback="True">
                <asp:ListItem>GMC</asp:ListItem>
                <asp:ListItem>Chevrolet</asp:ListItem>
                <asp:ListItem>Pontiac</asp:ListItem>
            </asp: radiobuttonlist >
        </TD>
        <TD NOWRAP>
            <asp: radiobuttonlist id="ModelsList" runat="server" />
        </TD>
    </TR>
</TABLE>
</form>
</body>
</html>
```

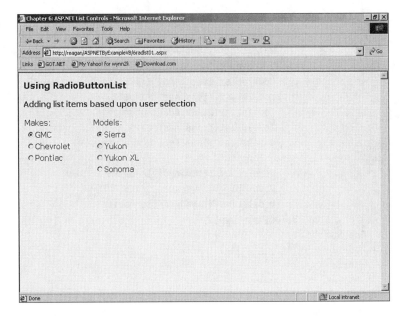

Figure 6.4: *The output from the code in Listing 6.10.*

You should have noticed that we introduced the RadioButtonList, the last list control of the chapter (woo-hoo!). We could just as easily have used any other two list controls, but I thought this was a good time to slip that one in. This example introduces two important methods of the Items collection: Clear and Add. Once the vehicle make is selected, the first thing we need to do is to remove all the models from the models list control. We do this simply by calling the Clear method on the control's Items collection. We now have an empty list to which we can add the corresponding vehicle models for the selected make. Now we can just call the Add method once for each model to be added to the list. Note that we are passing the model name as a string to the Add method; however, we could use this optional syntax:

```
ModelsList.Items.Add(New ListItem("Yukon XL"))
```

This second approach creates a new ListItem object and passes the object to the Add method. The first approach lets the list control create the ListItem object on the fly simply by passing in the item text. Either way is acceptable.

Removing Items with the Remove Method

Now that we've added items to the list controls, let's look at how to remove items in an example for the following scenario. You need to design an interface to maintain users and security groups for your new ASP.NET Web application. You need to have a list of available users and another list of current members of the security group. We'll make the second list control the members list, which initially will be empty. Listing 6.11 contains the full example. Please take a moment to look it over before we walk through it. Figure 6.5 shows the output.

EXAMPLE

Listing 6.11: Using the Items collection to handle multiple selections in a ListBox control (6lstb05.aspx).

```vb
<%@ Page language="vb" autoeventwireup="false" codebehind=""%>
<html>
<head>
<script language="VB" runat="server">
    Sub AddButton_Click(sender As Object, e As EventArgs)
        Dim Users as ListItemCollection = New ListItemCollection()
        Dim User as ListItem
        For Each User in UserList.Items
            If User.Selected Then
                Users.Add(User)
            End If
        Next
        For Each User in Users
                UserList.Items.Remove(User)
                GroupList.Items.Add(User)
        Next
    End Sub
    Sub RemoveButton_Click(sender As Object, e As EventArgs)
        Dim Users as ListItemCollection = New ListItemCollection()
        Dim User as ListItem
        For Each User in GroupList.Items
            If User.Selected Then
                Users.Add(User)
            End If
        Next
        For Each User in Users
                UserList.Items.Add(User)
                GroupList.Items.Remove(User)
        Next
    End Sub
</script>
</head>
<body>
<form runat="server">
<h3>Moving items between lists with Add and Remove</h3>
<TABLE WIDTH="300" BORDER="0" CELLSPACING="1" CELLPADDING="1">
    <TR>
        <TD NOWRAP>Users:</TD>
        <TD NOWRAP></TD>
```

Listing 6.11: continued

```
        <TD NOWRAP>Power Users:</TD>
    </TR>
    <TR>
        <TD NOWRAP>
            <asp:ListBox id="UserList" runat="server" Rows="4"
             selectionmode="Multiple">
                <asp:ListItem>Paula</asp:ListItem>
                <asp:ListItem>Chris</asp:ListItem>
                <asp:ListItem>Eric</asp:ListItem>
                <asp:ListItem>Wynn</asp:ListItem>
            </asp:ListBox>
        </TD>
        <TD NOWRAP>
            <asp:button text="->" runat="server" ID="AddButton"
             onclick="AddButton_Click"/>
            <br>
            <asp:button text="<-" runat="server" ID="RemoveButton"
            onclick="RemoveButton_Click"/>
        </TD>
        <TD NOWRAP>
            <asp:ListBox id="GroupList" runat="server" Rows="4"
             selectionmode="Multiple">
            </asp:ListBox>
        </TD>
    </TR>
</TABLE>
</form>
</body>
</html>
```

In this example, we've created a pair of event handlers for the Add and Remove buttons on the form. Because they essentially do the same thing, only in reverse, we'll only walk through one of them. In each case, we begin by declaring an array of type ListItem, which we've named UserArray. We then iterate through the array and test the Selected property of each item. If the item is selected, we simply add it to the opposite list control while removing it from the current list.

You may be wondering why we didn't iterate through the Items collection directly the same way we did in previous examples. We must perform the extra step in this case by copying the items to an array first because removing items from the collection while it is being iterated produces an error.

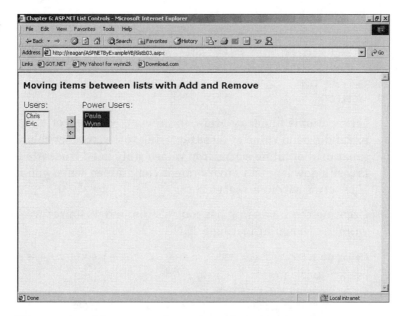

Figure 6.5: *The output from the code in Listing 6.11.*

Databinding and List Controls

Up to this point, we've introduced all four types of ASP.NET list controls and you learned how to manipulate each programmatically. In the next section, you'll learn how to automatically create the items in a list from an external data source and bind a list selection to that data source. Before we begin, let's take a quick look back at how we would databind list controls in previous versions of ASP.

For all its strengths, there are some aspects of previous versions of ASP that are just plain awkward. Take the code in Listing 6.12, for instance.

Listing 6.12: Databinding <select> tag in previous versions of ASP.

```
<SELECT NAME="STATUS">
    <OPTION VALUE="PENDING"
        <%If rs("Status") = "PENDING" Then Response.Write "selected"%>>
        PENDING
    </OPTION>
    <OPTION
       VALUE="ACTIVE"
      <%If rs("Status") = "ACTIVE" Then Response.Write "selected"%>>
          ACTIVE
    </OPTION>
    <OPTION
```

Listing 6.12: continued

```
        VALUE="INACTIVE"
        <%If rs("Status") = "INACTIVE" Then Response.Write "selected"%>>
            INACTIVE
    </OPTION>
</SELECT>
```

This example illustrates how, in previous versions of ASP, a task as simple as binding the value of a <select> tag to a recordset column required a great deal of inline script. You've probably been frustrated when your favorite development environment complained when you included server-side script within a <select> tag.

Creating the items in a list control from a datasource was equally awkward, as shown in Listing 6.13.

Listing 6.13: Databinding <options> in a <select> tag in previous versions of ASP.

```
<SELECT NAME="STATUS">
    <%Do While Not rs.EOF%>
        <OPTION VALUE="<%rs(0)%>"><%=rs(1)%></OPTION>
    <%rs.MoveNext
      Loop%>
</SELECT>
```

Why do I reminisce like this? Only to make you fully appreciate the simplicity you're about to see. Databinding the list of items in ASP.NET list controls is as easy as

- Creating or obtaining your datasource

- Setting the DataSource property of the list control

- Calling the DataBind method of the list control or Page object

Listing 6.14 creates a data source of cities in Texas and binds a DropDownList control to it. Figure 6.6 shows the databinding in action.

EXAMPLE

Listing 6.14: Databinding the items in a DropDownList control (6databind01.aspx).

```
<%@ Page language="vb"%>
<html>
<head>
    <script language="VB" runat="server">
        Sub Page_Load(sender As Object, e As EventArgs)
            Dim Cities as ArrayList = new ArrayList()
            Cities.Add ("Houston")
            Cities.Add ("Dallas")
            Cities.Add ("Austin")
            Cities.Add ("San Antonio")
            Cities.Add ("South Padre Island")
            CityList.DataSource = Cities
```

Listing 6.14: continued

```
            CityList.DataBind()
        End Sub
    </script>
</head>
<body>
    <form runat="server">
        <h3>Databinding list controls</h3>
        <asp:DropDownList id="CityList" runat="server"/>
    </form>
</body>
</html>
```

OUTPUT

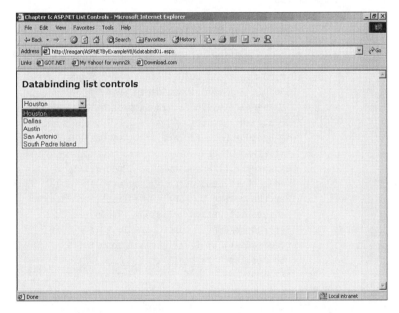

Figure 6.6: *The output from the code in Listing 6.14.*

In this example, we created the data source (in this case an array of cities in Texas), set the DataSource property of the list control equal to this array, and finally called the DataBind method of the control to populate the list. That's all there is to it! Keep in mind that the data source could just as easily have been some XML data or an ADO.NET data source. Just to prove it, we'll do that in the next example.

Using DataTextField and DataValueField Properties

In the previous example, both the value and the text of the list items were the same. However, in many instances we need to display some friendly text to the user while keeping some unique ID for the list item value.

Listing 6.15 illustrates an example that displays a list of products from the Northwind database in Microsoft SQL Server, and Figure 6.7 shows the output.

EXAMPLE

Listing 6.15: Specifying the `Text` and `Value` fields when databinding a `DropDownList` control (6databind03.aspx).

```vb
<%@ Page language="vb"%>
<%@ Import Namespace="System.Data"%>
<%@ Import Namespace="System.Data.SqlClient"%>
<html>
<head>
<script language="VB" runat="server">
    Sub Page_Load(sender As Object, e As EventArgs)
        If Not IsPostBack Then
            'Declare our SQL Statement
            Dim cmd As String = "SELECT ProductID, ProductName FROM Products"
            'Create our ADO SQL Adapter
            Dim DSAdapter As SqlDataAdapter
            DSAdapter = New SqlDataAdapter(cmd, _
                "server=localhost;uid=sa;pwd=;database=Northwind")
            'Create the DataSet
            Dim ProductsData As DataSet = New DataSet()
            'Fill the DataSet
            DSAdapter.Fill(ProductsData, "Products")
            ProductsList.DataSource = ProductsData.Tables("Products").DefaultView
            'Set the column to supply the list item value
            ProductsList.DataValueField = "ProductID"
            'Set the column to supply the list item text
            ProductsList.DataTextField = "ProductName"
            ProductsList.DataBind()
        End If
    End Sub
    Sub ProductsList_Change(Sender as Object, e as EventArgs)
        ProductSelection.Text = "You've selected Product #:" _
            & ProductsList.SelectedItem.Value
    End Sub
</script>
</head>
<body>
<form runat="server">
<h3>Using DataTextField and DataValueField</h3>
    Please select a product below:<br>
    <asp:DropDownList
        id="ProductsList"
        runat="server"
        onselectedindexchanged="ProductsList_Change"
```

Listing 6.15: continued

```
        autopostback="True"/>
    <asp:label id="ProductSelection" runat="Server" />
</form>
</body>
</html>
```

OUTPUT

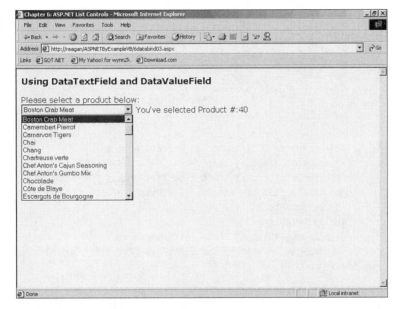

Figure 6.7: *The output from the code in Listing 6.15.*

In this example, we display values from the ProductName database column while setting the value for the list item equal to the ProductID column. Although this kind of databinding is pretty powerful, it's only half the story.

Databinding List Control Selections

As you learned in previous chapters, ADO.NET also lets you bind the values of your Web controls to data elsewhere on your Web form. Consider the example shown in Listing 6.16 (Figure 6.8 shows the output).

EXAMPLE

Listing 6.16: Databinding the selection in a DropDownList control (6databind02.aspx).

```
<%@ Page language="vb"%>
<html>
<head>
<script language="VB" runat="server">
    Sub Page_Load(sender As Object, e As EventArgs)
        If Not IsPostBack Then
            Dim Cities as ArrayList = new ArrayList()
            Cities.Add ("Houston")
```

Listing 6.16: continued

```
                Cities.Add ("Dallas")
                Cities.Add ("Austin")
                Cities.Add ("San Antonio")
                Cities.Add ("South Padre Island")
                CityList.DataSource = Cities
                CityList.DataBind()
                CityButtons.DataSource = Cities
                CityButtons.DataBind()
            End If
            Page.DataBind()
        End Sub
</script>
</head>
<body>
<form runat="server">
    <h3>Databinding list control selections</h3>
    Please select a city below:<br>
    <asp:radiobuttonlist id="CityButtons" runat="Server"
        onselectedindexchanged="CityButtons_SelectedIndexChanged"
        autopostback="True"/>
    You've selected:<br>
    <asp:DropDownList id="CityList" runat="server"
        SelectedIndex="<%# CityButtons.SelectedIndex%>"/>
</form>
</body>
</html>
```

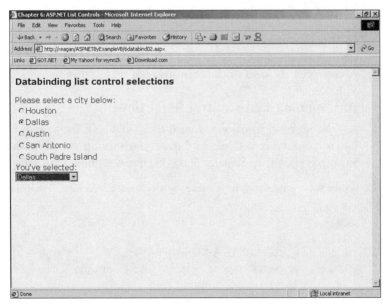

Figure 6.8: *The output from the code in Listing 6.16.*

We have added an additional list control to the form, this time a `RadioButtonList`. Just as before, we've bound each control to the `CityList` array to create the list items. Note that this time we've wrapped this code block inside an `If...Then` block, evaluating the `IsPostBack` property of the page. We do this so that the list items are created only the first time the page loads.

The idea is to change the selection in the drop-down list based on the selection in the first list, much as we did early in the chapter. You'll probably notice that this example required much less code. This is because of the new databinding features in ASP.NET Web controls that allow us to bind properties of our controls to external data sources. To bind the selection of the control in this case, we simply use the databinding syntax you learned in Chapter 3 to bind the `SelectedIndex` property of the `DropDownList` control to the same property in the `RadioButtonList` control. We then set the `AutoPostBack` property equal to `True` for the radio list so that we post back to the server whenever the selection changes. The actual databinding takes place with the last line of the `Page_Load` event handler with the call to `Page.Databind()`. We could just as easily have called the `DataBind()` methods of each control individually, but calling `Page.DataBind()` saves a great deal of code, especially when your Web forms become quite large.

Changing the Layout of List Controls

Up to this point, you've seen how to manipulate list control selections, create and remove items programmatically, as well as how to bind these controls to external data sources. Now we'll look at how to control the layout of the two list controls that support this feature, `CheckBoxList` and `RadioButtonList`.

Using `RepeatLayout`

The first tool at our disposal for changing the layout of these two list controls is the `RepeatLayout` property. This property has two possible values: `Table` (default) and `Flow`. When `RepeatLayout` is set to `Table`, the list items are rendered within a `<table>` so that the items are distributed evenly. When set to `Flow`, the list items flow according to the surrounding HTML on the page. Listing 6.17 illustrates the difference, and Figure 6.9 shows its output.

Listing 6.17: Changing the layout of a `RadioButtonList` control (6layout01.aspx).

EXAMPLE

```
<%@ Page language="vb"%>
<html>
<head>
<script language="VB" runat="server" ID=Script1>
    Sub RepeatLayoutList_Changed(sender As Object, e As EventArgs)
        Select Case RepeatLayoutList.SelectedItem.Value
            Case "Table"
                RadioList.RepeatLayout = RepeatLayout.Table
```

Listing 6.17: continued

```
                Case "Flow"
                    RadioList.RepeatLayout = RepeatLayout.Flow
            End Select
        End Sub
</script>
</head>
<body>
<form runat="server">
    <h3>Changing list control layout</h3>
    RepeatLayout:
    <asp:dropdownlist id="RepeatLayoutList" runat="Server"
        autopostback="True"
        onselectedindexchanged="RepeatLayoutList_Changed">
        <asp:listitem value="Table">Table</asp:listitem>
        <asp:listitem value="Flow">Flow</asp:listitem>
        </asp:dropdownlist>
    <asp:radiobuttonlist id="RadioList" runat="server">
        <asp:ListItem>Houston Texans</asp:ListItem>
        <asp:ListItem>New Orleans Saints</asp:ListItem>
        <asp:ListItem>Dallas Cowboys</asp:ListItem>
        <asp:ListItem>Tennessee Titans</asp:ListItem>
    </asp:radiobuttonlist>
</form>
</body>
</html>
```

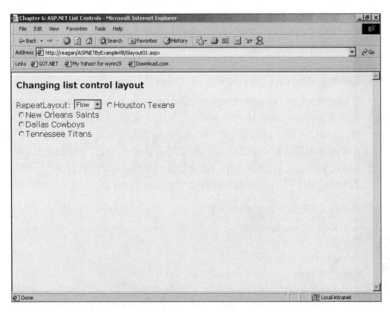

Figure 6.9: *The output from the code in Listing 6.17.*

By running the preceding example, you can see that using the drop-down menu to toggle the RepeatLayout property allows you to change the layout of the list items. We can also change the direction in which the items are repeated with another property: RepeatDirection.

A Change in Direction with RepeatDirection

Like the RepeatLayout property, RepeatDirection has two possible values: Vertical (default) and Horizontal. Listing 6.18 expands on the previous example to allow us to toggle not only the layout type, but also the direction. See Figure 6.10 for the output.

EXAMPLE

Listing 6.18: Changing the layout and direction of a RadioButtonList control (6layout02.aspx).

```
<%@ Page language="vb"%>
<html>
<head>
<script language="VB" runat="server" ID=Script1>
    Sub RepeatLayoutList_Changed(sender As Object, e As EventArgs)
        Select Case RepeatLayoutList.SelectedItem.Value
            Case "Table"
                RadioList.RepeatLayout = RepeatLayout.Table
            Case "Flow"
                RadioList.RepeatLayout = RepeatLayout.Flow
        End Select
    End Sub
    Sub RepeatDirectionList_Changed(sender As Object, e As EventArgs)
        Select Case RepeatLayoutList.SelectedItem.Value
            Case "Vertical"
                RadioList.RepeatDirection = RepeatDirection.Vertical
            Case "Horizontal"
                RadioList.RepeatDirection = RepeatDirection.Horizontal
        End Select
    End Sub
</script>
</head>
<body>
<form runat="server">
    <h3>Changing list control layout</h3>
    RepeatLayout:
    <asp:dropdownlist id="RepeatLayoutList" runat="Server" autopostback="True"
onselectedindexchanged="RepeatLayoutList_Changed">
        <asp:listitem value="Table">Table</asp:listitem>
        <asp:listitem value="Flow">Flow</asp:listitem>
    </asp:dropdownlist><br>
    RepeatLayout:
    <asp:dropdownlist id="RepeatDirectionList" runat="Server" autopostback="True"
onselectedindexchanged="RepeatDirectionList_Changed">
        <asp:listitem value="Vertical">Vertical</asp:listitem>
```

Listing 6.18: continued

```
        <asp:listitem value="Horizontal">Horizontal</asp:listitem>
        </asp:dropdownlist>
    <asp:radiobuttonlist id="RadioList" runat="server">
        <asp:ListItem>Houston Texans</asp:ListItem>
        <asp:ListItem>New Orleans Saints</asp:ListItem>
        <asp:ListItem>Dallas Cowboys</asp:ListItem>
        <asp:ListItem>Tennessee Titans</asp:ListItem>
    </asp:radiobuttonlist>
</form>
</body>
</html>
```

OUTPUT

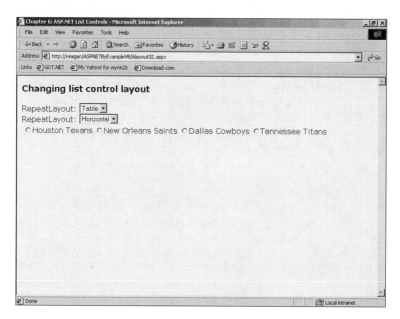

Figure 6.10: *The output from the code in Listing 6.18.*

We can go one step further with the layout of the list items by setting the number of columns in which the items are repeated in either the layout or direction combinations in the preceding example. We can change the column count simply by setting the RepeatColumns property, as the example in Listing 6.19 illustrates. (See Figure 6.11 for the output.)

EXAMPLE

Listing 6.19: Changing the column count of a RadioButtonList control (6layout03.aspx).

```
<%@ Page language="vb"%>
<html>
<head>
<script language="VB" runat="server" ID=Script1>
    Sub RepeatLayoutList_Changed(sender As Object, e As EventArgs)
```

Listing 6.19: continued

```
        Select Case RepeatLayoutList.SelectedItem.Value
            Case "Table"
                RadioList.RepeatLayout = RepeatLayout.Table
            Case "Flow"
                RadioList.RepeatLayout = RepeatLayout.Flow
        End Select
    End Sub
    Sub RepeatDirectionList_Changed(sender As Object, e As EventArgs)
        Select Case RepeatLayoutList.SelectedItem.Value
            Case "Vertical"
                RadioList.RepeatDirection = RepeatDirection.Vertical
            Case "Horizontal"
                RadioList.RepeatDirection = RepeatDirection.Horizontal
        End Select
    End Sub
    Sub RepeatColumnsValue_Change(sender As Object, e As EventArgs)
        RadioList.RepeatColumns = RepeatColumnsValue.Text
    End Sub
</script>
</head>
<body>
<form runat="server">
    <h3>Changing list control layout</h3>
    RepeatLayout:
    <asp:dropdownlist id="RepeatLayoutList" runat="Server"
        autopostback="True"
        onselectedindexchanged="RepeatLayoutList_Changed">
        <asp:listitem value="Table">Table</asp:listitem>
        <asp:listitem value="Flow">Flow</asp:listitem>
    </asp:dropdownlist><br>
    RepeatLayout:
    <asp:dropdownlist id="RepeatDirectionList" runat="Server"
        autopostback="True"
        onselectedindexchanged="RepeatDirectionList_Changed">
    RepeatColumns:
    <asp:textbox id="RepeatColumnsValue" runat="Server"
        ontextchanged="RepeatColumnsValue_Change"
        columns="1" autopostback="True"/>
        <asp:listitem value="Vertical">Vertical</asp:listitem>
        <asp:listitem value="Horizontal">Horizontal</asp:listitem>
        </asp:dropdownlist>
    <asp:radiobuttonlist id="RadioList" runat="server">
        <asp:ListItem>Houston Texans</asp:ListItem>
        <asp:ListItem>New Orleans Saints</asp:ListItem>
        <asp:ListItem>Dallas Cowboys</asp:ListItem>
        <asp:ListItem>Tennessee Titans</asp:ListItem>
    </asp:radiobuttonlist>
```

Listing 6.19: continued

```
</form>
</body>
</html>
```

OUTPUT

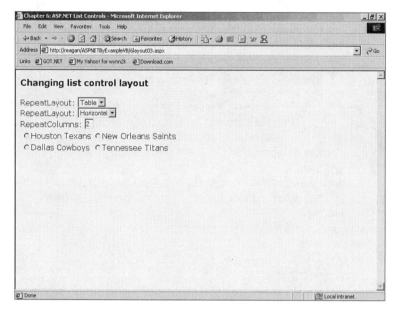

Figure 6.11: *The output from the code in Listing 6.19.*

Go ahead and experiment with changing the number of columns in different combinations of both layout and direction. These layout adjustments offer a great deal of control over how your list controls look on your forms. If you're a developer who likes to fine-tune your control layout, ASP.NET includes some additional properties.

Fine-Tuning List Control Layout

Aside from the coarse adjustments to layout that you can make with RepeatLayout, RepeatDirection, and RepeatColumns, ASP.NET also includes two additional properties for fine-tuning the layout of your list controls: Cellspacing and Cellpadding. I'm sure you're familiar with these two properties already from working with the HTML <TABLE> tag. Just like their counterparts for that HTML element, these two list control properties control the space between list items and the space within list items respectively. Note that this property is ignored when the RepeatLayout property is set to Flow. Listing 6.20 provides us with an example. (See Figure 6.12 for the output.)

Listing 6.20: Fine-tuning list control layout with `Cellspacing` and `Cellpadding` (6layout04.aspx).

```
<%@ Page language="vb"%>
<html>
<head>
<script language="VB" runat="server" ID=Script1>
    Sub RepeatLayoutList_Changed(sender As Object, e As EventArgs)
        Select Case RepeatLayoutList.SelectedItem.Value
            Case "Table"
                RadioList.RepeatLayout = RepeatLayout.Table
            Case "Flow"
                RadioList.RepeatLayout = RepeatLayout.Flow
        End Select
    End Sub
    Sub RepeatDirectionList_Changed(sender As Object, e As EventArgs)
        Select Case RepeatLayoutList.SelectedItem.Value
            Case "Vertical"
                RadioList.RepeatDirection = RepeatDirection.Vertical
            Case "Horizontal"
                RadioList.RepeatDirection = RepeatDirection.Horizontal
        End Select
    End Sub
    Sub RepeatColumnsValue_Change(sender As Object, e As EventArgs)
        RadioList.RepeatColumns = RepeatColumnsValue.Text
    End Sub
</script>
</head>
<body>
<form runat="server">
    <h3>Changing list control layout</h3>
    RepeatLayout:
    <asp:dropdownlist id="RepeatLayoutList" runat="Server"
         autopostback="True"
         onselectedindexchanged="RepeatLayoutList_Changed">
        <asp:listitem value="Table">Table</asp:listitem>
        <asp:listitem value="Flow">Flow</asp:listitem>
    </asp:dropdownlist><br>
    RepeatLayout:
    <asp:dropdownlist id="RepeatDirectionList"
        runat="Server" autopostback="True"
        onselectedindexchanged="RepeatDirectionList_Changed">
    RepeatColumns:
    <asp:textbox id="RepeatColumnsValue" runat="Server"
        ontextchanged="RepeatColumnsValue_Change"
        columns="1" autopostback="True"/>
        <asp:listitem value="Vertical">Vertical</asp:listitem>
        <asp:listitem value="Horizontal">Horizontal</asp:listitem>
        </asp:dropdownlist>
```

Listing 6.20: continued

```
<asp:radiobuttonlist id="RadioList" runat="server">
    <asp:ListItem>Houston Texans</asp:ListItem>
    <asp:ListItem>New Orleans Saints</asp:ListItem>
    <asp:ListItem>Dallas Cowboys</asp:ListItem>
    <asp:ListItem>Tennessee Titans</asp:ListItem>
</asp:radiobuttonlist>
</form>
</body>
</html>
```

OUTPUT

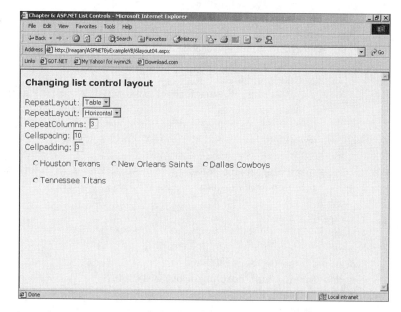

Figure 6.12: *The output from the code in Listing 6.20.*

Notice how the Cellspacing and Cellpadding properties are ignored when the layout mode of the list control is set to Flow. Even though all five of these layout properties only apply to two list controls, CheckBoxList and RadioButtonList, remember that you can tweak the look of all ASP.NET list controls by using CSS stylesheets.

Summary

Let's review what we've covered in this chapter. So far we've discovered how to:

- Use list controls on your Web forms to present the user with a list of choices from which to choose

- Get and set the selected items in a list control

- Create and remove list items programmatically

- Databind both the items collection and the selection property of each control

- Change the layout of the list controls that support this functionality

What's Next?

In the next chapter, we will take a look at ASP.NET rich controls. These controls will bring a degree of functionality to your Web forms more commonly associated with Windows-based forms.

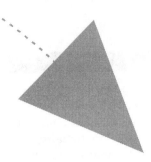

Using ASP.NET Rich Controls

ASP.NET includes a set of controls to provide advanced functionality for your Web forms, beyond the intrinsic controls found in HTML. The purpose of this chapter is to discuss two of these controls, AdRotator and Calendar, and get you started integrating them into your ASP.NET applications.

In this chapter you will learn

- What the properties, methods, and events of each of the ASP.NET rich controls are

- How to change the layout and display of these controls

- How to databind properties of the Calendar control

Introduction to Rich Controls

Unlike ASP.NET list controls, which all inherit from `ListControl` and therefore share specific common functionality, the rich controls discussed in this chapter are inherited from `WebControl`, so they have very little in common with one another except for providing more advanced functionality than intrinsic or list controls. We'll begin by discussing `AdRotator` and the changes to ad rotation since ASP 3.0.

Working with `AdRotator`

You'll recall that previous versions of ASP provided ad rotation functionality. However, as with all the other Active Server Components provided by Microsoft, it was in the form of a scriptable COM object used from within `<%...%>` tags, as shown in Listing 7.1.

Listing 7.1: Declaring the `AdRotator` control.

```
<%
Dim oAdRotator
Set oAdRotator = Server.CreateObject("MSWC.AdRotator")
Dim strAdHTML
StrAdHTML = oAdRotator.GetAdvertisment("ads.txt")
Response.Write(strAdHTML)
%>
```

In ASP.NET, ad rotation now gets a declarative syntax for greater simplicity. The preceding code simply becomes

```
<asp:AdRotator id="oAdRotator" AdvertisementFile="ads.xml" runat="Server" />
```

Table 7.1 shows a summary of the properties and events of the `AdRotator` control. Please take a moment to review them before we begin with an example.

Table 7.1: Properties and Events of the **AdRotator** *Control*

Name	Item	Description
AdCreated	Event	Raised when a new advertisement is created but before the control is rendered
AdvertisementFile	Property	Gets or sets path to the XML file containing configuration data for advertisements
KeywordFilter	Property	Gets or sets the keyword used to match advertisements to categories
Target	Property	Gets or sets the frame in which to load the URL of an ad when clicked

Let's begin by looking at an example of the `AdRotator` in action. We declare the `AdRotator` control as shown in Listing 7.2.

Listing 7.2: Declaring the AdRotator control (6ad01.aspx).

```
<%@ Page language="vb" debug="true"%>
<html>
<head>
<title>Chapter 7: ASP.NET Rich Controls</title>
</head>
<body>
    <form runat="server">
        <asp:AdRotator id="BooksRotator"
            AdvertisementFile="books_ads.xml" runat="Server" />
    </form>
</body>
</html>
```

Figure 7.1 shows the output from Listing 6.2.

OUTPUT

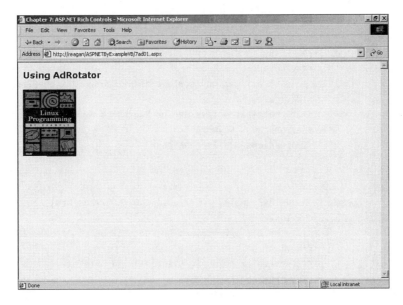

Figure 7.1: *The AdRotator control in action.*

If you're following along by running the examples in your browser, go ahead and refresh the page two or three times to see the ad rotation. When using the AdRotator control, the source, hyperlinks, and frequency of the ads are declared externally in the AdvertisementFile. Table 7.2 defines the properties for each Ad element found in this configuration file.

Table 7.2: Element Definitions for the `AdvertisementFile`

Name	Type	Description
AlternateText	Element	The text for the ALT tag for the image
ImageUrl	Element	The absolute or relative URL to the image to be displayed
Impressions	Element	The weight of the ad in the rotation frequency
Keyword	Element	The category for the advertisement when using the KeywordFilter property of the AdRotator
NavigateUrl	Element	The URL to load when the ad is clicked

In this example, we've named the `AdvertisementFile` "books_ads.xml". Listing 7.3 contains the XML source of the file.

Listing 7.3: The books_ads.xml `AdvertismentFile`.

```
<?xml version="1.0" encoding="utf-8" ?>
    <Advertisements>
        <Ad>

<ImageUrl>/ASPNETByExampleVB/ch07/ads//ch07/ch07/ads/asp3.jpg</ImageUrl>
            <NavigateUrl>
                http://www.mcp.com/que/detail_que.cfm?item=0789722402
            </NavigateUrl>
            <AlternateText>Active Server Pages 3.0 By Example</AlternateText>
            <Keyword>web</Keyword>
            <Impressions>50</Impressions>
        </Ad>
        <Ad>

<ImageUrl>/ASPNETByExampleVB/ch07/ads//ch07/ch07/ads/html.jpg</ImageUrl>
            <NavigateUrl>
                http://www.mcp.com/que/detail_que.cfm?item=0789722283
            </NavigateUrl>
            <AlternateText>HTML By Example</AlternateText>
            <Keyword>web</Keyword>
            <Impressions>50</Impressions>
        </Ad>
        <Ad>

<ImageUrl>/ASPNETByExampleVB/ch07/ads//ch07/ch07/ads/linuxprogramming.jpg
</ImageUrl>
            <NavigateUrl>
                http://www.mcp.com/que/detail_que.cfm?item=0789722151
            </NavigateUrl>
            <AlternateText>Linux Programming By Example</AlternateText>
            <Keyword>Linux</Keyword>
            <Impressions>50</Impressions>
        </Ad>
        <Ad>
```

Listing 7.3: continued

```
<ImageUrl>/ASPNETByExampleVB/ch07/ads//ch07/ch07/ads/linuxsocket.jpg</ImageUrl>
        <NavigateUrl>
              http://www.mcp.com/que/detail_que.cfm?item=0789722410
        </NavigateUrl>
        <AlternateText>Linux Socket Programming By Example</AlternateText>
        <Keyword>Linux</Keyword>
        <Impressions>50</Impressions>
    </Ad>
    <Ad>
        <ImageUrl>/ASPNETByExampleVB/ch07/ads/java2.jpg</ImageUrl>
        <NavigateUrl>
              http://www.mcp.com/que/detail_que.cfm?item=0789722666
        </NavigateUrl>
        <AlternateText>Java 2 Programming By Example</AlternateText>
        <Keyword>web</Keyword>
        <Impressions>50</Impressions>
    </Ad>
    <Ad>
        <ImageUrl>/ASPNETByExampleVB/ch07/ads/xml.jpg</ImageUrl>
        <NavigateUrl>
              http://www.mcp.com/que/detail_que.cfm?item=0789722429
        </NavigateUrl>
        <AlternateText>XML By Example</AlternateText>
        <Keyword>web</Keyword>
        <Impressions>50</Impressions>
    </Ad>
</Advertisements>
```

As you can see, in this example we are rotating ads of thumbnails of other books in this Que series. The ImageUrl element in each ad definition uses a relative URL for the image source, but we could just as easily have used an absolute URL to point to the original file on the Que Web site. For each ad, the NavigateURL actually does use an absolute URL to link to the product page for each book on the Web site. By setting the AlternateText value, we set the text the browser should display if the image is unavailable. This value is simply written to the ALT attribute in the HTML img tag output by the AdRotator control. This value is also displayed as a tooltip in most modern browsers.

The last two elements in the definition file provide the real heart of the AdRotator functionality: the ability to change the frequency and conditions of the ad rotation. The Keyword element sets the category for the advertisement. This category assignment determines if the ad is placed into the rotation, depending on whether it matches the corresponding KeywordFilter property of the AdRotator control. This allows us to filter ads on a page-by-page basis based on this category setting. We can also give a higher priority to some ads by setting the Impressions value. This value weights the frequency of each ad in the rotation proportionally, based on these values. The higher the Impressions value for a particular ad, the more often in proportion to the other ads it will appear in the ad rotation.

Suppose we are building an ad-supported Web-based discussion group for developers that includes banners at the top of each page. We would most probably want to display relevant advertisements for each forum, so let's expand the previous example by setting the KeywordFilter property for the AdRotator control (see Figure 7.2):

```
<asp:AdRotator id="BooksRotator" AdvertisementFile="books_ads.xml"
    runat="Server" KeywordFilter="web" />
```

OUTPUT

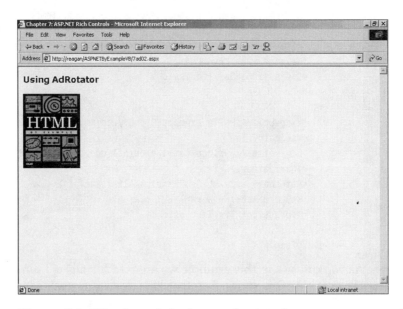

Figure 7.2: *Filtering ads by keyword using the* AdRotator *control.*

Now when we refresh the browser, the only advertisements rendered are those that match the "web" keyword setting in the AdvertisementFile. Now suppose that each of these ads for development books were linked to their corresponding product pages at Amazon.com, FatBrain.com, or some other online bookseller. We might want to give higher priority to the ads for those products for which we make the highest margin. As mentioned earlier, we would simply adjust the Impressions value for each ad in the XML file. Let's modify the AdvertisementFile as shown in Listing 7.4.

Listing 7.4: The modified books_ads.xml AdvertisementFile.

```
<?xml version="1.0" encoding="utf-8" ?>
    <Advertisements>
        <Ad>
```

Listing 7.4: continued

```
        <ImageUrl>/ASPNETByExampleVB/ch07/ads/asp3.jpg</ImageUrl>
        <NavigateUrl>
            http://www.mcp.com/que/detail_que.cfm?item=0789722402
        </NavigateUrl>
        <AlternateText>Active Server Pages 3.0 By Example</AlternateText>
        <Keyword>web</Keyword>
        <Impressions>10</Impressions>
    </Ad>
    <Ad>
        <ImageUrl>/ASPNETByExampleVB/ch07/ads/html.jpg</ImageUrl>
        <NavigateUrl>
            http://www.mcp.com/que/detail_que.cfm?item=0789722283
        </NavigateUrl>
        <AlternateText>HTML By Example</AlternateText>
        <Keyword>web</Keyword>
        <Impressions>1</Impressions>
    </Ad>
    <Ad>
        <ImageUrl>/ASPNETByExampleVB/ch07/ads/linuxprogramming.jpg</ImageUrl>
        <NavigateUrl>
            http://www.mcp.com/que/detail_que.cfm?item=0789722151
        </NavigateUrl>
        <AlternateText>Linux Programming By Example</AlternateText>
        <Keyword>Linux</Keyword>
        <Impressions>1</Impressions>
    </Ad>
    <Ad>
        <ImageUrl>/ASPNETByExampleVB/ch07/ads/linuxsocket.jpg</ImageUrl>
        <NavigateUrl>
            http://www.mcp.com/que/detail_que.cfm?item=0789722410
        </NavigateUrl>
        <AlternateText>Linux Socket Programming By Example</AlternateText>
        <Keyword>Linux</Keyword>
        <Impressions>1</Impressions>
    </Ad>
    <Ad>
        <ImageUrl>/ASPNETByExampleVB/ch07/ads/java2.jpg</ImageUrl>
        <NavigateUrl>
            http://www.mcp.com/que/detail_que.cfm?item=0789722666
        </NavigateUrl>
        <AlternateText>Java 2 Programming By Example</AlternateText>
        <Keyword>web</Keyword>
        <Impressions>1</Impressions>
    </Ad>
    <Ad>
        <ImageUrl>/ASPNETByExampleVB/ch07/ads/xml.jpg</ImageUrl>
```

Listing 7.4: continued

```
        <NavigateUrl>
            http://www.mcp.com/que/detail_que.cfm?item=0789722429
        </NavigateUrl>
        <AlternateText>XML By Example</AlternateText>
        <Keyword>web</Keyword>
        <Impressions>1</Impressions>
    </Ad>
</Advertisements>
```

Now save the file and refresh your browser. You should notice that *Active Server Pages 3.0 By Example* appears ten times more often than the other titles in the rotation.

Using the `AdCreated` Event

In all the examples so far in this chapter, we've used the `AdRotator` control to render ads consisting of images only. Often, however, Internet advertising consists of a banner ad and a hyperlink or descriptive caption. One way to accomplish this would be to couple the `AdRotator` control with a `Hyperlink` control, but how do we set the `NavigateUrl` property of the hyperlink for each ad dynamically? We do this by handling the `AdCreated` event of the `AdRotator` control, as shown in Listing 7.5.

Listing 7.5: Declaring the `AdRotator` control (6ad03.aspx).

```
<%@ Page language="vb" debug="true"%>
<html>
<head>
<title>Chapter 7: ASP.NET Rich Controls</title>
<script language="vb" runat="server">
    Sub BooksRotator_AdCreated(sender as Object, e as AdCreatedEventArgs)
        AdLink.NavigateURL = e.NavigateURL
    End Sub
</script>
</head>
<body>
<form runat="server">
    <p align="center">
    <asp:AdRotator id="BooksRotator"
        AdvertisementFile="books_ads.xml" runat="Server"
        keywordfilter="web" onadcreated="BooksRotator_AdCreated" />
    <br>
    <asp:hyperlink id="AdLink" runat="Server"
        Text="ClickHere" font-names="Arial" font-size="8pt"/>
    </p>
</form>
</body>
</html>
```

Figure 7.3 shows the output from Listing 6.5.

OUTPUT

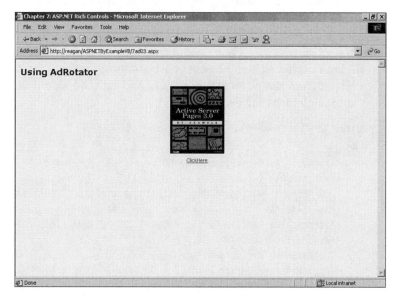

Figure 7.3: *Creating captions by handling the* AdCreated *event.*

In this example, we've added a Hyperlink control and the
BooksRotator_AdCreated event handler to the Web form. Note that the type
of the second argument for this event handler is AdCreatedEventArgs
instead of the usual EventArgs as with most Web control event handlers.
Table 7.3 defines the properties for the AdCreatedEventArgs class.

Table 7.3: Properties of the **AdCreatedEventArgs** *Class*

Name	Type	Description
AdProperties	Property	Gets a dictionary object with all the properties from the AdvertisementFile for the created ad
AlternateText	Property	Gets or sets the text for the ALT tag for the image
ImageUrl	Property	Gets or sets the URL for the created ad
NavigateUrl	Property	Gets or sets the URL to load when the created ad is clicked

In this example, we simply copy the URL for the ad to the hyperlink control
using the NavigateUrl property of the AdCreatedEventArgs class. Now we
have a linked caption for each ad in the rotation. But suppose we wanted to
change the text of the hyperlink to be more descriptive. Perhaps we would
like to include the title of the book in the caption. Although we could use
the AlternateText property of the AdCreatedEventArgs class to obtain this
value, let's take another approach that will introduce the extensibility built
into the AdRotator control.

The key to tailoring the `AdRotator` control for your own purpose is found in the `AdProperties` property of the `AdCreatedEventArgs` class. As defined in Table 7.3, this read-only property returns a dictionary object representing all the properties of the currently created ad as defined in the external `AdvertisementFile`. That means that we can define custom elements in this file and retrieve them at runtime via `AdProperties`. Listing 7.6 shows a snippet from the `AdvertisementFile` and how we would define a custom `Caption` element for each ad.

Listing 7.6: Using custom elements in the `AdvertisementFile`.

```
<Ad>
    <ImageUrl>/ASPNETByExampleVB/ch07/ads/asp3.jpg</ImageUrl>
    <NavigateUrl>
        http://www.mcp.com/que/detail_que.cfm?item=0789722402
    </NavigateUrl>
    <AlternateText>Active Server Pages 3.0 By Example</AlternateText>
    <Keyword>web</Keyword>
    <Impressions>10</Impressions>
    <Caption>Active Server Pages 3.0 By Example</Caption>
    <PercentOff>10</PercentOff>
</Ad>
```

Now let's change the event handler on the Web form to retrieve these two new values and dynamically change the caption for each ad in the rotation. Listing 7.7 shows the new code.

Listing 7.7: Dynamic captions with the `AdRotator` control (6ad04.aspx).

```
<%@ Page language="vb" debug="true"%>
<html>
<head>
<title>Chapter 7: ASP.NET Rich Controls</title>
<script language="vb" runat="server">
    Sub BooksRotator_AdCreated(sender as Object, e as AdCreatedEventArgs)
        AdLink.NavigateURL = e.NavigateURL
        AdLink.Text = "Save " & e.AdProperties("PercentOff") & _
            "% on " & e.AdProperties("Caption")
    End Sub
</script>
</head>
<body>
<form runat="server">
    <p align="center">
    <asp:AdRotator id="BooksRotator"
        AdvertisementFile="books_ads.xml" runat="Server"
        keywordfilter="web" onadcreated="BooksRotator_AdCreated" />
    <br>
```

Listing 7.7: continued

```
    <asp:hyperlink id="AdLink" runat="Server"
        Text="ClickHere" font-names="Arial" font-size="8pt"/>
    </p>
</form>
</body>
</html>
```

Figure 7.4 shows the output from Listing 7.7.

OUTPUT

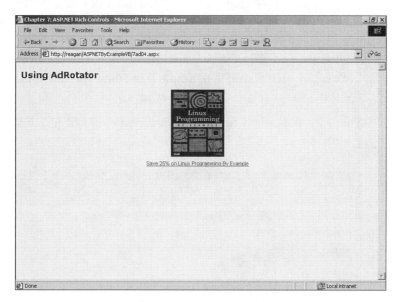

Figure 7.4: *Descriptive captions by using custom* AdvertisementFile *elements.*

Notice that we now build the caption dynamically and not only include the book title, but we also include the savings the customer can expect. These are but two simple examples of custom properties you can define for your ads to customize your implementation of the AdRotator control. I'm sure that you will find this extensibility useful in your own projects as you define custom attributes for your advertisements.

Up to this point in this chapter, you have seen how the AdRotator control simplifies ad rotation in ASP.NET. Now let's take a look at another new control and how it adds a great deal of functionality not inherent in previous versions of ASP.

Introduction to the Calendar Control

In the previous chapters, you've seen how ASP.NET simplifies a lot of tasks that were code-intensive in previous versions of ASP. Perhaps no other control included in ASP.NET illustrates this point better than a databound calendar. For most developers, the amount of code and intermingled HTML involved for such a job in ASP justified the purchase of a third-party server component. Now ASP.NET brings to Web development the GUI manipulation of date values that VB, C++, and Java developers have always enjoyed. However, as you will find out, the ASP.NET Calendar control doesn't forfeit any of the fine-grain layout and display control Web developers take for granted.

Let's begin with a simple example by adding the control to the Web form:

```
<asp:Calendar id="Cal" runat="server" />
```

That's all the code it takes to create a calendar in ASP.NET, as shown in Figure 7.5.

OUTPUT

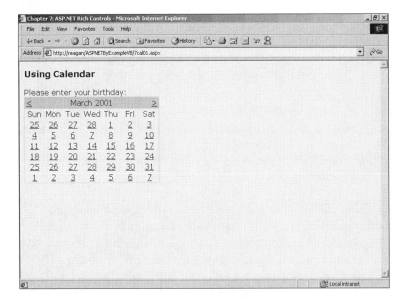

Figure 7.5: *A simple calendar using the ASP.NET* Calendar *control.*

Of course, at this point, the calendar is not very useful, so before we expand this example, let's look at the characteristics of the Calendar control. Take a moment to review this partial listing of the properties, methods, and events for the Calendar control in Table 7.4.

Table 7.4: Properties, Methods, and Events of the **Calendar** *Control*

Name	Type	Description
CellPadding	Property	Gets or sets the spacing between the cell borders and its contents
CellSpacing	Property	Gets or sets the spacing between cells
DayHeaderStyle	Property	Gets the current style for the day-of-the-week header row
DayNameFormat	Property	Gets or sets format for the day-of-the-week names
DayNameFormat	Property	Gets or sets format for the day-of-the-week names
DayRender	Event	Raised when a day cell is rendered
DayStyle	Property	Gets the current style for the day cells
FirstDayOfWeek	Property	Gets or sets the day of the week to display in the first column of the calendar
NextMonthText	Property	Gets or sets the text to display for the next month navigation link
NextMonthFormat	Property	Gets or sets the format for the month name for the Previous Month and Next Month buttons
NextPrevStyle	Property	Gets the current style for the Next and Previous selectors
OtherMonthDayStyle	Property	Gets the current style for the day cells from the previous month
PrevMonthText	Property	Gets or sets the text to display for the previous month navigation link
SelectedDate	Property	Gets or sets the currently selected date
SelectedDates	Property	Gets the collection of dates currently selected
SelectedDateStyle	Property	Gets the current style for the currently selected date
SelectionChanged	Event	Raised when the SelectedDate property changes in response to a user click
SelectionMode	Property	Gets or sets the format of the selection: Day, Week, Month
SelectMonthText	Property	Gets or sets the text for the month selection in the selector column
SelectorStyle	Property	Gets the current style for the week and month selectors
SelectWeekText	Property	Gets or sets the text for the week selection in the selector column
ShowDayHeader	Property	Gets or sets whether the day names header is displayed
ShowGridLines	Property	Gets or sets whether the calendar will display grid lines
ShowNextPrevMonth	Property	Gets or sets whether the next and previous month links are displayed
ShowTitle	Property	Gets or sets whether the calendar title is displayed

Table 7.4: continued

Name	Type	Description
TitleFormat	Property	Gets or sets how the month name is formatted in the calendar title
TitleStyle	Property	Gets the current style for the calendar title
TodayDayStyle	Property	Gets the current style for the current date on the calendar
TodaysDate	Property	Gets the value of the current date for the calendar
VisibleDate	Property	Gets or sets the value of the date that determines which month to render
WeekendDayStyle	Property	Gets the current style for the weekend days on the calendar
VisibleMonthChanged	Event	Raised when the user clicks the next or previous month links

Armed with this information, let's expand the previous example and actually do something useful with the control. Normally, we're most interested in performing some action when the user changes the date selection in a calendar control. With the ASP.NET `Calendar`, we do this by handling the `SelectionChanged` event. Consider the example in Listing 7.8.

Listing 7.8: Using the `Calendar` control to gather user input (7cal02.aspx).

```
<%@ Page language="C#"%>
<html>
<head>
<title>Chapter 7: ASP.NET Rich Controls</title>
<script language="C#" runat="server">
    void Cal_Change(Object sender, EventArgs e){
        BirthdayLabel.Text = "Your birthday is " + _
        Cal.SelectedDate.ToShortDateString();
    }
</script>
</head>
<body>
    <form runat="server">
        Please enter your birthday:
        <asp:Calendar id="Cal" runat="server" onselectionchanged="Cal_Change" />
        <br>
        <asp:label id="BirthdayLabel" runat="Server" />
    </form>

</body>
</html>
```

Figure 7.6 shows the output from Listing 7.8.

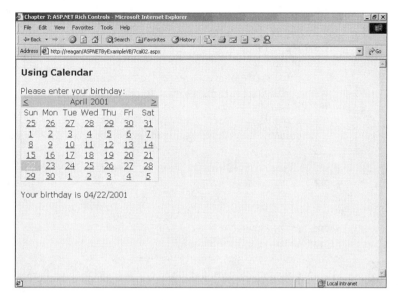

Figure 7.6: *Using the* Calendar *control to gather user input.*

In this example, we set up the event handler for the SelectionChanged event, which simply reads the SelectedDate property, to retrieve the user input. Because the SelectedDate property is of type System.DateTime, we can then use the built-in ToShortDateString method to return a formatted string to use for display in the label.

Using SelectionMode

Often, it is necessary for the user to input a range of dates instead of a single date selection. With the Calendar control, the SelectionMode property determines the selection behavior of the control. The property defaults to Day as you have just seen, but it also may be set to DayWeek, which allows both single days and single weeks to be selected, or DayWeekMonth, which allows single days, single weeks, or an entire month to be selected. This property also supports a fourth value of None if you would like to disable date selection. Listing 7.9 provides an example of selecting a date range with the Calendar control.

Listing 7.9: Allowing multiple date selection in the Calendar control.

```
<%@ Page language="C#" autoeventwireup="false"%>
<html>
<head>
<title>Chapter 7: ASP.NET Rich Controls</title>
<script language="C#" runat="server">
    void Cal_Change(Object sender, EventArgs e){
```

Listing 7.9: continued

```
        String VacationDates;
        String dStart;
        String dEnd;
        dStart = Cal.SelectedDates[0].ToShortDateString();
        dEnd = Cal.SelectedDates[Cal.SelectedDates.Count -
1].ToShortDateString();
        VacationDates = dStart + " thru " + dEnd;
        VacationLabel.Text = "Your requested vacation is " + VacationDates;


    }
</script>
</head>
<body>
    <form runat="server">
    Please enter your birthday:
    <asp:Calendar id="Cal" runat="server"
        onselectionchanged="Cal_Change"  selectionmode="DayWeekMonth"/>
    <br>
    <asp:label id="VacationLabel" runat="Server" />
    </form>
</body>
</html>
```

Figure 7.7 shows the output from Listing 7.9.

OUTPUT

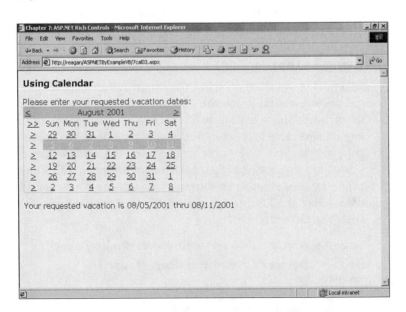

Figure 7.7: *Using the* Calendar *with multiple date selection.*

Because you can have only one birthday, we've changed this example to allow the user to request days off for an upcoming vacation. The only modifications necessary are to set the SelectionMode of the control, in this case DayWeekMonth, and then to modify the event handler to read the selected dates. The SelectedDates property returns a collection of System.DateTime values, which we can traverse using a For...Next loop or, as we did in this case, by reading the first and last values to get the date range. We can then display the values, pass them to a database query, or update other controls on the form.

Databinding and Calendar

Now that we've seen how to allow the user to select one or more dates with the Calendar control, let's look at how to set the default selection. In each of the samples so far, the calendar control has no default SelectedDate. Often, we would like to make the current date or the value of a database record the default selection. This can be accomplished easily by data binding the SelectedDate property to another variable, the value of another control, a database record, or an expression as in this example:

```
<asp:Calendar id="Calendar1"
   runat="server"
   SelectedDate="<%# Convert.ToDateTime(DateTime.Now) %>">
</asp:Calendar>
```

To activate the data binding, simply call the DataBind method:

```
Calendar1.DataBind();
```

Modifying Calendar Display

Now that you've seen how to use the Calendar control to display and input date values, let's look at some of its advanced layout features. Up to this point, we've been dealing with the control strictly from a functional perspective and haven't modified its display. Listing 7.10 illustrates how we can modify the look of the calendar control to achieve an almost infinite number of display possibilities.

Listing 7.10: Changing the look of the Calendar control.

```
<%@ Page language="VB" autoeventwireup="false"%>
<html>
<head>
<title>Chapter 7: ASP.NET Rich Controls</title>
</head>
<body>
    <form runat="server">
        <h3>Using Calendar</h3>
```

Listing 7.10: continued

```
Modifying the look of the Calendar control
<br><br>
<TABLE BORDER="0" CELLSPACING="1" CELLPADDING="1">
    <TR>
        <TD ALIGN="CENTER">
            Default Styling
            <asp:Calendar id="Cal" runat="server"
                selectionmode="DayWeekMonth"/>

        </TD>
        <TD ALIGN="CENTER">
            Small
            <asp:Calendar
                id="Cal2"
                runat="server"
                daynameformat="FirstLetter"
                titlestyle-font-size="8pt"
                titlestyle-font-names="Verdana"
                titlestyle-font-bold="True"
                todaydaystyle-backcolor="Gainsboro"
                todaydaystyle-font-bold="True"
                daystyle-font-size="8pt"
                daystyle-font-names="Verdana"
                dayheaderstyle-font-size="8pt"
                dayheaderstyle-font-bold="True"
                dayheaderstyle-font-names="Verdana"
                selectionmode="DayWeekMonth"
                nextprevstyle-font-names="Webdings"
                selectorstyle-font-names="Verdana"
                selectorstyle-font-size="6pt"
                nextmonthtext="4"
                nextprevstyle-font-underline="False"
                prevmonthtext="3"
            />
        </TD>
    </TR>
    <TR>
        <TD ALIGN="CENTER" colspan="2">
            Verbose:
            <asp:Calendar
                id="Cal3"
                runat="server"
                selectionmode="DayWeekMonth"
                nextmonthtext="Next Month"
                prevmonthtext="Previous Month"
```

```
                        daynameformat="Full"
                        titleformat="MonthYear"
                        dayheaderstyle-backcolor="#EEEECC"
                        titlestyle-backcolor="#009900"
                        titlestyle-forecolor="White"
                        selectorstyle-backcolor="#EEEECC"
                        selecteddaystyle-backcolor="#009900"
                        nextprevstyle-forecolor="White"
                        othermonthdaystyle-backcolor="LemonChiffon"
                        font-size="8pt" font-names="Verdana"
                        selectmonthtext="Select Month"
                        selectweektext="Select Week"
                    />
            </TD>
          </TR>
        </TABLE>

    </form>

</body>
</html>
```

Figure 7.8 shows the output from Listing 7.10.

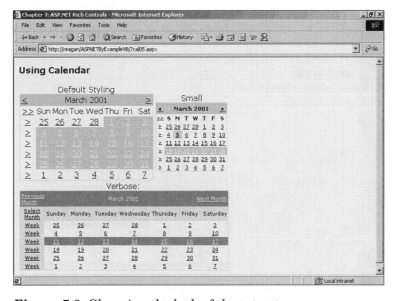

Figure 7.8: *Changing the look of the* Calendar.

Please note that in this example, all the display properties are set explicitly from within the Calendar control declaration. Many developers with Windows GUI experience will find this syntax natural because each display attribute is its own property for the control. However, most stylesheet-savvy Web developers might prefer a second method for controlling the display of the `Calendar` control (as well as most ASP.NET controls).

Using CSS to Control `Calendar` Display

One of the strongest selling points for moving to the .NET platform is the separation of code from presentation markup. One of the easiest ways to separate what your forms do from what they look like is by using Cascading Style Sheets (CSS). Listing 7.11 demonstrates how you can create cleaner, easier-to-manage code while garnering even more control over the display properties of the `Calendar` control.

Listing 7.11: Changing the look of the `Calendar` control by using CSS (7cal06.aspx).

```
<%@ Page language="VB" autoeventwireup="false"%>
<html>
<head>
<title>Chapter 7: ASP.NET Rich Controls</title>
<style>
.Cal {
font-family: Verdana;
font-size: 8pt;
border-top: solid 1 black;
border-bottom: solid 1 black;
border-left: solid 1 white;
border-right: solid 1 white;
}
.CalDayHeader {
background: #EFEFEF;
font-size: 10pt;
}

.CalDay A
{
text-decoration: none;
}
.CalNextPrev
{
font-size: 8pt;
}
.CalOtherMonthDay
{
background: #CCCCCC;
}
.CalOtherMonthDay A
{
```

Listing 7.11: continued

```
text-decoration: none;
}
.CalSelectedDay
{
border: solid 1 red;
background: white;
}
.CalSelector {
background-color: silver;
font-size: 6pt;
}
.CalTitle {
/* not currently working in Beta 1*/
}
.CalToday
{
background: blue;
}
.CalToday A
{
font-weight: bold;
text-decoration: none;
}
.CalWeekend A
{
background: #EFEFEF;
}
.CalWeekend A
{
text-decoration: none;
}
</style>
</head>
<body>
    <form runat="server">
        <h3>Using Calendar</h3>
        Modifying the look of the Calendar control
        <br><br>
        <asp:Calendar
            id="Cal"
            runat="server"
            selectionmode="DayWeekMonth"
            cssclass="Cal"
            dayheaderstyle-cssclass="CalDayHeader"
            daystyle-cssclass="CalDay"
            nextprevstyle-cssclass="CalNextPrev"
            othermonthdaystyle-cssclass="CalOtherMonthDay"
```

Listing 7.11: continued

```
            selecteddaystyle-cssclass="CalSelectedDay"
            selectorstyle-cssclass="CalSelector"
            titlestyle-cssclass="CalTitle"
            todaydaystyle-cssclass="CalToday"
            weekenddaystyle-cssclass="CalWeekend"
            titlestyle-font-size="12pt"
            titlestyle-font-bold="True"
            prevmonthtext="<img border='0' src='images/rew.gif'>"
            nextmonthtext="<img border='0' src='images/fwd.gif'>"
        />
    </form>

</body>
</html>
```

Figure 7.9 shows the output from Listing 6.11.

OUTPUT

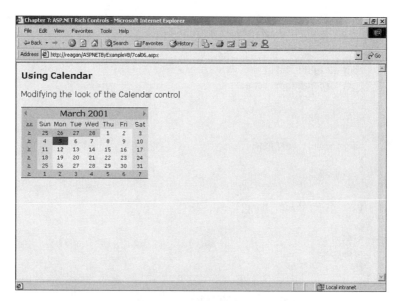

Figure 7.9: *Changing the look of the* Calendar *using style sheets.*

In this example, we've completely separated the display properties from the actual control declaration simply by assigning the CssClass property for each style unit of the calendar. These CSS classes are defined in the <style> section in the head of the document. We could just as easily have included these definitions in an external linked style sheet for an even greater degree of code separation. One of the benefits for using CSS classes instead of inline style properties—in addition to cleaner code—is the ability to reuse these class definitions. If you wanted to include two identical-looking calendar controls on the same page or on different pages, using inline style properties creates a great amount of duplicate code. Also, modifications made to one calendar would have to be copied to the second calendar control to keep the controls identical. By using CSS classes in linked style sheets, changes made to the style sheet cascade across the entire site. This greatly increases manageability by allowing Web designers to modify the look of the site without handling the actual Web form code.

Summary

Let's review what we've covered in this chapter. So far we've discovered how to

- Use the `AdRotator` control to present dynamic banner ads on the Web forms
- Use custom properties for the ads in the `AdvertisementFile` to customize ad rotation
- Use the `Calendar` control to display and input date values
- Databind a calendar control to an outside datasource
- Change the display of the `Calendar` control using both inline style properties and external CSS classes

What's Next?

In the next chapter, we will take a look at ASP.NET validation controls to validate user input. These controls greatly simplify data validation to reduce user input errors.

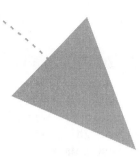

Using ASP.NET Validation Controls

One of the coolest sets of tools included in the ASP.NET toolbox has to be the validation controls. In Classic ASP, writing good validation logic that worked on the client (if the browser supported it) and on the server every time was difficult. It's not that they were rocket science to put together, but building the validation logic for a single user form could take hours and was a tedious and typically thankless job. That translates to "It didn't happen very often." Most of the time, some ASP error handling and checking for required fields was the extent of all but the most critical of data gathering forms. With ASP.NET's validation controls, there will no longer be an excuse not to provide strong client and server-side validation on every form, because it is just so easy and powerful.

In this chapter, you will

- Learn how web form validation works.

- Learn how to add validation to your ASP.NET pages.

- Learn how to use regular expressions to create powerful string validators.

- Learn how to combine form elements and validation controls.

Validating HTML Forms

As an ASP developer working with Classic ASP, one of the most frequent tasks I encountered involved developing HTML forms to gather user inputs, usually for storage in a database of some kind. Often, someone wanted to be able to *use* this data at some point in the future (though just as often, this was not the case), and when the time came to use the data, the clients invariably wanted the data to be in a clean, consistent format. There are at least a dozen different ways to display a telephone number, for example, but usually only one method was to be used for a particular application.

To accomplish this task with Classic ASP, I learned JavaScript to perform the client-side validation. Early on, I thought that client-side validation was *the* way to go, because it provided a better user experience, but I soon learned that it was not difficult to bypass client-side validation, and for this reason, if it was worth validating, it was worth validating on the server.

NOTE

For more on how to bypass client-side validation, see this link:

```
http://www.aspalliance.com/stevesmith/articles/19990611asptoday.asp
```

What Are Validation Controls?

The ASP.NET validation controls all inherit from the `ValidationControl` object, which itself inherits from the `Control` object. As you will see, one of the greatest things about the .NET Framework is its extensibility, allowing developers to build upon and extend existing objects to create better, richer objects. This is exactly what Microsoft has done with the validation controls that ship with ASP.NET. Each of these controls includes three parts, a client-side HTML representation of the control, client-side script, and server-side code.

The client-side script used is JScript/JavaScript, and the validation controls use the function library installed under the webroot folder in the /_aspx/[version]/script/WebUIValidation.js file for their client-side validation. This file is important to know about if you ever need to enable validation on a custom control you create, or want to customize the client-side behavior of a particular validation control. We will examine how these three separate parts of the control work together to help make validating user input simple and easy.

Client-Side Validation

As mentioned, the validation controls use the WebUIValidation.js file's JScript validation functions to perform validation on browsers that support it. This is referred to as client-side validation and is preferred over server-side validation because it offers the user a better, more responsive experience. It can be very frustrating to have to wait 5 or 10 seconds after each page request, only to find out after each submission that another form element is not valid. By performing all the validation client-side, the user doesn't have the delays that are commonly associated with server-side validation.

However, there are some problems with client-side validation that preclude its use as the sole means of validating user input. First of all, not all browsers support client-side scripting, so obviously we cannot use this approach everywhere. Second, it is not difficult for a malicious user to bypass client-side script by saving the Web form on the user's own machine, removing the validation script, and then submitting the form. If client-side validation were the only method used, this would pose a security hole, because the end user could potentially submit values that would confuse the ASP event handler or simply place garbage data into the application's database.

For these reasons, server-side validation is always performed by ASP.NET validation controls, and client-side validation is only done on those browsers that are known to support client-side scripting. This behavior can be further controlled by the developer through the use of the Page directive's ClientTarget property. By setting this property to "Downlevel", you force the validation controls to assume that the client has no client-side scripting capabilities, and so only server-side validation is used. With this setting, no Dynamic HTML (DHTML) is used, and every form submission will result in a round trip to the server. Similarly, by setting the property to "Uplevel", you force the validation controls to always use client-side validation (in addition to server-side) and DHTML, without checking to see whether the client supports these features.

Inserting a Validation Control

Inserting a validation control is no different from inserting any other control. If you are using Visual Studio .NET, you can simply drag the appropriate control onto your page's layout. Otherwise, simply insert the appropriate control within the HTML where you would like the validation's message to appear if the input is not valid. The following example demonstrates how to require a user to enter his or her name.

Perhaps the most common form of validation is simply to require that fields be filled in. The RequiredFieldValidator control does just this. Listing 8.1 shows the relevant code to make a text box entry required (that is, to ensure that the user enters some value).

EXAMPLE

Listing 8.1: Adding required validation to a text box.

```
<form method="post" runat="server">
<table>
    <tr>
        <td>
        Full Name:
        </td>
        <td>
        <asp:textbox runat="Server" columns="50" id="fullname">
        </asp:textbox>
        </td>
        <td>
        <asp:requiredfieldvalidator runat="Server" id="fullname_required"
        controltovalidate="fullname" errormessage="A name is required."
                display="dynamic">
        *
        </asp:requiredfieldvalidator>
        </td>
    </tr>
</table>
</form>
```

Figure 8.1 shows an example of what this page would look like if the user attempted to submit the form without providing a value for the fullname text box.

OUTPUT

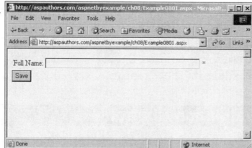

Figure 8.1: *A Simple Required Validator.*

In Figure 8.1, note the * to the right of the field. This is the default indicator that a field has failed a validation test. We'll see how to display more helpful validation feedback shortly.

NOTE

The examples for this chapter are available live online at:

http://aspauthors.com/aspnetbyexample/ch08/

One important thing to note is that all validator controls must be enclosed within server-side form tags. If you're not already doing so, I recommend that you follow Visual Studio's guidelines and simply place a server-side form on every .aspx page enclosing the entire contents of the <body>. This will save you a great deal of frustration trying to figure out why your controls are not behaving as you expect because you forgot the <form> tag.

In Listing 8.1, you see that the RequiredFieldValidator has a number of properties, as well as the contents of the tag, which in this case is simply a "*". The contents of the tag are the control's Text property. When a validator control is displayed, the Text property determines what is displayed by default. However, the ValidationSummary control uses the ErrorMessage property, not the Text property. We will see later in this chapter how we can use both the Text and ErrorMessage properties together to offer the user a detailed description of the errors encountered in their form submission. First, let's go over the properties and methods that are common to all validation controls.

Validation Control Properties

All validation controls inherit from the System.Web.UI.WebControls. BaseValidator class, and so they share the properties detailed in Table 8.1.

NOTE

You can view the complete class definition for this and any other .NET class by using the class browser application included with the SDK or available online at http://www.gotdotnet.com/quickstart/aspplus/samples/classbrowser/vb/ classbrowser.aspx.

Table 8.1: **BaseValidator** *Class Properties*

Property	Type	Description
ControlToValidate	String	The name of the control this validator is supposed to validate.
Enabled	Boolean	Determines whether or not the validator control is active.
EnableClientScript	Boolean	Determines whether or not client-side validation is used.
ErrorMessage	String	Describes the error message to be used if validation fails. Used by the ValidationSummary control.

Table 8.1: continued

Property	Type	Description
IsValid	Boolean	Is true if the ControlToValidate is valid and false otherwise. Set by the Validate() method.
Text	String	Describes the error message to be displayed on the page where the validator control is placed, if the validated control is not valid.
Display	ValidatorDisplay	[Dynamic|None|Static] Determines how the control is displayed on the page, if at all.

Validation Control Methods

All validation controls also expose the method described in Table 8.2.

Table 8.2: **BaseValidator** *Class Methods*

Method	Type	Description
Validate()	void	Causes the control to perform its validation and set the IsValid property.

RequiredFieldValidator Control

The simplest of the validation controls is the RequiredFieldValidator control. This control, which you saw in our first example, simply checks to ensure that a value has been entered for a particular form control. If the required field is missing, this control will display its text and set the page's IsValid property to false. The control's Text should prompt the user that she needs to fill in a value for the associated control.

The RequiredFieldValidator control inherits all the BaseValidator's properties described in Table 8.1, and also exposes its own property described in Table 8.3.

Table 8.3: **RequiredFieldValidator** *Class Additional Properties*

Method	Type	Description
InitialValue	String	Used to describe the initial value of the ControlToValidate. This is used to account for a default non-null value that should not be accepted, such as "Enter name here".

Note that if the InitialValue property is set, the RequiredFieldValidator will not be triggered by an empty (null) value in the ControlToValidate control. Basically, this validator simply compares InitialValue with the validated control's value, and if the two are the same, the validator concludes that the control is invalid.

Because we have already used this validator in an example, we will jump ahead to the next validation control before showing another example. The other validation controls are much more interesting than the RequiredFieldValidator, and we will see that by using these validators in concert, we are able to easily perform complex validation tasks that would have been very difficult, or at least tedious and time-consuming, using Classic ASP.

RangeValidator Control

The RangeValidator control is used to ensure that the input for a particular form field falls within a particular range of values. It extends upon the BaseValidator class's properties by adding three additional properties described in Table 8.4. To define a range of values for a control, it is necessary to know the minimum and maximum values of the range, as well as the type of data (numeric, date, and so forth) involved.

Table 8.4: **RangeValidator** *Class Additional Properties*

Method	Type	Description
MaximuumValue	String	The minimum valid value for the ControlToValidate.
MinimumValue	String	The maximum valid value for the ControlToValidate.
Type	ValidationDataType	The data type of value in the ControlToValidate. Must be one of the following: Currency, Date, Double, Integer, String.

In execution, the RangeValidator control is fairly simple. It examines the ControlToValidate's value, and determines whether or not it falls within the range specified by the RangeValidator's properties. If it does, the validator concludes that the control is valid. Otherwise, the RangeValidator concludes that the ControlToValidate is invalid. One common use of the RangeValidator control is to restrict the range of values one might enter for age. Listing 8.2 demonstrates how you might require users to enter ages between 18 and 65, for example. Figure 8.2 shows the output.

Listing 8.2: Adding range validation to a text box.

```
<%@ Page language="c#" ClientTarget="DownLevel" %>
<script language="C#" runat="server">
    void Page_Load()
    {
                if(Page.IsPostBack){
                    Validate();
        if(!IsValid){
            if(!age_required.IsValid){
                errorMessage.Text = "You must enter a value for age.<br>";
            }
            else if(!age_range.IsValid){
                errorMessage.Text = "Age must be between 18 and 65.<br>";
            }
        }
                }
    }
</script>
<HTML>
    <HEAD>
        <!DOCTYPE HTML PUBLIC "-//W3C//DTD HTML 4.0 Transitional//EN" >
    </HEAD>
    <body>
        <form method="post" runat="server">
            <asp:Label ID="errorMessage" Runat="server"></asp:Label>
            <table>
                <tr>
                    <td>
                        Age:
                    </td>
                    <td>
                        <asp:textbox runat="Server" columns="6"
                                                id="age"></asp:textbox>
                    </td>
                    <td>
                        <asp:requiredfieldvalidator runat="Server"
    id="age_required" controltovalidate="age" display="dynamic"
     errormessage="Age is required." EnableClientScript="False">
                            *
                        </asp:requiredfieldvalidator>
                        <asp:rangevalidator runat="Server" id="age_range"
    controltovalidate="age" display="dynamic"
    errormessage="Age must be an integer between 18 and 65." minimumvalue="18"
    maximumvalue="65" Type="Integer" EnableClientScript="False">
                            *
                        </asp:rangevalidator>
```

Listing 8.2: continued

```
                    </td>
                </tr>
            </table>
            <asp:button id="save_button" runat="Server"
                        text="Save"></asp:button>
        </form>
    </body>
</HTML>
```

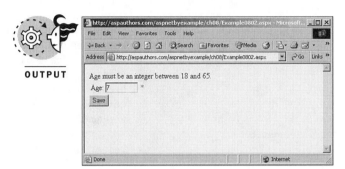

Figure 8.2: Example0802.aspx After Invalid Submit.

In this example, we've demonstrated how it is possible to use more than one validator control on a single form element. In this case, the age `TextBox` is required and its value must fall between 18 and 65. We've also shown how it is possible to use the `Page.IsValid` and validation controls' `IsValid` methods to capture and display detailed error messages in addition to a simple red asterisk (or other marker) next to the offending form element. We will see later in this chapter how another validation control, the `ValidationSummary` control, does a lot of this work for us and exposes a number of different display options.

One last item to note about Listing 8.2 is the very first line, where we added `'ClientTarget="DownLevel"'`. This was done to require the page to submit back to the server on each submission; otherwise the `errorMessage` control's `Text` would never have been set on browsers supporting client-side validation, because no invalid page would ever be submitted to the server.

CompareValidator Control

Often the validity of an item on a form can only be determined based on its relationship to other values on the form. For example, a form might ask the users how much money they would like to donate to a charity, and then ask them how much of their donation they would like to put toward, say, .NET programming training (it could happen…). It wouldn't make any sense for the second value to exceed the first value because it is limited by the total

amount the user has donated. In situations like these, the
CompareValidator can be used to ensure that the relationships between con-
trols on a form are valid. Table 8.5 describes the properties that make the
CompareValidator different from the BaseValidator class discussed earlier.

Table 8.5: **CompareValidator** *Class Additional Properties*

Method	Type	Description
ControlToCompare	String	The control to which the ControlToValidate should be compared.
Operator	ValidationCompareOperator	The type of comparison to be performed. One of: DataTypeCheck, Equal, GreaterThan, GreaterThanEqual, LessThan, LessThanEqual, NotEqual.
Type	ValidationDataType	The data type of value in the ControlToValidate. Must be one of the following: Currency, Date, Double, Integer, String.
ValueToCompare	String	Can be used instead of ControlToCompare to set a comparison value at design time.

As with the RangeValidator, we must specify a Type. This is because the
comparison only makes sense if the two values are of the same data type.
The kind of comparison must also be chosen, as the Operator property, and
should be fairly self-explanatory. The DataTypeCheck is the only one that
bears explanation. This value is simply used to ensure that the data type of
the ControlToValidate is the same as that of the ControlToCompare (or
ValueToCompare). Let's look at a simple example of how to use the
CompareValidator before going into any more detail. Listing 8.3 demonstrates how to force a user to enter a total amount to donate, followed by a
smaller or equal amount to put toward .NET programmer training. The
validator will simply display a "*" if the values are incorrect. Figure 8.3
shows the output.

EXAMPLE

Listing 8.3: Adding compare validation to a text box.

```
<%@ Page %>
<HTML>
    <HEAD>
        <!DOCTYPE HTML PUBLIC "-//W3C//DTD HTML 4.0 Transitional//EN" >
    </HEAD>
```

Listing 8.3: continued

```
    <body>
        <form method="post" runat="server">
            <asp:Label ID="errorMessage" Runat="server"></asp:Label>
            <table>
                <tr>
                    <td>
                        Total Donation:
                    </td>
                    <td>
                        <asp:textbox runat="Server" columns="6"
                                                    id="total_donation">
</asp:textbox>
                                                    .
                    </td>
                    <td>
                        <asp:requiredfieldvalidator runat="Server"
    id="total_donation_required" controltovalidate="total_donation"
    display="dynamic" errormessage="A total donation value is required.">
                                *
                        </asp:requiredfieldvalidator>
                        <asp:rangevalidator runat="Server"
    id="total_donation_range" controltovalidate="total_donation"
    display="dynamic" errormessage="Total dontation must be between $0 and
$5000."
    minimumvalue="0" maximumvalue="5000" Type="Currency">
                                *
                        </asp:rangevalidator>
                    </td>
                </tr>
                <tr>
                    <td>
                        Portion of above donation to
    apply toward .NET programmer training:
                    </td>
                    <td>
                        <asp:textbox runat="Server" columns="6"
    id="net_portion"></asp:textbox>
                    </td>
                    <td>
                        <asp:requiredfieldvalidator runat="Server"
    id="net_portion_required" controltovalidate="net_portion" display="dynamic"
    errormessage="A .NET portion value is required.">
                                *
                        </asp:requiredfieldvalidator>
                        <asp:CompareValidator Runat="server"
    ID="net_portion_compare" ControlToValidate="net_portion"
    ControlToCompare="total_donation" Operator="LessThanEqual"
    ErrorMessage="You cannot apply more toward .NET training than your total
donation."
```

Listing 8.3: continued

```
                Display="Dynamic" Type="Currency">
                              *

                        </asp:CompareValidator>
                        <asp:CompareValidator Runat="server"
        ID="net_portion_positive" ControlToValidate="net_portion" ValueToCompare="0"
        Type="Currency" Display="Dynamic" Operator="GreaterThanEqual"
        ErrorMessage=".NET portion must be a positive value.">
                              *

                        </asp:CompareValidator>
                    </td>
                </tr>
            </table>
            <asp:button id="save_button" runat="Server"
        text="Save"></asp:button>
        </form>
    </body>
</HTML>
```

OUTPUT

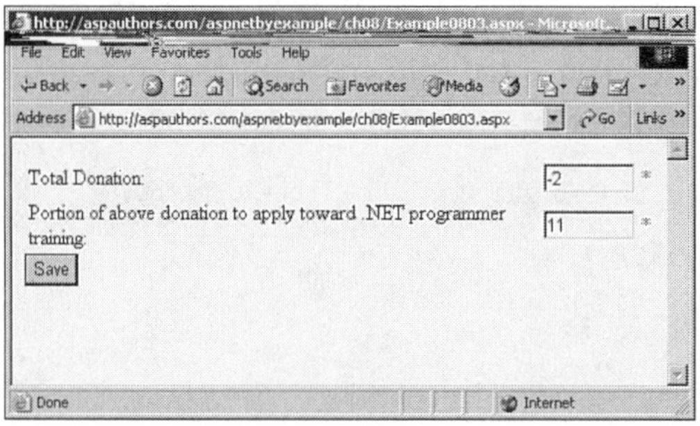

Figure 8.3: Example0803.aspx with invalid values.

For completeness, we continue to use the Required and Range validators in this example. However, the important validation to notice is the CompareValidator, which enforces the rule that states that the net_portion control's value cannot exceed the total_donation control's value. This would not prevent net_portion from being negative, however. For this reason, we used the second CompareValidator, net_portion_positive, to ensure that the net_portion control's value was greater than or equal to 0. This is an example of using the CompareValidator without ControlToCompare.

In many situations, more complicated patterns will be involved. For example, you might think that the RangeValidator would work for validating ZIP codes or telephone numbers, but in reality these kinds of values are much better validated by using regular expressions. We will briefly examine regular expressions and the .NET RegularExpressionValidator control in the next section.

RegularExpressionValidator Control

Before we go into this control, let's briefly discuss regular expressions, what they are, and how they are used. A complete coverage of regular expressions is well beyond the scope of this chapter (and this book!), but in this chapter we will provide you with a brief introduction to this powerful tool, along with a number of helpful examples and references to resources where you can find more information. Regular expressions are often the simplest, easiest way to search or compare strings, so they naturally can be very powerful when used to validate user input on forms.

A regular expression is a pattern of text that serves as a template for a particular character pattern. Strings can then be evaluated to determine whether any portion(s) of the string match the pattern described by the regular expression. Regular expression syntax includes specifications for many special metacharacters, that give these patterns a great deal of flexibility and power (and also sometimes make them look as if a drunken monkey was typing on the keyboard to produce the pattern). Nonetheless, regular expressions are a very powerful tool, that until recently have been largely limited to the UNIX world of computing.

Regular expressions were developed in the 1950s, believe it or not, by American mathematician Stephen Kleene, and were used to describe what he called "the algebra of regular sets." Ken Thompson, the principal inventor of UNIX, would later incorporate regular expressions into that operating system's search utilities. The first practical application of regular expressions was in the Unix editor called qed.

http://msdn.Microsoft.com/scripting/jscript/doc/reconearlybeginnings.htm

More recently, regular expressions have found their way into many different search engine utilities, JScript/JavaScript, and even recent versions of Microsoft's VBScript language.

At their simplest, regular expressions are just simple strings. If you have a string and you want it to match "abc", you could simply use the regular expression "abc". However, this expression would also match "123abc", "abc123", and "This string has abc in it". In order to restrict the pattern matching to JUST the string in the expression, it is necessary to use a couple of metacharacters, the caret ("^") and the dollar sign ("$"). The caret ("^") character matches the beginning of a string, and the dollar sign ("$") matches the end of a string. So to create a regular expression that will only match "abc", you would use the expression "^abc$". Now, this is pretty cool, but obviously the utility of matching a single, hard-coded expression is very limited. Let's move on to look at wildcard characters.

What if you want to match all strings that began with "abc" and ended with "123" regardless of any characters in the middle? Then you could use the expression "^abc*123$" because the asterisk ("*") character matches any number of characters. In this way, it works very much like the DOS * wildcard. To match a single character, you use the period (".)", and so "^abc.123$" would match "abca123" and "abc5123" but not "abcXX123".

Finally, you can match a range of characters by placing the character range within hard braces (or square brackets) "([   ])". The hyphen "(-)" character can be used to specify a range, or a list of characters can be placed in the braces. For example, "[12345]" and "[1-5]" would both match any numeric character from 1 to 5. Using the caret ("^")at the beginning of a bracket expression has the effect of inverting the match, so [^1-5] would match anything but a numeric character from 1 to 5.

Now, that should give you enough of a grip on regular expressions for us to start using them. Let's take a quick look at the `RegularExpressionValidator`'s one special property that makes it stand out from the `BaseValidator` class (see Table 8.6), and then we'll look at some examples.

Table 8.6: `RegularExpressionValidator` *Class Additional Property*

Method	Type	Description
ValidationExpression	String	The regular expression to be used to validate the `ControlToValidate`.

The `RegularExpressionValidator` control only exposes one property in addition to the standard properties common to all validator controls, the `ValidationExpression`. This property is set to the regular expression used by ASP.NET to match with the `ControlToValidate`, and the control will conclude that the `ControlToValidate` is valid if it finds that its contents match this expression. Listing 8.4 demonstrates how to validate a few common fields using the `RegularExpressionValidator` control.

EXAMPLE

Listing 8.4: Adding regular expression validation to a text box.

```
<%@ Page %>
<HTML>
    <HEAD>
        <!DOCTYPE HTML PUBLIC "-//W3C//DTD HTML 4.0 Transitional//EN" >
    </HEAD>
    <body>
        <form method="post" runat="server">
            <asp:Label ID="errorMessage" Runat="server"></asp:Label>
            <table>
                <tr>
                    <td>
```

Listing 8.4: continued

```
                            Email
                        </td>
                        <td>
                            <asp:textbox runat="Server" columns="30"
id="email"></asp:textbox>
                        </td>
                        <td>
                            <asp:regularexpressionvalidator runat="Server"
id="email_regex" controltovalidate="email" errormessage="" display="dynamic"
validationexpression="^[\w-\.]{1,}@([\w-]+\.)+[\w-]{2,3}$">
                                *
                            </asp:regularexpressionvalidator>
                        </td>
                    </tr>
                    <tr>
                        <td>
                            Phone
                        </td>
                        <td>
                            <asp:textbox runat="Server" columns="15"
id="phone"></asp:textbox>
                        </td>
                        <td>
                            <asp:regularexpressionvalidator runat="Server"
id="phone_regex" controltovalidate="phone" errormessage="" display="dynamic"
validationexpression="^[2-9]\d{2}-\d{3}-\d{4}$">
                                *
                            </asp:regularexpressionvalidator>
                        </td>
                    </tr>
                    <tr>
                        <td>
                            Social Security Number
                        </td>
                        <td>
                            <asp:textbox runat="Server" columns="15"
id="ssn"></asp:textbox>
                        </td>
                        <td>
                            <asp:regularexpressionvalidator runat="Server"
id="ssn_regex" controltovalidate="ssn" errormessage="" display="dynamic"
validationexpression="^\d{3}-\d{2}-\d{4}$">
                                *
                            </asp:regularexpressionvalidator>
                        </td>
                    </tr>
                    <tr>
```

Listing 8.4: continued

```
                        <td>
                            ZIP/Postal Code
                        </td>
                        <td>
                            <asp:textbox runat="Server" columns="15"
        id="zip"></asp:textbox>
                        </td>
                        <td>
                            <asp:regularexpressionvalidator runat="Server"
        id="zipregex" controltovalidate="zip" errormessage="" display="dynamic"
        validationexpression="^\d{5}-\d{4}|\d{5}|[A-Z]\d[A-Z]\s{1}\d[A-Z]\d$">
                                *
                            </asp:regularexpressionvalidator>
                        </td>
                    </tr>
                </table>
                <asp:button id="save_button" runat="Server"
        text="Save"></asp:button>
            </form>
        </body>
    </HTML>
```

This example uses four regular expressions, which validate commonly used form fields. Let's examine them in detail to see exactly how they are working before we conclude our coverage of the RegularExpressionValidator. First, and probably the most common of all, is the e-mail regular expression. In researching this chapter I quickly found at least half a dozen different e-mail validation regular expressions, each slightly different from the others in syntax and function. Some explicitly required that the last part of the domain name be either "com", "edu", "mil", "gov", "net", or "org". Others simply checked to ensure that an ampersand ("@") and a period (".") were present in the string to be checked. Given the fact that every country has its own top-level domain (TLD), and several new TLDs are slated to be introduced in the next year or two, I chose to simply check the pattern of the string, rather than the specific words involved. The regular expression used to validate an e-mail address in Listing 8.4 looks like this:

EXAMPLE

```
^[\w-\.]+@([\w-]+\.)+[\w-]{2,3}$
```

This regular expression uses a few metacharacters that we haven't yet covered, so we'll go over them now. Starting at the left, we've already discussed the caret ("^") character, which matches the beginning of the string. And we know that the "[ ]" brackets are used to contain lists of characters. In this case, the "\w" sequence is a special character sequence that matches any alphanumeric word sequence, including the underscore ""("_) character. It is functionally equivalent to "[A-Za-z0-9_]", but much shorter. Because hyphens and periods are also allowed in e-mail addresses, we also list the hyphen ("-") and the period ("\."). The period is a special character by itself, and so must be "escaped" by using the backslash "(\)"in order to reference the actual period. Next comes the plus "(+)" character. This character matches the preceding expression one or more times. In this case, it means that we will have any combination of alphanumeric characters, underscores, hyphens, and periods consisting of one or more of these values.

That brings us to the ampersand ("@") character, which simply matches the "@" character in the e-mail address. Following the "@", things are a bit more complicated. The use of parentheses ( ) is similar to those in mathematical expressions, as a means of grouping expressions. Inside the parentheses, we are matching any series of alphanumeric characters (including hyphens and underscores, but not periods), as represented by the expression "[\w-]+". This is then followed by the backslash and a single period to create the expression "(\.)". The entire expression in parentheses is then matched one or more times by adding a plus "(+)" to the end of it.

Finally, the last portion of the expression consists of "[\w-]{2,3}$". This uses the familiar "[\w-]" expression, but now we introduce yet another new metacharacter, the curly braces ({ }). Curly braces are used to designate an exact number of times to match the preceding expression, similar to the plus "(+)" but more specific. The curly braces include a minimum and maximum value (or if only one value is used, only that exact number of matches is allowed). In this case, we are only matching character strings that are two or three characters long. Lastly, we match the end of the string with the dollar sign "($)".

Okay, that was a lot to cover for one regular expression, but the good news is that you now know 90% of the most commonly used characters used in regular expressions. We'll see that the next three expressions are much easier to explain, now that you have this strong knowledge base. The next regular expression used in Listing 8.4 is for a phone number and matches patterns that look like this:

"ANN-NNN-NNNN"

EXAMPLE

where N is a numeric digit from 0 to 9, and A is a numeric digit from 2 to 9 (0 and 1 are not valid starting digits for phone numbers). Note that this regular expression only matches domestic U.S. telephone numbers, but it would not be difficult to modify this regular expression to suit another country's standard, or to support international extensions. The regular expression to match this pattern looks like this:

^[2-9]\d{2}-\d{3}-\d{4}$

You're familiar with the caret "(^)" and the dollar sign "($)" by now. The first character is matched by the "[2-9]" expression, which matches any number from 2 to 9. This is immediately followed by "\d{2}". The backslash followed by the letter d "(\d)" is a special metacharacter that matches any numeric digit; it is equivalent to "[0-9]". And of course we've already covered curly braces—this evaluates to exactly two occurences of "\d", or two numeric digits. This is followed by the hyphen "(-)", which matches the same character "(-)" in the phone number. Next we match exactly three numeric digits, another hyphen, and then exactly four numeric digits, with the remaining expression of "\d{3}-\d{4}", and that is it!

After you've seen the phone number regular expression, the social security number expression should be pretty self-explanatory. Its expression matches the pattern of "NNN-NN-NNNN", where N is any numeric digit.

^\d{3}-\d{2}-\d{4}$

This evaluates to exactly three numeric digits, a hyphen, exactly two numeric digits, another hyphen, and finally exactly four numeric digits. Simple, right?

The last regular expression we will examine matches a ZIP or postal code for the United States or Canada. This is a bit more complicated than the phone or SSN examples because there are three different options that are all valid. The ZIP code is valid if it consists of five numbers or five numbers, a hyphen, and four numbers. The Canadian postal codes, on the other hand, have the form of "ANA NAN" where N is a number from 0 to 9 and A is a capital letter from A to Z. The expression, then, is

^\d{5}-\d{4}|\d{5}|[A-Z]\d[A-Z] \d[A-Z]\d$

This introduces a few more new characters that we have yet to deal with. Going from left to right, we see that the first portion of the expression matches ZIP+4 patterns of exactly five digits, a hyphen, and exactly four digits, using the pattern "\d{5}-\d{4}". The next character, the pipe "(|)", is read as "or", and is used to separate multiple valid patterns. In this case, the next valid expression is "\d{5}", which is exactly five numeric digits (which matches a standard U.S. ZIP code). Next we encounter another pipe "(|)" character, which then leads to our third valid option. Although this looks fairly imposing, it is actually pretty straightforward. The first half of this expression is "[A-Z]\d[A-Z]" and simply matches any single capital letter, any single numeric character, and then any single capital letter. This is followed by a space, which simply matches a space in the postal code, and finally the expression "\d[A-Z]\d", which matches a single numeric character, a single capital letter, and finally another single numeric character.

You can find a lot more information on regular expressions in Microsoft's MSDN resource. Their scripting documentation includes a good article on regular expression syntax, located at `http://msdn.microsoft.com/scripting/vbscript/doc/jsgrpregexpsyntax.htm`. A quick search for regular expressions in any search engine will yield many more articles online. Finally, for a growing list of ready-made regular expressions and an online expression tester, visit the Regular Expression Library at `http://regexlib.com/`.

CustomValidator Control

Sometimes none of the previously covered validation controls are sufficient to properly validate user input. For instance, none of the preceding examples would be up to the task of validating that a credit card number was valid, or better yet, checking to make sure that that account had sufficient funds for the pending transaction. For situations like these that require the use of special business rules to validate the user input, the `CustomValidator` control is the tool to use. Table 8.7 details the additional properties specific to the `CustomValidator` control.

Table 8.7: **CustomValidator** *Class Additional Properties*

Method	Type	Description
ClientValidationFunction	String	The client-side function to use for `Uplevel` browser client-side validation.

The `CustomValidator` control also exposes a method, `ServerValidate`, that must be handled by the form's server-side code and referenced when the control is used with the `OnServerValidate=""` attribute. It is possible to create very advanced `CustomValidator` validation logic, but for this example, we will just check to see if the value entered is a perfect square (an integer raised to the power of 2) or not. Listings 8.5 and 8.6 show the ASPX file and its codebehind used for this validation. For this example, only server-side validation is being implemented, which is frequently all that is possible with custom validation because they often rely on remote data stores to perform their tasks.

Listing 8.5: Adding custom validation to a text box (Example0905.aspx).

EXAMPLE

```
<%@ Page language="c#" Codebehind="Example0905.aspx.cs" Src="Example0905.aspx.cs"
AutoEventWireup="false" Inherits="validate.Example0905" %>
<HTML>
    <HEAD>
        <!DOCTYPE HTML PUBLIC "-//W3C//DTD HTML 4.0 Transitional//EN" >
    </HEAD>
    <body>
        <form method="post" runat="server" ID="Form1">
            <asp:Label ID="errorMessage" Runat="server"></asp:Label>
            <table>
```

Listing 8.5: continued

```
            <tr>
                <td>
                    Enter a Perfect Square (the square of an integer):
                </td>
                <td>
                    <asp:textbox runat="Server" columns="30"
id="square"></asp:textbox>
                </td>
                <td>
                    <asp:CustomValidator Runat="server"
ID="square_custom" Display="Dynamic" OnServerValidate="validateSquare"
EnableClientScript="False">
                        *
                    </asp:CustomValidator>
                </td>
            </tr>
        </table>
        <asp:button id="save_button" runat="Server"
text="Save"></asp:button>
    </form>
</body>
</HTML>
```

EXAMPLE

Listing 8.6: Adding custom validation to a text box (Example0905.aspx.cs).

```
protected void validateSquare(object sender,
    System.Web.UI.WebControls.ServerValidateEventArgs e)
    {
        int _square;
        int _sqrt;

        try
        {
            _square = Int32.Parse(square.Text.ToString());
        }
        catch
        {
            e.IsValid = false;
            return;
        }
        try
        {
            _sqrt =
Int32.Parse(Math.Sqrt(Double.Parse(_square.ToString())).ToString());
        }
        catch
        {
            e.IsValid = false;
```

Listing 8.6: continued

```
        return;
    }
    e.IsValid = true;
}
```

This example takes advantage of error handlers to determine whether or not the square root of the value entered into the "square" text box is an integer. If no error is raised when converting the value itself or its square root into an integer value, the value entered must be a perfect square. Otherwise, the value must not be a perfect square. It is interesting to note that the event handler validateSquare does not return a value, but instead sets the value of the ServerEventArgs object's IsValid property to true or false, as appropriate. Although this is a very simple example, custom validation controls can be as simple or as complex as your business needs dictate.

ValidationSummary Control

We saw in our second example (refer to Listing 8.2) that it is possible to use the Page.IsValid property to dynamically display validation control ErrorMessage properties. This last control is built to do just this, but without our having to write any code. Simply by placing this control on the page and setting a few properties, we will achieve all the functionality we had in that earlier example, and then some.

Unlike all the previous controls, the ValidationSummary control does not inherit from the BaseValidator class. Instead, it is derived from the System.Web.UI.WebControls.WebControl class. Its important properties are detailed in Table 8.8.

Table 8.8: **ValidationSummary** *Class Properties*

Method	Type	Description
DisplayMode	ValidationSummaryDisplayMode	Determines how the errors are listed when the summary is displayed. One of "BulletList", "List", or "SingleParagraph".
HeaderText	String	Sets the header text to display the list of errors.
ShowMessageBox	Boolean	Determines whether or not a message box should be used to summarize the page's errors.
ShowSummary	Boolean	Determines whether or not a summary of all errors should be displayed.

The `ValidationSummary` control is the ideal way to summarize the validation error messages for an entire form. It includes several alternatives for layout and display, and can be placed anywhere within your form tags. To demonstrate how easy this control is to use, we will repeat the example from Listing 8.2 in Listing 8.7, but we will use the `ValidationSummary` control this time, instead of our own custom code.

EXAMPLE

Listing 8.7: Adding a `ValidationSummary` Control (Example0807.aspx).

```
<%@ Page %>
<HTML>
    <HEAD>
        <!DOCTYPE HTML PUBLIC "-//W3C//DTD HTML 4.0 Transitional//EN" >
    </HEAD>
    <body>
    <form method="post" runat="server">
    <asp:ValidationSummary Runat="server" ID="valsummary"
    DisplayMode="SingleParagraph"></asp:ValidationSummary>
    <table>
        <tr>
            <td>
                Age:
            </td>
            <td>
                <asp:textbox runat="Server" columns="6" id="age"></asp:textbox>
            </td>
            <td>
                <asp:requiredfieldvalidator runat="Server" id="age_required"
controltovalidate="age" display="dynamic" errormessage="Age is required.">
                    *
                </asp:requiredfieldvalidator>
                <asp:rangevalidator runat="Server" id="age_range"
controltovalidate="age" display="dynamic"
errormessage="Age must be an integer between 18 and 65." minimumvalue="18"
maximumvalue="65" Type="Integer">
                    *
                </asp:rangevalidator>
            </td>
        </tr>
    </table>
    <asp:button id="save_button" runat="Server" text="Save"></asp:button>
    </form>
    </body>
</HTML>
```

Note that in this example it is no longer necessary to disable client-side scripting or force the `ClientTarget` to be for a `DownLevel` browser. The result is the same as in the earlier example when there is an error, as we see in Figure 8.4.

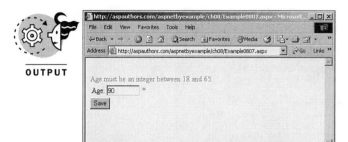

OUTPUT

Figure 8.4: *Example0807.aspx with some invalid data*

Bringing It All Together

By using the validation controls you learned about in this chapter, it is possible to create very sophisticated forms with a minimum of code. To demonstrate this capability, we will combine all the examples we have looked at so far in this chapter into one form, and combine this with a ValidationSummary control to provide a summary of all errors found on the form. This example also includes one new validation for ensuring that a user's password and confirmed password match.

In the interests of conserving space, we won't display the full source code for this example here. Figure 8.5 shows what the end result looks like with a few errors. You can see the live version of this example with full VB and C# source code at http://aspauthors.com/aspnetbyexample/ch08/. We will just look at the new functionality of this example in the text.

As you can see, we have added two fields to our form that weren't covered elsewhere in the chapter. These are the Password and ConfirmPassword fields. Normally the form elements for the input of these fields would be set to display asterisks instead of showing the values, but for the purposes of demonstration we are using standard cleartext text boxes. The password must be at least eight characters long, it is required, and the Confirm Password field must exactly match the password field in order for the form to be valid. The code for this is displayed in Listing 8.8.

OUTPUT

EXAMPLE

- Full Name is required.
- Email must be in the form of abc@xyz.com.
- Password must be at least 8 characters long.
- Confirmation password does not match password.
- A value for total donation is required.
- A portion to apply toward .NET programmer training is required.

Full Name:		*
Age:	3	
Email	steve	*
Password	abcd	*
Confirm Password	1234	*
Phone		
Social Security Number		
ZIP/Postal Code		
Total Donation:		*
Portion of above donation to apply toward .NET programmer training.		*
Enter a Perfect Square (the square of an integer):		

Save

Figure 8.5: *Culmination.aspx with some invalid input.*

Listing 8.8: Password validation (culmination.aspx).

```
<tr>
    <td>
        Password
    </td>
    <td>
        <asp:textbox runat="Server" columns="30" id="password"></asp:textbox>
    </td>
    <td>
        <asp:RequiredFieldValidator Runat="server" Display="Dynamic"
ControlToValidate="password" ErrorMessage="A password is required."
ID="password_required">
        *
        </asp:RequiredFieldValidator>
        <asp:RegularExpressionValidator runat="server" Display="Dynamic"
ControlToValidate="password"
ErrorMessage="Password must be at least 8 characters long."
ValidationExpression=".{8}.*" id="RegularExpressionValidator1">
        *
        </asp:RegularExpressionValidator>
    </td>
</tr>
<tr>
```

Listing 8.8: continued

```
    <td>
        Confirm Password
    </td>
    <td>
        <asp:textbox runat="Server" columns="30"
    id="password_confirm"></asp:textbox>
    </td>
    <td>
        <asp:RequiredFieldValidator Runat="server" Display="Dynamic"
    ControlToValidate="password_confirm"
    ErrorMessage="A confirmation password is required."
ID="password_confirm_required">
        *
        </asp:RequiredFieldValidator>
        <asp:CompareValidator Runat="server" Display="Dynamic"
    ControlToValidate="password_confirm" ControlToCompare="password"
Type="String"
    ErrorMessage="Confirmation password does not match password."
    ID="password_confirm_compare">
        *
        </asp:CompareValidator>
    </td>
</tr>
```

This excerpt includes a total of four validators. Two of these are RequiredField validators, and do not need any explanation. The RegularExpressionValidator used for the password text box uses a new regular expression syntax, the use of the period "(.)" and the asterisk "(*)" The period character in a regular expression matches any character. The "{8}" following the first period means that we want to see exactly eight instances of any character. The asterisk "*" operator matches the previous expression zero or more times. So, after we see eight characters, we want to see zero or more characters. Basically all this is doing is ensuring that the length of the password is at least eight characters long. This is a fairly trivial use for a regular expression, but by using a regular expression validator here, I have made it easy to enhance the restrictions placed on allowable passwords simply by editing the ValidationExpression. The last validator used here is the CompareValidator, which simply ensures that the Confirm Password text box's value exactly matches the Password text box's value.

Again, the full source code for this example is available on the book's support Web site, at (http://aspauthors.com/aspnetbyexample/ch08/), along with complete working examples.

One Step Beyond: VControls

Combining user controls (which we will cover in more detail in the next chapter) with validation controls can provide even greater re-use. For instance, the e-mail field is probably the most commonly seen form field, so why should you have to deal with the text box and several different validator controls every time you use one? The solution is to create what I've dubbed a VControl, or Validated Control. This is simply a user control that combines the necessary controls to display a single commonly used form field. An entire suite of VControls is a useful tool to have, and you can easily create your own library of them to suit your needs based on this example. I have created a variety of these tools, including VControls for e-mail, phone, zip code, SSN, and confirm password, which are available for free from http://www.aspsmith.com/vcontrols/. We're going to look at just one such control, the EmailBox VControl.

We have already seen how to validate an e-mail text box using validation controls. The EmailBox VControl uses this same method for its validation. User controls are similar to Server Side Include files from Classic ASP, but with much more power and flexibility. For this example, we will need to look at three files: the user control declarative code (the .ascx file), the user control codebehind code (the .cs or .vb file), and the page that uses the control (an .aspx file). Listing 8.9 displays the contents of EmailBox.ascx, the declarative portion of the user control.

EXAMPLE

Listing 8.9: EmailBox VControl user control (EmailBox.ascx).

```
<%@ Control Language="c#" AutoEventWireup="false" Codebehind="EmailBox.ascx.cs"
Src="EmailBox.ascx.cs" Inherits="ASPSmith.VControls.EmailBox" %>
<asp:textbox id="EmailTextBox" runat="server">
</asp:textbox>
<asp:literal id="Sep" runat="server">
</asp:literal>
<asp:regularexpressionvalidator id="EmailValidator" runat="server"
display="dynamic"
    ErrorMessage="Invalid Email Address. Expected format: abc@xyz.com"
    controlToValidate="EmailTextBox"
    ValidationExpression="^[\w-\.]+@([\w-]+\.)+[\w-]{2,3}$">
    *
</asp:regularexpressionvalidator>
<asp:requiredfieldvalidator id="EmailRequired" runat="server" display="dynamic"
    controlToValidate="EmailTextBox" ErrorMessage="An Email Address is required."
    Enabled="false">
    *
</asp:requiredfieldvalidator>
```

As you can see, this looks pretty much like an excerpt from an ASPX page. And for the most part, that is all that is going on here. The only thing that

makes this any different from, say, Example0904.aspx is the use of the
Literal control, Sep. We'll see how this is used in a moment. You'll learn
more about the implementation details of these kinds of files in the next
chapter. Now, let's have a look at Listing 8.10, the EmailBox codebehind,
which does most of the interesting work for this control.

EXAMPLE

Listing 8.10: EmailBox VControl user control codebehind (EmailBox.ascx.cs).

```
namespace ASPSmith.VControls
{
    using System;
    using System.Data;
    using System.Drawing;
    using System.Web;
    using System.Web.UI.WebControls;
    using System.Web.UI.HtmlControls;

    public class EmailBox : System.Web.UI.UserControl
    {
        public System.Web.UI.WebControls.RegularExpressionValidator
EmailValidator;
        public System.Web.UI.WebControls.TextBox EmailTextBox;
        public System.Web.UI.WebControls.RequiredFieldValidator EmailRequired;
        protected System.Web.UI.WebControls.Literal Sep;

        public ValidatorDisplay Display{
            get{
                return EmailValidator.Display;
            }
            set{
                EmailValidator.Display = value;
                EmailRequired.Display = value;
            }
        }
        public string ErrorMessage{
            get{
                return EmailValidator.ErrorMessage;
            }
            set{
                EmailValidator.ErrorMessage = value;
            }
        }
        public string ErrorIcon{
            get{
                return EmailValidator.Text;
            }
            set{
```

Listing 8.10: continued

```
                EmailValidator.Text = value;
                EmailRequired.Text = value;
            }
        }
        public bool isRequired    {
            get{
                return EmailRequired.Enabled;
            }
            set{
                EmailRequired.Enabled = value;
            }
        }
        public string RequiredErrorMessage{
            get{
                return EmailRequired.ErrorMessage;
            }
            set{
                EmailRequired.ErrorMessage = value;
            }
        }
        public string SeparatorHTML {
            get {
                return Sep.Text;
            }
            set{
                Sep.Text = value;
            }
        }
        public string Text{
            get{
                return Text;
            }
            set{
                EmailTextBox.Text = value;
            }
        }
        public string ValidationExpression{
            get{
                return EmailValidator.ValidationExpression;
            }
            set{
                EmailValidator.ValidationExpression = value;
            }
        }
        /// <summary>
        public EmailBox(){
            this.Init += new System.EventHandler(Page_Init);
```

Listing 8.10: continued

```
        }
        protected void Page_Load(object sender, System.EventArgs e){
            // Put user code to initialize the page here
        }
    }
}
```

The main portion of this class file is devoted to exposing public properties that can be set by the page that is using this control. For instance, if you want the e-mail address to be required, you simply set the IsRequired property to true. We'll see how to set these properties in the next example when we actually implement this control. There are eight properties that I chose to expose explicitly with this control, but notice also that the controls for the text box, separator, and validator are all declared as public. This means that all the methods and properties of these controls are exposed to the calling page as well, so by using this VControl you are not limited to the properties I have chosen to expose—you retain complete control over every part of the enclosed controls because they are publicly exposed.

Notice the use of the SeparatorHTML property to set the value of the Sep literal WebControl. This is included so that this VControl can be rendered in a table with the validation control in a separate table cell from the e-mail box, as is often the desired layout. By setting the separator to "</td><td>", it is easy to split the text box and the validator into separate table cells, for instance. You can see an example of this in Listing 8.11.

EXAMPLE

Listing 8.11: EmailBox VControl user control (Example0811.aspx).

```
<%@ Page AutoEventWireup="false" %>
<%@ Register TagPrefix="ASPSmith" TagName-"EmailBox"
Src="UserControls/EmailBox.ascx" %>
<HTML>
    <HEAD>
        <!DOCTYPE HTML PUBLIC "-//W3C//DTD HTML 4.0 Transitional//EN" >
    </HEAD>
    <body>
        <form method="post" runat="server">
            <asp:ValidationSummary Runat="server" ID="valsummary"
DisplayMode="List" />
            <table>
                <tr>
                    <td>
                        Email:
                    </td>
                    <td>
                        <ASPSmith:EmailBox id="EmailBox" runat="server"
isRequired="true" SeparatorHTML="</td><td>" ErrorIcon="<b>!</b>" />
```

Listing 8.11: continued

```
                    </td>
                </tr>
            </table>
            <asp:button id="save_button" runat="Server"
    text="Save"></asp:button>
        </form>
    </body>
</HTML>
```

As you can see, there are only a couple of non-HTML lines in this page. The second line simply tells the page where to find the user control, and will be covered in more detail in the next chapter. The ASPSmith:EmailBox control is the actual call to place the control on the page. Notice that the public properties we exposed can all be set as attributes here. For example, we have added some HTML to the SeparatorHTML property to split the text box and validation control into separate table cells, and we have changed the ErrorIcon from the default asterisk ("*") to a bold exclamation point "(!)". Also, just to demonstrate that these VControls will still work with ValidationSummary controls, we have added one of these to the page as well. The result, after an invalid e-mail is entered, is shown in Figure 8.6.

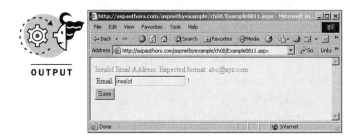

OUTPUT

Figure 8.6: Using the EmailBox VControl

Summary

That's all there is to it. As you can see, bundling commonly used form elements and their validation controls into VControls can save you a lot of development effort, especially if you frequently find yourself building forms like these. The beauty of validation controls in general is their ease of use, and with VControls, things can't get much easier. Look for a variety of free, ready-to-use VControls at ASPSmith.com/vcontrols/.

Validation controls are very easy to use and relatively simple in concept, but they add a great deal to the productivity of Web site developers, especially when compared to the amount of work required in Classic ASP to accomplish the same task. In this chapter, we looked at different kinds of validation and how validation has typically been done prior to .NET. We examined the `BaseValidator` class, from which all the other validation controls (except the Summary) are derived. We looked at examples of how to use the `RequiredFieldValidator`, `RangeValidator`, `CompareValidator`, `RegularExpressionValidator`, and `CustomValidator` controls. We then looked at the `ValidationSummary` control, which allows you to tie the results of many different validator controls together. Finally, we introduced the idea of user controls, which will be covered in detail in the next chapter, as a way to package frequently used validations and form inputs for use on many different forms.

What's Next?

In the next chapter, we will be covering user controls, which are an exciting way to easily encapsulate ASP.NET code in libraries. Although at first user controls sound an awful lot like Server Side Includes, you will see that they are much more powerful tools and very easy to use.

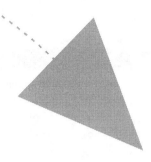

9

Using ASP.NET User Controls

One of the greatest promises of ASP.NET is smaller, easier-to-manage code. One of the ways Microsoft delivers on this promise is by providing Web developers the ability to create user controls in order to encapsulate functionality and facilitate reuse. Previously enjoyed only by Visual Basic, Java, and other GUI developers, the ability to create these user controls finally brings object-oriented concepts to Web-based GUI development. The purpose of this chapter is to give you an overview of user controls and get you started using them in your ASP.NET applications.

In this chapter you will

- Learn how ASP.NET user controls differ from `include` files in previous versions of ASP

- Learn how to create ASP.NET user controls to encapsulate logic and reuse code

- Learn how to expose properties, methods, and events from ASP.NET user controls

Introduction to User Controls

Chances are, if you are currently an ASP developer, the term *code reuse* conjures up images of a seemingly endless series of include files that has come to be known in Web development circles as *spaghetti code*. Aptly named, this phenomenon can be the byproduct of ASP include statements to include either subroutines or inline presentation markup used by more than one ASP page. While providing some benefits, such as allowing changes in included files to cascade across the site, the include statement makes debugging more difficult. Most of us have felt the pain of stepping through another developer's code searching through a chain of included files looking for a particular function declaration.

ASP.NET attempts to alleviate these headaches with the advent of user controls. User controls in their simplest form are really nothing more than a way for you to componentize your Web forms by combining one or more existing controls to function as a unit. In the same way that classes encapsulate logic in OOP design, controls encapsulate functionality in GUI design.

It must be noted here that user controls are not the only way of encapsulating functionality when creating ASP.NET applications. In the next chapter, we will discuss creating ASP.NET Custom Controls and in which scenarios they are preferable to user controls.

Before we delve into the creation of ASP.NET user controls, let's look briefly at some scenarios in which they should be considered:

- When UI elements are repeated often on many Web forms throughout an ASP.NET project. Like include statements, using user controls in this situation allows changes to cascade across the site.

- For complex Web forms with many UI elements. Breaking up the Web form into smaller controls makes maintenance easier.

- For team projects. Controls allow a natural division of work for team members.

Now, let's look at how we create user controls and use them in ASP.NET.

Creating ASP.NET User Controls

We create user controls much the same way that we create normal Web forms in ASP.NET; however, we normally denote that a file is to be used as a control by saving it with an .ascx file extension. Let's look at an example of a simple user control.

```
<asp:label text="Welcome to ASP.NET User Controls" runat="Server"/>
```

Yes, that's it. That's our entire control. Note that it's nothing more really than a Web form fragment, and in our control definition file we do not include `<html>`, `<head>`, `<body>`, or `<form runat="server">` tags. Listing 9.1 shows how we use our control on a Web form.

EXAMPLE

Listing 9.1 Implementing the User Control on a Web Form (91.aspx)

```
<%@ Page language="c#"%>
<%@ Register TagPrefix="ASPNETByExample" TagName="Welcome" Src="welcome.ascx" %>
<html>
  <body>
    <form method="post" runat="server">
        <ASPNETByExample:Welcome runat="server"/>
    </form>
  </body>
</html>
```

OUTPUT

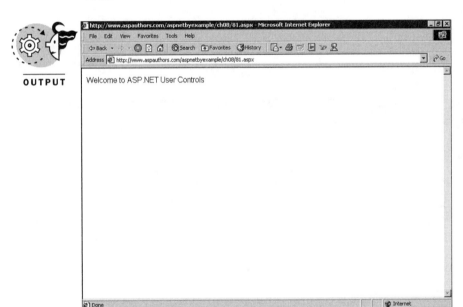

Figure 9.1: *The output of Listing 9.1, a simple welcome message user control.*

This control simply provides a label displaying our static welcome text. Let's look at another example to see how we would include script in our control to render a dynamic welcome message. Listing 9.2 includes the updated control to render a different welcome message depending on the time of day.

EXAMPLE

Listing 9.2 User Control to Display Dynamic Welcome Message Based on Time of Day (timeofday-welcome.ascx)

```csharp
<script language="c#" runat="server">
    void Page_Load(Object sender, EventArgs e)
    {
        int CurrentHour =  System.DateTime.Now.Hour;
        String WelcomeMessage = "";
        if (CurrentHour < 12) {
            WelcomeMessage = "Good Morning";
        }
        else if ((CurrentHour > 12) && (CurrentHour < 18)){
            WelcomeMessage = "Good Afternoon";
        }
        else {
            WelcomeMessage = "Good Evening";
        }
        Message.Text = WelcomeMessage;
    }
</script>
<asp:label id="Message" runat="Server"/>
```

OUTPUT

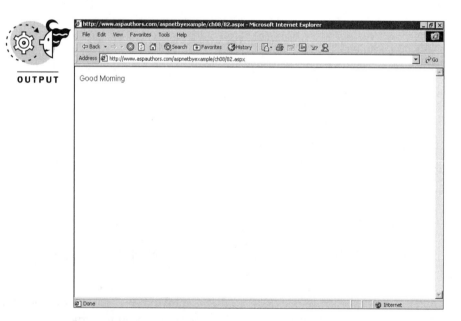

Figure 9.2: The output of Listing 9.2, the updated welcome message control (92.aspx).

Now you will note that the control determines which of three possible greetings to render based on the time of day the user accesses the page. As in

ASP 3.0 include files, our script is kept neatly in a control definition file which keeps our Web forms easier to manage.

At this point, you're probably wondering how user controls are much of an improvement over include files. You may have noticed that while we now have a descriptive tag to place on our Web form instead of a generic include statement, we've actually had to write more code to include this welcome message than we would have using include files under ASP 3.0. Now we'll begin to cover some of the features which set user controls apart from the include directive in earlier versions of ASP.

Creating Code-behind User Controls

Up until this point, the user controls we've been working with have contained both the declarative presentation markup and program logic in the same file. Just like ASP.NET Web forms, however, user controls support code-behind files. This allows us to make maintenance easier by separating the program logic and presentation markup into different files.

Now let's take our previous time-of-day user control and convert it into a code-behind user control. To do so, we remove everything except the presentation markup. This leaves us with a simple label control:

```
<asp:label id="Message" runat="Server"/>
```

Next, we create the code-behind file with the appropriate file extensions (either .cs for C# controls or .vb for VB.NET controls). We then include the system namespaces required for working with Web controls. In C# we do so with the using statement:

```
using System;
using System.Web.UI;
using System.Web.UI.WebControls;
```

In VB.NET, we reference the appropriate namespaces via the Imports statement:

```
Imports System
Imports System.Web.UI
Imports System.Web.UI.WebControls
```

Next we create a class for our user control that inherits from System.Web.UI.UserControl:

```
class TimeOfDayControl : UserControl
{
}
```

Or in VB.NET:

```
Class TimeOfDayControl
    Inherits UserControl
End Class
```

Once we've created the derived class, we need to declare instance variables for each server control in the .ascx file. Next, we need to add the appropriate code the class body to provide the functionality for the user control. We do this by moving the code over from our original control file. Listings 9.3 and 9.4 show the complete code-behind files.

Listing 9.3 C# Version of the Time of Day Code-behind Control (timeofdayctl.cs)

```
using System;
using System.Web.UI;
using System.Web.UI.WebControls;

class TimeOfDayControl : UserControl
{
    public Label Message;
    void Page_Load(Object sender, EventArgs e)
    {
        int CurrentHour =  System.DateTime.Now.Hour;
        String WelcomeMessage = "";
        if (CurrentHour < 12) {
            WelcomeMessage = "Good Morning";
        }
        else if ((CurrentHour > 12) && (CurrentHour < 18)){
            WelcomeMessage = "Good Afternoon";
        }
        else {
            WelcomeMessage = "Good Evening";
        }
        Message.Text = WelcomeMessage;
    }

}
```

Listing 9.4 VB.NET Version of the Time of Day Code-behind Control (timeofdayctl.vb)

```
Imports System
Imports System.Web.UI
Imports System.Web.UI.WebControls

Class TimeOfDayControl
    Inherits UserControl

    Public Message As Label;
    Sub Page_Load(sender As Object, e As EventArgs)
        Dim CurrentHour As Integer =  System.DateTime.Now.Hour
        Dim WelcomeMessage As String = ""
        If (CurrentHour < 12) Then
            WelcomeMessage = "Good Morning"
```

Listing 9.4 continued

```
        ElseIf ((CurrentHour > 12) And (CurrentHour < 18)) Then
            WelcomeMessage = "Good Afternoon"
        Else
            WelcomeMessage = "Good Evening"
        End If
        Message.Text = WelcomeMessage
    End Sub

End Class
```

Finally, we need to specify the code-behind file in the `.ascx` file. We do this with a simple @Control directive at the top of the file:

```
<%@ control inherits = "TimeOfDayControl" src = " timeofdayctl.cs" %>
```

Or for the VB.NET version:

```
<%@ control inherits = "TimeOfDayControl" src = " timeofdayctl.vb" %>
```

Note that both versions of these code-behind controls are functionally equivalent to our previous example. Next, we'll look at how to expose properties from user controls.

Defining Properties in User Controls

As we mentioned earlier, one of the handy features of the ASP 3.0 include statement was the ability to reuse portions of code across multiple ASP pages. However, since include files are processed before the containing ASP page is executed, code in included files is executed as if it were included inline within the containing page. This means that blocks of included code act more or less like parts grafted onto an ASP page. This can present a number of problems including these:

- Variable scope issues between includes that use the <%...%> syntax versus the <SCRIPT RUNAT=SERVER>...</SCRIPT> tags.

- No good way to dynamically include files. Include files can be conditionally executed; however, all includes are processed before the page executes so large include files are processed regardless of whether they're executed.

- While the ASP engine will not allow duplicate variables to be declared, duplicate function declarations do not produce an error, which can lead to unexpected results.

With ASP.NET user controls, developers can now encapsulate logic within self-contained components that allow for more sophisticated code reuse by setting property values and making method calls. Listing 9.5 shows an example of a login user control that exposes properties to the containing form.

Listing 9.5 Login User Control (login.ascx)

```csharp
<script language="c#" runat="server">

    private Boolean m_Secure = false;
    public String WelcomeMessage = "Welcome";

    void Login_Click(Object sender, EventArgs e){
        if (UsernameValidator.IsValid && PasswordValidator.IsValid){
            UnsecurePanel.Visible = false;
            Message.Text = WelcomeMessage + ", " + UserName.Text;
            SecurePanel.Visible = true;
            m_Secure = true;
        }
    }
    void Logout_Click(Object sender, EventArgs e){
        if (UsernameValidator.IsValid && PasswordValidator.IsValid){
            UnsecurePanel.Visible = true;
            UserName.Text = "";
            Password.Text = "";
            SecurePanel.Visible = false;
            m_Secure = false;
        }
    }

    public Boolean Secure{
        get{
            return m_Secure;
        }

        set{
            m_Secure = value;
        }
    }

</script>
<asp:panel id="UnsecurePanel" runat="Server">
    <asp:label runat="server" font-size="9pt">Username: </asp:label>
    <br>
    <asp:textbox id="UserName" runat="server" />
    <br>
    <asp:requiredfieldvalidator id="UsernameValidator"
        runat="server"  controltovalidate="UserName"
        errormessage="Please enter a username" style="color: red; font-size:
8pt"  />
    <br>
    <asp:label runat="server" font-size="9pt">Password: </asp:label>
    <br>
    <asp:textbox id="Password" runat="server" textmode="Password" />
```

Listing 9.5 continued

```
    <br>
    <asp:requiredfieldvalidator id="PasswordValidator" runat="server"
        controltovalidate="Password"
        errormessage="Please enter a password"
        style="color: red; font-size: 8pt" />
    <br>
    <asp:button id="Login" text="Login" runat="server" onclick="Login_Click"/>
</asp:panel>
<asp:panel id="SecurePanel" runat="Server" visible="false">
    <asp:label id="Message" runat="server"/><br>
    <asp:linkbutton id="Logout" runat="server" onclick="Logout_Click"
text="Logout" style="font-size: 8pt; color: blue;"/>
</asp:panel>
```

Figure 9.3 shows the output of Listing 9.5.

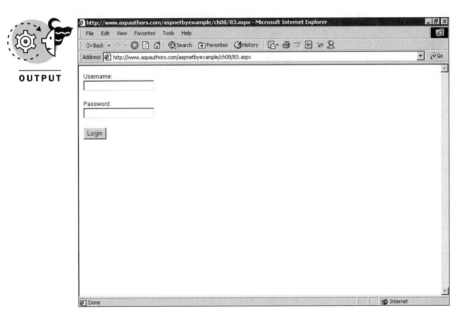

Figure 9.3: *The output of Listing 9.5, the login user control (login.ascx).*

Notice that the login control exposes two properties, Secure which we have defined using the get...set syntax to be read-only and WelcomeMessage as a public instance variable. We can set the WelcomeMessage property in a couple of ways. Normally we would want to set the required property values when declaring the control like this:

```
<ASPNETByExample:login id="UserLogin" runat="server" WelcomeMessage="Greetings"/>
```

Often, however, we need to set property values at runtime based on user input or some other dynamic value. We do this by setting the property value as we would any other property value:

```
UserLogin.WelcomeMessage = "Welcome";
```

Defining Methods in User Controls

We have seen how to expose properties from user controls, but there may be scenarios when it makes sense to expose methods to the containing Web form. To do so, we only need to declare our functions as `public`. Let's look at an updated version in Listing 9.6 of our login control to which we've add a new `Logoff` method.

EXAMPLE

Listing 9.6 Updated Login Control with `Logoff` Method (login2.ascx)

```
<script language="c#" runat="server">

    private Boolean m_Secure = false;
    public String WelcomeMessage = "Welcome";

    void Login_Click(Object sender, EventArgs e){
        if (UsernameValidator.IsValid && PasswordValidator.IsValid){
            UnsecurePanel.Visible = false;
            Message.Text = WelcomeMessage + ", " + UserName.Text;
            SecurePanel.Visible = true;
            m_Secure = true;
        }
    }
    void Logout_Click(Object sender, EventArgs e){
        if (UsernameValidator.IsValid && PasswordValidator.IsValid){
            Logoff();
        }
    }

    public Boolean Secure{
        get{
            return m_Secure;
        }

    }

    public void Logoff(){
        UnsecurePanel.Visible = true;
        UserName.Text = "";
        Password.Text = "";
        SecurePanel.Visible = false;
        m_Secure = false;
    }
```

Listing 9.6 continued

```
</script>
<asp:panel id="UnsecurePanel" runat="Server">
    <asp:label runat="server" font-size="9pt">Username:
</asp:label><br><asp:textbox id="UserName" runat="server" /><br>
    <asp:requiredfieldvalidator id="UsernameValidator" runat="server"
controltovalidate="UserName" errormessage="Please enter a username" style="color:
red; font-size: 8pt"  /><br>
    <asp:label runat="server" font-size="9pt">Password:
</asp:label><br><asp:textbox id="Password" runat="server" textmode="Password"
/><br>
    <asp:requiredfieldvalidator id="PasswordValidator" runat="server"
controltovalidate="Password" errormessage="Please enter a password" style="color:
red; font-size: 8pt" /><br>
    <asp:button id="Login" text="Login" runat="server" onclick="Login_Click"/>
</asp:panel>
<asp:panel id="SecurePanel" runat="Server" visible="false">
    <asp:label id="Message" runat="server"/><br>
    <asp:linkbutton id="Logout" runat="server" onclick="Logout_Click"
text="Logout" style="font-size: 8pt; color: blue;"/>
</asp:panel>
```

Now that we've added the `Logoff` method to our login control, we need to add code to our containing Web form to call the method. Listing 9.7 shows this modified Web form. Figure 9.4 displays the updated login control.

EXAMPLE

Listing 9.7 Updated Web Form That Calls the `Logoff` Method of the Login User Control (86.aspx)

```
<%@ Page language="c#"  %>
<%@ Register TagPrefix="ASPNETByExample" TagName="Login" Src="login2.ascx" %>
<html>
<head>
<script runat=server>
    void Logoff_Click(Object sender, EventArgs e){
        UserLogin.Logoff();
    }
</script>
  </head>
  <body>
    <form method="post" runat="server">
        <ASPNETByExample:login id="UserLogin" runat="server"
WelcomeMessage="Greetings"/>
        <br>
        <br>
        <br>
        <asp:button id="Logoff" runat="Server" text="Sign out"
onclick="Logoff_Click" />
    </form>
  </body>
</html>
```

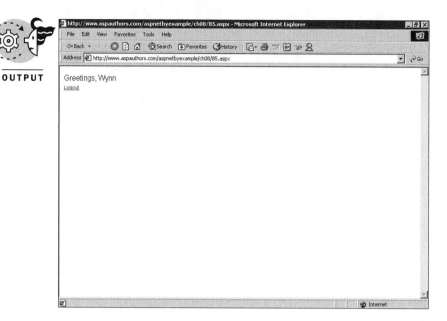

OUTPUT

Figure 9.4: *The output of Listing 9.6, the updated login control (login2.ascx).*

You'll note in this example we now can log the user off programmatically by calling the Logoff method of the user control. In our example, we test this functionality by calling Logoff from the event handler of a button on our containing page. In an actual application, however, perhaps the method would become more useful if called after a timeout check to determine if the user's current session had expired.

Raising Events from User Controls

In the previous examples we've discussed how the containing Web form communicates with user controls. There are occasions, however, when a user control needs to alert the containing Web form that its state has changed so that other controls on the form can be updated. We'll now examine how we create events in ASP.NET user controls.

Creating events in ASP.NET involves the following steps:

- Define a class that contains the data for the event (optional).

- Create an event *delegate*, a special object that allows an event sender to be connected to an event handler.

- Create a public event member whose type is an event delegate.

- Create a protected method that raises the event.

Let's look at each of these steps a little more in detail before we set out to create an event for our user control.

You've already become quite familiar with handling events for many of the built-in objects in ASP.NET. You may have noticed that the signatures for many of these event handlers are the same. Let's take a look at the Page_Load event as an example:

```
void Page_Load(Object sender, EventArgs e)
```

As with all ASP.NET event handlers, the first argument is the sender, or object that created the event. The second argument is the data for the event. In this example, the class is of type System.EventArgs, the base class for all event data in the .NET platform. We'll look at creating a custom class for event data a little later. The important thing to note here is that the data for your event must be of type System.EventArgs or derive from it.

After you have determined the class that will contain the data for your event, the next step in providing event functionality for your control is to create the event delegate. A delegate acts as a go-between for your control and the handler for your custom event. For those of you with C++ experience, delegates are similar to function pointers without many of the drawbacks. We will not spend too much time covering delegates in this context so please refer to the resources listed in this text to explore delegates further.

To create an event delegate we simply define the signature of the event handler:

```
public delegate void EventNameHandler(Object sender, EventDataType e);
```

Therefore, for an event named Click, our delegate would be defined as

```
public delegate void ClickHandler(Object sender, ClickEventArgs e);
```

After we have defined the delegate for our custom event, the next step in providing event functionality is to create a public event member whose type is the event delegate we just created. In the case of our Click event, our public event member would be defined as

```
public event ClickHandler Click;
```

Next, we create a protected method on our control that raises the event. The method must be named *On<EventName>*, so in our example, our method would be named *OnClick*. Listing 9.8 shows the method definition.

Listing 9.8 Protected OnClick Method to Raise the Click Event

```
protected virtual void OnClick(ClickEventArgs e)
{
    if(Click != null){
```

Listing 9.8 continued

```
        Click(this, e); // invokes the delegate
    }
}
```

The last step in providing custom events for your user control is to actually raise the event. To do so, we simply create an instance of the class that is to contain the event data and then call the protected method we just defined, passing it the event data. Listing 9.9 illustrates this step.

Listing 9.9 Creating the Event Data Class and Firing the Event

```
EventArgs evt = new EventArgs();
OnClick(evt);
```

For our Click example, we have selected the base class System.EventArgs to contain our event data. We'll cover firing events with custom event data classes in a later chapter.

Up until this point, our discussion of user control events may seem rather abstract. Let's walk through an example and put our theory into practice by adding event functionality to our login control. Please review the updated control in Listing 9.10 before we discuss the modifications.

EXAMPLE

Listing 9.10 Raising Events from a User Control (login3.ascx)

```
<script language="c#" runat="server">

    private Boolean m_Secure = false;
    public String WelcomeMessage = "Welcome";

    void LoginButton_Click(Object sender, EventArgs e){
        if (UsernameValidator.IsValid && PasswordValidator.IsValid){
            UnsecurePanel.Visible = false;
            Message.Text = WelcomeMessage + ", " + UserName.Text;
            SecurePanel.Visible = true;
            m_Secure = true;
            EventArgs evt = new EventArgs();
            OnLogin(evt);
        }
    }
    void LogoutButton_Click(Object sender, EventArgs e){
        if (UsernameValidator.IsValid && PasswordValidator.IsValid){
            Logoff();
        }
    }

    public Boolean Secure{
        get{
```

Listing 9.10 continued

```
            return m_Secure;
        }

    }

    public String User{
        get{
            return UserName.Text;
        }
    }

    public void Logoff(){
        UnsecurePanel.Visible = true;
        UserName.Text = "";
        Password.Text = "";
        SecurePanel.Visible = false;
        m_Secure = false;
        EventArgs evt = new EventArgs();
        OnLogout(evt);
    }

    // *** Define the Login Event
    // Delegate declaration
    public delegate void LoginHandler(object sender, EventArgs e);

    // Event declaration
    public event LoginHandler Login;


    // Raise the event by invoking the delegate,
    // sending "this", the current instance  of the class.
    protected virtual void OnLogin(EventArgs e) {
    if (Login != null) {
       Login(this, e);//Invokes the delegates.
        }
    }

    // *** Define the Logout event
    // Delegate declaration
    public delegate void LogoutHandler(object sender, EventArgs e);

    // Event declaration
    public event LogoutHandler Logout;

    // Raise the event by invoking the delegate,
    // sending "this", the current instance  of the class.
```

Listing 9.10 continued

```
    protected virtual void OnLogout(EventArgs e) {
    if (Logout != null) {
       Logout(this, e);//Invokes the delegates.
          }
    }

</script>
<asp:panel id="UnsecurePanel" runat="Server">
    <asp:label runat="server" font-size="9pt">Username:
</asp:label><br><asp:textbox id="UserName" runat="server" /><br>
    <asp:requiredfieldvalidator id="UsernameValidator" runat="server"
controltovalidate="UserName" errormessage="Please enter a username" style="color:
red; font-size: 8pt"  /><br>
    <asp:label runat="server" font-size="9pt">Password:
</asp:label><br><asp:textbox id="Password" runat="server" textmode="Password"
/><br>
    <asp:requiredfieldvalidator id="PasswordValidator" runat="server"
controltovalidate="Password" errormessage="Please enter a password" style="color:
red; font-size: 8pt" /><br>
    <asp:button id="LoginButton" text="Login" runat="server"
onclick="LoginButton_Click"/>
</asp:panel>
<asp:panel id="SecurePanel" runat="Server" visible="false">
    <asp:label id="Message" runat="server"/><br>
    <asp:linkbutton id="LogoutButton" runat="server" onclick="LogoutButton_Click"
text="Logout" style="font-size: 8pt; color: blue;"/>
</asp:panel>
```

You'll notice that in this example, we've extended our login user control example by adding two events, `Login` and `Logout`. Since these two custom events are declared in the same manner, we'll only walk through the steps in creating the `Login` event.

Since we are using the base `System.EventArgs` class to contain our event data, the first step in creating the `Login` event is to define our event delegate. In our example, we create our event delegate, `LoginHandler` as

```
public delegate void LoginHandler(object sender, EventArgs e);
```

Next, we create the public event member with the following syntax:

```
public event LoginHandler Login;
```

Note the type of this public event member is that of `LoginHandler`, the event delegate we created in the first step. Next we create a protected method to raise the event:

```
protected virtual void OnLogin(EventArgs e) {
    if (Login != null) {
       Login(this, e);  // Invokes the delegate.
    }
}
```

Finally, now that we are finished defining our custom `Login` event, we need to add code to fire the event at the appropriate time. We want to raise the `Login` event after the username and password have been validated, so we have added two new lines of code to our `LoginButton_Click` event handler:

```
EventArgs evt = new EventArgs();
OnLogin(evt);
```

In these two lines we simply create an instance of the `System.EventArgs` base class to contain our event data, and then we pass this event data to our protected `OnLogin` method. We now have a functional `Login` event for our login control. To test this new functionality, let's add an event handler for the `Login` event to our containing Web form.

If you will recall, we had added a sign-out button to our Web form to test our `Logoff` method. To test our new event functionality, let's hide or show this button based on whether the user is signed-in or not. To do so, we add two event handlers to our Web form:

```
void UserLogin_Login(Object sender, EventArgs e)
{
    LogoffButton.Visible = true;
}
void UserLogin_Logout(Object sender, EventArgs e)
{
    LogoffButton.Visible = false;
}
```

We create each of these event handlers as we have for the built-in events we have worked with until this point. Following convention, we name our event handler as the name of our control concatenated with an underscore and the name of our event. Our handler has no return type and its arguments must match those of the event delegate we created when defining the event from within our user control. Listing 9.11 contains the complete updated Web form. Figure 9.5 shows the output of this listing.

Listing 9.11 Updated Web Form with Event Handlers for the New `Login` and `Logout` Events (98.aspx)

```
<%@ Page language="c#"  %>
<%@ Register TagPrefix="ASPNETByExample" TagName="Login" Src="login2.ascx" %>
<html>
<head>
<script runat=server>
    void LogoffButton_Click(Object sender, EventArgs e){
        UserLogin.Logoff();
    }
    void UserLogin_Login(Object sender, EventArgs e)
    {
```

Listing 9.11 continued

```
        LogoffButton.Visible = true;
    }
    void UserLogin_Logout(Object sender, EventArgs e)
    {
        LogoffButton.Visible = false;
    }
</script>
  </head>
  <body>
    <form method="post" runat="server">
        <ASPNETByExample:login id="UserLogin" runat="server"
WelcomeMessage="Greetings"/>
        <br>
        <br>
        <br>
        <asp:button id="LogoffButton" runat="Server" text="Sign out"
onclick="LogoffButton_Click" />
    </form>
  </body>
</html>
```

OUTPUT

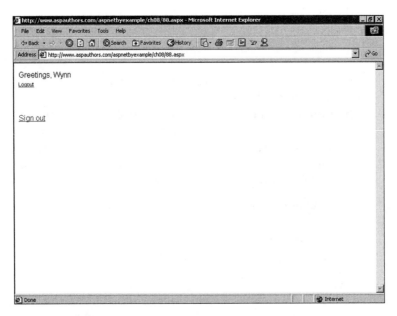

Figure 9.5: *The output of Listing 9.11, showing and hiding the sign-out button by handling the* Login *and* Logout *events.*

Summary

Let's review what we've uncovered in this chapter. So far we've discovered how to

- Use user controls to encapsulate logic and reuse portions of code when building Web forms.

- Expose properties and methods from user controls.

- Expose custom events from user controls to provide more advanced functionality.

What's Next?

In the next chapter we will take a look at ASP.NET applications. You'll gain a general understanding of the main ASP.NET application configurations components for developing and deploying your own applications.

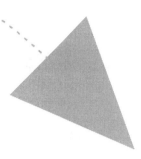

10

ASP.NET Applications

This chapter provides a general understanding of some of the main ASP.NET application configuration components you'll need to become familiar with as you develop and deploy your own applications. If you have developed any "Web applications" in Classic ASP, you probably felt like it was kind of an application, but it was really more like a bunch of Web pages simulating a real software application. ASP.NET is no longer a server-side scripting language, and your applications are not a bunch of dynamic Web pages. ASP.NET borrows from the success of ASP and will look familiar to ASP pros, but it is radically different.

In this chapter, you will

- Review some HTTP basics to understand how your ASP.NET application manages a remote client's session.

- Examine the key files and events in ASP.NET that help manage resources for client sessions.

- Look at some of the critical settings and requirements you'll need to know to deploy an ASP.NET application; with or without VS.NET.

- Code, configure, and compile an ASP.NET application that authenticates client access.

The source code for this chapter is a sample application that highlights this chapter's key concepts: Storing data at Application and Session object levels, Authentication with web.config, and setting cookies.

An ASP.NET application is composed of many different objects. Those objects might be Web pages, application services, security services, Web Services (detailed in Chapter 11, "ASP.NET and Web Services"), global application files, configuration files, resources such as DLLs and EXEs, and data stores like XML files. This chapter examines ASP's most critical application files, the scope of their control, the things they manage, what they look like, and how and when they are used.

HTTP Basics

ASP.NET handles its remote clients much the same way the family PC handles multiple local clients. By authenticating a user upon login, ASP.NET controls the scope of a client's session based on predetermined security privileges and personal settings. As soon as you start comparing how each system manages client and application communication, the similarities abruptly end. The family PC has complete control to create the most efficient environment for the client and the application. The Web server has virtually no control over the client and depends on the unreliability of the Internet. The family PC has the support of a robust message management communication protocol with all the bells and whistles. The Web server has a communication protocol just slightly more complex than the telegraph.

It's called HTTP (Hypertext Transfer Protocol) and the beauty is in its simplicity. A client makes an HTTP request by typing the URL of an HTML page she wants to view. The server processes the client's request and responds with an HTTP payload that contains the HTML data she asked for. HTTP Request + HTTP Response = Web Communication.

The clients and your server layer their HTTP request/response communications over another protocol I'm sure you've heard about: TCP/IP. TCP is the vehicle that transports HTTP payloads between the server and the clients. Just like a train, it has to separate its payloads into individual cars to hold its cargo. These cars are more commonly referred to as packets. An HTTP payload can contain HTML, XML, JPEGs, or MP3s; calls to remote programs; or just about anything else that can be converted to zeros and ones.

Your ability to extend the boundaries of the stateless HTTP protocol depends on your understanding of how ASP uses global variables at the application and client session levels. The events and variables that allow our applications to create a pseudo session state are stored in the global.asax file. As we discuss the internal structure of this file, you'll learn how we use the scope of certain variables and events to create a personalized environment that "remembers" each client between its HTTP requests. The global.asax file can be found within IIS's virtual root or within a directory that has been designated as an ASP application.

global.asax—A Good Place to Start and End

The *scope* of a variable or event in a software application refers to its place in your application's object hierarchy. The top of the object hierarchy for an ASP.NET application is the Application object. The top of the object hierarchy in terms of how you manage each client that interacts with the application is the Session Object. When you create variables at these levels (global) they are accessible to every object that was created after them. The events for these objects reside in the global.asax file, which you can see in Figure 10.1.

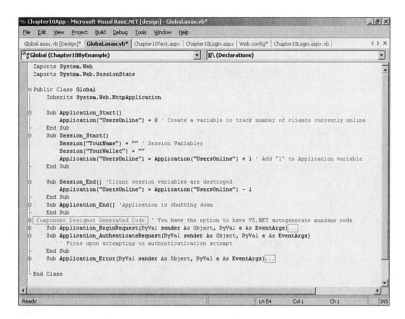

Figure 10.1: *The global.asax in VS.NET project.*

Events

Events happen. An alarm signals when it's time for you to wake up and go to work. The ringer on your telephone notifies you when someone is calling. The flip of a light switch illuminates a room. Each of these appliances help you manage and prioritize events that should make your life a little more efficient.

In object-oriented programming, you also use events to make your applications more efficient. In ASP.NET the events that have the power to start and stop your applications can be manipulated within your global.asax file.

ASP.NET adds new events to the global event file (formerly called global.asa in ASP), but the structure is extremely similar. First, let's talk about the events that have been part of ASP for a while and are still very much part of ASP.NET.

Application_OnStart

The first person that hits your Web application will inadvertently prompt ASP to fire the Application_OnStart event contained in the global.asax file. This event will not fire again. This event is where you should initialize global variables that you need to share across every user session. For example, what if you wanted to display the number of people that are currently connected to your application? Ironically, our sample application has just

such a feature. When the application first starts, we declare a variable
within the scope of the Application object.

```
Sub Application_OnStart()
        Application("UsersOnline") = 0
End Sub
```

All you have to do now is increment or decrement the value of this variable
every time we start or end a client session. We'll use the `Session` object's
`Start` and `End` events to house that portion of the code.

```
Sub Session_OnStart()
Application("UsersOnline") = Application("UsersOnline") + 1
  End Sub
```

```
Sub Session_OnEnd()
Application("UsersOnline") = Application("UsersOnline") - 1
  End Sub
```

Ultimately, the performance of your application is limited by its available
resources, and the variables you create at this level will require dedicated
resources the entire time your application is running. Just remember that
the only way to free up the resources a variable is using is to destroy the
object that created it. In other words, if you created a variable within
`Application` object's scope and you need to clear it out of memory, a simple
call to the `Application_OnEnd` event will do the trick.

Session_OnStart

HTTP is a stateless protocol, which means that it does not have a built-in
mechanism for maintaining information about each client in between each
new page they request. HTTP only cares about delivering the right
response for each requested page. HTTP is kind of like a fast food employee
who is responsible for the quick preparation and delivery of sandwiches for
every customer's order. It is so busy making sure that the customers get
exactly what they requested, it doesn't have time to focus on who ordered
what, and which sandwiches are for repeat customers.

The session event gives HTTP a little help with its impersonal approach to
customer service. Each time a new user accesses your application, the
`Session_OnStart` event is fired and ASP automatically assigns the visitor a
unique 32-bit Session ID. ASP sends this ID in the form of a cookie that
resides on the client's machine for the duration of his or her interaction
with your application. Every page request that follows that initial cookie
transaction will include that ID in the HTTP headers. Variables that you
use within this event's scope—including the Session ID—are created when
a client enters and are destroyed when the client's session ends.

ASP.NET will store and manage the variables associated with each customer session, but without that session ID included in each request's HTTP headers, it has no way of associating clients with their variable data. If ASP doesn't see the ID in the headers, it will assume it's a new client and issue a new ID.

Now that you have a technical sense of how ASP.NET uses the Session event to maintain a kind of pseudo-state for clients over HTTP, let's talk about a real world ASP implementation. Since ASP uses a pseudo-state, it's only appropriate for us to use a pseudo "real-world" application—like the one included with this chapter. Let's take a look at where and when we store the variables that are unique to a client's session.

When you make your first request for a specific page, our application issues a session ID cookie and allocates some of its memory to make room for the variables we want to store. We'll use the Session object to create two variables: YourName and YourWallet. We can add, edit, or delete this information any time during the client's session.

```
Sub Session_OnStart()
        Session("YourName") = ""
        Session("YourWallet") = ""
```

We'll use the *YourName* variable to provide a personal touch for our visitors during their session. As a user attempts to log in to our application, we will extract their name from a textbox control and write it to this session variable. We'll add and extract the data using code like:

```
Session("YourName") = "GlennC"
lblClientName.Text = Session("YourName")
' Extracted into a label's text property
```

If they have been authorized to view the Chapter10Text.aspx page, we have secret buttons hidden throughout the text that will demonstrate incremental changes to the *YourWallet* variable. A click on the button will perform a routine similar to the one we use for storing a count of connected users within the Application Object.

```
Application("UsersOnline") = Application("UsersOnline") + 1
```

The first page of our application prompts you for some authentication information before it allows access to any additional data. One possible option—and the one I selected to show—stores usernames and passwords in a file called web.config which we will talk about later. In the meantime, just remember that it is an XML-based file that we use to store our application's critical configuration information.

Session_OnEnd

Like the Session_OnStart event, Session_OnEnd is fired only once per client
visit. The server, the client, or the application developer can trigger this
event, which will permanently destroy all of a client's session data. You can
set an IIS server to automatically terminate a session if there has been no
activity from that client for longer than the set time. The client can exit the
application at any time, and our Session_OnEnd event will end the session
accordingly. The ASP programmer can also terminate a session by making a
call to this event from within his application. Here's the code we saw earlier
that subtracts a user from the total count of current users.

```
Application("UsersOnline") = Application("UsersOnline") - 1
```

Application_OnEnd

An Application_OnEnd event is also only fired once and will clean up its
global application variables. It is only triggered by restarting the application or if the application times out after a set period of inactivity.

NEW .NET APPLICATION EVENTS AND "DOT" DIRECTIVES

The new events that Microsoft has added to the global.asax file provide us
with improved control over each HTTP request and response. There are six
new events that are fired for every incoming HTTP Request before we pass
the request to the .NET Web service. We can authenticate client requests,
we can obtain session state information, and we can even avoid the complete roundtrip altogether if we have a response that has already been
processed and cached. If your Web service or ASP page encounters an error
while processing the request, and you don't have code to handle the error,
the Application_Error event is your last chance to handle or log any elu-
sive errors. If they are not handled, your HTTP response will include a
pretty HTML page, which contains an ugly application error message.

After the Web service or aspx page has prepared an HTTP response for the
client, there are four events that are fired just before a response is delivered to the client. These events are really beyond the scope of this book and
would probably only deserve an honorable mention in an intermediate
book.

As you've seen in previous examples, many of the objects that you will want
within your application are not readily accessible. You have to *import* a
pointer to those objects. We call these pointers directives because they point
(or direct) the system to the correct location of the objects that contain the
functionality we want to use.

ASSEMBLIES

Assemblies are compiled applications. By default they end up as .dll or .exe files in the \bin directory underneath your application's root. An assembly is made up of your application's source code compiled into Microsoft's Intermediate Language (MSIL, or more simply IL), an XML-based text that describes your application's code and contents, and may also include binary files and additional assemblies that your application needs. Your application is Just-In-Time (JIT) compiled a second time into native machine code on the ASP.NET server.

Configuring Your Application

Before ASP.NET, moving an ASP application from a testing environment to a production server was typically the most difficult portion of a project's life cycle. An external DLL would need its own deployment package to handle the appropriate registry entries. The server would need to be restarted. Security settings and policies had to be manually configured. A simple oversight while setting up NT, IIS, ASP, or DCOM could have disastrous consequences for everything and everyone.

ASP.NET simplifies this process. Ultimately, the server administrator maintains all the control, but the developer can deliver a single package that will handle all of the system level configuration requirements for your application. This deployment package will contain everything that web server needs to run your application. It might include security settings for roles, policies, or even encryption methods. It can install and configure the appropriate DCOM and security settings for external DLLs. Nobody will have to restart the server or worry about how the installation might affect other applications running on the server.

When you release a new version of your application, you will deliver a similar package. The administrator will double-click your package and for a short time, the new and older versions of your application will run side-by-side. ASP.NET will direct new client sessions to the newer version of your application, and as soon as it recognizes that there are no longer any client sessions dependent on the older version, it will no longer be used. Once again, this process does not require the system or server to be restarted.

The file that you will use to configure most of system and application level settings for your application is called the WebConfig. The Web.config file is a simple XML file that allows you to configure system settings, security settings, application settings, and session settings for your application. We'll discuss it in greater detail in a bit.

As we discussed earlier, if all the application developers adhere to one common standard (XML), everyone's applications will be able to communicate and share services and data—regardless of the actual programming language they were developed in. XML looks like a bunch of <HTML-ISH> tags, yet the tags only exist to describe and organize the data it contains. A parsed XML document looks like a tree of self-describing branches of data that contain self-describing data elements. It uses something called a "namespace" to make sure the client knows that the data within all the <titles> elements are referring to the <titles> of books, not the book authors' job <titles> elements. The only "presentation data" the XML file might include is a reference to some XSL. XSL is just an optional way to help transform the XML data into something more visually appealing.

XML is a strongly typed language, meaning that the code must be well formed with perfect syntax. In HTML, if you forget a closing </tag> here or there, the client's browser of choice will usually ignore your oversights and assemble the code the best it can. Breaking or bending XML coding standards, however, will always produce less than ideal results.

With a little well-formed XML and a web.config file, you've got all the power the server administrator never wanted you to have. In fact, she would be in a straightjacket right now if you asked her to configure half of the items .NET allows you to deploy and configure programmatically. It's kind of like your very own portable system administrator. On the other hand, you don't have to use it if you don't want to. If you feel comfortable with inheriting the systems' global settings, you don't need web.config at all. But if you want your application to terminate a session that has been inactive for more than five minutes (IIS's default is 20 minutes), a few simple lines of XML gives you all the power you need.

What Web.config Looks Like and Where to Find It

You can put a web.config file within an ASP application root directory or any of its subdirectories. Its mere presence is enough to override IIS's global settings with its own. Figure 10.2 shows the web.config file that we are using to authenticate clients for the application that accompanies this chapter.

NOTE

Every web.config file needs to start with a <Configuration> tag and end with a </Configuration> to wrap the setting for your application.

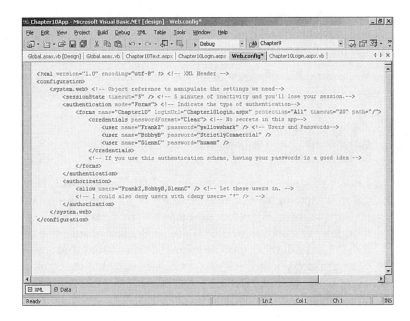

Figure 10.2: *Web.config is an XML-based configuration file that allows you to programmatically customize a variety of runtime settings for your application.*

Setting up Web.config

As you've probably noticed, the emphasis on consistent object-oriented programming (OOP) standards is a major part of .NET's initiative. There's really nowhere to run and hide from OOP these days, so if you're intimidated by it, get over it quick. You can make anything as complicated or simple as you choose to see it. Despite any overly complicated and abstract explanations you've heard in the past, the fact is, it's quite simple.

Establishing a reference to an object is a lot like putting a shortcut on your computer desktop. When you need quick access to a program on your hard drive, it makes more sense to place a tiny pointer on your desktop than it does to reinstall that application to your desktop. While you can give it a unique name to differentiate it from the other shortcuts on your desktop, it's still just a data store for the string variable that points to the real deal. Similarly, when you make a reference to an object in your code, the instance of that object is created with a pointer to its memory location.

Section Handlers

In order to configure a setting, you have to have a reference to the class object that manages those settings. For example, if you wanted to configure settings based on someone's browser capabilities, you need to make sure you include a reference to that class before you can manipulate the related settings.

You can add a reference to one of these classes, referred to as "configuration section handlers," by using code similar to the following:

EXAMPLE

```
<Configsections>
<add name ="objCoolBrowserCapReference"
type="System.Web.HTTPBrowserCapabilities$SectionHandler" />
</Configsections>
```

I know this object reference looks a little intimidating, but all it's really doing is turning the variable name you just added into a powerful class object a team of Microsoft developers wrote just for you. I know, I just upset a bunch of tightly wound OOP know-it-alls because the truth is that it didn't turn anything into anything! It's just like that shortcut we put on your desktop earlier. It's just an object variable that holds a pointer the compiled code. Nonetheless, the code above adds the appropriate reference so that you can configure browser capability settings.

<SessionState>

The <SessionState> handler gives your application control over five session state settings. Three of these settings are all related to storing sessions on a remote server, so they're grouped under the first bullet.

- Remote Session Storage—By default, each session state is stored on the server. For applications that support a large number of clients, you might want to free up some system resources by storing each session state on a different server. In order to accomplish this feat, you'll need to change three state settings within the SessionStateModule$SectionHandler class:

  Set inproc="false" to indicate that you want the session in another server's process space. You'll also need to point to the server (for example, server="MyCoolStateServer") that will be storing the session data for your application. Finally, you should specify a remote port number by assigning the appropriate port number. port="YourPortNumber" setting.

- Cookieless—Some clients don't like applications that use cookies. As we stated earlier, the Session ID is critical for us to be able to manage a client's session. Our only alternative is to encode a session ID into all of the URL strings a client can click. We can force ASP to do this for us by changing the cookieless property to "true". Its default setting is false to indicate that it should use a cookie to hold the session ID data. By the way, cookieless session management is much slower!

- TimeOut—The last setting allows you to control how long a client is allowed to be inactive before we should terminate the session. You simply set the timeout property equal to the number of minutes (for example, timeout="13").

DEPLOYING <Assemblies>

In the past, an ASP application was an organized collection of HTML pages with ASP code embedded within them. Deploying an ASP application required someone to manually duplicate the exact same environment that had existed on the machine it was tested on. This included the same directory structure and related files, IIS and security settings, and DNS entries for database access. If your ASP application made reference to an external DLL, you had to consider a deployment package for that executable, security privileges, and registry entries, as well as the impact these settings might have on other applications running on the same server.

In ASP.NET our applications are compiled into self-describing assemblies that function in many ways like self-extracting zip files. An assembly might include compiled code, the application's directory structure, system and application settings, versioning information, class libraries, and any external files or executable the code refers to. If your application requires an older 32-bit COM-based DLL, the file is added to the assembly like any other file, yet it will also include the appropriate registry and configuration data the server will need during the installation process. In other words, everything is automatically installed and configured to recreate the same environment that existed on the machine it was compiled on.

VS. Net's interface makes this process even easier, but you don't need VS.Net to achieve the same results. All VS.Net is doing is supplying you with user-friendly prompts that will handle the underlying details for you. The <assemblies> directive in the web.config file is used for adding and removing additional assemblies that will be passed to the compiler.

For example, let's say that you had just finished coding a .NET dll that replaces an older COM dll for one of your ASP.NET programs. Your trial version of VS.NET has just expired and you have ten minutes to build an updated version of your application. By making a few slight modifications to your code and the web.config file, you could essentially remove the old DLL and recompile it with the new one. Your web.config file might look like the following:

```
<assemblies>
<add assembly="YourNewDllComponent"/><remove assembly="YourOldDLLComponent" />
</assemblies>
```

```
<WebServices>
```

Let's say that your friend's company in Alaska just finished building an application that retrieves real-time data about their wireless phone customers' phone usage. (For example, is their phone turned on? are they on a call? does their phone have the most recent flash upgrade installed?) Because your company handles service calls for them, he asks that you provide his customers an online interface that automatically upgrades their phone's software for them and guides them through the installation process. This will keep his customers happy, and will save everyone tons of time and money. Since his application is already set up as a Web Service (and was written in ASP.NET of course), you can retrieve the services he exposes to you and present the data in a browser.

The real techies might be curious whether I am implying that ASP.NET can handle events asynchronously. The answer is yes. What this means is that while your application is waiting for Event A to finish, it can handle other Events B, C, and D. In other words, you could incrementally update a control on a client's Web page that indicates the progress of their phone's installation. At the same time, the user could be updating their account data, which gets passed to your friend's database.

The following chapter will describe Web Services in much greater detail, but at this point just remember that you configure a variety of Web Service settings in web.config.

Authentication and Authorization in web.config

HTML Forms Authentication is a new feature for ASP and its settings are configured in the web.config file. It provides the developer a number of techniques to validate a client's credentials and control their access privileges accordingly. After we determine that a client is a valid user, we issue a cookie that stores their credentials in an encrypted key. Each time a validated client requests a new page, the key is passed in their HTTP Request headers so ASP will not have to revalidate their credentials.

```
<authentication>
```

There are four authentication mode settings your applications can use. You set the value of each authentication mode with the following syntax:

```
<authentication mode="Cookie">
```

- None—"None" means that your application doesn't have any authentication requirements. None means no, yes?

- Windows—Also occasionally referred to as NT Authentication, it will validate a client's credentials based on its NT system's users and their permissions. NT creates an NT session ID that it uses to control the client's access based on its own security permissions.

- Cookie—Although it's not the most secure approach to authentication, a client can pass a locally stored cookie to validate clients.

- Passport—Microsoft has a pretty nifty new client authentication service called MS Passport Web Services, and it's free.

`<cookie>`

If you are using a cookie to validate clients, there are three cookie mode settings.

- `cookie`—Your cookie needs a name. It's important to make sure each cookie has a unique name to avoid conflicts with other application's cookies. A cookie setting might look like:

  ```
  <cookie cookie="UniqueCookieName">
  ```

- `DecryptionKey`—By default, your system will automatically generate a unique encryption key for its clients with the "autogenerate" setting. You can also provide your own key to encrypt the data, but this is really only necessary when your application spans a range of systems within a server farm. In other words, don't worry about it for now.

- `loginurl`—When clients first hit application resources that require authentication, you can direct them to a specific page to validate their credentials. Your new and improved cookie code might look like this now:

  ```
  <cookie cookie="UniqueCookieName" loginurl="AuthenticationPage.aspx"/>
  ```

We don't use cookies to authenticate users in our sample application, but if you peek inside this chapter's sample application, you'll notice an example of how to set and check for cookies in your own applications.

`<credentials>`

We also have the option to store people's user names and passwords within the web.config file. While storing credentials within the web.config is not an ideal approach for applications that need to validate the credentials of hundreds of clients, it's a perfect approach for smaller applications that only need to validate the credentials for a few clients. Larger applications will probably want to store credentials in a database.

There are three password format settings you can use to store the clients' credentials:

- Clear—Usernames and passwords are not encrypted.

- SHA1—Passwords are encrypted and validated against the SHA1 algorithm.

- MD5—Passwords are encrypted and validated against the MD5 algorithm.

Both of the encryption algorithms require a reference to a special API that executes the algorithms. To keep things simple, here's some credential syntax for "clear" credential storage:

```
<Credentials PasswordFormat="Clear"/>
```

<user>

Storing client usernames and passwords for authenticating client credentials is easy.

```
<user name="GlennC" password="human"/>
```

<authorization>

Even if our user has valid credentials we need to either "allow" or "deny" them access to our application. If we want to allow Frank and Bobby access, but deny Glenn, our syntax might look like:

```
<allow users="FrankZ", "BobbyB"/>
<deny users="GlennC"/>
```

If we wanted to assign access privileges to anonymous users, we could either "deny" or "allow" their access with one of the following:

```
<allow users="*"/>
```

```
<deny users="*"/>
```

I should also note that there is a "roles" property setting you can assign when allowing or denying user access. You can customize user access privileges even further by assigning this property value to the name of role on the system. For example, if I want Frank and Bob to have Administrator privileges, I would modify their code to look like:

```
<allow users="FrankZ", "BobbyB" roles="Administrator"/>
```

Building a Simple Authentication Application

In the sections that follow is a simple authentication application that uses Forms-based Authentication to control login access to a page with this chapter's text. The source code highlights the major points of discussion in this chapter and includes a few extras. If you don't have VS.NET yet, I've also included a few short movies that show the application running in this environment. You can find these files on the Web site.

The Application Root

Before we dig into the code, the first step after you have ASP.NET installed is to open your Internet Service Manager and make sure the application is registered accordingly. Just drag and drop the Chapter10App directory onto your system and create a virtual directory for it. If you look at the figure below, you'll see that I've named my application Chapter10App. The root domain name is planetdev.com so the URL for this application would look like `http://www.planetdev.com/Chapter10App`. In Figure 10.3, you can see the main files for our application as they appear in the Internet Service Manager window.

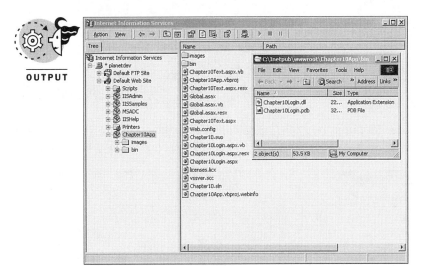

OUTPUT

Figure 10.3: *The Chapter 10 Application as it appears in the Internet Service Manager.*

If you right-click the applications root directory, and select Properties, you'll see an interface that allows you to configure some general settings as well as security, HTTP, and Session settings for your application. You can programmatically change much of the same information in your web.config file, but you should at least become familiar with the server administration GUI as well. In Figure 10.4 you'll see the property settings window as well as the settings you can change if you click the Configuration button.

Now that you've got everything configured the way you want, let's look at a simple high-level diagram that describes the relationships of the objects that drive the application (see Figure 10.5).

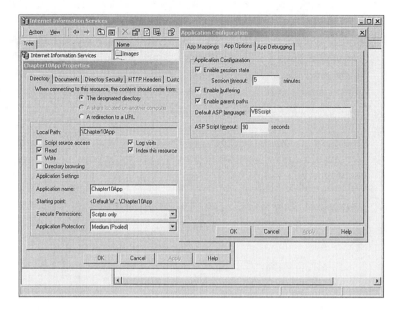

Figure 10.4: *You can configure settings for your application through the Internet Service Manager GUI or programmatically in the web.config file.*

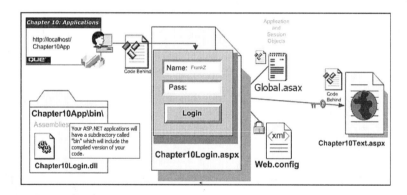

Figure 10.5: *A beginner-friendly diagram of the file relationships in this chapter's ASP.NET application.*

This application is even simpler than the diagram looks. As we discussed earlier, when someone makes a request (HTTP Request) to the URL where your application resides, it starts a chain of events that include declaring session variables, defining configuration and security settings, and executing the code behind the requested aspx page that handles events. The Chapter10Login.aspx page will work with the global.asax and web.config files to configure the data storage and configuration settings for a new client session. It will also import and inherit functionalities that will authenticate a user's login. When a user submits their username and password, it will use the data stored in the web.config file to authenticate the client. If the client is authorized, he will be directed to the Chapter10Text.aspx page. If he is denied access, the label control on the Chapter10.aspx page will ask him to resubmit his data.

Before we dive into some new code let's get a more detailed look at the global and configuration setting files you've already seen in this chapter.

Note: You will see many of the same comments in the source code of the application itself.

GLOBAL.ASAX, WEB.CONFIG

Both of these files are critical to defining your ASP.NET application's execution (runtime) environment. The first job of the global.asax file is to import the critical .NET class libraries that are used throughout the application. The web.config file will be used to manage the security roles and privileges for clients requesting its services.

The first two lines of the global.asax file import two of the System namespace's class libraries that are required for ASP.NET applications.

```
Imports System.Web
Imports System.Web.SessionState
```

As mentioned earlier in the book, an important part of learning how to build .NET applications is learning what the included .NET class libraries can do for you. .NET's class library is organized a bit like the directory of folders and files on your hard drive. Your operating system prefers that you use backslashes "\" to navigate to a specific file or folder (such as c:\Windows\WebFiles\. Object Oriented Programming compilers prefer that we use a dot "." to navigate the class hierarchy (for example, System. Web.Session

```
Public Class Global
    Inherits System.Web.HttpApplication
```

After we have imported our namespace classes, we begin the code that describes this file as a public class, which will need to inherit functionality found in the HttpApplication class.

Listing 10.1: Events and variable declarations in the global.asax file. (global.asax)

EXAMPLE

```
Sub Application_OnStart()
      Application("UsersOnline") = 0
End Sub

      Sub Session_OnStart()
          Session("YourName") = ""
          Session("YourWallet") = ""
          Application("UsersOnline") = Application("UsersOnline") + 1
```

Listing 10.1: continued

```
        End Sub


Sub Session_OnEnd()
Session objects are destroyed and the Application variable is updated.
Application("UsersOnline") = Application("UsersOnline") - 1
End Sub

Sub Application_OnEnd()
Application is shutting down all objects are destroyed
End Sub
```

We've already discussed this section of code earlier in the chapter, so I'll just give you a history of what has happened since the client called your application—ignore the end events for now. Assuming it's the very first client HTTP request, the ASP.NET will load and fire the Application_ OnStart event and create a variable called *UsersOnline*. It has also fired the Session_OnStart event and created two variables.

```
    Public Sub New()
        MyBase.New()
    End Sub
```

I should also note that the New method replaces the Class_Initialize event some of you VB programmers might be familiar with.

```
Sub Application_BeginRequest(ByVal sender As Object, ByVal e As EventArgs)
        ' Fires at the beginning of each HTTP request
End Sub

Sub Application_AuthenticateRequest(ByVal sender As Object, ByVal e As
EventArgs)
        ' Fires when attempting to authenticate the user
End Sub

Sub Application_Error(ByVal sender As Object, ByVal e As EventArgs)
        ' Fires when an error occurs
End Sub
```

These are the new events ASP.NET added to what used to be the global.asa in Classic ASP. The extended functionality is good to know about but I don't need it for this simple application.

AUTHORIZED XML

ASP.NET gives source code authors the power and responsibility to configure their own applications and system-level settings. In the past these settings were contained in IIS meta tables and set by the system administrator. Now you can use the web.config file to handle everything for you. In our Chapter10App, I've chosen to use Forms-based authentication to demonstrate how we can use web.config to configure and authorize users' names and passwords and their credentials.

NOTE: The objects you will want to make reference to and configure are case sensitive. *Keep the appendix for this book handy!*

```
<configuration>
<system.web>
<sessionState timeout="5" />
```

The <configuration> tag is the wrapper for specific settings you will use in your application. The first line includes a reference to the Web classes in the System namespace. Once I have this reference, I can access a multitude of properties that include booting clients after five minutes of inactivity.

```
<authentication mode="Forms">
<forms name="Chapter10" loginUrl="Chapter10Login.aspx" protection="All"
timeout="20" path="/">
```

The code you see above sets our application's authentication mode to Forms. In order for you to use this authentication model, make sure you have set the proper page URL that manages the form-based login process.

```
<credentials passwordFormat="Clear">
<user name="FrankZ" password="yellowshark">
<user name="BobbyB" password="StrictlyCommercial" />
<user name="GlennC" password="human" />
</credentials>
</forms>
</authentication>
```

Here is where we define our users and any credential settings. In this case I have chosen to keep things simple by setting the passwordFormat to Clear. You can change it to one of the encryption schemes we mentioned earlier if you'd like.

```
<authorization>
<allow users="FrankZ,BobbyB,GlennC" />
<deny users="*"/>
</authorization>
</system.web>
</configuration>
```

Before we close any open XML tags, we indicate the users we will grant access and everyone else will be denied.

CHAPTER10LOGIN.ASPX.VB

Figure 10.6 shows the HTML page as it would appear to a client who visits the application. The code behind page that manages the user events at the server is called Chapter10Login.aspx.vb.

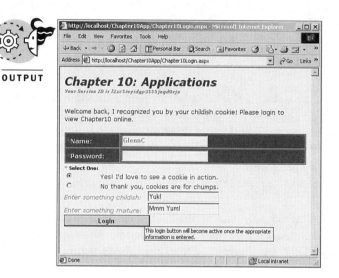

OUTPUT

Figure 10.6: *The main page of our application (Chapter10Login.aspx) as it appears in Internet Explorer.*

This is the page and code that really does all the work. I must note, however, that while writing this entire application, I never wrote a bit of HTML (and I loved every minute of it). The presentation code (Chapter10Login.aspx) is completely separate from the code behind page. I'm only going to mention the aspx page because I haven't even looked at its code since I made sure it inherited my code behind page. The only line of code you or I should care about in that aspx page is the first line:

```
<%@ Page Language="vb" AutoEventWireup="false"
➥ Codebehind="Chapter10Login.aspx.vb"
➥ Inherits="Chapter10ByExample.Chapter10LoginCode"%>
```

The code above is essentially inheriting the code behind page's class object called Chapter10LoginCode. In my project file I had assigned the application namespace as "Chapter10ByExample" so I drill down the hierarchy separating objects with the dot. You'll see that by inheriting that one class, I've also inherited 90 percent of this application's logic.

In this case we'll import the security class that we use for authentication in the code below. The second line establishes that this is a public class object named Chapter10LoginCode.

```
Imports System.Web.Security
Public Class Chapter10LoginCode
```

The line you see below inherits the System's Page object, which our aspx page needs to inherit from in order to expose the event handlers in this file.

```
Inherits System.Web.UI.Page
```

The following lines were generated automatically by VS.NET as I dragged controls from my toolbox and dropped them onto my Web page. All they are saying is that the code behind page should listen for events coming from objects which have inherited it.

```
Protected WithEvents txtName As System.Web.UI.WebControls.TextBox
Protected WithEvents txtPass As System.Web.UI.WebControls.TextBox
Protected WithEvents lblMessage As System.Web.UI.WebControls.Label
Protected WithEvents txtCookie As System.Web.UI.WebControls.TextBox
Protected WithEvents btnYes As System.Web.UI.WebControls.RadioButton
Protected WithEvents btnNo As System.Web.UI.WebControls.RadioButton
Protected WithEvents lblCookie As System.Web.UI.WebControls.Label
Protected WithEvents cmdLogin As System.Web.UI.WebControls.Button
```

The following section of code represents the event handlers that are fired as a user interacts with our aspx page. One incredibly exciting feature I must mention, which I used in this application and was mentioned earlier in the book, is a control's autopostback feature. It allows you to update a control without reloading the entire page. For example, in this application, if a user is denied access I simply update a label control to indicate they are not an authorized user. All you have to do is change a control's autopostback property to "True" and handle the events accordingly. The code below shows the autopostback feature and also checks to see if they have added a cookie to their system previously.

EXAMPLE

Listing 10.2: The 'Code Behind' Reading and Writing a Cookie to a User's System (*Chapter10Login.aspx.vb*)

```
Private Sub Page_Load(ByVal sender As System.Object, ByVal e As System.EventArgs)
Handles MyBase.Load

lblSessionID.Text = "Your Session ID is " & Session.SessionID
' Show them their Session ID

Dim objCookie As HttpCookie 'By importing the System.Web namespace
➡ you can create an instance of the HTTPCookie Class
objCookie = Request.Cookies("Chapter10")

If Not IsNothing(objCookie) Then 'If the value is not null then we can great them
accordingly
lblMessage.ForeColor = lblMessage.ForeColor.Black()
lblMessage.Text = "Welcome back, I recognized you by your childish cookie!
```

Listing 10.2: continued

```
➥ Please login to view Chapter10 online."

ElseIf Session("YourName") = "" Then
' We're checking a Session Object variable for any string data.
      lblMessage.ForeColor = lblMessage.ForeColor.Black()
      lblMessage.Text = "Welcome, please login to view Chapter10 online."
Else
' Ok, something's strange here! They have a string data in their
' Session("YourName") variable. They must have been sent back to us.
      lblMessage.ForeColor = lblMessage.ForeColor.Black()
lblMessage.Text = "Unauthorized Access: I'm sorry " &
Session("YourName") & ", please check your username and password " &
" and try again."
End If


End Sub
```

VS.NET automatically creates a Page_Load event for your Web forms as you add them to your project. First, we'll use this event to check to see if they have our cookie on their system. When you save a cookie on a user's system, they will be passing the cookie data in their HTTP headers. We can request to see them (if they exist), and we can also edit them if we like. In order to check for a cookie, we have to have a reference to the HTTPCookie class, which is part of the System.Web namespace. If the cookie is not Null then we know they have been here before. Then we check the Session Object data to see if the Session("YourName") variable contains any string data. If it's empty, it's pretty safe to assume they haven't tried to log in yet. If that variable has string data, it indicates that they either left the section of the app that requires access and need to login, or that they have been rejected by our security class.

The following code simply halts the login process if the length of string data submitted looks suspicious.

EXAMPLE

Listing 10.3: Using server-side code to manage client events. (Chapter10Login.aspx.vb)

```
Private Sub cmdLogin_Click(ByVal sender As System.Object,
➥ ByVal e As System.EventArgs) Handles cmdLogin.Click

    If Len(txtName.Text) <= 5 Then
        lblMessage.ForeColor = lblMessage.ForeColor.Red()
        lblMessage.Text = "Please enter a username."
        Exit Sub
    End If
    If Len(txtPass.Text) <= 3 Then
```

Listing 10.3: continued

```
        lblMessage.ForeColor = lblMessage.ForeColor.Red()
        lblMessage.Text = "Please enter a password."
        Exit Sub
    End If
```

If everything looks good we'll write a little cookie to their system before proceeding to the section of code that handles the authentication process.

```
If btnYes.Checked = True Then
        Response.Cookies("Chapter10")("Childish") = txtCookie.Text
        Response.Cookies("Chapter10")("Mature") = txtCookie2.Text
        Response.Cookies("Chapter10").Expires = "3/3/2039"
End If
```

When you send the HTTP response, you simply load it with your cookie(s). If cookies are enabled on the client browser, it's extremely simple to save (persist) this data on their machine. This data is now stored on their system and will exist in their headers across all their sessions until the cookie expires or they have deleted it. While it would have been very easy to authenticate users with cookies, I avoided it because of the level of abuse I have seen recently by deceitful Web sites who are pooling their resources together to share cookie data. If you would like more info on this issue, a search for "WebBugs" will lead you in the right direction. In the meantime, let's look at the authentication method we did choose.

EXAMPLE

```
    If FormsAuthentication.Authenticate(txtName.Text, txtPass.Text) = True Then
        Session("YourName") = txtName.Text
 Response.Redirect("Chapter10Text.aspx?Name=" & txtName.Text)
    Else
lblMessage.Text = "Unauthorized Access: I'm sorry "
➥ & Session("YourName") & ", please check your username and password and try
again."
    End If
```

```
End Sub
```

Since we have imported our security classes and configured them in web.config, we can now use a method to test them out. The FormsAuthentication.Authenticate method requires two arguments that we have extracted from the text property of the txtName and txtPass controls. If the system recognizes them from our web.config file, it returns a Boolean "True" to indicate they are authorized. Figure 10.7 shows what an authorized user will see. If they are authorized to enter, we redirect them to the Chapter 10 text and send them on their way with a query string that includes their name. We'll extract this from their HTTP headers in the Page_Load event of the Chapter10Text.aspx.vb page.

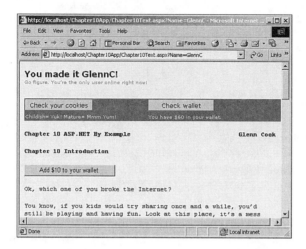

Figure 10.7: *The application will check the usernames and passwords stored in the web.config file to authenticate a user's access to Chapter10Text.aspx.*

Listing 10.4: Handling client-side events with server-side code to update controls in the client's browser. (Chapter10Login.aspx.vb)

```vb
Private Sub btnYes_CheckedChanged(ByVal sender As System.Object,
➥ ByVal e As System.EventArgs) Handles btnYes.CheckedChanged

' NOTE: By assigning both of these radio buttons a shared group name .NET treat
' them like a control array
cmdLogin.Enabled = False
lblCookie.Visible = True
txtCookie.Visible = True
    lblCookie2.Visible = True
txtCookie2.Visible = True
End Sub

Private Sub btnNo_CheckedChanged(ByVal sender As System.Object,
➥ ByVal e As System.EventArgs) Handles btnNo.CheckedChanged
        cmdLogin.Enabled = True
        lblCookie.Visible = False
        txtCookie.Visible = False
        lblCookie2.Visible = False
        txtCookie2.Visible = False
End Sub
```

Listing 10.4: continued

```
Private Sub txtCookie_TextChanged(ByVal sender As System.Object,
➥ ByVal e As System.EventArgs) Handles txtCookie.TextChanged
        cmdLogin.Enabled = True
End Sub
End Class
```

The event routines you see above perform a little code behind magic to enable or disable the login button and cookie related controls. For example, if a user selects the Yes radio button indicating they want to see a cookie work, the label and textbox controls (*lblCookie, lblCookie2, txtCookie, txtCookie2*) will suddenly appear on the page. When the *btnYes_CheckedChanged* event fires, we change those control's Visible settings from "False" (I had set this at design time) to "True", making them appear to the user. No HTML, no DHTML, no JavaScript! Check the HTML source in your browser if you still don't believe me.

Deploying your ASP.NET Application

The beauty of this section, and deploying .NET applications is in its simplicity. It's so easy I dare not over-describe it or you might interpret my babble as something complicated. All I can say is that in five years you'll be telling younger programmers, "I remember when we used to have to register those components with our bare hands ..."

Assembly Deployment: \bin

Drop your compiled assemblies into your application's \bin directory and ... well, that's it. Your assemblies already have their own metadata and you don't need regsvr32 to register your components. You'll notice that as you "Build and Browse" your application in VS.NET, it is automatically recompiling your assemblies and dropping them in the /bin directory so all you really need to do is go get them. Just make sure you've got your /global.asax, your web.config, and your /bin and you're done.

What If I Need to Update My DLL?

If your application needs a newer version of a compiled component, whatever you do, do not stop the Web server! Otherwise, you won't be able to see your application automatically update itself while it's running. As we mentioned earlier, all you or your server administrator will need to do is install the new file(s) over the old.

It's just as easy to delete an application. You don't have to worry about unregistering all of your apps' dependencies. Just highlight, and delete.

Summary

ASP.NET applications are compiled programs that deliver data and services to clients over a simple protocol called the Hypertext transfer protocol. These applications might deliver HTML data over HTTP to a browser but can also exchange data and services with any program—running locally or remotely—that also uses non-proprietary XML standards for sharing data.

HTTP is a stateless protocol responsible for sending data over a lower level network protocol called TCP/IP (a.k.a. "The Internet Protocol"). As a client communicates with an ASP.NET application, ASP.NET uses cookies stored on the client's machine and/or query strings (variable data appended onto hyperlinks) to manage the client's session state in between each request and response. This data is embedded in each HTTP request and response so that our application can uniquely identify and manage each client's session.

The global.asax file handles events for the Application and Session Objects. We store data for each client session by declaring variables within the Session object's events. We store data that is shared across all clients with variables scoped within the Application Object's events.

The web.config file allows an ASP.NET application developer to programmatically define the system and application level settings for their program. It can include everything from authentication to managing web farms. In the past, even if it were a possibility, most of these items would have to be done manually by the server's administrator.

ASP.NET applications are compiled into assemblies that contain all of the files and configuration data one needs to deploy their application on any ASP.NET capable system. Even if your ASP.NET application is dependent on a COM-based external DLL, it is included in the assembly and automatically installed and configured properly.

What's Next?

In the next chapter, we look at one of ASP.NET's most exciting components, its XML Web Services. Web Services allow our applications to connect and securely exchange data and services over the Internet. Using industry-wide accepted standards like XML and SOAP (Simple Object Access Protocol) which is an ASP.NET application, we are able to provide services as well as use other program's services and data.

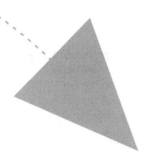

11

ASP.NET and Web Services

A Web Service is an application that delivers a service across the Internet using the standards and technologies defined in the Web Services architecture. After such services have been written, they can be utilized (consumed) by a client application written in any language on any platform as long as it has access to the appropriate client-side versions of these technologies. In addition, a Web Service can be published in a Web Services directory and queried using a standard discovery protocol. These directories are designed to provide potential consumers of Web Services with an easy way to locate vendors that provide exactly the services they require.

In this chapter you will

- Review some of the previous generation technologies that the Web Services architecture builds upon to better understand the problems that Web Services are meant to overcome.

- Examine each major specification and technology that together comprise the Web Services architecture.

- Start building your own Web Services and the clients that will consume them.

Distributed Computing: Many Things to Many People

In the Internet economy, distributed computing architectures are primarily employed to increase application performance and scalability. By using clusters of low-cost servers to host their online applications rather than rely on a single (albeit large and powerful) system, e-commerce sites gain the ability to easily add new servers to handle increased load during periods of peak activity and avoid the expense and delay associated with upgrading or replacing a single system stretched beyond its capacity. Just as important, they gain increased reliability because the loss of one or two servers in a cluster simply increases the load on the remaining servers until the failed nodes are replaced.

Microsoft, Sun Microsystems, and the Object Management Group, along with many others, provide competing protocols and platforms for creating *distributed object applications*, the type of distributed computing services designed to enhance the scalability and reliability of e-commerce and other mission-critical systems. These systems are all similar in that they provide applications with remote access to data and functionality hosted on servers across a network as well as a wide array of architectural "plumbing" services such as support for remote message queues and distributed transactions. At the same time they attempt to hide the complexity associated with these services by creating the illusion that all of the remote objects, data, and services in use are actually hosted on the programmer's workstation. Quite an accomplishment, to say the least!

In general, all of the aforementioned solutions adequately address the need to create distributed applications that are scalable and reliable. A new problem arises, however, when these systems are required to communicate and share data and services with each other across the Internet. Consider, for example, what occurs when two banks merge to form a single business entity. The distributed systems in one bank could be implemented using Microsoft technologies exclusively, whereas the other bank's systems could be implemented using a combination of Java and Oracle technologies with a few legacy mainframe applications thrown in for good measure. Obviously, the IT departments in both companies would have to figure out a way to make these systems interoperate and present a seamless banking experience to their customers as rapidly as possible.

The unfortunate truth, however, is that today interoperability among these competing technologies can only be achieved at great effort and expense using complex middleware solutions designed to bridge the rather large gaps between them. Like CORBA and Java-based solutions, Microsoft's existing object technology, COM+, does not communicate well with other technologies, presenting a serious problem to those tasked with the unenviable chore of making them work together. In addition, the unpredictable nature of the Internet means that slow network connections, and even connection failures, are the rule rather than the exception. Again, none of the existing crop of distributed object technologies were designed to tolerate these conditions. Even worse, most corporate firewalls are configured by default to prevent the "wire protocols" these technologies use to communicate from entering or leaving the internal networks they are installed to protect which in turn precludes any of them from being widely adopted as an Internet standard.

The good news, on the other hand, is that Microsoft's Web Services architecture, a key component of the .NET initiative and the subject of this chapter, is specifically designed to solve the seemingly intractable problem of interoperability among heterogeneous systems. In fact, Web Services go one step further and address a number of other problems specifically associated with the development of distributed applications designed to communicate over the Internet.

What Is a Web Service?

As mentioned in the introduction, a Web Service can be loosely defined as an application that delivers a service across the Internet in a platform-independent and language-neutral fashion. To accomplish this feat, Web Services rely on several XML protocols based on open standards that are collectively known as the Web Services architecture. In addition to providing cross-platform interoperability, a Web Service can also be published to an Internet directory and queried using an industry standard discovery protocol called Universal Description, Discovery, and Integration (UDDI). UDDI is itself implemented using XML and is designed to provide programmers with an easy way to locate the services they require.

A good example of the potential use of the Web Service architecture is a credit card verification system. Utilizing the Web Services architecture, a financial institution can expose an existing credit card verification system by building a Web Services access layer and publishing it to a UDDI service discovery directory. Later, a potential consumer of credit card verification services can perform a search against the same directory and discover the verification service with minimal effort. After discovering the service, the client simply downloads the service's "contract," the document that describes the service's capabilities and programmatic interface, and adapts his or her application to utilize the service accordingly.

Of course, we glossed over a few issues, such as how one might pay for such a service, acquire the requisite security credentials to access the service, and similar nontrivial details, but from a technological standpoint, this is how the Web Services architecture works at its most basic level.

Now that our introduction to distributed computing is out of the way, we're ready to plunge right in and tackle the specifications and technologies that make up the Web Services architecture.

Coming Clean About SOAP

To allow two different systems to interoperate the Web Services architecture utilizes an XML-based messaging format known as SOAP. SOAP, which stands for Simple Object Access Protocol, acts as a sort of universal wire protocol to mediate communications between Web Services and client applications. SOAP is at the core of the Web Services architecture and is meant to replace DCOM, RMI, IIOP, and other proprietary wire protocols whenever access in a heterogeneous environment is a requirement.

The reason why SOAP succeeds at providing interoperability among heterogeneous systems where other protocols fail lies in the fact that it utilizes XML to provide a standard, yet extensible, data representation and messaging format. In short, SOAP allows any system, whether it is based on COM, Java, CORBA, or even plain old RPC, to communicate with any other system as long as both understand the SOAP protocol. Furthermore, SOAP is able to circumvent the aforementioned limitations imposed by firewalls by operating across standard Web protocols like HTTP and HTTPS. These standard Web protocols, and the TCP ports commonly associated with them, are almost always accessible across network boundaries because they're the same ones that carry standard HTML documents. This also means that Web Services based on the SOAP protocol are URL-addressable using a standard Web browser.

SOAP has been submitted by Microsoft, IBM, Ariba, and other partners for consideration as a standard to the W3C, and it appears to be on track for recommendation by that body. A Java implementation of the SOAP protocol is well underway under the guidance of the Apache Foundation. Both of these factors bode very well indeed for the future of application interoperability among these systems.

WSDL: A Service Contract Language

Another key standard in the Web Services architecture is the Web Services Description Language, or WSDL for short. Whereas SOAP is responsible for providing a platform-neutral protocol for transporting data types and inter-application messaging, WSDL is an XML grammar responsible for exposing the methods, arguments, and return parameters exposed by a particular Web Service. As such, it plays basically the same role that the various dialects of IDL (Interface Definition Language) do within the CORBA and COM architectures. In essence, WSDL provides everything a programmer needs to consume a Web Service from defining the structure of SOAP method calls to providing code-completion and other similar capabilities within the developer's IDE.

Disco and UDDI—The Discovery Protocols

Disco and UDDI are similar in that they are both protocols used to discover the existence and capabilities of Web Services on the Internet. They differ, however, in their scope. If a developer knows that a particular URL hosts one or more Web Services, but is not aware of the capabilities offered, he or she can request an XML-formatted discovery document from the server revealing this information using the Disco protocol. If, however, as is often the case, the developer does not know beforehand the URL associated with the type of Web service he or she is trying to locate, it is necessary to query a UDDI business registry. UDDI business registries can (and probably will) be implemented themselves as Web Services and allow potential consumers of Web Services to more easily connect with the appropriate supplier.

NOTE

Although a discussion of the advanced query mechanisms and XML data structures provided by UDDI is beyond the scope of this chapter and, indeed, this book, a quick visit to Microsoft's Web site or to the UDDI homepage at `http://www.uddi.org` should serve as a good starting point for exploring this topic.

TIP

To demonstrate that the Web Services architecture is more than just a set of specifications, you should visit the following Web sites and witness firsthand the power of Web Services to transform the Web into a useful medium for hosting distributed applications.

- Microsoft Passport at `http://www.passport.com`
- Microsoft bCentral at `http://www.bcentral.com`
- Microsoft Terraserver at `http://terraserver.microsoft.net`

Writing Web Services

Now that we have a better understanding of the protocols and standards involved in creating a Web Service, we're finally ready to write one of our own. The good news is that although there are a large number of fairly complex protocols at work under the hood, the quality of Microsoft's tools and compilers hides almost of all of this complexity from us. As you'll see, a few simple keywords and command-line parameters are all that you'll really need to make fully functional Web Services a part of your next application. In addition, Visual Studio .NET provides a number of visual tools that make creating and consuming Web Services even easier.

The ASP.NET Pipeline and Handler Architecture

The first thing you'll notice when writing Web Services with ASP.NET is that their filenames end with the .asmx file extension. This unique extension allows IIS to identify the file as a Web Service and invoke the appropriate .NET runtime Web request handler to process it. The .NET runtime employs a modular pipeline architecture to process different types of Web requests. This pipelined architecture allows multiple request handlers to process a single Web request sequentially, and the modular design allows administrators to configure the order in which handlers are executed and developers to replace existing handlers or create new ones. Common request handlers include those required to execute .aspx, .asmx, and .asp file types, log application events, authenticate users, and perform session management functions.

Writing Our First Service

Let's start our project by creating a subdirectory called `testService` in our Web server's root directory. Next, open Notepad and save the empty file to the `testService` directory you just created with the filename `testService.asmx`.

Processor Directives

Processor directives are located at the beginning of global.asax, .aspx, and .asmx files and are used to configure certain compiler settings and to indicate to ASP.NET the nature of the content it is about to process. For our simple Web Service, we just need to specify the language and class name associated with the service. To accomplish this, we type the following into our newly created `testService.asmx` file:

EXAMPLE

```
<%@ WebService Language="c#" Class="testService" %>
```

The code for our first Web Service is fairly straightforward, so we'll just enter it directly into Notepad as shown in Listing 11.1.

EXAMPLE

Listing 11.1: A simple Web service using the `[WebMethod]` attribute (`11ASP01.cs.asmx`).

```
using System;
using System.Web.Services;

public class testService {
    [WebMethod]
    public string HelloWorld(string name) {
        return "Why, hello " + name + "!";
    }
}
```

The [WebMethod] Attribute

Everything you just typed in should look pretty familiar by now. Note our use of the System.Web.Services namespace. By referencing this namespace, we gain access to the [WebMethod] service attribute. This attribute is used to tag the HelloWorld(string name) method as being accessible via our Web service. Think of the [WebMethod] attribute as a sort of superpublic access modifier extending access to the method across the Internet. You can't get any more public than that!

Thanks to the dynamic nature of the ASP.NET runtime, our service will be automatically compiled the first time we attempt to access the service. All that's left is for us to test the service! Save the changes you've made to the testService.asmx file if you haven't done so already and then fire up your favorite Web browser and point it to http://localhost/testService/testService.asmx. At this point you should be presented with a generic Web Service interface similar to that shown in Figure 11.1.

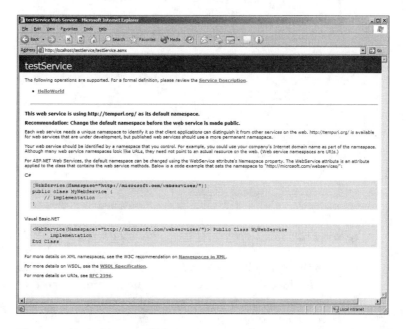

Figure 11.1: *Generic Web Service interface provided by ASP.NET.*

This interface is generated automatically by the ASP.NET runtime by examining the metadata associated with the compiled Web Service class as represented in its WSDL service contract. The WSDL service contract was likewise generated automatically by ASP.NET by examining the actual compiled class file associated with the service through a process known as reflection.

Each method marked with the [WebMethod] attribute (and therefore accessible via the Web Service) is listed in the Web Method Reference material along with information about what input parameters it requires and what values, if any, it returns. Moreover, a form-based interface that can be used to invoke the method for testing purposes is also provided.

Before we invoke our service's HelloWorld method to test the service, let's take a look at the WSDL file that ASP.NET has provided for us. Click the link entitled WSDL Contract and you should see the WSDL contract document as shown in Figure 11.2.

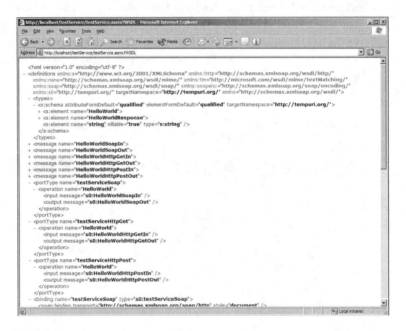

Figure 11.2: *WSDL contract associated with the HelloWorld Web Service.*

The first thing you'll notice is that the WSDL file returned to your browser is a well-formed XML document. The next thing to note is that this document describes three possible protocol bindings for the Web Service method HelloWorld. These bindings correspond to the SOAP, HTTP POST, and HTTP GET protocols respectively.

When we submit our name as a string value to the HelloWorld method, we will be using the HTTP POST protocol as defined in the service contract. According to the service contract, we can then expect to receive a string encoded using XML as a return value. The importance and value of the WSDL document cannot be understated because it allows a client application written in any language on any platform to understand the service's interface and execute against it.

Let's move on and actually test our Web Service. Use your browser's back button to return to the Web Service interface generated by ASP.NET and type your name (or the name of someone close to you whom you'd like to impress) in the form field. When you click the Invoke button, you will be presented with a screen similar to Figure 11.3 displaying the HTTP response generated by our service.

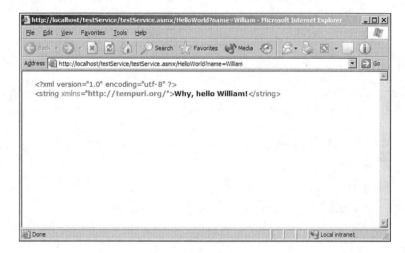

Figure 11.3: *HTTP response generated by the HelloWorld Web Service.*

Here we see that the return value has been encoded using XML within a `<string>` tag. If we had invoked the method programmatically using SOAP (as opposed to using an HTTP method from our Web browser), this tag would have been used by the client proxy to convert the value into a native string data type.

Generating a Client Proxy

The client proxy is what gives us the illusion that we are working with a simple local object when in fact much more is going on under the hood and over the Internet. It's important to emphasize that the client proxy is generated automatically for us by a simple .NET utility based on the WSDL contract provided by the ASP.NET runtime, making our job even easier. Let's generate a client proxy for our new service and use it to access our service programmatically over the Internet.

We'll start by creating a subdirectory called `testServiceClient` in the root of our c drive. Next, we'll open a command prompt, navigate to the `testServiceClient` directory, and issue the following command to generate the client proxy for our service:

TIP

If you're sure you've installed the .NET SDK properly but the command line reports that wsdl.exe and csc.exe are not recognized as "internal or external" commands, you might need to add the directories associated with these programs to your path. At the time of this writing, the default install paths for these programs were `C:\Program Files\Microsoft.NET\FrameworkSDK\Bin` and `C:\WINNT\Microsoft.NET\Framework\v1.0.2914`. Because these locations are likely to change by the time you read this tip, you should search your hard drive for wsdl.exe and csc.exe to find the proper paths to include for your system.

EXAMPLE

```
wsdl /language:CS /out:testServiceProxy.cs http://localhost/testService/
➥ testService.asmx?wsdl
```

After issuing this command, you should see something similar to Figure 11.4 as output on your display:

OUTPUT

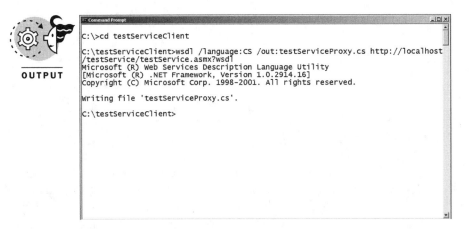

Figure 11.4: *Creating a Web Service client proxy from the command line.*

And that's it! We now have a client proxy that will allow us to program against our Web Service from within any .NET application from anywhere on the Internet! Before we use the proxy as part of a client application, however, let's take a closer look at the command-line parameters we used. The `/language:CS` parameter indicates that we want the application to generate our client proxy as C# code. Notice that we supplied a URL to access the service directly rather than the service's WSDL file. Although we could have provided the WSDL file ourselves by specifying the URL of the service, instead we save an extra step and ensure that our proxy will work against the latest version of the service. The `/out:` parameter indicates the location and filename where we'd like the proxy source code to be generated. Although C# code is generated by default, you can easily use the `/language:` parameter to specify a different target language, such as Visual Basic.

Now let's take a look at Figure 11.5 showing the client proxy code that Wsdl.exe generated to gain some insight into how we'd write such a proxy ourselves if .NET hadn't been nice enough to do the job for us.

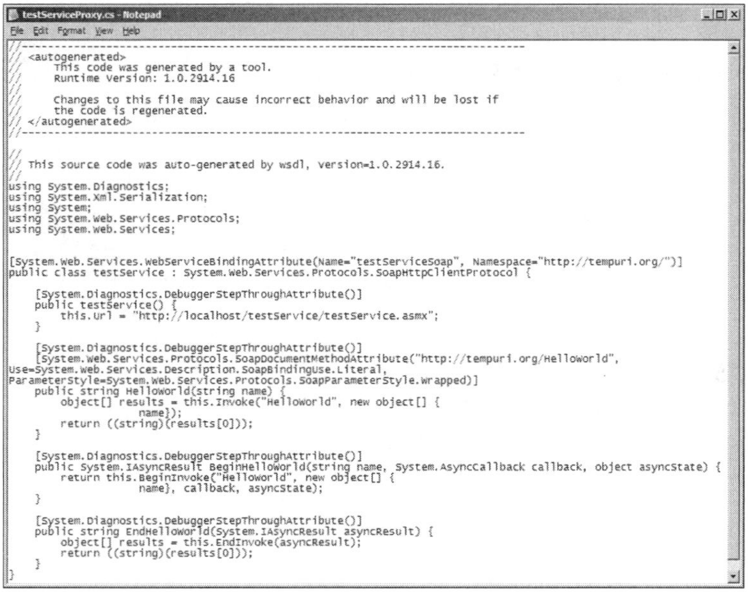

```
testServiceProxy.cs - Notepad
File Edit Format View Help
//------------------------------------------------------------------------------
// <autogenerated>
//     This code was generated by a tool.
//     Runtime Version: 1.0.2914.16
//
//     Changes to this file may cause incorrect behavior and will be lost if
//     the code is regenerated.
// </autogenerated>
//------------------------------------------------------------------------------

//
// This source code was auto-generated by wsdl, Version=1.0.2914.16.
//
using System.Diagnostics;
using System.Xml.Serialization;
using System;
using System.Web.Services.Protocols;
using System.Web.Services;


[System.Web.Services.WebServiceBindingAttribute(Name="testServiceSoap", Namespace="http://tempuri.org/")]
public class testService : System.Web.Services.Protocols.SoapHttpClientProtocol {

    [System.Diagnostics.DebuggerStepThroughAttribute()]
    public testService() {
        this.Url = "http://localhost/testService/testService.asmx";
    }

    [System.Diagnostics.DebuggerStepThroughAttribute()]
    [System.Web.Services.Protocols.SoapDocumentMethodAttribute("http://tempuri.org/HelloWorld",
Use=System.Web.Services.Description.SoapBindingUse.Literal,
ParameterStyle=System.Web.Services.Protocols.SoapParameterStyle.Wrapped)]
    public string HelloWorld(string name) {
        object[] results = this.Invoke("HelloWorld", new object[] {
                    name});
        return ((string)(results[0]));
    }

    [System.Diagnostics.DebuggerStepThroughAttribute()]
    public System.IAsyncResult BeginHelloWorld(string name, System.AsyncCallback callback, object asyncState) {
        return this.BeginInvoke("HelloWorld", new object[] {
                    name}, callback, asyncState);
    }

    [System.Diagnostics.DebuggerStepThroughAttribute()]
    public string EndHelloWorld(System.IAsyncResult asyncResult) {
        object[] results = this.EndInvoke(asyncResult);
        return ((string)(results[0]));
    }
}
```

Figure 11.5: *HelloWorld Web Service client proxy code.*

Immediately after the comment lines at the beginning of the file, we see references to several system libraries. Although `System.xml.Serialization` has been included by default, our client proxy does not use it. XML serialization is an advanced feature that allows complex data types, such as datasets and other system and user-defined classes, to be converted to XML so that they can be transmitted using SOAP. We'll see an example of this later in the chapter.

Also worth mentioning is `System.Web.Services.Protocols`. You'll notice that our client proxy class `TestService` inherits from this library's `SoapHttpClientProtocol` class. Here we see the beauty of object-oriented design in action. All our proxy class has to do in order to utilize the networking, protocol, serialization, and marshalling services that comprise the Web Services architecture is to simply inherit this functionality from the `SoapHttpClientProtocol` class.

The no argument constructor for the client proxy sets the URL parameter of the superclass to the address of the Web Service so that communication between the client and server can take place. Next, a public `HelloWorld` method is defined that invokes our Web Service's `HelloWorld` method and casts the result to a native string data type from the generic object type returned. Because our proxy will have to wait for a response from the Web Service after we've invoked the `HelloWorld` method, two utility methods are defined to handle this in an asynchronous fashion.

A Simple Web Service Client

Web Services won't change the world unless there are clients out there who use them—so let's get to work! Now that we've generated our proxy class, we just need to type our test client code into Notepad, save it, compile the test client and proxy classes together, and then run the program. Launch Notepad, type in the bit of code in Listing 11.2, and then save the file as `testServiceClient.cs` in the `C:\testServiceClient` directory.

EXAMPLE

Listing 11.2: A simple Web Service client (11ASP02.cs).

```
using System;
class testServiceClass {
    static void Main() {
    testService myTest = new testService();
    string response = myTest.HelloWorld("William");
        Console.WriteLine(response);
    }
}
```

Again, this is pretty much boilerplate code. In fact, we don't even need to specify any `using` statements to reference any special libraries because all of the architectural plumbing associated with remote access to Web Services is handled by the proxy class. All that there is left for us to do is to create an instance of the `TestService` class and call the `HelloWorld` method on it.

Before we can run our client application, however, we will need to compile both the `TestService` proxy and our new `testServiceClass` using the following command:

EXAMPLE

```
csc /r:System.Web.dll,System.Web.Services.dll,System.XML.dll,System.dll
➥ testServiceClient.cs testServiceProxy.cs
```

Here we are using the `/r:` parameter to indicate to the C# compiler which system libraries will be utilized by our application. In addition, we specify which source files we'd like to compile. The resulting executable is called testServiceClient.exe. If you run this application, you should receive output similar to that in Figure 11.6.

At this point, it is useful to take a look at a simplified version of the SOAP message that is actually being sent to the Web Service when you run the client.

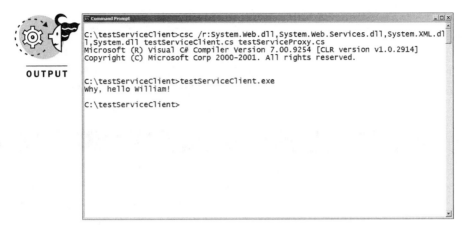

```
C:\testServiceClient>csc /r:System.Web.dll,System.Web.Services.dll,System.XML.dl
l,System.dll testServiceClient.cs testServiceProxy.cs
Microsoft (R) Visual C# Compiler Version 7.00.9254 [CLR version v1.0.2914]
Copyright (C) Microsoft Corp 2000-2001. All rights reserved.


C:\testServiceClient>testServiceClient.exe
Why, hello William!

C:\testServiceClient>
```

Figure 11.6: Sample output from testServiceClient.

EXAMPLE

```xml
<?xml version="1.0"?>
<soap:Envelope xmlns:soap="http://schemas.xmlsoap.org/soap/...>
    <soap:Body>
        <HellowWorld xmlns="http://tempuri.org">
            <name>William</name>
        </HelloWorld>
    </soap:Body>
</soap:Envelope>
```

As you can see, the SOAP message itself is made up of two major sections. The SOAP envelope identifies the various XML namespaces associated with SOAP messaging and contains the SOAP body, which carries the actual message being sent between systems. A third element, the SOAP header, is optional and carries data about the message such as that relating to transactions, authentication, and payment.

The body contains, at a minimum, the name of the method that is being invoked and any argument values that are passed to it. Here we see that one argument, name, with the value William is being passed to the HelloWorld method. Notice that it's very easy to read and understand a SOAP message as opposed to those encoded by binary protocols such as DCOM, RMI, and IIOP. Also notice that there is nothing Microsoft-proprietary going on here—it's all just straight XML and SOAP.

Now let's look at a simplified response message:

EXAMPLE

```xml
<?xml version="1.0"?>
<soap:Envelope xmlns:soap="http://schemas.xmlsoap.org/soap/...>
    <soap:Body>
        <HellowWorldResult xmlns="http://tempuri.org">
            <result>Why, hello William!</result>
```

```
        </HelloWorldResult>
    </soap:Body>
</soap:Envelope>
```

A SOAP response looks remarkably similar to a request. Here we see that `Why, hello William!` is returned as a result of the invocation of the `HelloWorld` method.

Advanced Topics

Yes, creating Web Services really is this simple. However, writing a "good" Web Service usually isn't. So far we've glossed over several important issues you're going to face when you try to implement your own Web Services.

First, there's the issue of complex types. How do we send custom classes of our own devising to clients that may reside on a different platform and be written in a wholly different language? Second, we all know the Internet is an unruly place, so what happens when delays interrupt our service in mid-transaction? Do the service and client application just stall until the connection is restored, or is there a better way to handle the situation? The answers to these questions are not overly complex, but they will add additional complexity to your application.

Also, if you're an old hand at Web application programming in the Windows environment, you're probably asking yourself, "How do I access all of the application support services that were provided under the Windows DNA model?" Specifically, you want to know how to use Microsoft Message Queue Server (MSMQ) and Microsoft Transaction Server (MTS) from within your Web Services. The fact is that both of these technologies are tightly integrated into the .NET architecture and programming model and are therefore available for you to use within your Web Services. The caveat, however, is that not all of these features are available as part of the SOAP protocol, so if you intend for your Web Services to interoperate with those hosted on non-Microsoft platforms, you will run into some limitations.

In this section we'll learn how to handle complex types and make our Web Service applications more resilient to the depredations that the Internet will inflict upon them. We'll also take a quick look at how and when MTS and MSMQ are used within Microsoft's implementation of the Web Services architecture. Near the end of the section, we'll take some time to gaze into our crystal ball and try to imagine how messaging and transaction handling functionality could evolve away from Microsoft's current proprietary MSMQ and MTS implementations to eventually become a part of the SOAP protocol itself.

Returning Complex Types

As mentioned previously, complex data types such as datasets and user-defined types (structs and classes) can be transmitted using SOAP. This feat is accomplished through a process known as XML serialization. XML serialization in turn depends upon another process known as reflection. Reflection represents the .NET runtime's ability to examine and expose the internal structure of any .NET class. XML serialization takes this structural information, combines it with the actual data associated with an object of the reflected class, and transforms the result into an XML message suitable for transmission via the SOAP protocol. The inverse of this process allows the original object to be recreated by the SOAP message recipient.

To demonstrate, let's modify our testService application to return a complex data type. First, modify the testService.asmx file to resemble Listing 11.3.

EXAMPLE

Listing 11.3: A Web Service that returns a complex type (11ASP03.cs.asmx).

```
<%@ WebService Language="C#" Class="testService" %>

using System;
using System.Web.Services;

public class Greeting {
    public String name;
    public String salutation;
    public String honorific;
}

public class testService {
    [WebMethod]
    public Greeting HelloWorld(string name) {
        Greeting myGreeting = new Greeting();

        myGreeting.name = name;
        myGreeting.salutation = "Why, hello";
        myGreeting.honorific = "Dr.";

        return myGreeting;
    }
}
```

What we've done is added a simple class called Greeting with three public member variables to our Web Service. Then, we modified the original testService class to create a new instance of the Greeting class, populate its member variables, and return the Greeting object as a result whenever the HelloWorld method is invoked.

Next, point your browser to http://localhost/testService/testService.asmx and invoke the HelloWorld method using your name as the parameter. The result that you see on your screen should look similar to the following and is the XML serialization of the Greeting class's structure and data.

OUTPUT

```
<?xml version="1.0" encoding="utf-8" ?>
<Greeting xmlns:xsi="http://www.w3.org/2001/XMLSchema-instance"
➥ xmlns:xsd="http://www.w3.org/2001/XMLSchema" xmlns="http://tempuri.org/">
    <name>William</name>
    <salutation>Why, hello</salutation>
    <honorific>Dr.</honorific>
</Greeting>
```

Again, it's important to note that SOAP is an open standard officially submitted to the W3C. Just as a .NET client application can easily deserialize this XML representation back into a native .NET object, a SOAP-enabled Java or CORBA runtime could just as easily deserialize it into a Java or CORBA object.

NOTE

It's technically incorrect to say that SOAP can serialize and deserialize an object instance. When we use the word *object* or *class*, we automatically imply behavior (methods) as well as data (attributes). As a result, we should be careful to observe that what SOAP is really doing is transmitting the data associated with an object instance and not the object instance itself. By way of comparison, serialization in the Java world is capable of transmitting both an object's data and behavior across a network. This functionality can be simulated, however, by casting a SOAP-encoded complex type to a local class type that implements the relevant behavior and data representation capabilities.

Let's try one more example of returning a complex data type. This time, we'll return a dataset object to the client using the SOAP protocol. You might not have SQL Server installed, so we'll just reconstitute a serialized dataset to get things going. When our dataset is reconstituted, it will act no differently than if a production SQL Server system had provided the information. The dataset, serialized as XML and presented in Listing 11.4, can either be typed in exactly as given or, better yet, downloaded from our Web site. In either case, you should name the file authors.xml and place it in the c:\inetpub\wwwroot\testService directory along with our other Web Service files.

EXAMPLE

Listing 11.4: Sample XML dataset(11ASP04.xml).

```
<?xml version="1.0" standalone="yes"?>
<NewDataSet>
    <authors>
        <au_lname>Arnaud</au_lname>
        <au_fname>Clay</au_fname>
```

Listing 11.4: continued

```
        <au_id>22187</au_id>
    </authors>
    <authors>
        <au_lname>Bulla</au_lname>
        <au_fname>Brent</au_fname>
        <au_id>22314</au_id>
    </authors>
    <authors>
        <au_lname>Caudron</au_lname>
        <au_fname>Tom</au_fname>
        <au_id>77612</au_id>
    </authors>
</NewDataSet>
```

Next, we will create a new Web Service called `testDSService.asmx` that will return to the caller a dataset representing the contents of the `authors.xml` file. Again, you'll need to type the code in Listing 11.5 into Notepad and save the file as `testDSService.asmx` and place it in the `c:\inetpub\ wwwroot\testService` directory along with our other Web Service files.

EXAMPLE

Listing 11.5: A Web Service that returns a dataset (11ASP05.cs.asmx).

```
<%@ WebService Language="C#" Class="testDSService" %>

using System;
using System.Web.Services;
using System.Data;
using System.Xml;

public class testDSService {

    [WebMethod]
    public DataSet getDataSet() {

        DataSet ds = new DataSet();
        ds.ReadXml(@"c:\inetpub\wwwroot\testService\authors.xml");

        return ds;
    }
}
```

The `testDSService` class is fairly straightforward. If you'd like to test it before moving on, just point your browser to `http://localhost/testService/ testDSService.asmx` and click the Invoke button. What you'll see is the serialized XML representation of the dataset returned to your browser—a neat trick but not all that useful in this format.

The real power of .NET's ability to serialize complex data types using XML and SOAP becomes apparent when our Web Service is consumed by a client application. Our next step, therefore, is to build such a client. To accomplish this, we will follow the pattern we outlined previously:

- Create the Web Service proxy using the Wsdl.exe utility.
- Create the Web Service client application using Notepad.
- Compile the client code and Web Service proxy classes using the C# compiler.

To create the proxy class that our client will use to talk to our new Web Service, go into the `C:\testServiceClient` directory and issue the following command:

```
Wsdl.exe /language:CS /out:testDSServiceProxy.cs http://localhost/
➡ testService/testDSService.asmx?WSDL
```

EXAMPLE

Next, launch Notepad and type in the code in Listing 11.6. Once you're done save the file as `testDSServiceClient.cs` in the `C:\testServiceClient` directory.

Listing 11.6: Sample Web Service client that retrieves a dataset (`11ASP06.cs`).

EXAMPLE

```csharp
using System;
using System.Data;

class testDSServiceClass {

    static void Main() {

        testDSService myTest = new testDSService();

        DataSet response = myTest.getDataSet();

        Console.WriteLine("DataSet retrieved...here comes the data!");
        foreach(DataRow row in response.Tables["authors"].Rows)
            Console.WriteLine(row["au_lname"].ToString());
    }
}
```

Lastly, issue the following command to compile the service proxy and client classes and then run the resulting executable.

```
csc /r:System.Web.dll,System.Web.Services.dll,System.XML.dll,System.dll,
➡ System.Data.dll testDSServiceClient.cs testDSServiceProxy.cs
```

EXAMPLE

The results should look similar to Figure 11.7.

OUTPUT

Figure 11.7: Sample output from testDSServiceClient.

When execution reaches line 10, we retrieve the DataSet object from our Web Service and then proceed to iterate through each row, printing the last name of each author in the table as we go along. Pretty simple, isn't it? In fact, this example is so simple that you might be in danger of failing to appreciate what life would be like without the .NET framework and Web Services architecture to lend a helping hand. Even in a relatively simple homogeneous environment composed of similarly versioned Microsoft products, it can still be an onerous and time-consuming process to marshal and unmarshal data across a remote connection and then reconstitute this data in a type-safe way on the client side. Now imagine just how difficult this would be to do in a completely generic cross-platform manner across a variety of HTTP protocols. Now imagine doing so in a manner almost completely seamless to the client application developer. The mind reels! And all of this effort would have nothing to do with the actual business logic you were attempting to implement on top of all of this plumbing code. Furthermore, chances are good that you would not have the time to make an equivalent system totally generic across all object types and would be forced to reinvent this code (perhaps using design patterns) for every project that required similar services!

Asynchronous Processing

Although the examples we have looked at so far have helped to demonstrate the key concepts associated with programming Web Services, these same applications would never stand up to the punishment that can and will be inflicted on them by the Internet. Any real-world scenario involving deployment across the Internet has to account for long delays in message delivery as well as outright delivery failure. Moreover, because you'll probably be using third-party services that you have no direct control over, your own applications have to be resilient even when services they depend upon are temporarily unavailable.

One basic problem inherent to all of our examples thus far is that they have been programmed to process SOAP responses synchronously. What this means is that when your application invokes a method exposed by some Web Service, it will stop in its tracks and won't resume execution until it receives a response. This is called *blocking* and is a bad thing when it comes to making your Web Services scalable, responsive, and resistant to failure. This might not seem like much of a problem when running Web Services on a development workstation or local area network, but it will quickly become a huge problem when you try to deploy your application on the Internet.

Fortunately, most of the work required to support the asynchronous processing of SOAP responses has already been done for us and is just sitting there in our service proxy code waiting to be used by our client! Take another look at the TestDSServiceProxy.cs file and take particular note of the following two methods:

EXAMPLE

```
public System.IAsyncResult BegingetDataSet(System.AsyncCallback callback,
➡ object asyncState) {
    return this.BeginInvoke("getDataSet", new object[0], callback, asyncState);
}
public System.Data.DataSet EndgetDataSet(System.IAsyncResult asyncResult) {
    object[] results = this.EndInvoke(asyncResult);
    return ((System.Data.DataSet)(results[0]));
}
```

All we have to do to enable our client to process SOAP responses asynchronously is to modify our code to use the methods provided by the proxy for this purpose. Consider the code in Listing 11.7.

EXAMPLE

Listing 11.7: Sample asynchronous Web Service client (s).

```
using System;
using System.Data;

class testDSServiceClass {
    static IAsyncResult asyncResult;

    static void Main() {
    testDSService myTest = new testDSService();

        // Begin asynchronous call to retrieve authors list dataset...
        asyncResult = myTest.BegingetDataSet(null, null);

        // Poll for completion.  This effectively blocks but proper threading
```

Listing 11.7: continued

```
        // would allow this operation to be carried out asynchronously...
        while(!asyncResult.IsCompleted);

        // Get the results!
        DataSet response = myTest.EndgetDataSet(asyncResult);

        Console.WriteLine("DataSet retrieved...here comes the data!");
        foreach(DataRow row in response.Tables["authors"].Rows)
        Console.WriteLine(row["au_fname"].ToString());
    }
}
```

When we execute the `BegingetDataSet(null, null)` method exposed by our
Web Service proxy, we are passed back an instance of `IAsyncResult`. This
object communicates with the Web Service on our behalf in a non-blocking
fashion. Next, we enter into a conditional loop that polls our `IAsyncResult`
object repeatedly until it indicates that it has received a response from the
Web Service. Although this is tantamount to blocking within the context of
our current application, we could also have continued with some other processing and polled for completion periodically, perhaps within a separate
thread of execution.

When the `IAsyncResult` object indicates that a response to our request has
been received, we execute the `EndgetDataSet(asyncResult)` method and
then proceed to process the resulting `DataSet` object.

Transaction Support

Failure happens. When someone kicks the plug out of the wall, a system
board component fails, or sunspot activity twiddles a crucial bit in your L2
cache, even the most crashproof of systems will fail. To make matters
worse, if a crash happens in the middle of processing an important batch of
instructions, your application could be left in an inconsistent state. Using
transaction services such as those provided by MTS, however, can minimize
the risk of catastrophic (or even just annoying) data loss in mission-critical
systems.

Without going into great detail, transactional systems recover gracefully
from failure by monitoring all operations that occur within the boundaries
of a specified transaction. If all operations are successful, all resources
involved in the transaction are told to commit modified data to persistent
storage. If even one operation is unsuccessful, however, all resources
involved are instructed to roll back any modifications to data that were
made and act as if the entire transaction had never happened. Although
such a policy might seem like overkill, the reality is that it's almost always
better to do nothing than to do something wrong. The ubiquitous check

cashing example is often called upon to reinforce this notion. Imagine that your bank account deposit routine crashes in the middle of processing that $1,000.00 check you just sent to your mortgage company. After the smoke clears, it turns out that the debit to your account has occurred, but the corresponding credit was never made to your lender. Ouch! No wonder this example is always used to emphasize why an all-or-nothing approach to transaction handling is a good idea!

Although a full description of MTS and its programming model is beyond the scope of this chapter, it is relevant to note that at a basic level all you need to do to transaction-enable a particular Web Service method is to modify the WebMethod attribute to look like the following:

```
[WebMethod(Transaction=Transaction.Required)]
```

There are a number of additional options other than just the Transaction.Required parameter that you can use to control your methods transactional behavior. Although enabling transactions within your own Web Services is easy enough, using transactions in an effective and efficient way is a complex subject and designing good transaction support into large, complex systems is still a tough job. What Microsoft has done for us, however, is bundle the basic transactional services we need with the OS and expose this functionality in a very intuitive way. The rest, as always, is up to you.

Programming Web Services with Microsoft Visual Studio .NET

Now that we've paid our dues and learned how to do things the hard way, we'll take a look at support for Web Services in Visual Studio .NET. Although the Web Services architecture is based on well-defined XML standards, the devil—at least for the developer—is in the details. As a result, Microsoft hopes to differentiate itself in the market for Web Services by providing tools for developers that can automate the creation, testing, and debugging of Web Services and thereby increase developer productivity. For the rest of this chapter, we'll focus on learning how to create and consume Web Services within the context of the Visual Studio .NET development environment.

Creating Web Services in Visual Studio .NET

As with other types of projects supported by Visual Studio .NET, creating a new Web Service follows the same familiar New Project Wizard paradigm. To get started, choose File, New, Project to open the New Project dialog box. Then, from the Visual C# Projects folder, select ASP.NET Web Service. We'll also give our new Web Service a distinctive name, in this case testVSWebService, and ensure that the Location parameter is set to specify our local machine at http://localhost. When we're finished, the New Project dialog box should look like Figure 11.8.

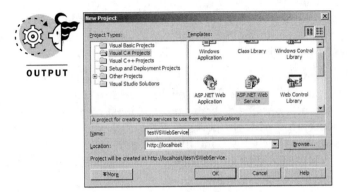

OUTPUT

Figure 11.8: Visual Studio .NET's New Project dialog box.

Next, click OK and wait for the system to trundle through the process of populating our new project with a number of supporting files. When the process is complete, the Solution Explorer window should look like Figure 11.9.

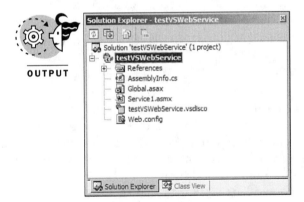

OUTPUT

Figure 11.9: The Solution Explorer view displays files associated with your solution and related projects.

You'll notice a lot of files here that we didn't create when hand-coding and compiling our previous Web Services using the command-line tools. Most of these files contain boilerplate Visual Studio .NET configuration data. A few, however, will warrant our attention a little later on. For now, though, let's test our Web Service to make sure everything is working properly.

Because Web Services built using Visual Studio .NET use ASP.NET's code-behind feature, we'll need to compile our application before we can view its default interface. Use of the code-behind feature has a few other implications that we'll consider in a short while. To build the project, just press Ctrl+Shift+B or choose Build, Rebuild All. Next, right-click on Service1.asmx, the default name for our new Web Service, and select View in Browser to test the service.

As you might have noticed, our new Web Service is a little thin on functionality. Conveniently, Microsoft provides a few lines of sample code that we can use to make our new service do something at least semi-useful. To view the source code associated with the service, right-click on Service1.asmx in Solution Explorer and select View Code from the pop-up menu. Next, scroll down to the bottom of the file and uncomment the following lines by removing the preceding double slash marks.

EXAMPLE

```
//    [WebMethod]
//    public string HelloWorld()
//    {
//        return "Hello World";
//    }
```

Rebuild the project and view it in the browser once again to test your changes. Adding your own functionality proceeds similarly in that you just have to add new methods to implement your business logic and include the [WebMethod] attribute to expose them across the Internet.

Visual Studio .NET Project Structure

After seeing all of the files listed in Solution Explorer, you might have asked yourself, "Isn't Visual Studio .NET supposed to make my life as a developer easier and less complicated?" In fact, there are a few more files that Visual Studio .NET hides from our view to reduce the amount of confusing clutter on the screen. To view them, just click the Show All Files icon in the Solution Explorer minitoolbar and then expand all of the nodes in the project. The results should look similar to Figure 11.10.

As you've seen in previous chapters, many of these files are just glue holding the Visual Studio .NET solution and its project files together. A few others store various bits of configuration data about our application that are usually modified using the Visual Studio .NET interface. The files that we don't usually need to worry about when building Web Services with Visual Studio .NET (or that aren't specific to Web Service projects) are testVSWebService.sln, Service1.asmx.resx, AssemblyInfo.cs, Web.config, Global.asax and Global.asax.cs, testVSWebService.csproj, testVSWebService.csproj.webinfo, and of course, bin\testVSWebService.dll and bin\testVSWebService.pdb.

Figure 11.10: *In the Solution Explorer, the Show All Files option has been enabled.*

.ASMX AND .ASMX.CS/.ASMX.VB FILES

Of the remaining files, the two most important are `Service1.asmx` and `Service1.asmx.cs`. Together, these two files constitute a Web service that has been built using the code-behind approach. The code-behind approach is designed to clearly separate the browsable files accessible to users of our service (located in `.asmx` files) from the code that actually implements the service (located in `.asmx.cs` files). In practice this just means that the processing directive now lives alone in the `.asmx` file and is modified to point to the implementation stored in the `.asmx.cs` file. Let's take a look at the modified processing directive from `Service1.asmx`.

```
<%@ WebService Language="c#" Codebehind="Service1.asmx.cs"
Class="testVSWebService.Service1" %>
```

EXAMPLE

Notice that the `Codebehind` parameter points to the C# source file that implements our Web Service. In addition, the `Class` parameter indicates the specific .NET namespace and class our Web Service derives its functionality from. Now let's look at the contents of `Service1.asmx.cs` in a little more detail.

```
using System;
using System.Collections;
using System.ComponentModel;
using System.Data;
using System.Diagnostics;
using System.Web;
using System.Web.Services;

namespace testVSWebService
{
```

EXAMPLE

```
/// <summary>
/// Summary description for Service1.
/// </summary>
public class Service1 : System.Web.Services.WebService {
    public Service1() {
        //CODEGEN: This call is required by the
        // ASP.NET Web Services Designer
        InitializeComponent();
    }

    #region Component Designer generated code
    /// <summary>
    /// Required method for Designer support - do not modify
    /// the contents of this method with the code editor.
    /// </summary>
    private void InitializeComponent() { }
    #endregion

    /// <summary>
    /// Clean up any resources being used.
    /// </summary>
    protected override void Dispose( bool disposing ) { }

    // WEB SERVICE EXAMPLE
    // The HelloWorld() example service returns the string Hello World
    // To build, uncomment the following lines then
    // save and build the project
    // To test this Web Service, press F5

//      [WebMethod]
//      public string HelloWorld() {
//          return "Hello World";
//      }
    }
}
```

The first thing to note is the inclusion of a lot of additional namespaces. This is pretty typical of tool-generated code. In this case, the namespaces relevant to Web Services and Web applications in general are included along with those necessary to enable ASP.NET's form designer.

You'll also notice that Visual Studio .NET includes a default namespace for our Web Service derived from the name of our project as well as copious comments (often in pseudo-XML format) that we can parse out into a help file if we ever get the urge. In addition, you'll find two protected methods, InitializeComponent() and Dispose(), that you'll see in most if not all ASP.NET applications built with Visual Studio .NET.

The important difference to note between our hand-coded Web Services and those generated by Visual Studio .NET is the use of `System.Web.Services. WebService` as a base class. By deriving from this class, our Web Service has access to the ASP.NET intrinsic objects for managing session state including the `Application`, `Session`, and `Request` objects. Although our simple examples don't require these services, it's important to realize that more complex Web services, especially those involving state management and session security, will need to use the services that these objects provide.

.VSDISCO FILES

Another important file generated by Visual Studio .NET is `testVSWebService.vsdisco`. As of the time of this writing, Microsoft's SDK defines a `.vsdisco` file as *"An XML-based file that contains links (URLs) to resources providing discovery information for a Web Service."* Because the Disco protocol is currently in a state of flux, I'll leave it at that for now and refer you to the documentation that comes with the Microsoft .NET SDK. I certainly have my doubts as to whether what I'm looking at today when I browse a .vsdisco file will look anything at all like what you'll be seeing on your screen after the publication of this book. The important thing to realize is that Visual Studio .NET will automatically generate the documents necessary to allow potential users of your Web Services to poll your Web server and "discover" what you've made available. Of course, you can always choose not to deploy the `.vsdisco` file if you would like the presence of your services to remain private.

It is also important to note that while Disco and UDDI are similar in that they are both used by third parties to "discover" Web Services, they differ greatly in terms of scope. Whereas UDDI directories provide lists of services available from a range of enterprises across a range of servers, Disco is primarily designed to allow third parties to enumerate the services installed on a particular Web server.

Consuming Web Services in Visual Studio .NET

Before we close the book (or at least the chapter) on Web Services let's create a simple Web application to consume a Web Service using Visual Studio .NET. We'll start off by creating a new ASP.NET Web application called `testVSWebServiceClient` on our local machine. If you need a refresher on how to use the New Project Wizard to accomplish this task, refer back to the section "Creating Web Services in Visual Studio .NET."

When our ASP.NET Web application project has been created, we'll add a reference to the Web Service we want to consume by selecting Project, Add Web Reference. The resulting dialog box should look similar to that pictured in Figure 11.11.

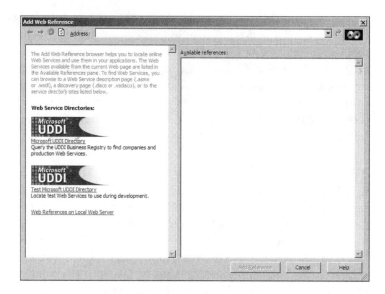

Figure 11.11: *The Add Web Reference dialog box automates the process of adding support for Web Services to your project.*

As its name implies, the Add Web Reference dialog box allows you to add references to Web Services to your Visual Studio .NET projects. Conceptually, the process of adding a reference to a Web Service is almost identical to adding a reference to a type library or COM object. As with type libraries and COM objects, adding a reference to a Web Service exposes its methods for use within our application and enables the Visual Studio .NET IDE to provide us with code-completion and other productivity enhancements.

Services can be referenced by searching UDDI directories, specifying a disco file located on a local or remote server, or by providing the URL of a known service. For the purpose of this exercise, we'll choose the Web References on Local Web Server link. At this point, the list of Available References displayed will include all of the Web Services available on our local machine. From this list, select the testVSWebService.vsdisco link and then click the Add Reference button.

We'll also need some way to invoke our Web Service and to display its results. From the toolbox, drop a button and a label onto the WebForm1.aspx form designer. Next, double-click the button to edit the Button1_Click event and insert the following code to invoke the Web Service:

```
localhost.Service1 myService = new localhost.Service1();
Label1.Text = myService.HelloWorld();
```

EXAMPLE

The code listed here is simple enough. The first line creates an instance of the Web Service proxy class called `myService` and the second line invokes its `HelloWorld()` method and assigns the result to the label's text property. Notice that by default the namespace of our Web Service is the URL of the server that hosts it. We can easily change this name in the Solution Explorer if we want to make it something a bit more meaningful, which is probably a good idea in production code. Also notice that after you type the service's namespace and subsequent trailing dot (that is, after typing `localhost.` into the IDE), code-completion kicks in and displays a list of available methods exposed by the service just as if it were a class or COM object local to our machine.

To see our client in action, build the project and then press F5 to begin execution. A simple Web form will be displayed containing the button and label we added previously. All that's left is for you to click the button and watch in awe as hundreds of thousands of lines of code churn under the hood of the OS to produce the result depicted in Figure 11.12.

Figure 11.12: A Web Application client consuming a Web Service.

Before we move on, a few additional items are worth mentioning. First, debugging Web Service and Web Service client applications using Visual Studio .NET is identical to debugging other ASP.NET applications. If you are debugging a Web Service on your local machine, it is trivial to step back and forth between client code to service code as long as both the service and client projects are located within the same Visual Studio .NET solution. In this configuration, Web Services and the applications that consume them are a true joy to work with and the productivity gains associated with using the Visual Studio .NET IDE versus the command-line tools come clearly into focus.

Also, as with other types of ASP.NET applications, deploying a Web Service from a development to a production machine can usually be accomplished just by copying the application's Web directory structure from one server to another. Another option is to use the Web Setup Project wizard to create an `.msi` installation package the same way you would with any ASP.NET application. Yet another option is to use the Web Hosting option available from the Visual Studio Start Page. This option is great for validating that your service will really work when accessed remotely across the Internet and is definitely useful when trying to impress your friends and coworkers.

TIP

For more information on publishing your Web Services to UDDI, see Microsoft's UDDI SDK at `http://uddi.microsoft.com` or visit `http://www.uddi.org` for more information.

Summary

Although we have focused on the implementation of Web Services using Microsoft's ASP.NET architecture, similar technologies provided by both Sun and IBM exist for those enmeshed in the world of Java programming. Although at the time of this writing these tools were, at least in this author's opinion, less well-integrated and "user-friendly" than their Microsoft counterparts, it is important even for dyed-in-the-wool Microsoft-only developers to realize that it is relatively easy for Web Services to be created and consumed by applications written using different platforms and tools.

TIP

For more information on Web Services within the context of Java development, you should visit a few of the following Web sites for more extensive and up-to-date information.

- IBM's DeveloperWorks Web-Services Homepage (`http://www.ibm.com/developerworks/webservices/`)

- Apache SOAP Implementation (`http://xml.apache.org/soap/index.html`)

Before coming to a (seemingly inevitable) conclusion regarding the success or failure of the Web Services architecture, let's review the benefits it provides:

- Virtually seamless interoperability between heterogeneous systems

- The ability to connect organizations through firewalls without compromising security

- Broad industry support from virtually every major player in the software development market

- An open, standards-based architecture

Given the importance of these factors to corporations attempting to provide integrated business services over the Internet, it is fair to say that rarely has so much potential been realized in a product that requires so little in the way of deployment costs and retraining.

What's Next?

Now that you've conquered Web services, we'll take a look at how to augment, reuse, and extend the functionality of the built-in ASP.NET server controls. By using custom controls you can achieve greater flexibility in how you design your ASP.NET application In addition, custom controls can be deployed and distributed as compiled code allowing you to keep your original source code private.

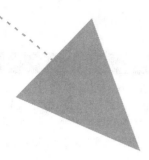

12

Custom ASP.NET Server Controls

One of the most exciting things about ASP.NET is that it is built on top of the .NET Framework, a very powerful platform with which to build applications. It is this platform that makes it possible for us easily to build on and extend the controls that ship with ASP.NET, adding any customized functionality that we need for our applications.

In this chapter we will

- Define what we mean by Controls and Components
- Compare Custom Controls with User Controls
- Examine some third-party controls
- Build a Custom Control
- Use a Custom Control in an ASP.NET page
- Build a Composite Control
- Build a Templated Control

Custom Controls Defined

We've seen quite a variety of controls so far in this book, and in this chapter we're adding one more: custom controls. However, we're going to also look at *components* at the end of the chapter, so it would help if we had a good understanding of just what a *control* is, compared to a *component*, or even just a simple *class*.

According to the .NET documentation, a *control* is defined as any object that is derived, either directly or indirectly, from the `System.Web.UI.Control` class. All the controls discussed in earlier chapters derive from this class at some point in their hierarchy. Apart from this distinction, the primary difference between a control, and any other custom piece of functionality, is that it renders User Interface (UI) logic. A *component*, on the other hand, is an object that performs some behind-the-scenes logic for an application but is not a part of the application's UI. One common type of component retrieves data from a database; these are typically referred to as data access components. Finally, a *class* is simply a blueprint for an object, and in the .NET world, both *controls* and *components* are built using *classes*.

All the samples in this chapter are in C#. The VB.NET versions of the samples can be viewed at `http://aspauthors.com/aspnetbyexample/ch12/`.

Custom Controls Versus User Controls

In Chapter 9, you learned how to build your own user controls to encapsulate frequently used pieces of your ASP.NET pages. Custom controls serve a purpose that is very similar to user controls, and in fact often you will find that the same task could be accomplished using either a user control or a custom control. User controls are designed to be used for large sections of your ASP.NET pages, and in fact they were originally going to be named Pagelets. User controls are typically easier to build and deploy than custom controls, because you can place all your HTML logic and other controls into the .ascx file, and you can deploy the user control without having to compile it first. Custom controls, on the other hand, must handle all their user interface logic programmatically, and must be compiled into assemblies and distributed before they can be used.

Writing a custom control of your own in an editor like Visual Studio.NET usually requires more effort than writing a user control, since user controls have all the same visual designer support that ASP.NET pages (Web forms) have. However, once built, custom controls can be added to the visual designer toolbox and then dragged and dropped onto other pages, whereas user controls have less support with regard to designer integration (though this may change with the release version of Visual Studio.NET).

An additional benefit of custom controls is reuse across applications. User controls cannot be shared across application domains, and so if you have more than one Web application that could benefit from the same user control, your only recourse is to copy the control to every Web application that requires it. This makes updating the control a nightmare, because it must then be redeployed. A custom control can be deployed to individual applications, or it can be placed in the Global Assembly Cache (GAC) on the server, which will make it available to all applications on that server. The GAC is beyond the scope of this book to cover, and unless you are writing commercial controls, you typically will not need to install to the GAC. Another nice feature of Visual Studio.NET is that it allows you to add references to assemblies on your development machine. This makes sharing assemblies easy, since you can just drop them all in a common Assemblies folder, and then reference them as needed from various Web applications. Visual Studio.NET will then copy the needed assembly DLLs to the Web application's /bin folder whenever you compile the application.

Third-Party Custom Controls

As this book is going to print, there are already a number of custom controls available separately from the base install of ASP.NET. Microsoft has released a suite of Web controls that includes a TreeView, a ToolBar, and a TabStrip, and in fact once ASP.NET is released these may be integrated into the framework. Other vendors and authors are offering controls as well, most of them for free at this time, though certainly once .NET is released we will start to see some commercially licensed controls available. Here are several controls that are available today, some of which include source code, and so could make good examples for how to build your own custom controls.

Internet Explorer WebControls

The Internet Explorer WebControls collection of four controls is designed to facilitate user interface authoring. Although the name might suggest otherwise, these controls are designed to produce working HTML for all the commonly used browsers. In addition, however, the collection takes advantage of many of the advanced features of Internet Explorer 5.5 and later versions, such as DHTML behaviors. You can download this control suite from:

```
http://msdn.microsoft.com/library/default.asp?url=/workshop/WebControls/
webcontrols_entry.asp
```

This package includes the following four controls:

- **MultiPage** enables the definition of collections of PageView elements, which can then be paged through one at a time.

- **TabStrip** simplifies the authoring of tabbed menus for site navigation.

- **Toolbar** acts as a container for other controls which can be used to create a toolbar similar to the toolbars commonly used in Microsoft Windows applications.

- **TreeView** provides a means of rendering data in a hierarchical fashion, such as a listing of folders, subfolders, and files.

ASPSmith VControls

Although they are still in development, I have written a set of controls called ASPSmith VControls, which encapsulate validation of common form elements, such as e-mail, telephone number, ZIP code, and so on. You can download this suite of controls from

```
http://aspsmith.com/vcontrols/
```

Right now, the following VControls are available, although by the time you are reading this more will probably be available: EmailBox, PhoneBox, ZipBox, PostalCodeBox, CreditCardBox, UrlBox, SsnBox.

SoftArtisans TreeView

SoftArtisans, a well-known ASP component vendor, has released a free TreeView control that functions similar to the Internet Explorer WebControl TreeView, but has several different features. You can download this control from

```
http://www.softartisans.com/softartisans/treeview.html
```

Other Controls

You will find a large number of controls and components available online. A good place to start your search for the control you need is the 411ASP.NET directory, whose .NET components section is at this URL:

```
http://www.411asp.net/home/components/
```

Creating a Custom Control of Our Own

As usual, we'll start with the obligatory Hello World example. In this case we're going to create a custom control that does nothing more than output the text "Hello World". We will see shortly how we can do this by inheriting from existing controls, such as the Label, but for now, we will simply inherit from the base class Control. The source code for our control is listed in Listing 12.1.

Listing 12.1: A C# Hello World Control, HelloWorld.cs

```
namespace ASPNETByExample
{
    public class HelloWorld : System.Web.UI.Control
```

EXAMPLE

Listing 12.1: continued

```
    {
        protected override void Render(System.Web.UI.HtmlTextWriter htwOutput)
        {
            htwOutput.Write("Hello World");
        }
    }
}
```

Examining this code line-by-line, we see first that we have declared a name-space for our control, called ASPNETByExample. Within this namespace, we declare our class, HelloWorld, which inherits from the System.Web.UI.Control class. This allows us to use all the methods and properties that the Control class makes available to us, one of which is the Render() method. Since we want to control the output of our control ourselves, we override the Render() method with our own declaration, which we define with the same parameters as the Control.Render() method. In this case, the method takes a single para-meter, a reference to an HtmlTextWriter object, called htwOutput. This object is used to output HTML to the Response stream, which in turn is sent to the user's browser. The method that we're most concerned with is the Write() method, which we have used here to output the text "Hello World".

DETERMINING BROWSER SUPPORT

One of the great benefits of using custom controls is the ability to customize the output based on the client's browser. You can use the Page.Request.Browser class's proper-ties to determine if the current browser supports a particular feature. For example, to test if the browser supports JavaScript, you could use this code:

```
if (Page.Request.Browser.JavaScript)
    // Do something requiring JavaScript
else
// Don't use Javascript
```

Having written our control, we must now compile it into an assembly, copy the assembly to the /bin folder of our Web application, reference the assem-bly on one of our ASP.NET pages, and finally place an element on the page where we want our control rendered. That's a seemingly daunting amount of work, especially compared to the amount of effort needed to access a user control to do the same thing. Let's take a look at what's involved, first with the command line and then with Visual Studio.NET.

Command Line Building and Deployment

To build our control, we will use the csc command (vbc if you are using the .vb file from the Web site). These programs can be found in the %SystemRoot%\ Microsoft.NET\Framework\v1.0.2914 directory (note that for the release of .NET, the v1.0.2914 will probably change). The %SystemRoot% variable is just the drive letter that your operating system is installed on, and will usually be C. So, assuming that you've found the csc.exe (vbc.exe) file, you can compile the HelloWorld.cs file into an assembly called HelloWorld.dll with the following command:

```
csc /t:library /out:HelloWorld.dll HelloWorld.cs
```

This results in the file, HelloWorld.dll, being created in the same directory as our HelloWorld.cs source file. To use this assembly in an ASP.NET application, we need to copy it to the Web application's folder on the hard drive, and place it in a folder called *bin* within the Web's folder.

Visual Studio.NET Building and Deployment

To build the control using Visual Studio.NET, we need to perform the following steps. First, we must create a new project for this control.

1. Open VS.NET and select New Project from the Start Page.

2. Under the Visual C# Projects tab, choose a Class Library template, and name it **HelloWorld**.

3. Click OK and wait while VS.NET sets up the project.

   By default, VS.NET starts with a class named Class1.cs. Obviously, we don't want a class named Class1.cs.

4. In the Solution Explorer, right-click the Class1.cs file, choose Rename, and name it **HelloWorld.cs**.

5. Delete the contents of the file and replace them with the code in Listing 12.1.

   Now we're almost ready to build the file. However, since we are using the System.Web.UI.Control object in our class, we need to add a reference to the System.Web namespace to our project.

6. In the Solution Explorer, right-click on References and then select Add Reference.

7. In the .NET tab, scroll down to the System.Web.dll Component, choose Select and then click OK.

   You should see System.Web listed in the References tab under Solution Explorer now. You're now ready to build the project.

8. Choose Build, and then select Build (or use the hotkey Ctrl+Shift+B, which is much faster).

   In the Output window, you should see this if your build was successful:

```
-------------------- Done --------------------

Build: 1 succeeded, 0 failed, 0 skipped
```

Your assembly will be in your project's bin folder, and by default should be named HelloWorld.dll. To use this assembly in your ASP.NET application, you will need to copy it to the Web's bin folder.

Referencing the Control from ASP.NET

Now that you've built your control and copied it to your Web application's bin folder, you're ready to access it from an ASP.NET page. To do this, we need to add a directive to the top of the page similar to how we set up a page to use a user control. For this control, we will use the following page directive:

```
<%@ Register TagPrefix="Hello" Namespace="ASPNETByExample"
Assembly="HelloWorld" %>
```

This directive tells the ASP.NET compiler that, whenever it sees a control with a tag prefix of "Hello", it should look for the corresponding control in the `ASPNETByExample` namespace found in the HelloWorld assembly. Note that you do not need to have a separate `Register` tag for every control you want to use on a page, unless they are all in different assemblies and namespaces. You could put a whole suite of control in a single namespace and assembly, and have access to all these controls using just one Register directive. The complete source code for our ASP.NET page is shown in Listing 12.2 below.

Listing 12.2: HelloControl.aspx

```
<%@ Register TagPrefix="Hello" Namespace="ASPNETByExample"
 Assembly="HelloWorld" %>
<html>
    <body>
        <Hello:HelloWorld runat="server" />
    </body>
</html>
```

That's it. Note that, as with all ASP.NET controls, you need to be sure that you add the `Runat="server"` tag to the control's declaration. When you view this page, you'll see a blank Web page with just the words "Hello World". You can see this example live at this book's supporting Web site, found at:

```
http://aspauthors.com/aspnetbyexample/ch12/
```

Building On Existing Controls

By overriding the `Render()` method of the base `Control` class, you can build very powerful controls. However, often you will find that there is an existing control that has most of the functionality you need. In this case, it is often much more efficient to simply inherit from the control that has most of your functionality. A common example of this kind of control would be a DropDownList that you would like to have pre-populated. Consider a form that has many yes or no questions on it. You might want to have a DropDownList with options for Yes, No, and a blank default option. You could create a custom control from scratch with this functionality, but you would not have any of the built-in functionality of the DropDownList Web control, such as handling PostBacks, unless you built it into your control. Rather than reinventing the wheel, you could just inherit from the DropDownList control itself, and add the necessary functionality needed to support your YesNoDropDownList. Listing 12.3 shows the complete source of our new control.

EXAMPLE

Listing 12.3: A YesNoDropDownList, YesNoDropDownList.cs

```
namespace ASPNETByExample
{
    public class YesNoDropDownList : System.Web.UI.WebControls.DropDownList
    {
        public string Value
        {
            get
            {
                return this.SelectedItem.Value.ToString();
            }

            set
            {
                this.Items.FindByValue(value).Selected = true;
            }
        }
        public YesNoDropDownList()
        {
            this.Items.Add("");
            this.Items.Add("No");
            this.Items.Add("Yes");
        }
    }
}
```

This control is a bit more complicated than our HelloWorld control, but is still pretty simple. We're still using our ASPNETByExample namespace, but this time instead of declaring our class as inheriting from Control, we are inheriting from System.Web.UI.WebControls.DropDownList. Note that, although we are not directly inheriting from Control, we still have access to all its behavior just as before, because DropDownList inherits (indirectly) from Control.

Just to make things a bit more interesting, I defined a `Value` property for this control, to make it easier to get or set the value of the `DropDownList`. The `get` just returns the value of the selected item, and the `set` searches for an item that matches what is passed into it and sets that item to be selected if it is found (the code right now will raise an exception if you try to set its value to an item that isn't in the list; we would add proper error handling to a production control). This property just makes it easier to work with our control, and also lets us set the value of the control declaratively on our ASP.NET page simply by adding a `value="Yes"` attribute to the control's declaration (as we shall see in a moment). Finally, the `YesNoDropDownList()` constructor is called whenever our control is created, and the constructor is responsible for creating the items in our list. In this case, it simply adds a blank option, a "No" option, and a "Yes" option, which will appear in that order on our page.

To test our control, we can use a simple ASP.NET page like the one listed in Listing 12.4.

EXAMPLE

Listing 12.4: YesNo.aspx

```
<%@ Register TagPrefix="YN" Namespace="ASPNETByExample"
Assembly="YesNoDropDownList" %>
<!DOCTYPE HTML PUBLIC "-//W3C//DTD HTML 4.0 Transitional//EN" >
<html>
    <body>
        <form id="YesNo" method="post" runat="server">
            Are we having fun yet?
            <YN:YesNoDropDownList
                runat="server"
                id="fun"
                value="Yes"
            />
            <asp:Button Runat="server" text="Go" />
            <hr />
            <h1>
                <%=fun.Value%>
            </h1>
        </form>
    </body>
</html>
```

This page looks very similar to our HelloControl.aspx page, with a few additions. First, since we want to use `PostBacks`, we need to make sure that our controls are all within a `<form runat="server">` tag. Next, you'll notice that we have set a default value for our tag of "Yes" by using the `Value` property, which is not case sensitive in our ASP.NET page even though it is case sensitive in our C# class (which is why we can't rely on case distinctions for public properties in C# classes). Then, we've added a button so that we can test sub-missions of our page. When you click the button, you will see whatever your selection was in big letters at the bottom of the screen.

NOTE

This example can be seen live online at
`http://aspauthors.com/aspnetbyexample/ch12/`.

Extending existing Web controls can provide a lot of functionality, and as you saw here, it is fairly easy to accomplish. One of the advantages of using this technique is that you don't have to worry about handling `PostBacks` yourself. However, there are limits to what you can do with just one of these controls. Consider, for instance, if you wanted to be sure that some-one always selected either Yes or No from your `YesNoDropDownList`. You would have to add a `RequiredFieldValidator` control (covered in Chapter 7) to every page that used the `YesNoDropDownList` to handle this. Although this solution would work, it would be much better if you could just include the `RequiredFieldValidator` functionality in with your control. One way to do this would be to override some more methods of the `DropDownList`, but again, why reinvent the wheel when there are already validation controls built into ASP.NET that we can use? The solution here is to use a *composite control*—a custom control made up of two or more other controls.

Creating Composite Controls

Composite controls are a bit more advanced than the controls we have seen thus far, but they are still fairly simple to build. For one thing, you still do not need to worry about handling `PostBacks`, because you can rely on all the features of the included controls to work just as if they were placed on the page themselves. Composite controls, because they typically encapsulate several pieces of UI code, are very close in function to user controls, so you will want to consider the differences between user controls and custom con-trols before you decide which method to use to create the functionality you need.

For this example, we will simply give the user the option of making the `YesNoListBox` required. To do this, we will actually go ahead and use our existing `YesNoListBox` control and include it along with a `RequiredFieldValidator` in a new control called `ReqYesNoListBox`. The complete code for this new control is in Listing 12.5.

Listing 12.5: ReqYesNoDropDownList.cs

```csharp
using ASPNETByExample;
using System.Web.UI.WebControls;
namespace ASPNETByExample
{
    public class ReqYesNoDropDownList : System.Web.UI.Control,
System.Web.UI.INamingContainer
    {
        // Declare child controls
        protected YesNoDropDownList ynList;
        protected RequiredFieldValidator ynRequired;

        public ReqYesNoDropDownList()
        {
            this.ynList = new YesNoDropDownList();
            this.ynRequired = new RequiredFieldValidator();
            ynList.ID = "YesNo" + this.UniqueID;

            ynRequired.ControlToValidate = ynList.ID;
            ynRequired.Display = ValidatorDisplay.Dynamic;
            ynRequired.Enabled = true;
            ynRequired.EnableViewState = false;
            ynRequired.Text = "*";
            ynRequired.ErrorMessage     = "You must select either Yes or No.";
        }

        public string Value
        {
            get
            {
                return this.ynList.Value;
            }

            set
            {
                this.ynList.Value = value;
            }
        }

        protected override void CreateChildControls()
        {
            this.Controls.Clear();
            this.Controls.Add(ynList);
            this.Controls.Add(ynRequired);
        }
    }
}
```

USE Trace **TO DEBUG CUSTOM CONTROLS**

If you want to add Trace statements to your custom controls so that you can debug their execution using ASP.NET's built-in tracing support, you need to reference the HttpContext.Current instance. For example, the following line of code would output a line to the trace results of the ASP.NET page that the control was listed on:

System.Web.HttpContext.Current.Trace.Write("Render","Rendering...");

Because we're going to be using our existing YesNoDropDownList control, I've gone ahead and included the ASPNETByExample namespace, along with the System.Web.UI.WebControls namespace, which holds the definition for the RequiredFieldValidator control. As with our HelloWorld control, we are inheriting from the Control class. This time, however, we are also implementing the INamingContainer interface. This interface is important to custom controls, because it ensures that any control created on an ASP.NET page will have a unique ID on the page. When building custom controls, you should always use this interface. You only need to worry about this if you are inheriting directly from Control—all the existing Web controls already implement this interface (so, for example, our YesNoDropDownList doesn't need to specify this interface, since DropDownList already implements it).

After declaring the controls that we will include in our composite control, we initialize their values in the ReqYesNoDropDownList() constructor. There's a little bit of a trick to note here. Since validator controls require a ControlToValidate property to be set, you need to know the name of the YesNoDropDownList. However, unless we set its ID ourselves, we have no way of knowing what unique ID the ASP.NET processor will give to this control. Worse, if we just hard-coded the ID field, we would never be able to use more than one of our controls on a page, because the names would conflict. The solution to this problem is to create an ID dynamically using the UniqueID of our composite control as part of the name of the child control. In this way, we can know the name of the control for the validator to reference, and we can still have as many of these composite controls on a page as we want.

After dealing with the issue of IDs, we set some default properties for the RequiredFieldValidator, ynRequired. Because these child controls are declared as protected, the user cannot access any of these properties directly, so the only way they can be set is within the composite control. If you want your control's child controls to be available to users directly, you can either declare them as public (which is not usually recommended), or you can set up properties that map to the child control's properties. This is what we have done for the YesNoDropDownList Value property. Our

ReqYesNoDropDownList exposes a public property of Value, which simply delegates its sets and gets to the ynList child control.

Finally, we come to the most important method of a composite control, the CreateChildControls() method. This method is similar to Render() in that it is built into the Control object and must be overridden in our composite control in order for us to use it. In this case, we are programmatically adding our child controls to this control's Controls collection, using the collection's Add() method. The controls are automatically rendered by the Control class in the order in which we have added them.

NOTE

It is quite possible to build custom controls that inherit from other custom controls, ad infinitum. Some very powerful suites of controls can be built in this fashion. If you have several layers of controls that need to render user interface logic, either with the Render() method or the CreateChildControls() method, you can make sure that your superclass performs its rendering by using the base keyword in C# (which is analogous to the MyBase keyword in VB.NET, or the super keyword in Java). So, within the Render() method, you would call base.Render(), and within the CreateChildControls() method, you would call base.CreateChildControls().

To test out our new control, let's take a look at ReqYesNo.aspx, which is listed in its entirety in Listing 12.6.

EXAMPLE

Listing 12.6: ReqYesNo.aspx

```
<%@ Register TagPrefix="YN" Namespace="ASPNETByExample"
Assembly="YesNoDropDownList" %>
<!DOCTYPE HTML PUBLIC "-//W3C//DTD HTML 4.0 Transitional//EN" >
<html>
    <body>
        <form id="YesNo" method="post" runat="server">
            You must answer yes or no:
            <YN:ReqYesNoDropDownList runat="server" id="fun" />
            <asp:Button Runat="server" text="Go" />
            <hr />
            <asp:ValidationSummary Runat="server" />
            <h1>
                <%=fun.Value%>
            </h1>
        </form>
    </body>
</html>
```

For this test, we've modified the YesNo.aspx file so that it uses the ReqYesNoDropDownList (which was compiled into the same assembly as before), and removed the default value for the list so that the user will have to choose either Yes or No. We've also added a ValidationSummary control to display any error messages that are generated by our validation controls. Attempting to submit the form without choosing a value results in the error message being displayed, as in Figure 12.1.

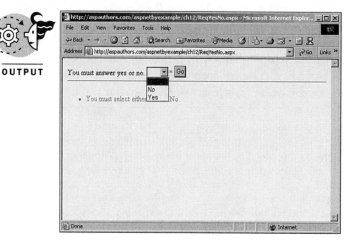

OUTPUT

Figure 12.1: *Testing our required YesNo DropDownList.*

Now that we have seen how to build custom controls from scratch or by inheriting from existing controls, let's dig a little bit deeper and look at some of the more advanced options available. Note that control-building techniques could easily fill a book themselves, so we will only be able to provide cursory coverage of some of these topics.

When developing your own controls, there are several more advanced pieces of functionality that you may want to add. These include

- Handling control events
- Handling PostBacks
- Using templates
- Raising events
- Databinding

These techniques are covered in the rest of the chapter.

Handling Control Events

All custom controls inherit from the System.Web.UI.Control class, which defines the events described in Table 12.1.

Table 12.1: **System.Web.UI.Control** *Events*

Event	Method To Override	Description
DataBinding	OnDataBinding(EventArgs e)	Occurs when the server control binds to a data source.
Dispose	Dispose()	Occurs when a server control is released from memory, after the Unload() event.
Init	OnInit(EventArgs e)	Occurs when the server control is initialized.
Load	OnLoad(EventArgs e)	Occurs when the server control is loaded into the Page object.
PreRender	OnPreRender(EventArgs e)	Occurs when the server control is about to render to its containing Page object.
Unload	OnUnload(EventArgs e)	Occurs when the server control is unloaded from memory.

These events describe the life cycle of all controls in ASP.NET, including all the built-in controls. As a control moves through its life cycle of creation and destruction, which happens on every page request, it will go through some or all of the following phases in the order described in Table 12.2.

Table 12.2: Control Life Cycle

Phase	What the Control Should Be Doing in This Phase
Constructor	Anything required for the entire state of the control that cannot be put off until the Initialize phase. This should be used sparingly, since acquiring resources could probably be delayed until a later phase, resulting in a more efficient control.
Declarative Properties	Declarative properties set on the ASP.NET page are set. Any objects that need to exist for this stage should be created either in the constructor or, optimally, should be created by a separate method called by the property setter only if needed.
Initialize (Init)	Initialize settings needed during the rest of the lifetime of the event.
Track ViewState	Perform custom logic to manage saving ViewState for the control.
Load ViewState	Use the LoadPostData method to perform custom logic to load ViewState into the control's properties. Only occurs if IPostBackDataHandler is implemented.
Programmatic Properties	Properties set programmatically in the ASP.NET page's Load event are process.

Table 12.2: continued

Phase	What the Control Should Be Doing in This Phase
Load	Perform actions common to all requests. At this point, the state of the control has been restored and all form controls reflect client-side data.
PostBack DataChanged Event	Raise events in response to changes in state between the current and previous PostBack. Only occurs if IPostBackDataHandler is implemented.
Raise PostBack Event	Handle the client-side event (such as OnClick) that caused the PostBack. Only occurs if IPostBackEventHandler is implemented.
PreRender	Last chance to modify the contents of a control, and have those changes persisted to ViewState, before the control is rendered.
Save ViewState	The ViewState collection is converted to a string and persisted to the client as a hidden form field.
Render	The HTML output for the control is sent to the client.
OnUnload	Occurs as the control is about to be released from memory.
Dispose	Called immediately after OnUnload.
Class Destructor	Typically should not be used. The Dispose event tends to take its place and in fact where Dispose is used, it seems that the class's destructor is not executed.

Notably missing from this list is the CreateChildControls() method, which is used to create the controls tree for a control. It is not listed in this life cycle diagram because it could be called during one of several phases, including the Load, DataBinding, and Render phases. Basically, this control is called whenever the ASP.NET page framework needs the controls tree to exist. You can ensure that this event is called prior to your accessing properties of child controls in your property setters and getters by calling the EnsureChildControls() method within these routines. This method checks to see if the CreateChildControls() method has already been called, and calls it only if it hasn't already been called.

Understanding the life cycle of a control can be very useful when developing a complex custom control of your own. It can be very frustrating when you are trying to reference child controls in your declarative properties and you are getting null reference exceptions because the child controls don't exist yet. A good way to debug such situations is to trace through your code so you can see the order in which the events are being performed. You can easily do this using the VS.NET debugger, but that doesn't make nearly as good an example as demonstrating how to do this using the Trace feature that is built into ASP.NET.

We're going to build an extension to our Hello World control that handles all the events described above and output `Trace` statements as each event is begun and completed. Some of these events will only be fired on `PostBack`, and some, like the ones that occur after `Render`, will not appear at all in the trace results because the page has already been rendered by the time these events are executing. In order to show the difference between setting properties declaratively within our control tag on the .aspx page, and setting them programmatically in our `Page_Load` event, we are also tracing whenever our property is set. Listing 12.7 shows the complete source code of our new class, HelloLifeCycle.cs.

Listing 12.7: HelloLifeCycle.cs

```csharp
using System;
using System.Collections.Specialized;
using System.Web.UI;

namespace ASPNETByExample
{
    public class HelloLifeCycle : System.Web.UI.Control,
        IPostBackEventHandler, IPostBackDataHandler
    {
        System.Web.HttpContext cx;
        public HelloLifeCycle()
        {
            cx = System.Web.HttpContext.Current;
            cx.Trace.Write("HelloLifeCycle","Begin Constructor");
            cx.Trace.Write("HelloLifeCycle","End Constructor");
        }
        ~HelloLifeCycle()
        {
            cx.Trace.Write("HelloLifeCycle","Begin Destructor");
            cx.Trace.Write("HelloLifeCycle","End Destructor");
        }
        public string property
        {
            set
            {
                cx.Trace.Write("Property Set","Set Property: " + value);
            }
        }
        protected override void OnInit(EventArgs e)
        {
            cx.Trace.Write("OnInit","Begin OnInit");
            base.OnInit(e);
            cx.Trace.Write("OnInit","End OnInit");
        }
```

Listing 12.7: continued

```
    protected override void OnLoad(EventArgs e)
    {
        cx.Trace.Write("OnLoad","Begin OnLoad");
        base.OnLoad(e);
        cx.Trace.Write("OnLoad","End OnLoad");
    }
    protected override void OnDataBinding(EventArgs e)
    {
        cx.Trace.Write("OnDataBinding","Begin OnDataBinding");
        base.OnDataBinding(e);
        cx.Trace.Write("OnDataBinding","End OnDataBinding");
    }
    protected override void OnPreRender(EventArgs e)
    {
        cx.Trace.Write("OnPreRender","Begin OnPreRender");
        base.OnPreRender(e);
        cx.Trace.Write("OnPreRender","End OnPreRender");
    }
    protected override void Render(System.Web.UI.HtmlTextWriter htwOutput)
    {
        cx.Trace.Write("Render","Begin Render");
        htwOutput.Write("Hello World Life Cycle");
        cx.Trace.Write("Render","End Render");
    }
    protected override void OnUnload(EventArgs e)
    {
        cx.Trace.Write("OnUnload","Begin OnUnload");
        base.OnUnload(e);
        cx.Trace.Write("OnUnload","End OnUnload");
    }
    public override void Dispose()
    {
        cx.Trace.Write("Disposed","Begin Disposed");
        base.Dispose();
        cx.Trace.Write("Disposed","End Disposed");
    }
    protected override void LoadViewState(object savedState)
    {
        cx.Trace.Write("LoadViewState","Begin LoadViewState");
        base.LoadViewState(savedState);
        cx.Trace.Write("LoadViewState","End LoadViewState");
    }
    protected override object SaveViewState()
    {
        cx.Trace.Write("SaveViewState","Begin SaveViewState");
        try{return base.SaveViewState();}
        finally{
```

```
                cx.Trace.Write("SaveViewState","End SaveViewState");
            }
        }
        protected override void TrackViewState()
        {
            cx.Trace.Write("TrackViewState","Begin TrackViewState");
            base.TrackViewState();
            cx.Trace.Write("TrackViewState","End TrackViewState");
        }
        public virtual void RaisePostDataChangedEvent()
        {
            cx.Trace.Write("RaisePostDataChangedEvent","Begin
RaisePostDataChangedEvent");
            cx.Trace.Write("RaisePostDataChangedEvent","End
RaisePostDataChangedEvent");
        }
        public virtual bool LoadPostData(string postDataKey,
            NameValueCollection postCollection)
        {
            cx.Trace.Write("LoadPostData","Begin LoadPostData");
            try{return true;}
            finally
            {
                cx.Trace.Write("LoadPostData","End LoadPostData");
            }
        }
        public void RaisePostBackEvent(String eventArgument)
        {
            cx.Trace.Write("RaisePostBackEvent","Begin RaisePostBackEvent");
            cx.Trace.Write("RaisePostBackEvent","End RaisePostBackEvent");
        }
    }
}
```

As you can see, this class has a lot of repeated code. Basically, it inherits from Control and implements the IPostBackEventHandler and IPostBackDataHandler interfaces. Next, it establishes a class variable, cx, to hold a reference to the System.Web.HttpContext.Current object, which lets us access the calling page's intrinsic properties and methods, such as Trace. The rest of the code is fairly self-explanatory. For the property, I output the value of the property in the trace output so that we can see whether it was set declaratively or programmatically (because I'm going to pass it the string "Declarative" or "Programmatic" depending on where I am setting it). For the methods that override the Control class, I make sure to call the base.MethodName() method, which is just a good habit to get into for these methods. Now, to actually see this control in action, we need an ASP.NET page to hold the control and implement tracing so we can follow the life cycle of the control. Listing 12.8 describes our ASP.NET page for testing this control.

Listing 12.8: HelloEvents.aspx

```
<%@ Page Language="C#" Trace="True" %>
<%@ Register TagPrefix="Hello" Namespace="ASPNETByExample" Assembly="HelloWorld"
%>
<%@ Import Namespace="ASPNETByExample" %>
<script runat="server">
void Page_Load(){
    hello.property = "Programmatic";
}
</script>
<html>
    <body>
        <form runat="server">
            <Hello:HelloLifeCycle runat="server" ID="hello"
property="Declarative" />
            <asp:Button runat="server" Text="PostBack" ID="btnPostBack" />
        </form>
    </body>
</html>
```

As you can see, in this code I am just placing the control on the page, with a declarative property setting of Declarative and a programmatic property setting (in Page_Load) of Programmatic. The btnPostBack button is there so that we can generate a PostBack and observe the object life cycle both with and without a PostBack. Since the PostBack is more interesting, you can see the trace output for this page after a PostBack in Figure 12.2.

Now that we have seen *when* these events take place, let's examine *how* to implement some of them, starting with using PostBacks and ViewState in your own custom controls.

Handling PostBacks

All custom controls can take advantage of the built-in ViewState property of the Control component to handle retaining their value through PostBacks. The use of ViewState can be controlled through the EnableViewState property of a control, or at the Page level with the EnableViewState property of the Page. When used, ViewState is stored in an encrypted hidden form field called __VIEWSTATE, which you can examine by viewing the source of an ASP.NET page in your browser (assuming it is using ViewState).

OUTPUT

Trace Information			
Category	**Message**	**From First(s)**	**From Last(s)**
aspx.page	Begin Init	0.013249	0.000118
aspx.page	End Init	0.013675	0.000087
aspx.page	Begin LoadViewState	0.013759	0.000083
aspx.page	End LoadViewState	0.013891	0.000133
aspx.page	Begin ProcessPostData	0.014278	0.000387
aspx.page	End ProcessPostData	0.014433	0.000154
aspx.page	Begin ProcessPostData Second Try	0.014889	0.000087
aspx.page	End ProcessPostData Second Try	0.014977	0.000088
aspx.page	Begin Raise ChangedEvents	0.015060	0.000083
aspx.page	End Raise ChangedEvents	0.015142	0.000082
aspx.page	Begin Raise PostBackEvent	0.015222	0.000080
aspx.page	End Raise PostBackEvent	0.015383	0.000161
aspx.page	Begin PreRender	0.015475	0.000091
aspx.page	End PreRender	0.015737	0.000087
aspx.page	Begin SaveViewState	0.016685	0.000450
aspx.page	End SaveViewState	0.017071	0.000089
aspx.page	Begin Render	0.017153	0.000082
aspx.page	End Render	0.018272	0.000552
HelloLifeCycle	Begin Constructor		
HelloLifeCycle	End Constructor	0.013031	0.013031
OnInit	Begin OnInit	0.013341	0.000091
OnInit	End OnInit	0.013425	0.000084
OnLoad	Begin OnLoad	0.014716	0.000102
OnLoad	End OnLoad	0.014803	0.000087
OnPreRender	Begin OnPreRender	0.015563	0.000088
OnPreRender	End OnPreRender	0.015651	0.000088
Property Set	Set Property: Declarative	0.013132	0.000101
Property Set	Set Property: Programmatic	0.014613	0.000181
Render	Begin Render	0.017625	0.000472
Render	End Render	0.017720	0.000095
SaveViewState	Begin SaveViewState	0.016145	0.000408
SaveViewState	End SaveViewState	0.016235	0.000090
SaveViewState	Begin SaveViewState	0.016892	0.000208
SaveViewState	End SaveViewState	0.016982	0.000089
TrackViewState	Begin TrackViewState	0.013506	0.000081
TrackViewState	End TrackViewState	0.013588	0.000082

Control Tree

Done — Internet

Figure 12.2: Trace information for HelloEvents.aspx.

Let's update our `HelloWorld` control to accept a property, and use `ViewState` to persist this property across multiple `PostBacks`. We'd like to be able to say hello to someone in particular, so we'll add a `PersonName` property to the control, and then have it render "Hello" + `PersonName` instead of "Hello World". In order to utilize `ViewState`, we'll reference the `ViewState` collection in our set and get methods of the property. The complete source for this updated control is found in Listing 12.9.

EXAMPLE

Listing 12.9: HelloPerson.cs

```
namespace ASPNETByExample
{
    public class HelloPerson : System.Web.UI.Control
    {
        public string PersonName
        {
            get
            {
                return ViewState["PersonName"].ToString();
            }
            set
```

Listing 12.9: continued

```
            {
                ViewState["PersonName"] = value;
            }
        }
        protected override void Render(System.Web.UI.HtmlTextWriter htwOutput)
        {
            htwOutput.Write("Hello " + PersonName);
        }
    }
}
```

As you can see, this is not very different from the other controls we have built thus far, except for the get and set methods of our PersonName property, which use the ViewState collection of the Control object to store state information for this control. Note that the collection is specific to this control, so if we were to put more than one HelloPerson control on a page, and set each one's PersonName property to something different, we would not have any collisions; everything would work fine.

To test this control, we can build a simple ASP.NET page like the one shown in Listing 12.10.

EXAMPLE

Listing 12.10: HelloPerson.aspx, C#

```
<%@ Page Language="C#" %>
<%@ Register TagPrefix="Hello"
Namespace="ASPNETByExample" Assembly="HelloWorld" %>
<%@ Import Namespace="ASPNETByExample" %>
<script runat="server">
void Page_Load(){
    if(!IsPostBack){
        hello.PersonName = "Steve";
    }
}
</script>
<html>
    <body>
        <form runat="server">
            <Hello:HelloPerson runat="server" id="hello" />
            <br />
            <asp:Button Runat="server" Text="PostBack" />
        </form>
    </body>
</html>
```

In the Page_Load event handler for this page, we check to see if the current instance of the page is due to a PostBack by using the Page.IsPostBack property. If it is not a PostBack, such as when the page is first loaded, we set the PersonName property of our HelloPerson control (named hello in the code) to Steve. Note that, in the event of a PostBack, we do not set any value.

Clicking on the button will result in the control retaining its original value of "Hello Steve". If we add Trace="true" to the Page directive of the page, we will be able to see even more information, such as the size of the ViewState for this control (36 bytes), the __VIEWSTATE contents, and the start and end of the PostBackEvent event in the Trace Information.

You can perform more advanced operations related to ViewState and PostBacks, such as comparing the value of the posted data with the current value of the control to see if it has changed, or responding to a PostBack event by raising an event of its own. These advanced techniques are beyond the scope of this book to cover, but are accomplished by implementing interfaces such as the IPostBackDataHandler and IPostBackEventHandler. Searching for these in the .NET documentation or online should help you get started with building controls that use these features.

Using Templates

Within your custom control, it is possible to add support for user-defined templates, such as the ones that you learned about in Chapter 5, "HTML/Web Controls." Again, one of the great things about ASP.NET is that you have as much control over your custom controls as Microsoft has when they build their controls. If you see a feature of an existing control, such as the Repeater, that you'd like to implement in your own custom control, you can!

Templates are all about user interface. They allow your control to define one or more templates that can be customized by the user. Your control then defines when and how these templates are rendered. A common use for templates in the list controls was to have an ItemTemplate and an AlternateItemTemplate, which made it easy for users to define a different look for alternating items in a list. Headers and footers are also common candidates for templating.

We can only provide one simple example of a templated control, but this will give you a taste of what is involved. A more thorough investigation into the details of building templated controls is left as an exercise for the reader.

For this example, we will build on our HelloWorld control once more. We need to create two separate classes, one for the control itself, and another for its template. For a more advanced control with many templates, each additional template would require its own class to be defined.

Templates are only really useful if you have multiple properties or data elements within your custom control. If there is only one string to output, for example, then any formatting required could simply be applied to the control, and there is no need for a template. In order to make a template worthwhile for our HelloWorld example, we will be creating three properties for our control: ToPerson, FromPerson, and Message. This control will then render these properties, with the help of a template if one is provided.

All templated controls should implement the INamingContainer interface covered earlier, to ensure that any child controls created are given unique names. The controls must also include several attributes in their class definition to ensure that they are handled properly by the ASP.NET runtime. The first attribute, ParseChildren, must be applied to the class as a whole, and is used to tell ASP.NET to treat any inner (child) tags within your control's tags as properties of your control. The syntax for this, in C#, looks like the following (specifying the name of the parameter is optional):

```
[ParseChildren(true)]
//or
[ParseChildren(ChildrenAsProperties = true)]
```

This attribute should be placed immediately before (typically on the line above) your class definition.

The second attribute that is used is TemplateContainer. This attribute is applied to any template definitions, which are properties of the control of type ITemplate. The TemplateContainer attribute needs to be passed the type of the class that is defined to handle the specific template. For example, in our HelloTemplate example, we use

```
[TemplateContainer(typeof(MessageTemplateContainer))]
```

The complete source for our templated control is shown in Listing 12.11, below.

EXAMPLE

Listing 12.11: Templated Hello World Control, (HelloTemplate.cs)

```
using System;
using System.Web.UI;

namespace ASPNETByExample
{
    [ParseChildren(true)]
    public class TemplatedHelloWorld : Control, INamingContainer
    {
        private ITemplate messageTemplate;
        private String toPerson = null;
        private String fromPerson = null;
        private String message = null;
```

Listing 12.11: continued

```
private Control myTemplateContainer;

protected override void OnDataBinding(EventArgs e)
{
    EnsureChildControls();
}

[TemplateContainer(typeof(MessageTemplateContainer))]
public ITemplate MessageTemplate
{
    get
    {
        return messageTemplate;
    }
    set
    {
        messageTemplate = value;
    }
}


public String ToPerson
{
    get
    {
        return toPerson;
    }
    set
    {
        toPerson = value;
    }
}
public String FromPerson
{
    get
    {
        return fromPerson;
    }
    set
    {
        fromPerson = value;
    }
}
public String Message
{
    get
```

Listing 12.11: continued

```
            {
                return message;
            }
            set
            {
                message = value;
            }
        }

        protected override void CreateChildControls ()

        {

            if (MessageTemplate != null)
            {
                // Use user-defined template for rendering
                myTemplateContainer =
                    new MessageTemplateContainer(this);
                MessageTemplate.InstantiateIn(myTemplateContainer);
                Controls.Add(myTemplateContainer);
            }
            else
            {
                // Use the default rendering
                Controls.Add(new LiteralControl("<b>To:</b> " +
                    ToPerson + "<br/>"));
                Controls.Add(new LiteralControl("<b>From:</b> " +
                    FromPerson + "<br/>"));
                Controls.Add(new LiteralControl("<b>Message:</b><p>" +
                    Message + "</p>"));
            }


        }

    }

    // Keeps a backpointer to the parent control to access its properties
    public class MessageTemplateContainer : Control, INamingContainer
    {
        private TemplatedHelloWorld parent;
        public MessageTemplateContainer(TemplatedHelloWorld parent)
        {
            this.parent = parent;
        }
```

Listing 12.11: continued

```
        public String ToPerson
        {
            get
            {
                return parent.ToPerson;
            }
        }
        public String FromPerson
        {
            get
            {
                return parent.FromPerson;
            }
        }
        public String Message
        {
            get
            {
                return parent.Message;
            }
        }
    }
}
```

Let's go over this code—it's more complicated than anything we've done so far. First we define our class, deriving from Control as usual and implementing INamingContainer. Next we declare our instance variables, which we'll use later. The first method we come to is OnDataBinding(). It is a good practice to always override this method and call EnsureChildControls() so that if any of the controls within a template utilize databinding, we are assured that the controls have been created before ASP.NET attempts to bind them to their data source(s).

We then define our properties, which include an ITemplate called MessageTemplate, which includes the TemplateContainer attribute. This property is used to provide a reference to the MessageTemplateContainer class, so that it can be invoked to handle the contents of a MessageTemplate template. Then we declare our three string properties: ToPerson, FromPerson, and Message.

The last method in the TemplatedHelloWorld class is the CreateChildControls() method, which defines the behavior of our control based on the existence of a template. If a template is supplied, then an instance of MessageTemplate will exist, and we will use the user-defined template to render our properties. Otherwise, the default behavior for this class is to output its properties in three LiteralControls.

The `MessageTemplateContainer` class is created with a reference to the `TemplatedHelloWorld` class passed into its constructor, which it sets to the local parent variable. This control can then access `TemplatedHelloWorld`'s properties through this reference, as it does in each of its properties. No rendering logic is required in this control, as it will render its contents automatically using the `Control` objects `Render()` method. Its properties are accessed within the template by using the `Container.PropertyName` syntax with `<%# %>` tags, as we shall see in Listing 12.12, which shows the source for an ASP.NET page that tests this control.

EXAMPLE

Listing 12.12: HelloTemplate.aspx

```
<%@ Register TagPrefix="Custom" Namespace="ASPNETByExample"
Assembly = "HelloWorld" %>
<HTML>
    <body>
        <form runat="server" ID="Form1">
            Using Template:
            <br />
            <Custom:TemplatedHelloWorld
                id="hello1"
                ToPerson="World"
                FromPerson="Steve"
                Message="Hello!"
                runat="server">
                <MessageTemplate>
                    <table bgcolor="#CCCCCC">
                    <tr bgcolor="#9999FF">
                        <th>TO</th>
                        <th>FROM</th>
                        <th>MESSAGE</th>
                    </tr>
                    <tr bgcolor="#EEEEEE">
                        <td>
                            <%# Container.ToPerson %>
                        </td>
                        <td>
                            <%# Container.FromPerson %>
                        </td>
                        <td>
                            <%# Container.Message %>
                        </td>
                    </tr>
                    </table>
                </MessageTemplate>
            </Custom:TemplatedHelloWorld>
            <hr />
```

Listing 12.12: continued

```
            Default (no template):
            <br />
            <Custom:TemplatedHelloWorld
                id="hello2"
                ToPerson="World"
                FromPerson="Steve"
                Message="Hello!"
                runat="server" />
        </form>
    </body>
</HTML>
```

This page includes two instances of our TemplatedHelloWorld control, one with and one without a template. The first instance uses a template to output the contents of the control as cells in a row of an HTML table. The second instance simply outputs the contents of the control using the default rendering defined in the control. Note that in both cases, we are setting the parameters on the control. The results of viewing this page in a browser can be seen in Figure 12.3.

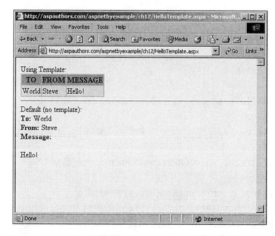

Figure 12.3: Working with templated custom controls.

Raising Events

Sometimes you will want to raise events of your own from within your controls. For example, a validation control might raise an event to let its parent control know that it found an invalid element. Although not necessary for many kinds of controls and a bit more advanced, custom events can be a powerful tool. A simple example of raising an event and handling it from an ASP.NET page is really all that we have room for in this chapter, but it should give you an idea of how this works and get you started if you need to build an event-raising control of your own.

Just to keep things simple, we're going to add an event to our `HelloPerson` class that we used earlier in the chapter. We have decided that if this control's `PersonName` property is left blank, that this is "event-worthy" and should raise a `PersonNameRequired` event. Because we are not doing anything too fancy with our event, like returning a custom data structure, we can take advantage of the default data structures `System.EventArgs`, `System.EventHandler`, and `System.Web.UI.Control.Events`.

In order to wire up an event, we need to define two items in our class: an event and an event-handler routine. There are several ways to define these items; the technique described here is the one recommended by the documentation as being the most optimized for performance. Once the event is defined in the class, it is still necessary that something cause the event to be raised. In our example, we are going to check the value of the `PersonName` property during the pre-render phase of our control's life cycle, and raise the event there if we find that the `PersonName` property is not set. The complete source of our new control, HelloPersonEvents.cs, is in Listing 12.13.

EXAMPLE

Listing 12.13: Raising Events From Your Control (HelloPersonEvents.cs)

```
using System;
namespace ASPNETByExample
{
    public class HelloPersonEvents : System.Web.UI.Control
    {
        private static readonly object PersonNameRequiredEvent = new object();

        protected virtual void OnPersonNameRequired(EventArgs e)
        {
            EventHandler onPersonNameRequiredHandler =
                (EventHandler)Events[PersonNameRequiredEvent];
            if (onPersonNameRequiredHandler != null)
                onPersonNameRequiredHandler(this, e);
        }

        public event EventHandler PersonNameRequired
        {
            add
            {
                Events.AddHandler(PersonNameRequiredEvent, value);
            }
            remove
            {
```

Listing 12.13: continued

```
                Events.RemoveHandler(PersonNameRequiredEvent, value);
        }
    }

    public string PersonName
    {
        get
        {
            if(ViewState["PersonName"]!=null)
                return ViewState["PersonName"].ToString();
            else
                return "";
        }
        set
        {
            ViewState["PersonName"] = value;
        }
    }

    protected override void OnPreRender(EventArgs e)
    {
        base.OnPreRender(e);
        if((PersonName == null) || (PersonName.Length == 0))
        {
            OnPersonNameRequired(EventArgs.Empty);
        }
    }

    protected override void Render(System.Web.UI.HtmlTextWriter htwOutput)
    {
        htwOutput.Write("Hello " + PersonName);
    }
    }
}
```

Note that both the OnPersonNameRequired routine and the
PersonNameRequired event rely on the Events collection, which is exposed by
System.Web.UI.Control. This collection manages event handlers for us,
allowing us to enable support for an event in just a few lines of code.

In order to actually raise an event, you need to call its handler from within
the control. In this case, the OnPreRender method does a check to see if the
PersonName property is empty, and if it is, it calls OnPersonNameRequired(),
passing it an empty EventArgs parameter.

Of course, raising the event is only half the story. It's up to the ASP.NET
page to actually do something when this event occurs. In this case, the page
will display an error message to notify the user that they need to provide a

value for the control, providing functionality similar to that of the RequiredFieldValidator control. The complete source code of the test page is in Listing 12.14.

EXAMPLE

Listing 12.14: Handling Events from Controls (HelloPersonEvents.aspx)

```
<%@ Page Language="C#" %>
<%@ Register TagPrefix="Hello" Namespace="ASPNETByExample" Assembly="HelloWorld"
%>
<%@ Import Namespace="ASPNETByExample" %>
<script runat="server">
void Page_Load(){
    hello.PersonName = person.Text;
}
void hello_PersonNameRequired(object sender, EventArgs e) {
    Error.Text = "You must enter a value for the textbox.";
}
</script>
<html>
    <body>
        <form runat="server">
            <Hello:HelloPersonEvents
                runat="server"
                id="hello"
                OnPersonNameRequired="hello_PersonNameRequired"
            />
            <br />
            <asp:TextBox Runat="server" ID="person" Text="Steve" />
            <asp:Button Runat="server" Text="PostBack" />
            <br />
            <asp:Label
                Runat="server"
                ID="Error"
                ForeColor="Red"
                EnableViewState="False"
            />
        </form>
    </body>
</html>
```

There are two key things to note about this page. First, in the declaration of the control, the OnPersonNameRequired event is defined to invoke the hello_PersonNameRequired event handler. Second, looking at this event handler in the page's source code, we see that it looks just like any other event, and can participate in the page's execution freely. In this case we use it to set the value of an error Label. Now, when this page is loaded, if no value is set in the TextBox (and thus no value is copied to the HelloPersonEvents control), the PersonNameRequired event will fire and result in the red error message being displayed.

You can view this example live online at http://aspauthors.com/aspnetbyexample/ch12/.

Databinding

Databinding is one of the many powerful features built into ASP.NET controls that you can take advantage of in your own custom controls. The details of how you bind your control to a data source can get very complicated, but you can use this technique to create powerful controls like the DataGrid control that ships with ASP.NET. Unfortunately, databinding is generally best used with templates, and any really useful example would be beyond the scope of this book. To learn more about how to build databound templated controls, consult the documentation and quick-start tutorials that ship with the .NET Framework SDK.

Building Components

As we learned in the beginning of the chapter, another custom tool you can build with .NET is a component. A component is similar to a control, but doesn't inherit from the Control class and typically doesn't render any UI. A common use for components is to encapsulate business logic or data access logic. In this section, we will create a simple SalesTax component and demonstrate how to use it in an ASP.NET page. For more on components, refer to the IBuySpy case study in Chapter 14.

To create a component, we simply write a class just as we did with our initial HelloWorld control. However, for a component we don't need to inherit from anything (although we can if we choose to), so for this example just declaring the class is sufficient. The complete listing for our SalesTax component is in Listing 12.15.

EXAMPLE

Listing 12.15: SalesTax.cs

```
namespace ASPNETByExample
{
    public class SalesTax
    {
        static double taxRate = 0.06;

        public static double computeTax(double price)
        {
            return price * taxRate;
        }
    }
}
```

Summary

In this chapter, you learned how to extend the many different controls that we have covered in order to add additional functionality to them, as well as how to build your own completely customized controls. In fact, even with all the material covered in this chapter, it is only scratching the surface of what can be done with custom controls. With custom controls, you have a huge amount of control over how your application works. Further, the ease of installation of these controls (compared to COM objects) coupled with their power is sure to create a large market for third-party controls once ASP.NET is released. In many cases this will allow you to buy the functionality you need off-the-shelf, rather than build it yourself. Finally, this chapter briefly covered custom components, which are a key part of most significant applications. Components are covered in more detail in Chapter 14, as part of the IBuySpy architecture.

What's Next?

ASP.NET includes a lot of great new features, including a lot of support for debugging. Using these features, and development tools such as Visual Studio.NET, it is much easier to debug Web applications than it ever was with classic ASP and COM. Chapter 13 covers debugging with ASP.NET.

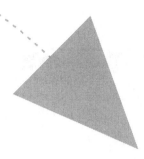

13

Debugging ASP.NET Overview

Okay, so you've jumped into .NET programming, and you've built your first (or tenth or hundredth) ASP.NET page. It compiles just fine, but it refuses to work right, returning the wrong value or stopping execution unexpectedly. What now? Returning to your ASP roots, you prepare to start inserting `Response.Write` statements throughout the code. But wait! There is a better way! Among its many improvements to ASP, ASP.NET provides several application-level improvements to the process of debugging, and Visual Studio.NET goes further to include a debugger that allows you to step through your code line by line, just as if it were a local VB application. So don't add that `Response.Write`—read on and see how things are done in ASP.NET.

In this chapter, you will

- Use Page directives to debug

- Create Web.config directives

- Become familiar with `System.Diagnostics` tools

- Set up Visual Studio.NET's integrated debugger

- Uncover Common ASP.NET bugs

ASP.NET Debugging Features

ASP.NET includes several new features to aid debuggers that weren't included with Classic ASP. The first of these is the Trace object, which allows programmers to include debug output in their pages that can be controlled using page-level or application-level directives. Trace is a new intrinsic object that, like Response, Request, Server, and so on, is directly accessible in your ASP.NET code. When deactivated, these statements are not included in the compiled version of the page. As a result, there is no performance hit as there would have been in Classic ASP code, like that shown in Listing 13.1. Using this kind of code resulted in extra overhead from the function call involved and the If-Then statements that had to be executed every time the page was executed. If these kinds of constructions are used throughout an application, this overhead can quickly add up and impede scalability.

EXAMPLE

Listing 13.1: Source code for classicdebug.asp.

```
Dim sql
Dim book_id
book_id = Request("book_id")
Call Debug("Book ID: " & book_id)
sql = "SELECT * FROM mytable WHERE mycolumn = " & book_id
Call Debug(sql)

'Insert database code here

Function Debug(myString)
    If Session("debug") = "" Then Session("debug") = 0
    If Session("debug") = 1 Then
        Response.Write myString & "<br>"
    End If
End Function
```

System.Trace

The Trace object in ASP.NET provides you with the same debugging functionality and much more, without impeding the performance of our application (at least, not when tracing is turned off!). By simply turning Tracing on for a page, you get a great deal of information about the execution of the page, including elapsed time information. Figure 13.1 shows a simple ASP.NET trace example, for the HelloWorldVB.aspx example used in Chapter 2, "An Introduction to ASP.NET." The source code is listed in Listing 13.2, and is identical to the source in Chapter 2 except for the addition of the Trace="True" statement in the Page directive.

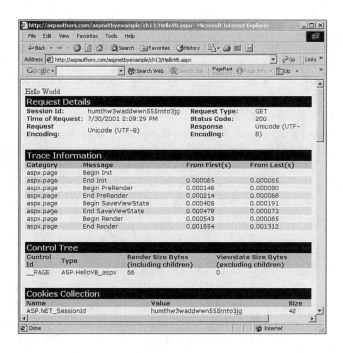

Figure 13.1: *An ASP.NET trace example.*

EXAMPLE

Listing 13.2: Source code for HelloVB.aspx

```
<%@ Page Language="VB" Trace="True"%>
<html>
<head>
</head>
<body>
<%
Response.Write("Hello World")
%>
</body>
</html>
```

Trace Output

With tracing enabled, you get a wealth of information about the execution of your code. There are eight main sections of the trace output page: Request Details, Trace Information, Control Tree, Cookies Collection, Headers Collection, Form Collection, Querystring Collection, and Server Variables. The different collections are only displayed if they have values to display, so frequently some will be omitted from trace output.

Request Details

This section of the trace output contains simple metadata about the page execution, such as when it occurred and what kind of request (GET or POST) it was. The session ID and HTTP status code are also included.

Trace Information

The Trace Information section is the area where your Trace.Write() or Trace.Warn() statements will appear (we'll cover these methods in detail shortly). It lists messages in a table view, including the category of the message and the message text. Also included is the time since the previous message (From Last) and a running tally of the time since the page began execution (From First).

Control Tree

ASP.NET controls are covered in Chapters 5 through 9. Any controls that are used on the page are listed in this section of the trace output, along with their memory size in bytes (because controls can include other controls, the size is listed both with and without child controls). The ASP.pagename_aspx control (where pagename is the name of your ASP.NET page) will be listed here even if no other controls are used on the page, because the Page object is used to render the trace output and is the base class for all ASP.NET pages.

Cookies Collection

Any cookies sent by the client in the request header are displayed in this section.

Headers Collection

The Headers collection displays the HTTP headers that were passed to the server with this request.

Form Collection

The Form collection displays any form values that were POSTed to the page.

Querystring Collection

The Querystring collection displays any querystring values that were appended to the URL or the result of a GET form submission.

For classic ASP developers, this is the Request.ServerVariables collection that you are familiar with. If you're unfamiliar with this collection, it includes many name-value pairs, such as the server name, IP address, client IP address, page path, and much more. This collection often has information that is useful when debugging.

Implementing Tracing

Now let's take a look at the actual implementation of the Trace class, shown in Listing 13.3. We'll just examine the VB version of the class prototypes; the C# or JScript versions can be viewed using the class browser application that ships with the .NET SDK (or available at http://docs. aspng.com/quickstart/aspplus/doc/classbrowser.aspx), under the System.Web.TraceContext object.

EXAMPLE

Listing 13.3: VB prototype for the Trace class.

```
Public Warn (category As String, message As String)
Public Warn (category As String, message As String, errorInfo as Exception)
Public Write (category As String, message As String)
Public Write (category As String, message As String, errorInfo as Exception)
```

Note that both Trace.Warn and Trace.Write are examples of *overloaded* methods. That is, more than one method definition exists for a given name, and the one that is used depends on the *signature*, or number and type of parameters, that is used to invoke the method. In the case of these two methods, the effect is that the errorInfo parameter is essentially optional—whether or not it is used affects the method's behavior, but it is not a required parameter.

The category parameter is used to group a set of messages together, for instance, if you wanted to signal that you were in a particular subroutine, or a particular iteration of a loop. The message string is your actual message that you are outputting—this can be anything you like. If your program encounters an exception that you handle, you can use Trace or Warn to report that exception, using the errorInfo parameter. Let's look at how each of these parameters is used in an example. Listing 13.4 demonstrates how you might make use of tracing to debug a function, by displaying the status of the function in different states and iterations.

EXAMPLE

Listing 13.4: Source code for tracedebug.aspx.

```
<%@ Page Language="VB" Trace="False"  %>
<script runat="server" language="vb" Option="Strict">

Function Factorial (base as Integer) as Integer
```

Listing 13.4: continued

```
    If base <=0 Then
        Trace.Warn("Factorial", "Invalid base value: " & base)
        Exit Function
    ElseIf base = 1 Then
        Trace.Write ("Factorial", "Exit condition met, returning.")
        Return base
    Else
        Trace.Write("Factorial","Recursing, new value: " & base-1)
        Return base * Factorial(base-1)
    End If
End Function
</script>
<html>
<head>
</head>
<body>
<%
    Response.Write(Factorial(-1) & "<br>")
    Response.Write(Factorial(5) & "<br>")
%>
</body>
</html>
```

This code produces the output displayed in Figure 13.2.

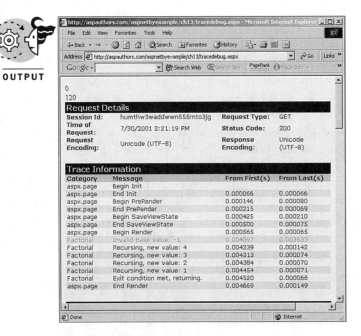

Figure 13.2: *Tracing output.*

Notice the difference in effect between Warn and Write (you may need to view this page yourself to see the difference, because the black-and-white figure probably doesn't demonstrate it). Warn displays the message line in red, whereas Write displays it in black. This is really the only difference between the two commands, but it does allow you to differentiate between simple logging and more important messages.

System.Trace.TraceContext

When you use Trace, you are using an instance of the TraceContext class defined in the System.Web namespace.TraceContext supports the following two properties:

- IsEnabled. Boolean that returns true if tracing is enabled.

- TraceMode. Used to set or determine the sorting method used when outputting trace information.

IsEnabled is provided so that debugging logic beyond simple trace statements can be encapsulated in if statements and only executed when the page is actually in debug mode. For example, if you looped through a collection and output the contents using Trace, you would want to enclose the entire loop in an If Trace.IsEnabled Then statement so that you wouldn't have the overhead of the loop when the application was not being debugged.

TraceMode determines the order in which tracing output is displayed. By default, trace output is listed sequentially, in order of execution. This corresponds to the TraceMode value of SortByTime. The other option for TraceMode is SortByCategory, which lists trace output sorted by category first, and then by time.

TIP

In Custom Components, you can use tracing if you reference the System.Web namespace and use the HttpContext.Current object to get a reference to the current context. For example:

System.Web.HttpContext.Current.Trace("category","message");

Exception Handling

In Classic ASP with VBScript, error handling was rudimentary at best. It consisted of two states, ON and OFF, which were controlled by the statements On Error Resume Next and On Error Goto 0. JScript ASP was a bit better than its counterpart, having added support for Try...Catch in a later version of the scripting engine, but no such improvement was ever seen in VBScript, which remained Microsoft's default language for building Active

Server Pages. Try and Catch blocks trace their origins back to C/C++, after which JavaScript/Jscript was modeled.

Enter ASP.NET, with which Microsoft has finally incorporated powerful exception-handling features into all the languages used, including VB.NET. It now becomes possible to do things that were difficult or extremely awkward in classic ASP. Further, when combined with Trace and some System.Diagnostics libraries, it is possible to build error handling into ASP.NET pages that would only have been possible in compiled COM objects with classic ASP pages. Listing 13.5 demonstrates this capability. The results of Listing 13.5 are displayed in Figure 13.3.

EXAMPLE

Listing 13.5: Source code for logerror.aspx.

```vb
<%@ Page Language="VB" Trace="True"  %>
<script runat="server" language="vb" Option="Strict">

Function Factorial (base as Integer) as Integer
    If base <=0 Then
        Err.Raise(-1,"Factorial","Invalid value for Factorial")
    '
    'we forget our exit condition here...
    '
    'ElseIf base = 1 Then
    '    Trace.Write ("Factorial", "Exit condition met, returning.")
    '    Return base
    Else
        Trace.Write("Factorial","Recursing, new value: " & base-1)
        Try
            Return base * Factorial(base-1)
        Catch E As Exception
            Trace.Warn ("Factorial: " & base, "Error in Factorial call.", E)
        End Try
    End If
End Function
</script>
<html>
<head>
</head>
<body>
<%
    Try
        Response.Write(Factorial(-1) & "<br>")
    Catch E As Exception
        Trace.Warn ("Main: -1", "Error calling Factorial", E)
    End Try
    Try
```

Listing 13.5: continued

```
        Response.Write(Factorial(5) & "<br>")
    Catch E As Exception
        Trace.Warn ("Main: 5", "Error calling Factorial", E)
    End Try
%>
</body>
</html>
```

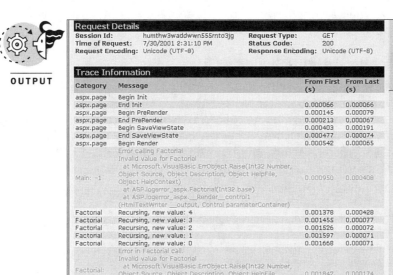

Request Details			
Session Id:	humthw3waddwwn555rnto3jg	Request Type:	GET
Time of Request:	7/30/2001 2:31:10 PM	Status Code:	200
Request Encoding:	Unicode (UTF-8)	Response Encoding:	Unicode (UTF-8)

Trace Information			
Category	Message	From First (s)	From Last (s)
aspx.page	Begin Init		
aspx.page	End Init	0.000066	0.000066
aspx.page	Begin PreRender	0.000145	0.000079
aspx.page	End PreRender	0.000213	0.000067
aspx.page	Begin SaveViewState	0.000403	0.000191
aspx.page	End SaveViewState	0.000477	0.000074
aspx.page	Begin Render	0.000542	0.000065

Main: -1	Error calling Factorial
	Invalid value for Factorial
	  at Microsoft.VisualBasic.ErrObject.Raise(Int32 Number, Object Source, Object Description, Object HelpFile, Object HelpContext)
	  at ASP.logerror_aspx.Factorial(Int32 base)
	  at ASP.logerror_aspx.__Render__control1 (HtmlTextWriter __output, Control parameterContainer)
		0.000950	0.000408

Factorial	Recursing, new value: 4	0.001378	0.000428
Factorial	Recursing, new value: 3	0.001455	0.000077
Factorial	Recursing, new value: 2	0.001526	0.000072
Factorial	Recursing, new value: 1	0.001597	0.000071
Factorial	Recursing, new value: 0	0.001668	0.000071

Factorial: 1	Error in Factorial call.
	Invalid value for Factorial
	  at Microsoft.VisualBasic.ErrObject.Raise(Int32 Number, Object Source, Object Description, Object HelpFile, Object HelpContext)
	  at ASP.logerror_aspx.Factorial(Int32 base)
	  at ASP.logerror_aspx.Factorial(Int32 base)
		0.001842	0.000174

aspx.page	End Render	0.002313	0.000470

Done — Internet

Figure 13.3: *Built-in error handling.*

Note that in this example, we have broken the Factorial function such that it has no valid exit condition, but rather raises an error when an invalid value is sent to it. Demonstrating the usage of the Try and Catch statements in VB, we cause this exception to be raised both directly from the main page execution as well as from within a recursive call to the function. If you're unfamiliar with Try, Catch, and Finally, consider this really quick explanation. Basically, you want your code to attempt (or try) to execute whatever is in the Try block. However, if any errors are thrown, they are caught by the Catch block (with a reference to the exception passed in, E in Listing 13.5). Although not demonstrated in this code listing, the Finally block provides a third block of code that is executed regardless of whether there were any errors encountered in the Try block. The Finally block is most often used to execute any "cleanup code" that is required to release resources used in the Try or Catch blocks. Getting back to the example in

Listing 13.5, in both Try blocks, when the exception is encountered, we trap it with a Catch statement and use Trace.Warn to display the error information.

By passing the exception, E, to the Warn (or Write) method of Trace, the details of the exception are written out in addition to whatever message is sent in the message parameter. Essentially, this is the same as if the exception's ToString method were called and appended to the method parameter. This provides a simple way to output detailed error information for debugging purposes.

Application-Level Debugging

In addition to page-level tracing, we can also enable or disable tracing for our entire application. This is done through the web.config utility that was discussed in detail in Chapter 10, "ASP.NET Applications." By adding the setting described in Listing 13.6, we enable tracing for our entire application. The various settings and their effects are described in Table 13.1. Note that this setting must be made in the Web.config file located in the application root, not in a subdirectory's Web.config.

EXAMPLE

Listing 13.6: The web.config settings to enable application tracing.

```
<!--Sample trace setting -->
<trace enabled="true" localOnly="false" requestLimit="10"
     pageOutput="false" traceMode="SortByTime" />
```

Table 13.1: The web.config Settings

Property	Effect	Description
enabled	[true | false]	Setting this to true enables application-level tracing. The default is false.
localOnly	[true | false]	This property must be set to true in order to view the application Trace from a remote machine. The default is false.
requestLimit	[int]	This setting determines how many requests to keep in memory for the application, and is used by the Trace.axd tool when displaying trace results. The default is 10.
pageOutput	[true | false]	This setting determines whether or not every page in the application displays tracing output. When this is set to false, but enabled is set to true, trace output is still available through the use of the Trace.axd utility, described in the next section. The default is false.
traceMode	[SortByCategory | SortByTime]	This determines how individual trace items are sorted in the trace output. The default is SortByTime.

Application-level tracing allows you to view trace output for every page in your application, either on each page or through a centrally organized page called Trace.axd. The Trace.axd page does not actually correspond to a file on the Web server, but rather makes use of an HTTP handler to detect the request for this file and respond with the dynamically generated tracing information. HTTP handlers are similar to ISAPI extensions, and are a fairly advanced technique that is beyond the scope of this book. You can learn more about them at `http://docs.aspng.com/quickstart/aspplus/doc/httphandlers.aspx`. An example of a Trace.axd file is shown in Figure 13.4.

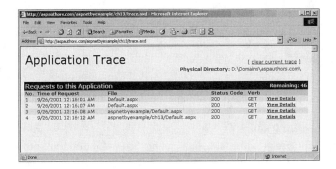

Figure 13.4: *A Trace.axd file.*

The Trace.axd file has two views. The default view displays a list of up to (`requestlimit`) pages that have trace information. Clicking on the View Details link for any of these pages brings up its trace output, which is identical to the trace output that you saw in Figure 13.2 for a page using page-level tracing.

System.Diagnostics Tools

The .NET Framework includes a number of tools in the `System.Diagnostics` namespace that are useful for gathering debugging information. A common tool used to track Windows Distributed internet Applications (DNA) applications is the event log. A major disadvantage of using events to log debugging information was the fact that you couldn't generally access the event log without direct access to the server (either physically or through a remote control application). Using the `System.Diagnostics` namespace, it is very easy to build an event log viewer in ASP.NET, so that you can see your events without having to access the server directly.

Logging Events

The System.Diagnostics namespace offers many useful functions, and logging events is just one of them. A common place where you may want to log events is in response to system errors, so that you can track them down at a later date. The easiest way to do this is to add an Application_Error function to your global.asax file. Listing 13.7 shows how to configure an error event handler for your ASP.NET application.

EXAMPLE

Listing 13.7: global.asax Application_Error function (C#).

```
public void Application_Error(Object sender, EventArgs e)
{
        string LogName = "ASPAlliance";
        string ErrorMessage;

        ErrorMessage = "URL: " + Request.Path;
        ErrorMessage += " Error: " +
                Server.GetLastError().ToString();

        // Create event log if it doesn't exist
        if (!System.Diagnostics.EventLog.SourceExists(LogName))
        {
        System.Diagnostics.EventLog.CreateEventSource(LogName, LogName);
        }
        System.Diagnostics.EventLog Log = new
System.Diagnostics.EventLog();
        Log.Source = LogName;
        Log.WriteEntry(ErrorMessage,
System.Diagnostics.EventLogEntryType.Error);
}
```

The first two lines of this function set the event log name to the name of our application and build our event string from the page's URL and exception that caused this event to be raised, which is available through the use of the this keyword (the me keyword in VB).

We determine whether this log has been created already by using the SourceExists method of the System.Diagnostics.EventLog namespace. This returns true if the name we pass exists, and false otherwise. If the log doesn't exist, we create it by using the CreateEventSource function, passing the LogName variable for both the event source and the event log name. Finally, we create an instance of the EventLog class, set its source to our application's name, and use its WriteEntry method to log the error message, specifying an event type of Error using the EventLogEntryType class (which has properties for each possible event type).

To test that this is working, create a simple ASPX page in your application that creates a variable, assigns it to zero, and then attempts to divide by it.

You should note that the error is captured by this event handler and logged to an event log. You can read the event log on the Web server by using the Administrative Tools – Event Viewer utility, or you can write an ASP.NET page to read the event log, as we will now do.

Reading Event Logs

Logging events is great, but only if you can read them—preferably without having to be logged on locally to the Web server. The next example is a full-featured event viewer that you can copy to any .NET-enabled Web server. The complete source is available from this book's Web site—we will just look at the interesting parts here. Listing 13.8 displays the code that is used to retrieve the events and bind them to our repeater control, or delete them.

NOTE

View This Example Live:

http://aspauthors.com/aspnetbyexample/ch13/events.aspx

EXAMPLE

Listing 13.8: events.aspx (C#).

```
protected void Page_Load(object sender, EventArgs e)
{
        try{
            if (!IsPostBack)
            {
                    BindEvents();
            }
        }
        catch{
            Response.Write("There were errors in the processing of your
request.");
        }
    }

    private void BindEvents()
    {
            int i;

            // Get an array with all of the event logs on the server
            EventLog[]elArray = EventLog.GetEventLogs(".");

            // Populate a SELECT box with the different event logs
            logs.DataSource = elArray;
            logs.DataTextField = "Log";
            logs.DataValueField = "Log";
```

Listing 13.8: continued

```
                logs.DataBind();

                for (i=0;i<logs.Items.Count;i++)
                {
                    try{
                        logs.Items[i].Text =
                                        logs.Items[i].Text +
                                        " (" + elArray[i].Entries.Count +
                                        " rows)";
                    }
                    catch(Exception e){
                        // do not display the restricted logfiles
                        Trace.Write("BindEvents",
                                        "Cannot Access " +
                                        logs.Items[i].Text);
                        Trace.Write("BindEvents","",e);
                        logs.Items.Remove(logs.Items[i]);
                        i--;
                    }
                }
        }

        protected void getMessages_Click(object sender,

                                                        EventArgs e)
        {
            GetLogEntries();
        }

        protected void clearLog_Click(object sender, EventArgs e)
        {
            EventLog el = new EventLog();
            el.MachineName = ".";
            el.Log = logs.SelectedItem.Value.ToString();
            el.Clear();
            el.Close();
            BindEvents();
            GetLogEntries();
        }

        protected void GetLogEntries()
        {
            EventLog el = new EventLog();
            el.MachineName=".";
            el.Log = logs.SelectedItem.Value.ToString();
            System.Collections.ArrayList alEvents =
```

Listing 13.8: continued

```
                new System.Collections.ArrayList(el.Entries);
        alEvents.Reverse();
        messages.DataSource = alEvents;
        messages.DataBind();
        el.Close();
    }

    protected string GetEventTypeDesc(EventLogEntryType elet)
    {
        switch(elet)
        {
            case EventLogEntryType.Error:
                return "Error";
            case EventLogEntryType.Warning:
                return "Warning";
            case EventLogEntryType.Information:
                return "Information";
            case EventLogEntryType.SuccessAudit:
                return "Success Audit";
            default:  //EventLogEntryType.FailureAudit
                return "Failure Audit";
        }
    }
}
```

In the Page_Load function, we first bind a list of all event logs on this
machine to a drop-down box control called logs. This is accomplished using
the GetEventLogs() method, and passing it a "." to represent the local
machine. The resulting array is then used as the data source for our drop-
down list. To make the list more useful, we then loop through it and append
the number of events in each log to the displayed text, using the
Entries.Count property of the EventLog object.

Clicking on the button to display messages in a log calls the getMessages_
Click method, which in turn simply calls GetLogEntries. GetLogEntries
retrieves the event log referenced in the drop-down list, reverses the order
by using an array, and then binds the repeater control messages to the
array. By default, messages are listed in order from oldest to newest, so the
Reverse is necessary to make the events display most recent first, like the
Windows Event Viewer application.

Clearing an event log is accomplished simply by instantiating an Eventlog
object, setting it to the log described by the drop-down list logs, and using
the Clear() method.

That's it! I recommend that you use event logging only for events that happen infrequently, or else your logs will get very large very quickly. For most
times when you're actively debugging, the Trace function is better, but if

you have a production application and you want to know if it is misbehaving, event logging may be the way to go. And with this application, you won't have to log on to the server itself to view the event logs!

Other `System.Diagnostics` Tools

The `System.Diagnostics` tools offer a lot of functionality for debugging and monitoring of your ASP.NET applications. Although we don't have time to cover much more in detail, I do want to demonstrate how easy it is to display performance counter values through this library. For this example, we'll display how many users are logged on to the Web server (total for all webs), something impossible to do using classic ASP without a custom component.

If you are using Visual Studio.NET, you can use the Server Explorer to locate performance counters that you would like to include in your ASP. NET page, and just drag them onto the page. However, even without Visual Studio.NET, taking advantage of Windows performance counters in your .NET application is really very easy. Listing 13.9 demonstrates how to set up a counter object. You can view this example live and download the complete source from this book's support Web site.

EXAMPLE

Listing 13.9: perfActiveSessionsCS.aspx (C#).

```
protected void Page_Load()
{
if (!IsPostBack)
{
    System.Diagnostics.PerformanceCounter SessionsActiveCounter;
    SessionsActiveCounter = new System.Diagnostics.PerformanceCounter ();
    SessionsActiveCounter.CategoryName = "ASP.NET Applications";
    SessionsActiveCounter.InstanceName = "__Total__";
    SessionsActiveCounter.CounterName = "Sessions Active";
    SessionsActiveCounter.MachineName = ".";
    lblUsers.Text = SessionsActiveCounter.NextValue().ToString();
}
}
```

Performance counters are exposed by the `System.Diagnostics.PerformanceCounter` class. To use a counter object, simply provide it with some required properties, such as the category and name of the counter, the instance of the counter if it has more than one, and the machine name of the server on which the counter resides. That's it. To get the scalar value of a counter at any given instant, use the `RawValue` constant. In this example, we are displaying the total active sessions for the Web server (for ASP.NET) in a label control on the page.

NOTE

See a demonstration of how to use performance counters in your ASP.NET pages live at `http://aspauthors.com/aspnetbyexample/ch13/`.

Visual Studio.NET

If you are developing with Visual Studio.NET, its integrated debugger will allow you to step through your ASP.NET application, including all components and Web controls, as it executes on your server. To configure your project for debugging, make sure you complete a few steps first. However, after this is done, you will find that debugging with VS.NET is definitely the way to go, and something that has long been lacking from ASP development tools.

The first step to getting your project ready to use the Visual Studio.NET debugger is to make sure your web.config file has an element for compilation debug mode that is set to true, as in Listing 13.10.

EXAMPLE

Listing 13.10: The web.config settings to enable debugging.

```
<compilation debugMode="True" />
```

Frequently Encountered Bugs

If you're a veteran VBScript/ASP developer, here are a few things to watch out for as you debug your ASP.NET pages. These are the kinds of mistakes you'll probably find yourself making as you transition from ASP to ASP.NET programming.

Runat="Server"

Script blocks and controls all need to be marked with the attribute `RUNAT="Server"` if you want them to be processed by ASP.NET. It's especially common to forget this on FORM tags. Remember, if you want to take advantage of ASP.NET's form-handling capabilities, the form itself must have a `RUNAT="Server"` attribute. Further, you can only have one form per page that is configured this way. If you think you need more than one form, you probably don't. Consider using more than one button-click event handler instead, but only one form. You will find that nearly any page you design can be built successfully using just one server-side FORM tag. Also note that, if you omit the FORM entirely, your web controls will fail, which is another common mistake to watch out for.

Type Mismatches

Type mismatches are rarely a problem in the weakly typed VBScript environment, but you may find them to be a common problem as you move to a strongly typed VB or C# programming language. Get to know the typecasting syntax of your language of choice, and make use of the framework documentation to ensure that you are using parameters and return types that are correct. Although somewhat common, these bugs are usually pretty easy to find, thanks to the fact that the ASP.NET compiler is pretty good about giving useful error information for these errors.

VB/VBScript Syntax

If you've primarily used VBScript (and perhaps VB6 or earlier) for your ASP development, going to VB.NET may result in some other common mistakes apart from type mismatches. In fact, quite a number of things have changed between VBScript/VB6 and VB.NET. Here are a few tips to remember for your ASP.NET development—of course, this is far from an exhaustive list of the differences between VBScript and VB.NET. You will find additional information about VB.NET in Appendix C.

Parameters Are Passed ByVal by Default

In previous versions of Visual Basic, parameters were passed ByRef by default. Starting with VB.NET, this has changed, and the default is now ByVal. This may result in unexpected results if legacy functions are migrated to .NET without taking this into account. I recommend that you always explicitly specify ByVal or ByRef for each parameter in your functions so that changes to the default behavior do not adversely affect your code as it is ported from one platform or version to another.

Calling Procedures

In previous versions of Visual Basic, there were two ways to call procedures (Subs). You could use the Call keyword and enclose the arguments in parentheses, as in the following example:

```
Call mySub({parameters})
```

Or you could simply refer to the procedure by name and list any parameters after it separated by commas (without parentheses), as in the following example:

```
mySub {parameters}
```

With VB.NET, this second option is no longer supported. Calls to procedures and calls to functions share the same syntax, in that both are required to list any parameters inside parentheses. This is typically how other languages behave, so personally I think this is a welcome change.

However, if you are in the habit of listing your parameters after a procedure call with no parentheses, you might not appreciate this change, because your code will fail to compile. The Call keyword can still be used optionally in VB.NET, so a procedure call looks like this:

```
{Call} mySub ({parameters})
```

Date and Time

The VB/VBScript functions Date() and Time() have been replaced in VB.NET with Today() and TimeOfDay(). Trying to use the old function names will result in compile errors.

Dim Syntax

It is unlikely that the Dim syntax will cause any bugs for most developers, because the change tends to make code that behaves more intuitively. However, I think it is worth noting here, because it is an important change from VB6 to VB.NET (it's not really an issue in VBScript, where everything is Variant). In previous versions of VB, the following statement would result in the creation of three variables: Variant x, Variant y, and Integer z:

```
Dim x, y, z As Integer
```

To create three integers with one Dim statement, each variable's type must follow each and every variable. With VB.NET, this has been changed so that the preceding line would result in the creation of three integers. This is more intuitive and makes for code that is easier to read. However, under VB.NET, you can no longer Dim variables of different types on one line. All variables in a single Dim statement must share the same type.

Wend Is Now End While

While loops in VB.NET are closed with an End While, not with the keyword Wend as in previous versions. If you are writing functions that need to coexist in both VB.NET and earlier versions, consider using the Do While...Loop syntax, which provides the same functionality and operates the same in both VB.NET and earlier versions (and also supports the Exit Do short circuit syntax to exit the loop). Using the familiar While...Wend syntax will cause you problems in VB.NET.

Summary

Debugging is an important part of software development, and with Classic ASP, it was generally a challenge. ASP.NET goes a long way toward bringing the process of debugging up to the level that developers have come to expect from established languages like Visual Basic or Visual C++. The tracing and diagnostic libraries of the .NET framework make it much easier to determine what your code is doing, and Visual Studio.NET's integrated debugger makes it easy to step through ASP and component code even when it involves several different languages.

NOTE

For a more complete reference on debugging ASP.NET applications, consider *Debugging ASP.NET*, from New Riders Publishing, by Jonathan Goodyear and Brian Peek.

What's Next

In Chapter 14, we will take a look at a case study of how to build a successful e-commerce site using ASP.NET. For this study, we will be looking at the Microsoft-designed site, IBuySpy.com, the complete source code of which is available online at the Web site. We will walk through how the site was designed and implemented using ASP.NET best practices, and with the help of the designers, shed some light on why as well as how they did the things they did.

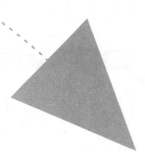

14

Case Study: E-commerce with ASP.NET

In this chapter, you will learn how Microsoft recommends using .NET to build scalable, maintainable Internet solutions for e-commerce. Microsoft, in cooperation with Vertigo Software, has provided a complete working e-commerce Web site to demonstrate how easy it is to use ASP.NET to build Web applications. This application is available online and is called IBuySpy.com (IBS).

Building a Web Store—IBuySpy.com

`IBuySpy.com` is a humorous, fictitious retail site that lists, sells, and tracks transactions for high-tech spy gear. The purpose of IBuySpy is to provide a working example of how to build an online storefront using ASP.NET, and it is available with complete documentation and source code. The entire site is available for demonstration and download from `http://www.ibuyspy.com`. The goal of this case study is to provide insight into the design decisions that went into creating the site, as well as to highlight some of the more interesting techniques that were used in its creation.

As we go though the chapter, it will help if you are familiar with the site and ideally if you have it available to reference, either online or installed locally. Microsoft continues to update the site, and at the time of this writing, the IBS Store is currently in Beta 2, build 0711. By the time you are reading this, several more builds will probably have occurred, but for the most part the site should remain unchanged. Because the IBuySpy team themselves will be reviewing this chapter before it goes to print, it's very likely that some of the recommended improvements will be implemented on the public site by the time this book reaches stores.

In this chapter, we're going to first take a look at the high-level design of the site. We will then examine how certain features were implemented for the IBS store.

IBuySpy Store Design

The IBS store is designed to provide a learning tool for ASP.NET developers. As such, the code is short, sweet, and to-the-point. Everything is well documented, and in general the simple approach is taken toward most tasks. This makes the site very easy to understand for developers who are new to ASP.NET. However, it also means that for some parts of the application, only a foundation is provided, not a complete solution. When the IBS method differs from how a real-world application should be designed, I will note the difference and why Microsoft chose to implement it the way they did.

Sources

In this chapter, I will occasionally quote members of the IBuySpy development team. The IBuySpy team includes Scott Guthrie and Susan Warren of Microsoft and Mike Amundsen and Bob Lair of Vertigo Software. This group designed and built the first version of the IBuySpy store in just four weeks. All four of these individuals are very helpful, and in particular Scott and Susan were able to answer many of my questions as I prepared this case study. Rob Howard, of Microsoft, was also very helpful.

The IBuySpy.com Web site and all of its source code is available for free to the public. You are welcome to use this code as a base for your own applications and to extend and modify it however you see fit. The only restriction placed upon the IBuySpy applications is that the installation files not be redistributed, to ensure that the latest builds are always available from the IBuySpy.com Web site.

Design Considerations

Let's examine some of the design considerations that Microsoft had when preparing to build the IBS store. One of the things that makes developing with Microsoft tools so much easier than with many other vendors' offerings is the wealth of documentation and sample material they provide to developers. `IBuySpy.com` is not the first sample application Microsoft has used to demonstrate its technology. For example, the Duwamish bookstore (`http://duwamishonline.com`), originally devised as a sample desktop application, has been around for years and continues to evolve today into a distributed .NET application. Similarly, the FMStocks sample (`http://fmstocks.com`) application provides a great example of how to build a scalable Windows DNA application on Windows NT or 2000, and is also being revised to support .NET. Both of these sample applications are available at Microsoft's MSDN site, `http://msdn.microsoft.com`. Susan Warren notes: "The IBuySpy apps are intentionally implemented as simply as possible to facilitate learning. FMStocks, on the other hand, was intended to be a more general architecture prototype and specifically to show off the benefits/implementation of COM+ services."

The primary goal in designing IBuySpy was that it be simple and easy to understand. To this end, the application was designed in a modular fashion using a small number of subsystems. Because many people would use the application as a basis for developing more advanced applications, IBS was designed to be extensible and followed good coding and architectural guidelines. In the overview of the application, three design goals are cited: minimal code, high performance, and scalability. We will see in this chapter how all three of these goals were met by the application.

If IBuySpy had been designed to meet some transactions-per-second benchmark (as FMStocks was), it would have been developed somewhat differently. For one thing, it would probably have used COM+ for transaction management. The existing IBuySpy store doesn't even use transactions or deal with the payment process at all. This is left as an exercise for the reader. But remember, this was not IBuySpy's goal.

Architecturally, IBuySpy's application logic was divided into several well-known layers. Unlike previous sample applications, however, IBuySpy did not include separate data access layer (DAL) and business logic layer (BLL) components. This helped keep the number of components and total code required for the application to a minimum.

COMPONENT ARCHITECTURE

In software application design, it helps to isolate the logical parts of the program into separate layers. For example, one might group all data access rules in one layer (the Data Access Layer, or DAL), and all business logic in another layer (the Business Logic Layer, or BLL). This would allow for easier modification at a later date. Thus, if (or more likely, when) business rules change, only the business layer objects need to be modified, or if the data store changes, only the data access layer objects need to be updated.

Figure 14.1 describes how the different layers of an application are frequently broken up across different physical or logical boundaries. Desktop applications, the classical example, were traditionally built with everything on the same machine and in the same logical space. Client/server applications tend to follow the two-tier design displayed. Most Windows DNA applications are built using something like the three-tier design (FMStocks 2000 follows this architecture). Finally, it is possible to distribute every layer across multiple machines to provide the greatest scalability and reliability, and the N-tier design demonstrates this.

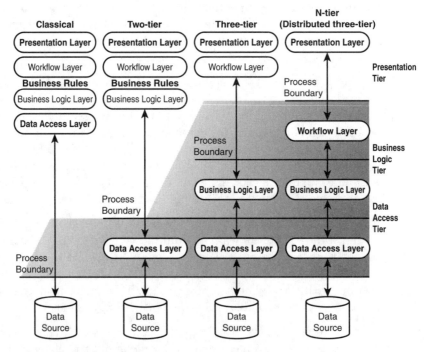

Figure 14.1: *Tiered application architectures.*

At first, the IBuySpy team designed the application with separate layers of components for data access and for business rules. However, they found that the BLL was merely serving as a pass-through layer, and wasn't actually adding any benefits to the application. Experience from FMStocks had taught Vertigo and Microsoft that "having a 'pluggable' data layer (which would also justify the Biz layer) is also only 'sometimes' worthwhile. Most of the time [it] is just more code, and doesn't improve scalability or maintainability." (Susan Warren)

Currently, IBuySpy's architecture, as shown in Figure 14.2, is most closely related to the two-tier design. As you can see, its architecture is compressed into basically two layers—the pages themselves—which include presentation, context, and business logic—and a set of data access layer objects.

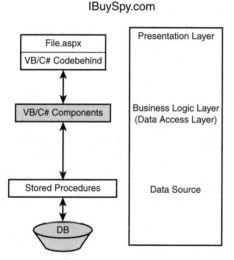

Figure 14.2: *IBuySpy architecture.*

Figure 14.3 displays a tree view of the classes used in the IBuySpy application. If you look at the IBuySpy namespace, the distinction between pages and data access layer components is easy to see. The Components namespace lists all the data access classes, and the Pages namespace lists all the ASP.NET pages used in the application.

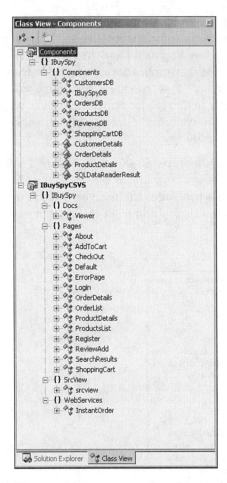

Figure 14.3: IBuySpy *class hierarchy.*

Note that each main object in the application, such as a Customer or an Order, has its own DAL component associated with it. This is similar to other Microsoft sample sites, such as FMStocks, and is a good way to organize your components. This system allows all related functionality for a particular part of your application to be encapsulated into one class. Meanwhile, general functions or tools that are needed by the entire application should be placed in a "library" component, or an application class. This is basically what the IBuySpyDB class does. IBuySpyDB simply exposes the connection string used by the application to access the back-end database

APPLICATION-LEVEL SETTINGS

The IBuySpy web.config file makes an excellent template for new developers to use when building their own ASP.NET applications. It includes a number of best practices for storing application-wide variables like connection strings, securing certain pages with a login screen, and configuring customer error handling. For reference, the entire web.config file is listed in Listing 14.1, but you can also view the most current version online at the IBuySpy Web site (http://www.ibuyspy.com).

Listing 14.1: IBuySpy store web.config.

```xml
<?xml version="1.0" encoding="utf-8" ?>
<configuration>
    <!-- application specific settings -->
    <appSettings>
        <add key="ConnectionString"
             value="server=localhost;uid=sa;pwd=;database=store" />
    </appSettings>
    <!-- forms based authentication -->
    <system.web>
        <!-- enable Forms authentication -->
        <authentication mode="Forms">
            <forms name="IBuySpyStoreAuth" loginUrl="login.aspx"
                protection="All" path="/" />
        </authentication>
        <!-- enable custom errors for the application -->
        <customErrors mode="RemoteOnly" defaultRedirect="ErrorPage.aspx" />
        <!-- disable session state for application -->
        <sessionState mode="Off" />
    </system.web>
    <!-- set secure paths -->
    <location path="Checkout.aspx">
        <system.web>
            <authorization>
                <deny users="?" />
            </authorization>
        </system.web>
    </location>
    <location path="OrderList.aspx">
        <system.web>
            <authorization>
                <deny users="?" />
            </authorization>
        </system.web>
    </location>
    <location path="OrderDetails.aspx">
        <system.web>
            <authorization>
                <deny users="?" />
            </authorization>
        </system.web>
    </location>
</configuration>
```

You learned about the web.config file in Chapter 10, "ASP.NET Applications." In ASP, there were many different ways to store connection information, and many different myths about which one was the best. Most experienced ASP developers stored the connection information in an application variable that was set in Application_OnStart. Although this is still an option with ASP.NET, I do not recommend it for several reasons. The first reason is that, logically, database connection information is an application configuration piece of data, and so it should reside in the web.config with the other configuration data. More importantly, though, there is the question of security. If you store your connection string in an application variable, and you *ever* decide to use Trace on a public Web page, your database connection information will be exposed to the world within the Trace dump, because it lists the contents of all application and session variables. I first ran into this on ASPAlliance.com, because I was preparing a tutorial on tracing. I quickly learned that storing database connection information in the application scope was *not* a good idea if you are planning to use Trace as part of your application, for the reasons I already mentioned.

In Chapter 3, we discussed some different ways to migrate ASP-based login pages to ASP.NET. The simplest and most effective way to accomplish this is through the technique used by IBuySpy. The <location> attributes allow you to manage your file security in one central location for your application. However, there is one limitation to using the web.config file: Only the root web.config file has authority to set permission configuration (or, for that matter, debug configuration) information for the application. If, for some reason, you absolutely do not have access to the root web's web.config file, you will need to find an alternative way to secure your pages, such as the user control discussed in Chapter 3.

Finally, there are two other application-wide settings that IBuySpy uses to enhance its performance. I consider these to be application settings because they are done on every page, but the actual implementation of these two best practices requires code on each individual ASP.NET page that uses them. The first item is the use of session state, and this is disabled by using the EnableSessionState="False" Page directive. You should use this on every page in your application that does not require session information, because it reduces the amount of resources the page will require on the server. The second directive is similar, and determines whether or not controls on a page should maintain their viewstate between postbacks. This should only be used for pages that post back to themselves—any other page should disable this functionality by using the EnableViewState="False" attribute in the Page directive. Tracking viewstate requires resources both when the page is rendered and also in the form of network bandwidth, because the (often large) viewstate data must be passed to and from the client with each request. Obviously, this should only be done when necessary.

NOTE

You can also control viewstate on individual controls by setting the EnableViewState property. You should disable viewstate for any control that doesn't use it to guarantee optimum performance.

DATABASE DESIGN

The IBuySpy store uses just seven small database tables to store all the data required for the site. These tables and their relationships (as installed) are listed in Figure 14.4. Note that there are a few omissions to the database that should be corrected in a production application, such as adding a foreign key from OrderDetails to Products on ProductID, and also adding a primary key on Reviews. However, because the application currently doesn't allow any way for users to violate data integrity on these tables, the lack of these constraints is not terribly important to IBuySpy as a sample application. I mention them here only for the sake of absolute correctness. Of course, if you were to build on this design and use it for a production application, you would want to ensure that your database integrity was guaranteed through the proper use of keys and constraints.

One thing that is worth noting in this design is that the ShoppingCart table does not have any relationship with the Customers table. Anonymous users are thus allowed to create shopping carts without having to first log in and register themselves. This is a good practice in an e-commerce site because it lowers the barriers between the customer and the buying process. Only when they commit to the purchase by clicking on Check Out are the users required to register or log in.

Another best practice to note in the database design for IBuySpy is the use of stored procedures for all of the site's data access. All data access in the IBuySpy application is done through stored procedures, which are called by separate DB components. This is done because stored procedures perform better and are easier to maintain than hard-coded SQL statements. As you build new applications and rebuild existing applications using ASP.NET, you should follow IBuySpy's example: Do not succumb to the temptation to place hard-coded SQL in your applications.

Functional Overview

As a mock e-commerce site, IBuySpy.com must provide a number of functions in order to allow the user to browse the site's products and make a purchase decision. Because it is only a sample site, it doesn't need to worry about details like credit card validation, secure access to ordering pages that transmit credit card numbers, inventory tracking, or various shipping methods. Nonetheless, it does provide an excellent starting point for a real Web-based retail store, providing functions like the ability to browse products, add items to a shopping cart, manage that cart across separate sessions, and check out. Registration and login are also handled neatly by the application.

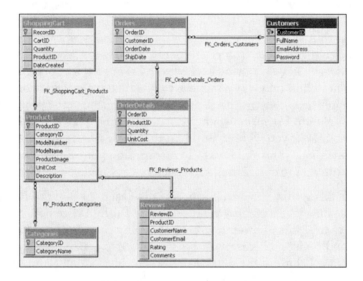

Figure 14.4: IBS database schema.

LIST PRODUCTS

Of course, no catalog store would be complete without a way to list the products available. IBuySpy does this using several different methods. On the home page, a featured product is displayed, as well as a listing of the most popular items. Clicking on any of the categories on the left menu brings up a list of products in that category, complete with small image, price, and links to obtain more information or to add the item to the shopping cart. The home page for the IBuySpy store is shown in Figure 14.5.

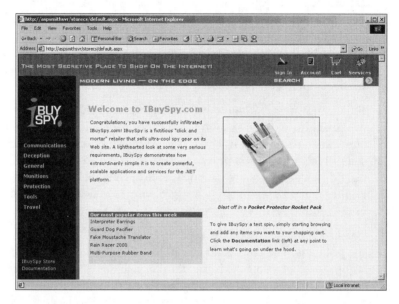

Figure 14.5: *The IBuySpy home page.*

The popular items listing uses a user control to encapsulate the functionality. This is an excellent way to design your pages, because it provides better opportunities for code re-use and makes it easier to construct a template page and then just drag and drop the controls you want onto it. The featured item is hard-coded onto the page, so that it is always the Pocket Protector Rocket Pack. Obviously, this isn't ideal, because it requires the developer to edit the actual Web page in order to change the featured item, introducing potential for error. We'll see how to convert this into a user control as well later in this chapter.

Of course, the main product listing pages are the category listings and the search results page. These two pages both use the same DataList code to display the listing of products, but again, they are not user controls. Because of this, although the two pieces of code are meant to be identical, it is very easy for a developer to make a change in one and not the other, introducing unwanted behavior. For example, in one early release of the site, there was a bug on the SearchResults.aspx page that resulted in the word "ProductID" appearing next to each search result. The same code was used by both the ProductsList.aspx page and the SearchResults.aspx page to list the products, and most likely a change was made to one of these files without updating the other file, resulting in the bug.

This minor mistake made it past the testing phase because the same code was used in two places using two different copies of the code. An update to one was not reflected in the other. This is one of the primary advantages of code reuse, and this is one reason why user controls are so powerful. They provide a very easy way to encapsulate reusable pieces of code in your applications. Later in this chapter, we will redesign the SearchResults.aspx and ProductsList.aspx pages to use a User Control.

The last thing we should look at on these pages is how they get to the data for the products. The data is all stored in a SQL Server database and accessed using stored procedures. If the data for each search or category were being cached so that it would be available for other pages, it would make sense to use a DataSet to extract the data because DataSets can be easily serialized and cached. However, DataSets are bigger and slower than DataReader objects, so the first hit to the page would suffer. Further, IBuySpy is using output caching to cache the contents of the rendered page, so there is no need to cache the data itself. Thus, the DataReader provides better performance in this scenario.

In response to the question of why IBS chose to use a custom data type as the return type for their DAL components that return a single record, instead of a standard DataReader or DataSet, Susan Warren replied:

> We used the Details class type ("struct") for those queries that return a single record. This makes for much more grokkable [understandable] databinding in the UI layer. (I can bind to CustomerDetails.FullName instead of DataSet. Tables["Customers"][0]["FullName"]. It's also strongly typed, so you get statement completion and design-time syntax checking from VS.NET. Because there's no biz logic reason for disconnected data, we used DataReaders to render the UI, for performance reasons. In several places we used DataSets in order to have a disconnected object we could cache.

ADD ITEMS TO CART

Using ASP.NET, developers are encouraged to create their pages so that they submit back to themselves using a "postback." One of the lessons we can learn from IBuySpy is in what instances this technique is not a good idea. A good example of this involves the AddToCart functionality.

Although the product listing and search result pages could each have implemented the AddToCart function as a postback method on each of these pages, this was not done for several reasons. Postbacks require maintaining viewstate, which is expensive especially on pages that have a lot of server controls, because data for each control must be rendered and sent over the wire. Also, because the functionality of adding an item to the cart could be called from other pages apart from the list pages (such as the home page, for instance), segregating this functionality into its own page helps keep the code logically separated and easier to reuse.

The actual AddToCart.aspx page doesn't really have any presentation logic to it at all. It simply uses its Page_Load event to add an item to the user's shopping cart before redirecting the page to the ShoppingCart.aspx page. This is a good example of how to implement general functions in an application when the functions do not require much user interaction and can be called from many different pages.

One last note for developers who are building international e-commerce sites: most countries don't use shopping *carts*; they use shopping *baskets*. If you want your customers to intuitively understand your store, and your audience extends beyond North America, you may want to use a "basket" instead of a "cart" to hold your wares.

MANAGE CART

The ShoppingCart.aspx page is probably the most complicated page in the whole IBuySpy application. It uses a DataGrid to render the contents of the user's shopping cart, providing the user with controls to use to update quantities or delete items. DataGrids, described in Chapter 4, offer developers a great deal of flexibility and power, but of course with all this flexibility comes the requirement to write a decent amount of code to implement a particular behavior. This is the main reason why the ShoppingCart.aspx and ShoppingCart.cs (or .vb) files are each a few pages long—there is a lot going on with the DataGrid. For this reason, this page makes an excellent study example of how to use DataGrids.

The way anonymous and registered users' carts are handled by this page is interesting. The CartID is used to identify the cart, and consists of a dynamically generated GUID for anonymous users and the CustomerID for known users. Whenever a user logs in or registers with the store, part of the process of authenticating the user includes migrating her cart information from anonymous to registered. This step uses a method called migrateCart in the ShoppingCartDB component, and basically all it does is update the `CartID` of the cart in question to be the `CustomerID` of the current customer.

The rest of the implementation of the shopping cart and the `DataGrid` is well documented within the IBuySpy source code, so I won't spend any more time on it here.

CHECK OUT CART

Of course, before you can finalize a transaction on an e-commerce site, you have to go through the obligatory checkout process. IBuySpy.com is no different, and offers users the option of "Final Check Out" from the Shopping Cart page. There are really only two things to note about this page. First, it requires a registered user, and will send an anonymous user to the Login.aspx page before allowing her to proceed. This is all controlled in the web.config file, which we looked at earlier. Second, the page calls a component that calls a stored procedure that creates the order, and returns an order ID to give to the customer. Apart from repeating the mantra of "use stored procedures for your data access," there isn't much else to say about this bit of functionality. Notice that by encapsulating security and data access in separate parts of the application, the CheckOut.aspx page is kept very small. The actual programming code takes less than 30 lines of code, and the whole page including HTML is less than two pages long.

REGISTER USERS

With the IBuySpy application, it doesn't take much to register yourself as a customer. A name, an e-mail address, and a password are all you need. However, although this page is simple, it does demonstrate an important concept that will come into play when we look at the Login.aspx page. User registration is one of the best places to use validation controls (discussed in Chapter 7), because this will help ensure that your database holds valid customers and not garbage data. Of course, validation can only do so much, but at the very least you should protect your customers from themselves by ensuring that their e-mail address is valid and that their password matches what was typed in the Confirm Password box. Furthermore, if you are certain to validate your user's username and password during registration, you can perform the same validation checks on your login page, and avoid the need to hit the database for login requests that are invalid according to your validation rules. Note that if you choose to use validation as the first stage to authenticating users, you must make sure that your validation logic for the registration page matches the validation logic of your login page. The easiest way to do this is to make the fields (for example, username and password and their validation controls) of the registration page into one or two User Controls.

LOGIN USERS

Although the complete login code for the IBuySpy store takes several pages, the real work is all done in one method that is called when the login button is clicked. Because this is an important piece of code and only a few lines long, it is included here as Listing 14.2. The comments provide most of the information we need to follow the code (and a VB version is available on the IBuySpy.com Web site).

Listing 14.2: IBuySpy's login code, Login.cs, C#.

```csharp
void LoginBtn_Click(Object sender, ImageClickEventArgs e) {

    // Only attempt a login if all form fields on the page are valid
    if (Page.IsValid == true) {

        // Save old ShoppingCartID
        IBuySpy.ShoppingCartDB shoppingCart =
            new IBuySpy.ShoppingCartDB();
        String tempCartID = shoppingCart.GetShoppingCartId();

        // Attempt to Validate User Credentials using CustomersDB
        IBuySpy.CustomersDB accountSystem =
            new IBuySpy.CustomersDB();
        String customerId =
            accountSystem.Login(email.Text, password.Text);

        if (customerId != null) {

            // Migrate any existing shopping cart items
            // into the permanent shopping cart
            shoppingCart.MigrateCart(tempCartID, customerId);

            // Lookup the customer's full account details
            IBuySpy.CustomerDetails customerDetails =
                accountSystem.GetCustomerDetails(customerId);

            // Store the user's fullname in a cookie
            // for personalization purposes
            Response.Cookies["IBuySpy_FullName"].Value =
                customerDetails.FullName;

            // Make the cookie persistent only if the user
            // selects "persistent" login checkbox
            if (RememberLogin.Checked == true) {
                Response.Cookies["IBuySpy_FullName"].Expires =
                    DateTime.Now.AddMonths(1);
            }
```

Listing 14.2: continued

```
            // Redirect browser back to originating page
            FormsAuthentication.RedirectFromLoginPage(customerId,
                RememberLogin.Checked);
        }
        else {
            Message.Text = "Login Failed!";
        }
    }
}
```

There really is a lot more going on here than just your typical login functionality of looking up a user and password in the database and returning true or false. The first thing we do here is ensure that the login form was valid—no sense wasting resources hitting the database if the form isn't even filled out properly, right? When we know the form is valid, we take the current shopping cart and store its ID so that we don't lose it when we log in the customer.

The actual authentication is performed with the following block of code:

```
// Attempt to Validate User Credentials using CustomersDB
IBuySpy.CustomersDB accountSystem =
    new IBuySpy.CustomersDB();
String customerId =
    accountSystem.Login(email.Text, password.Text);
```

Here, the IBuySpy component accountSystem is instantiated and its Login method is called on to perform the login, which returns a customerID if successful and null otherwise. In the case of a null return, we simply return with a "Login Failed" message.

However, if the login was successful, our work is not yet done. This page does a few more things that are good tricks to know for your own applications. First, we migrate the shopping cart so that the CartID is now the CustomerID instead of an anonymous GUID. Next, we grab the customer's details and use them to store personalized data in a cookie (in this case, the customer's name). This cookie will expire when the user closes the browser, unless we set its Expires property, which is the next step. If the user stated that we should remember his login information, we update the cookie's expiration date to be a month from now, making it so that the user will only have to log in once per month as long as he checks the box to remember his login. Finally, we use the built-in FormsAuthentication class's RedirectFromLoginPage method to send the user to the page he was originally attempting to access, passing along his CustomerID and also whether or not he wants to persist his login cookie.

If you are building a site that will require users to log in—and most sites do have at least a few pages that are restricted from public access—the IBuySpy login page is an excellent place to start.

EXPOSE WEB SERVICE

Web services are just cool. We covered them in Chapter 11, "ASP.NET and Web Services," and IBuySpy exposes two methods through its InstantOrder Web service: OrderItem and CheckStatus. Both of these services require the user to send her username and password as parameters, and then perform their function using the other parameters that are passed. The sheer beauty of ASP.NET is that implementing Web services is almost trivial. Listing 14.3 shows the OrderItem Web method (in C#— the VB version is available at http://www.ibuyspy.com). Note that the whole thing is only ten lines of actual code, about half of which deals with validating the user's credentials.

Listing 14.3: The OrderItem Web method, InstantOrder.cs.

```
[WebMethod(Description="The OrderItem method enables a remote client
➥to programmatically place an order using a WebService.", EnableSession=false)]
public OrderDetails OrderItem(string userName, string password,
    int productID, int quantity) {

    // Login client using provided username and password
    IBuySpy.CustomersDB accountSystem = new IBuySpy.CustomersDB();
    String customerId = accountSystem.Login(userName, password);

    if (customerId == null) {
        throw new Exception("Error: Invalid Login!");
    }

    // Add Item to Shopping Cart
    IBuySpy.ShoppingCartDB myShoppingCart = new IBuySpy.ShoppingCartDB();
    myShoppingCart.AddItem(customerId, productID, quantity);

    // Place Order
    IBuySpy.OrdersDB orderSystem = new IBuySpy.OrdersDB();
    int orderID = orderSystem.PlaceOrder(customerId, customerId);

    // Return OrderDetails
    return orderSystem.GetOrderDetails(orderID);
}
```

That is all there is to it! Notice that in this case we are actually returning an OrderDetails object as the return type for this method. This is done by serializing the object into XML, as we covered in Chapter 11, ASP.NET and

Web Services. You can definitely see that Web services are going to be extremely popular in the next few years, because exposing them to the world is such an easy task, thanks to the Microsoft .NET Framework.

PERFORMANCE—CACHING

Although not really a store function, no study of IBuySpy would be complete without a look at some of its performance-enhancing features, particularly caching. The initial version of the store relied on output caching and custom use of the .NET caching API. Although this yielded very good performance, the release version of the store now includes fragment caching, which allows portions of pages to be cached. This is much easier to work with than the caching API, especially for new developers, and makes it very easy to cache individual portions of ASP.NET pages.

Some Recommended Improvements

There are some things we can do to improve and extend the existing IBS store, and provide a great learning exercise. To begin, let's go ahead and make a few of the improvements we discussed as we went over the site. The first thing we could do to improve the site would be to make the Featured Item section of the home page a user control, so that we could add featured items to any page we wanted in the future.

FEATURED ITEM USER CONTROL

Instead of hard-coding the umbrella rocket on the home page of IBuySpy.com, we would prefer to use a user control to display the day's featured item, which we could then specify using a Web-based edit page (much like the IBuySpy Portal's user controls), or in the web.config file, so that we can manage which product is featured without having to edit the actual page.

Listing 14.4 describes the user control, FeaturedItem, that we use to accomplish this task. This particular implementation uses data stored in the web.config file, but you could easily create a file or database table to store the featured item or items, or have it randomly select an item from all of those available.

Listing 14.4: FeaturedItem user control _FeaturedItem.ascx (C#).

```
<%@ Control Language="C#" %>
<%@ Import Namespace="System.Data.SqlClient" %>
<%@ OutputCache Duration="3600" VaryByParam="None" %>

<script language="C#" runat="server">
    public int ProductID = 0;
    public String Product_Ad_Phrase;
    protected IBuySpy.ProductDetails featuredItem;
```

Listing 14.4: continued

```
    void Page_Load(Object Src, EventArgs E ) {

            // If no ProductID was specified, look it up from the Config.Web file
            if (ProductID == 0){
                    try{
                            ProductID =
Int32.Parse(ConfigurationSettings.AppSettings["FeaturedItem"]);
                            Product_Ad_Phrase = (string)
ConfigurationSettings.AppSettings["FeaturedItemPhrase"];
                    }
                    catch{
                            // If none set, default to Pocket Protector Rocket
Pack
                            ProductID =373;
                            Product_Ad_Phrase = "Blast off in a ";
                    }
            }

        try{
            IBuySpy.ProductsDB productCatalog = new IBuySpy.ProductsDB();
            featuredItem = productCatalog.GetProductDetails(ProductID);
        }
        catch{
            FeaturedItemSpan.Visible = false;
        }
    }
</script>
<span id="FeaturedItemSpan" runat="server">
        <img src='ProductImages/<%=featuredItem.ProductImage %>'
            width="309" border="0">
        <br/>
            
        <span class="NormalDouble"><i><%=Product_Ad_Phrase%> 
        <a href='ProductDetails.aspx?productID=<%=ProductID %>'>
        <span class="ProductListHeader"><b>
        <%=featuredItem.ModelName %></b></i></span></a></span>
</span>
```

Now, in order to use this control on the home page (Default.aspx), we need to add the following line to the top of the page:

```
<%@ Register TagPrefix="IBuySpy" TagName="FeaturedItem"
➥Src=" _FeaturedItem.ascx" %>
```

and then replace the existing HTML that displays the Umbrella Rocket with this tag:

```
<IBuySpy:FeaturedItem ID="FeaturedItem" runat="server" />
```

Now, this control exposes public properties for the product ID and description, so you could manually specify the featured product from this page if you wanted to. However, we would like to manage this from the web.config file, so we will leave these properties blank, and the control will default to the web.config values.

To set up the values in the web.config file, we need to add two nodes to the appsettings node, `FeaturedItem` and `FeaturedItem_Ad_Phrase`. The entire appsettings element is shown following:

```
<add key="ConnectionString"
    value="server=localhost;uid=sa;pwd=;database=store" />
<add key="FeaturedItem" value="374" />
<add key="FeaturedItemPhrase" value="Protect your stuff with a" />
```

These two nodes set the product ID for the featured product, and a brief ad blurb to describe it, which replaces the original store's "Blast off with a" blurb. Incidentally, if our Products database had had a field for this, we wouldn't have needed to store it here. That would make for another enhancement to add to this application.

That's it! Now, if we view the home page after making the changes just described, it will look like the page in Figure 14.6.

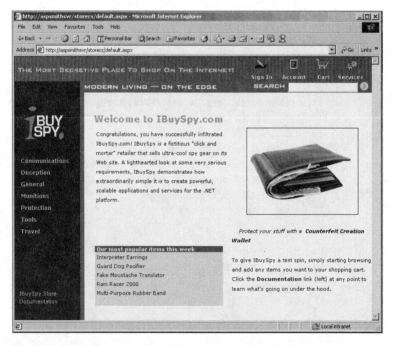

Figure 14.6: *Revised IBuySpy.com home page.*

ListItems USER CONTROL

As we saw earlier in the chapter, copying functionality between pages instead of encapsulating it in custom controls or user controls is a bad practice and can lead to errors. Listing 14.5 shows what a user control to replace the existing DataList controls on the SearchResults and ProductsList pages would look like. Using this control greatly simplifies these two pages, and enhances the ProductsList page by adding a message for the case where no items are found.

Listing 14.5: ListItems user control _ListItems.ascx (C#).

```
<%@ Control Language="C#" %>
<%@ Import Namespace="System.Data.SqlClient" %>
<%@ OutputCache Duration="3600" VaryByParam="*" %>

<script runat="server">

    public SqlDataReader DataSource;

    void Page_Load(Object sender, EventArgs e) {
        MyList.DataSource = DataSource;
        MyList.DataBind();

        // Display a message if no results are found
        if (MyList.Items.Count == 0) {
            ErrorMsg.Text = "No items matched your query.";
        }
    }

</script>

<asp:DataList id="MyList" RepeatColumns="2" runat="server">
    <ItemTemplate>
        <table border="0" width="300">
            <tr>
                <td width="25">
                     
                </td>
                <td width="100" valign="middle" align="right">
                    <a href='ProductDetails.aspx?productID=<%# DataBinder.Eval
➥(Container.DataItem, "ProductID") %>'>
                        <img src='ProductImages/thumbs/<%# DataBinder.Eval
➥(Container.DataItem, "ProductImage") %>'
                                        width="100" height="75" border="0">
                    </a>
                </td>
                <td width="200" valign="middle">
```

Listing 14.5: continued

```
                    <a href='ProductDetails.aspx?productID=<%# DataBinder.Eval
➥(Container.DataItem, "ProductID") %>'>
                        <span class="ProductListHead">
                            <%# DataBinder.Eval(Container.DataItem, "ModelName")
%>
                        </span>
                        <br>
                    </a><span class="ProductListItem"><b>Special Price: </b>
                        <%# DataBinder.Eval(Container.DataItem, "UnitCost",
"{0:c}") %>
                    </span>
                    <br>
                    <a href='AddToCart.aspx?productID=<%# DataBinder.Eval
➥(Container.DataItem, "ProductID") %>'>
                        <span class="ProductListItem">
                        <font color="#9D0000"><b>Add To Cart<b></font>
                        </span>
                    </a>
                </td>
            </tr>
        </table>
    </ItemTemplate>
</asp:DataList>
<img height="1" width="30" src="Images/1x1.gif">
<asp:Label id="ErrorMsg" class="ErrorText" runat="server" />
```

Implementing the list on the ProductList.aspx and SearchResults.aspx pages simply requires adding a Register directive to the top of each of these pages, and replacing the existing data list code with the user control call. The Register directive would look like this:

```
<%@ Register TagPrefix="IBuySpy" TagName="ItemList" Src="_ListItems.ascx" %>
```

The call to the user control would then be:

```
<IBuySpy:ItemList ID="ItemList1" runat="server" />
```

Finally, the DataList code in the Page_Load event needs to be updated to refer to the ItemList control, like so (this example is from the SearchResults.aspx page):

```
ItemList1.DataSource =
    productCatalogue.SearchProductDescriptions(Request.Params["txtSearch"]);
ItemList1.DataBind();
```

One more feature that we might add to the site to improve it would be the ability for users to update their profile and change their name or password. We'll conclude the chapter with this example.

LET USERS UPDATE THEIR PROFILE

The Register.aspx page provides a form for users to sign up for the IBuySpy Web site, but once they have done so, they cannot modify their settings afterward. Adding this functionality is fairly straightforward—we are just going to copy the Register.aspx file to EditUser.aspx and change the action to update the user's settings rather than inserting a new user. The main part of the form can remain the same, but we've changed the button's name to UpdateBtn. Listing 14.6 shows the script block for the new EditUser.aspx page (the complete page is available online at http://aspauthors.com/aspnetbyexample/ch14/).

Listing 14.6: Script block for EditUser.aspx (C#)

```
<script runat="server">
void Page_Load(){
    if(!Page.IsPostBack){
    // Calculate end-user's shopping cart ID
    IBuySpy.ShoppingCartDB cart = new IBuySpy.ShoppingCartDB();
    String cartId = cart.GetShoppingCartId();

    // cartId is also the customer ID
    IBuySpy.CustomersDB custDB = new IBuySpy.CustomersDB();
    IBuySpy.CustomerDetails custDetails = custDB.GetCustomerDetails(cartId);

    // Populate the form with the customer's current values
    Name.Text = custDetails.FullName;
    Email.Text = custDetails.Email;
    Password.Text = custDetails.Password;
    ConfirmPassword.Text = Password.Text;
    }
}

void UpdateBtn_Click(Object sender, ImageClickEventArgs e){

    // Only attempt a login if all form fields on the page are valid
    if (Page.IsValid == true) {
        // Calculate end-user's shopping cart ID
        IBuySpy.ShoppingCartDB cart = new IBuySpy.ShoppingCartDB();
        String cartId = cart.GetShoppingCartId();

        // Update Customer Information In CustomersDB database
        IBuySpy.CustomersDB accountSystem = new IBuySpy.CustomersDB();
        accountSystem.UpdateCustomer(cartId, Name.Text, Email.Text,
Password.Text);

        Response.Redirect("ShoppingCart.aspx",true);
    }
}
</script>
```

In the Page_Load method we retrieve the customer's ID by using the GetShoppingCartId, since this ID is the same as the customer's ID. To ensure that this has a value, we will set up the EditUser.aspx page in the web.config file so that it requires the user to login to access the page. Once we have the ID, we use the CustomersDB object to retrieve a CustomerDetails struct, which has all of the information we need. Finally, we set the values of our four form fields with the appropriate values from the database.

When the user clicks the submit image, it will launch the UpdateBtn_Click event handler (because there is an OnClick="UpdateBtn_Click" attribute on the ImageButton). This method looks identical to the click handler in the Register.aspx page, except instead of adding a customer, we are calling a new method of the CustomersDB object, UpdateCustomer(). This method did not exist in the original IBuySpy application—we had to add it, along with a new stored procedure. The UpdateCustomer() method is shown in Listing 14.7, and must be added to the CustomersDB.cs file in the Components folder. Before the change will take effect, the mk.bat file must be executed from within the components folder as well.

Listing 14.7: UpdateCustomer() method (CustomersDB.cs)

```
public void UpdateCustomer(string customerId, string fullName,
    string email, string password)
{
    // Create Instance of Connection and Command Object
    SqlConnection myConnection = new
        SqlConnection(ConfigurationSettings.AppSettings["ConnectionString"]);
    SqlCommand myCommand = new SqlCommand("CustomerUpdate", myConnection);

    // Mark the Command as a SPROC
    myCommand.CommandType = CommandType.StoredProcedure;

    // Add Parameters to SPROC
    SqlParameter parameterCustomerID =
        new SqlParameter("@CustomerID", SqlDbType.Int, 4);
    parameterCustomerID.Value = Int32.Parse(customerId);
    myCommand.Parameters.Add(parameterCustomerID);

    SqlParameter parameterFullName =
        new SqlParameter("@FullName", SqlDbType.NVarChar, 50);
    parameterFullName.Value = fullName;
    myCommand.Parameters.Add(parameterFullName);

    SqlParameter parameterEmail =
        new SqlParameter("@Email", SqlDbType.NVarChar, 50);
```

Listing 14.7: continued

```
    parameterEmail.Value = email;
    myCommand.Parameters.Add(parameterEmail);

    SqlParameter parameterPassword =
        new SqlParameter("@Password", SqlDbType.NVarChar, 50);
    parameterPassword.Value = password;
    myCommand.Parameters.Add(parameterPassword);

    myConnection.Open();
    myCommand.ExecuteNonQuery();
    myConnection.Close();
}
```

Comparing this method to the AddCustomer() method, we see that it is almost identical, except that it doesn't return a value, and it takes customerId as a parameter. These methods are very well documented on the IBuySpy Web site, so won't go into any more detail on what this page is doing. Assuming you've already read the ADO.NET chapter, you should have no trouble following this code anyway. The UpdateCustomer() method calls the CustomerUpdate stored procedure, which we have added to the store database. The source for this procedure is displayed in Listing 14.8, below, and can be added to your sql server database by simply typing the entire listing into the query analyzer and running it.

Listing 14.8: CustomerUpdate stored procedure.

```
CREATE PROCEDURE CustomerUpdate
(
    @CustomerID  int,
    @FullName    nvarchar(50),
    @Email       nvarchar(50),
    @Password    nvarchar(50)
)
AS

UPDATE Customers SET
    FullName = @FullName,
    EMailAddress = @Email,
    Password = @Password
WHERE CustomerID = @CustomerID
```

Once this is done, the last change is to add the EditUser.aspx page to the list of pages that require the user to log in, which is done in the web.config file. Listing 14.9 shows the node that should be added to the main configuration node (with the other location nodes).

Listing 14.9: Securing the EditUser.aspx page (web.config)

```
<location path="EditUser.aspx">
    <system.web>
        <authorization>
            <deny users="?" />
        </authorization>
    </system.web>
</location>
```

Now your users will be able to update their name and password and email for their accounts by using this page. Add a link somewhere on the site to the EditUser.aspx page, and this feature will be active for everyone who uses your site. Adding additional features that require data access that isn't already in the DB components will generally require changes like the ones we have just covered here, including new stored procedures and updates to the appropriate DB component. Using these techniques you can easily adapt the IBuySpy store archtitecture to support your own commercial Internet storefront.

Summary

One thing that really makes Microsoft stand alone as a programming tools vendor is their dedication to providing developers with all the resources they could need to be successful. From online support like MSDN to their outstanding support for authors, Microsoft demonstrates their commitment to supporting developers. The IBuySpy application, which will include a store, portal, and news site by the time .NET is officially released, is just one more example of how Microsoft helps developers to be productive with their tools.

IBuySpy.com encapsulates many of Microsoft's best practices for developing solutions using .NET. In this chapter, you learned how the IBuySpy.com store was designed and architected, and also why the designers made their decisions. You learned which choices were made because they are the best way to do a certain task, and which ones were made in the interest of keeping the sample application simple and approachable by novice developers. The examples in this chapter all built upon the existing framework provided by IBuySpy.com, which itself is fully available for download, and as you worked through the examples in this chapter you installed your own IBuySpy.com store.

What's Next

The references in Appendixes A through E should provide you with a good resource as you are learning .NET. I hope you've had a look at them before this point in the book! Remember, for all the source code, live examples, errata, and updates, visit this book's supporting Web site at http://aspauthors.com/aspnetbyexample/.

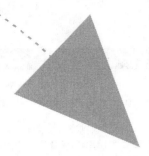

ASP.NET Syntax

This appendix reviews the overall syntax for using ASP.NET, including overall page structure, forms, database access and data binding, use of controls, and debugging. In many ways, an ASP.NET page is very similar to a traditional ASP page, with slight changes to accommodate the change from VBScript (or JScript) to Visual Basic or C#. For example:

```
<%@ Page Language="Visual Basic"%>
<html>
<head>
</head>
<body>
<%
Response.Write("Hello World")
%>
</body>
```

(The syntax is the same for C#, with a change in the Language parameter and a semicolon added to the Response.Write line.)

There are, of course, many more issues to consider.

File Structure

An ASP.NET page (as opposed to a control, service, and so on) can be written in any number of languages. The most common are Visual Basic and C#. An ASP.NET page generally has several items:

- **Page directives.** Information provided to the compiler about the page. For example, a directive indicating that the page uses C# as its default language is written as follows:

```
<%@ Page language="C#" %>
```

  Directives normally appear at the top of the page, but may appear anywhere. (Page directives are detailed in the section "Page Directives.")

- **Scripting.** Code that is executed either by the server or the client. Several different formats exist for server-executed code:

```
<% Code written here is executed %>
<%= Code written here is evaluated and the results are output %>
<script runat="server" id="progID" language="VB">
    Code written here
</script>
```

  Adding the `runat="server"` attribute and value instructs the server to execute the code when the page is called.

- **Comments.** Text that either provides description or represents code that should not be executed, as indicated by the fact that it's surrounded by `<%--` and `%-->` rather than `<% %>`:

```
<%-- Code (or comments) written here will not be executed. --%>
```

- **Controls.** Predefined or custom code called via an XML element, sometimes including namespace information:

```
<form method="post" runat="server">
    <asp:label id="Label1" runat="Server"></asp:label>
</form>
```

- **Content.** Neither code nor controls, represents text that is part of the resulting HTML page.

```
<h1>Title of the Page</h1>
```

Putting these components together results in the following ASP.NET page code:

```
<%@ Page Language="VB" Trace="False" %>
<script runat="server">
Sub Page_Load(Src As Object, E As EventArgs)
    <%-- Set initial text for first_name control --%>
    If Page.IsPostBack Then
```

```
            output.Text = "You entered " & first_name.Text & "."
        End If
    End Sub
    </script>
    <html>
    <head><title>Sample Form</title></head>
    <body>
    <asp:Label runat="server" id="output" />

    <form runat="server" id="form1">
        Please enter a name: <asp:Textbox runat="server" id="first_name" />
        <asp:Button runat="server" Text="Submit" />
    </form>

    </body></html>
```

Page Parameters

The Page directive allows you to specify parameters that are used when the page is compiled. Only one Page directive is allowed on a page, so all parameters must be part of the same directive, as in the following example:

```
<%@ Page AspCompat="true" Buffer="true" Trace="false" %>
```

Available Page parameters are AspCompat, AutoEventWireup, Buffer, ClassName, ClientTarget, CodePage, CodeBehind, CompilerOptions, ContentType, Culture, Debug, Description, EnableSessionState, EnableViewState, EnableViewStateMac, ErrorPage, Explicit, Inherits, Language, LCID, ResponseEncoding, Src, Strict, Trace, TraceMode, Transaction, and WarningLevel.

The Page directive can only be used on an .aspx page.

Other Directives

The Page parameters are not the only page directives that can be used on an ASP.NET page. Other directives, such as Control (which can only be used in a user control), or Import, which imports a namespace or control into a page, use the same syntax as the Page parameters.

```
<%@ Import Namespace="System.Net" %>
<%@ Register TagPrefix="LoginModule" TagName="LoginModule" Src="login.ascx" %>
```

Potential page directives are Page, Control, Import, Implements, Register, Assembly, OutputCache, and Reference. Each has its own list of parameters.

Adding Code-Behind Pages

One of the strengths of ASP.NET is the ability to build a page that is linked to external code files. The Inherits directive tells the compiler from which class your page inherits. The source code can reside in any file, but when your pages run, the server looks for the compiled code in the /bin directory or in the Global Application Cache (GAC). Visual Studio.NET, on the other hand, uses the CodeBehind page parameter to determine the organization of files in the project menu and, more importantly, where to find the code referenced in the Inherits directive. For example:

```
<%@ Page language="c#" Inherits="MyPrj.StoredProc" CodeBehind="StoredProc.cs" %>
```

You can then reference class functions from within the page. The server ignores the CodeBehind page parameter, but the Src parameter serves the same purpose, allowing the server to locate and compile the code. A page that carries both the CodeBehind and Src parameters can be used with certainty in both environments.

Forms

Most of the functions that had to be specifically programmed in traditional ASP are now handled by form controls:

```
<%@ Page Language="VB" Trace="False" %>
<script runat="server">
Sub Page_Load(Src As Object, E As EventArgs)
    If Not Page.IsPostBack Then
        won.Items.Add("Yes")
        won.Items.Add("No")
    Else
        Dim resultTxt as String
        resultTxt = "Hello, " & first_name.Text & ".  "
        if won.SelectedItem.Text = "yes" then
            resultTxt += "Congratulations!"
        else
            resultTxt += "So sorry."
        end if
        output.Text =  resultTxt
    End If
End Sub
</script>
<!DOCTYPE HTML PUBLIC "-//W3C//DTD HTML 4.0 Transitional//EN"
            "http://www.w3.org/TR/REC-html40/loose.dtd">
<html>
<head>
<title>Survey</title>
</head>
<body>
<form runat="server" id="form1">
    First Name: <asp:Textbox runat="server" id="first_name" /><br />
    Have you ever won anything?
```

```
                    <asp:DropDownList runat="server" id="won" /><br />
    <asp:Button runat="server" Text="Submit Answers" />
</form>
<asp:Label runat="server" id="output" />
</body>
</html>
```

Alternatively, the `DropDownList` could have been written as:

```
<asp:DropDownList runat="server" id="won">
    <asp:ListItem value="yes" runat="server">Yes</asp:ListItem>
    <asp:ListItem value="no" runat="server">No</asp:ListItem>
</asp:DropDownList>
```

Other form controls include `CheckBox`, `CheckBoxList`, `ImageButton`, `ListBox`, `RadioButton`, and `RadioButtonList`.

Dealing with Data

With ADO.NET, you have new capabilities for both retrieving and using data. Your application can retrieve data directly into a `DataReader` much like the classic ASP `RecordSet`, or into a temporary, in-memory database structure called a `DataSet`. This `DataSet` can then be used to populate structures such as `DataGrids` and `Repeaters`, used to display the information.

Creating a Connection with ADO.NET

The most common source for data is a database, so before you retrieve any data, you will have to create a connection. Three different objects for creating a connection are included in `System.Data.SQL`: `DBConnection`, `OleDbConnection`, and `SQLConnection`. `DBConnection` is a general class inherited by all other classes. `OleDbConnection` is much like traditional ADO (and was, in fact, called `ADOConnection` in earlier versions of .NET), in that it is not database-specific. `SQLConnection` is optimized for making connections to Microsoft SQL Server databases. Make a connection by using a connection string or DSN:

```
OleDbConnection cn =
    new OleDbConnection("userid=sa;password=;database=nrthwnd;server=myServer")
```

or

```
OleDbConnection cn = new OleDbConnection("northwind", "sa", "manager")
```

Commands

It is the command objects that execute the actual SQL statements. Like connections, there are three versions of commands: `DBCommand`, `OleDbCommand`, and `SQLCommand`. To use them, set a connection and command text, and execute it.

```
OleDbCommand cmd = new OleDbCommand();
cmd.Connection = cn;
cmd.CommandText =
        "insert into products (prod_id, prod_name) values (232, 'Cushions')";

nCount = cmd.ExecuteNonQuery();
```

or the alternate syntax:

```
OleDbCommand cmd = new OleDbCommand(
        "insert into products (prod_id, prod_name) values (232, 'Cushions')",
        cn);
nCount = cmd.ExecuteNonQuery();
```

You can also use a command object to execute a stored procedure, passing both IN parameters and OUT parameters, and accessing the OUT parameter values.

```
OleDbCommand cmd = new OleDbCommand();
cmd.Connection = cn;
cmd.CommandText = "MyProcedure";
cmd.CommandType = CommandType.StoredProcedure;
OleDbParameter TempParam;

TempParam = new OleDbParameter("myInParam",OleDbDataType.VarChar,2);
TempParam.Value = "CA";
cmd.Parameters.Add(TempParam);

TempParam = new OleDbParameter("myOutParam", OleDbDataType.Int);
TempParam.Direction = ParameterDirection.Output;
cmd.Parameters.Add(TempParam);

cmd.ExecuteNonQuery();

Label1.Text = cmd.Parameters["myOutParam"].Value.ToString();
```

Retrieving Data

The most commonly executed statements return a set of data, which can be viewed in a number of ways. The simplest is to create a DBDataReader, OleDbDataReader, or SQLDataReader, populated by the execution of the command object:

```
OleDbCommand cmd = new OleDbCommand("select * from products", cn);

OleDbDataReader dr;
cmd.Execute(out dr);

while (dr.Read())
{
```

```
        Label1.Text += dr["pid"] + ": " + dr["prod_name"] + "<br>";
}
```

For more complex data retrieval needs, extract data into a DataSet. A DataSet can take data from more than one command and can create keys similar to those created for data integrity in the actual database.

```
DataSet ds = new DataSet();

OleDbDataAdapter prodCmd = new OleDbDataAdapter();
prodCmd.Connection = cn;
prodCmd.CommandText =
            "select * from products p1, pricing p2 where pid = priceid";
prodCmd.Fill(ds, "productInfo");

OleDbDataAdapter priceCmd = new OleDbDataAdapter("select * from orders", cn);
priceCmd.Fill(ds, "orders");

DataColumn prodId = ds.Tables["productInfo"].Columns["pid"]
DataColumn orderProdId = ds.Tables["orders"].Columns["pid"]
DataRelation productOrdersRel = new DataRelation("productOrders",
                                          prodId,
                                          orderProdId)
```

DataSets and XML

You can also populate a DataSet with XML and use a DataSet to output XML:

```
DataSet ds = new DataSet();
ds.ReadXml(Server.MapPath("products.xml"));
Response.ContentType="text/xml";
StringWriter s = new StringWriter();
ds.WriteXmlData(s);
Response.Write (s.ToString());
```

Viewing Data

When you have the data, you can create a view that can be filtered or sorted. You can then bind this view to a DataGrid or other control.

```
        DataView dv = ds.Tables["orders"].DefaultView;
        String orderid = formOrderid.Text;
        dv.Sort = "pid";
        dv.RowFilter = "orderid = " + orderid;

        DataGrid1.DataSource = dv;
        DataGrid1.DataBind();
```

Databinding Syntax

Databinding applies to more than just `DataGrids`. The page itself can also bind data to controls and to sections of the page.

```
<%@ Page language="VB" %>
<script language="VB" runat="server">
Sub Page_Load(Src As Object, E As EventArgs)
    Page.DataBind()
End Sub
</script>
<html>
<head><title>Page Data</title></head>
<body>
    <h2>Data Binding for Fun and Profit</h2>
    <form action="myPage.aspx" method="post" runat="server">
        Please enter another movie:
        <asp:TextBox id="movie" runat="server" />
        <asp:Button runat="server" Text="Submit Choice" />
    </form>
    <p>The last title you entered was <%# movie.Text %>.</p>
</body>
</html>
```

When `Page.DataBind()` executes, all sections of the page within `<%# %>` are populated. You can also use databinding to bind a control, as in:

```
<asp:Label id="lastChoice" Text="<%# movie.Text %>" />
```

Databinding is also used in a slightly more generic context, such as in using a `DataGrid`, `Repeater`, or other templated control. In this case, the static `DataBinder.Eval()` method allows you to specify a particular piece of data:

```
<asp:Repeater id="Repeater1" runat="server">
    <template name=HeaderTemplate>
        <h1>Products</h1>
    </template>

    <template name="ItemTemplate">
        <%# DataBinder.Eval(Container.DataItem, "pid") %> --
        <%# DataBinder.Eval(Container.DataItem, "prod_name") %>
        $<%# DataBinder.Eval(Container.DataItem, "price") %>
    </template>

    <template name="SeparatorTemplate">
        <hr>
    </template>
</asp:Repeater>
```

Using Controls

Controls are compiled code residing in .DLL files that can be accessed by the server. In many cases, these controls are part of the .NET Framework, but you can also create and use custom controls.

Declaring a Control

In order for a control to be visible to the application, it must be registered with the server. In traditional ASP, this was accomplished with regsrvr32. exe, and required you to shut down all Web services to make a change. In ASP.NET, registration is accomplished when the page is run via the Register directive:

```
<%@ Register TagPrefix="cust" Namespace="MyCustomCtrls" Assembly="MyDLLFile" %>
```

The preceding example assumes that the MyDLLFile.DLL file is in the bin directory for the application.

Referencing a Control

After the control is registered, add it to the page with the proper name-space alias to make it available from within the code.

```
<script runat="server" language="VB">
function UserRanking
    UserRanking = Scores.TopScore
end function
</script>
<html>
<head><title>Ranking Page</title></head>
<body>
<cust:Rankings id="Scores" sport="baseball" maxRanking="1000" runat="server" />
Your top score is <%= UserRanking %>.
</body>
</html>
```

Debugging

Rather than printing comments to your pages or using other jury-rigged debugging, you can use ASP.NET's built-in debugging features.

System.Trace

The System.Trace class allows you to output both information and warn-ings, depending on the situation, using Trace.write() and Trace.warn(). You can combine these with exception handling to provide extensive debug-ging information.

```
<%@ Page Language="VB" Trace="True" %>
<script runat="server" language="VB">
```

```
Function Savings (price as Double, discount as Double) as Double
    if TraceContext.isEnabled then
        Response.write "<!-- Tracing enabled.  Sort mode is " & _
                                        TraceConect.TraceMode&"-->"
    else
        Response.write "<!-- Tracing disabled. -->"
    end if

    dim temp as Double
    try
        Trace.write("SavingsCategory",
                "Attempting calculation: price="&price&" discount="&discount)
        temp = discount/price
    catch E as Exception
        Trace.warn("SavingsCategory", "Invalid savings or price:", E)
        temp = 0
    finally
        return temp
    end try
end Function
</script>
<html>
<head><title>Debugging Example</title></head>
<body>
    This week's discount is <%= Savings(299.99, 50.00) %>.
</body>
</html>
```

The `Trace` methods both allow you to choose whether to include exception information:

```
Public Warn (category As String, message As String)
Public Warn (category As String, message As String, errorInfo as Exception)
Public Write (category As String, message As String)
Public Write (category As String, message As String, errorInfo as Exception)
```

Application-Level Tracing

The `global.asax` file gives you an opportunity to add generic error handling, which can include event log information:

```
<script runat="server" language="C#">

public void Application_Error(Object sender, EventArgs e){
    string LogName = "ASPAlliance";
    string ErrorMessage = "URL: " + Request.Path + " Error: "
                                + this.LastError.ToString();

    // Create event log if it doesn't exist
    if (!System.Diagnostics.EventLog.SourceExists(LogName))
```

```
    {
        System.Diagnostics.EventLog.CreateEventSource(LogName, LogName);
    }
    System.Diagnostics.EventLog Log = new System.Diagnostics.EventLog();
    Log.Source = LogName;
    Log.WriteEntry(ErrorMessage,System.Diagnostics.EventLogEntryType.Error);
}
</script>
```

Configuration

You can turn on tracing for the application through the web.config file. This file may contain a number of different sections, all specified via XML, but the relevant sections for turning on tracing are shown in the sample web.config file that follows. This example sets tracing to be enabled (the default is False), to allow up to 20 simultaneous tracing requests (the default is 10), to output tracing information at the bottom of each page (the default is for it to be available only in the trace utility), for tracing information to be listed chronologically (it can also be listed by category), and for the trace utility to be available only locally, on the server.

```
<configuration>
    <configSections>
        <sectionGroup name="system.web">
            <section name="trace"
                     type="System.Web.Configuration.TraceConfigHandler">
        </sectionGroup>
    </configSections>

    <system.web>
        <trace enabled="true" requestLimit="20" pageOutput="true"
               traceMode="SortByTime" localOnly="true" />
    </system.web>
</configuration>
```

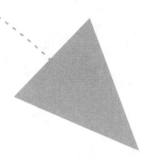

ADO.NET Object Model

ADO.NET consists of the namespaces and classes that manage accessing backend databases. In total ADO.NET consists of five namespaces and hundreds of classes. We don't have room to list all the namespaces and classes so we will detail only the three most commonly used namespaces (System.Data, System.Data.OleDb, and System.Data.SqlClient) and only the most commonly used classes within those namespaces. Figure B.1 shows the ADO.NET architecture that includes the most commonly used classes.

If you need information about the namespaces or classes not listed here please refer to the reference that is included in the documentation for the .NET SDK.

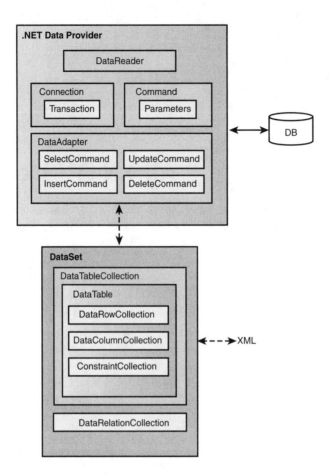

Figure B.1: *You will probably use these classes in ADO.NET.*

System.Data Namespace

The System.Data namespace consists mainly of classes that make up ADO.NET. ADO.NET allows a developer to build components that manage data from data sources.

DataColumn Object Members

The DataColumn class represents the schema of a column in a DataTable object. Tables B.1 through B.4 list the constructor, properties, and methods for the DataColumn class.

Table B.1: **DataColumn** Constructor

Name	Parameters	Description
DataColumn	none	Initializes a new instance of the DataColumn class.
DataColumn	columnName (String)	Initializes a new instance of the DataColumn class with the specified name.
DataColumn	columnName (String) dataType (Type)	Initializes a new instance of the DataColumn class with the specified name and data type.
DataColumn	columnName (String) dataType (Type) expr (String)	Initializes a new instance of the DataColumn class with the specified name, data type, and expression.
DataColumn	columnName (String) dataType (Type) expr (String) type (MappingType)	Initializes a new instance of the DataColumn class with the specified name, data type, expression, and value that determines whether the column is an attribute.

Table B.2: **DataColumn** Properties

Name	Type	Description
AllowDBNull	Boolean	Retrieves or sets a value indicating whether null values are allowed in this column for rows in this table.
AutoIncrement	Boolean	Retrieves or sets a value indicating whether the column automatically increments the value of the column for new rows added to the table.
AutoIncrementSeed	Long	Retrieves or sets the starting value for a column that has its AutoIncrement property set to true.
AutoIncrementStep	Long	Retrieves or sets the increment used by a column with its AutoIncrement property set to true.
Caption	String	Retrieves or sets the caption for this column.
ColumnMapping	MappingType	Retrieves or sets the MappingType of the column.
ColumnName	String	Retrieves or sets the name of the column within the collection.
Container	IContainer	Retrieves the container for the component.
DataType	Type	The type of data stored in the column.
DefaultValue	Object	Retrieves or sets the default value for the column when creating new rows.

Table B.2: continued

Name	Type	Description
DesignMode	Boolean	Retrieves a value indicating of the component is in design mode.
Expression	String	Retrieves or sets the expression used to either filter rows, calculate the column's value, or create an aggregate column.
ExtendedProperties	Property Collection	Retrieves the collection of custom user information.
Namespace	String	Gets or sets the namespace of the DataColumn.
Ordinal	Integer	Retrieves the position of the column in the collection.
Prefix	String	Gets or sets the XML prefix that aliases the DataTable's namespace.
ReadOnly	Boolean	Retrieves or sets a value indicating whether the column allows changes after a row has been added to the table.
Site	ISite	Retrieves or sets the site of the component.
Table	DataTable	Retrieves the DataTable the column belongs to.
Unique	Boolean	Retrieves or sets a value indicating whether the values in each row must be unique.

Table B.3: **DataColumn** *Methods*

Name	Parameters	Description
Dispose	none	Disposes the component.
Dispose	disposing (Boolean)	Releases the unmanaged resources used by the MarshalByValue Component and optionally releases the managed resources.
Equals	obj (Object)	Determines whether the specified object is the same instance as the current object.
Equals	objA (Object) objB (Object)	Determines if the specified object instances are equal.
GetHashCode	none	Serves as a hash function for a particular type.
GetService	service (Type)	Gets the implementer of the IServiceProvider.
GetType	none	Retrieves the type of the object.
ToString	none	Returns a string that represents the current object.

Table B.4: **DataColumn** *Event*

Name	Description
Disposed	Adds an event handler to listen to the Disposed event of the component.

DataRow **Object Members**

The DataRow class represents a row of data in a DataTable. Tables B.5 and B.6 list the properties and methods for the DataRow class.

Table B.5: **DataRow** *Properties*

Name	Type	Description
HasErrors	Boolean	Retrieves a value indicating whether there are errors in the collection.
Item	Object	Retrieves or sets data stored in the column.
ItemArray	Object	Retrieves or sets all the values for this row through an array.
RowError	String	Retrieves or sets the custom error description for a row.
RowState	DataRowState	Retrieves the current state of the row in regard to its relationship to the RowsCollection.
Table	DataTable	Retrieves the DataTable for which this row has a schema.

Table B.6: **DataRow** *Methods*

Name	Parameters	Description
AcceptChanges	none	Commits all changes made to this row since the last time this method was called.
BeginEdit	none	Begins an edit operation on a DataRow object.
CancelEdit	none	Cancels the current edit on the row.
ClearErrors	none	Clears the errors for the row, including the RowError and errors set with SetColumnError.
Delete	none	Deletes the row.
EndEdit	none	End the edit occurring for this row.
Equals	obj (Object)	Determines whether the specified object is the same instance as the current object.
Equals	objA (Object) objB (Object)	Determines if the specified object instances are equal.

Table B.6: continued

Name	Parameters	Description
GetChildRows	relation (DataRelation)	Retrieves the child rows of this DataRow using the specified DataRelation.
GetChildRows	relationName (String)	Retrieves the child rows of this DataRow using the named DataRelation.
GetChildRows	relation (DataRelation) version (DataRowVersion)	Retrieves the child rows of this DataRow using the specified DataRelation and DataRowVersion.
GetChildRows	relationName (String) version (DataRowVersion)	Retrieves the specified version of the child rows using the specified DataRelation.
GetColumnError	columnIndex (Integer)	Retrieves the error description for the column using the specified index.
GetColumnError	columnName (String)	Retrieves the error description for the column using the specified name.
GetColumnError	column (DataColumn)	Retrieves the error description for the column using the specified DataColumn.
GetColumnsInError	none	Retrieves an array of columns that have errors.
GetHashCode	none	Serves as a hash function for a particular type.
GetParentRow	relationName (String)	Retrieves the parent row of a DataRow using the specified relation name.
GetParentRow	relation (DataRelation)	Retrieves the parent row of a DataRow using the specified DataRelation.
GetParentRow	relationName (String) version (DataRowVersion)	Retrieves the parent row of a DataRow using the specified relation name and the specified DataRowVersion.
GetParentRow	relation (DataRelation) version (DataRowVersion)	Retrieves the parent row of a DataRow using the specified DataRelation and the specified DataRowVersion.
GetParentRows	relation (DataRelation)	Retrieves the parent rows of a DataRow, using the specified DataRelation.
GetParentRows	relationName (String)	Retrieves the parent rows of a DataRow, using the specified relation name.

Name	Parameters	Description
GetParentRows	relationName (String) version (DataRowVersion)	Retrieves the parent rows of a DataRow, using the specified relation name and the specified DataRowVersion.
GetParentRows	relation (DataRelation) version (DataRowVersion)	Retrieves the parent rows of a DataRow, using the specified DataRelation and the specified DataRowVersion.
GetType	none	Retrieves the type of the object.
HasVersion	version (DataRowVersion)	Retrieves a value indicating whether a specified version exists.
IsNull	column (DataColumn)	Retrieves a value indicating whether the specified DataColumn contains a null value.
IsNull	columnName (String)	Retrieves a value indicating whether the specified named column contains a null value.
IsNull	columnIndex (Integer)	Retrieves a value indicating whether the column with the specified index contains a null value.
IsNull	column (DataColumn) Version (DataRowVersion)	Gets a value indicating whether the specified DataColumn and DataRowVersion contains a null value.
RejectChanges	none	Rejects all changes made to the row since the AcceptChanges method was last called.
SetColumnError	columnName (String) error (String)	Sets the error description for a specified named column.
SetColumnError	column (DataColumn) error (String)	Sets the error description for a specified DataColumn.
SetColumnError	columnIndex (Integer) error (String)	Sets the error description for a column with a specified index.
SetParentRow	parentRow (DataRow)	Sets the parent row of a DataRow with the specified DataRow.
SetParentRow	parentRow (DataRow) relation (DataRelation)	Sets the parent row of a specified DataRow with the specified DataRow and DataRelation.

Table B.6: continued

Name	Parameters	Description
SetUnspecified	column (DataColumn)	Sets the value of a DataColumn with the specified name to unspecified.
ToString	none	Returns a string that represents the current object.

DataSet Object Members

The DataSet class represents an in-memory cache of data. Tables B.7 through B.10 list the constructor, properties, methods, and events for the DataSet class.

*Table B.7: **DataSet** Constructor*

Name	Parameters	Description
DataSet	none	Initializes a new instance of the DataSet class.
DataSet	info (SerializationInfo) context (StreamingContext)	Initializes a new DataSet class with the SerializationInfo and StreamingContext.
DataSet	name (String)	Initializes a new instance of the DataSet class with the specified name.

*Table B.8: **DataSet** Properties*

Name	Type	Description
CaseSensitive	Boolean	Retrieves or sets a value indicating whether string comparisons within DataTable objects are case sensitive.
Container	IContainer	Retrieves the container for the component.
DataSetName	String	Retrieves or sets the name of the DataSet.
DefaultViewManager	DataViewManager	Retrieves a custom view of the data contained by the DataSet.
DesignMode	Boolean	Retrieves a value indicating the component is in design mode.
EnforceConstraints	Boolean	Retrieves or sets a value indicating whether constraint rules are followed when an update operation is performed.

Name	Type	Description
ExtendedProperties	PropertyCollection	Retrieves the collection of custom user information.
HasErrors	Boolean	Retrieves a value indicating whether there are errors in any of the rows in any of the tables of this DataSet.
Locale	CultureInfo	Retrieves or sets the locale information used to compare strings within the table.
NameSpace	String	Retrieves or sets the namespace of the DataSet.
Prefix	String	Retrieves or sets an XML prefix that aliases the namespace of the DataSet.
Relations	DataRelationCollection	Retrieves the collection of relations that link tables and allow navigation from parent tables to child tables.
Site	ISite	Retrieves or sets the site of the component.
Tables	DataTableCollection	Retrieves the collection of tables contained in the DataSet.

Table B.9: **DataSet** *Methods*

Name	Parameters	Description
AcceptChanges	none	Commits all changes made to this DataSet since it was loaded or the last time the AcceptChanges method was called.
BeginInit	none	Begins the initialization of a DataSet that is used on a form or used by another component.
Clear	none	Clears the DataSet of all data.
Clone	none	Clones the structure of the DataSet.
Copy	none	Copies both the structure and data for this DataSet.
Dispose	none	Releases the resources used by the MarshalByValueComponent.

Table B.9: continued

Name	Parameters	Description
Equals	obj (Object)	Determines whether the specified object is the same instance as the current object.
Equals	objA (Object) objB (Object)	Determines if the specified object instances are equal.
GetChanges	none	Returns a copy of the DataSet that contains all changes made to the DataSet since it was loaded or the AcceptChanges method was called.
GetChanges	rowStates (DataRowState)	Returns a copy of the DataSet that contains all changes made to the DataSet since it was loaded or the AcceptChanges method was called, filtered by DataRowState.
GetHashCode	none	Serves as a hash function for a particular type.
GetService	service (Type)	Get the implementer of the IServiceProvider.
GetType	none	Retrieves the type of the object.
GetXml	none	Retrieves an xml representation of the data stored in the DataSet.
GetXmlSchema	none	Retrieves the XSD schema for the XML representation of the data in the DataSet.
HasChanges	none	Retrieves a value indicating whether the DataSet has changes.
HasChanges	rowStates (DataRowState)	Retrieves a value indicating whether the DataSet has changes, filtered by DataRowState.
InferXmlSchema	stream (Stream) nsArray[] (String)	Infers the XML schema from the specified Stream object into the DataSet.
InferXmlSchema	fileName (String) nsArray[] (String)	Infers the XML schema from the specified file into the DataSet.
InferXmlSchema	reader (TextReader) nsArray[] (String)	Infers the XML schema from the specified TextReader into the DataSet.
InferXmlSchema	reader (XmlReader) nsArray[] (String)	Infers the XML schema from the specified TextReader into the DataSet.

Name	Parameters	Description
Merge	rows[] (DataRow)	Merges the DataSet with an array of DataRow objects.
Merge	table (DataTable)	Merges the DataSet with a specified DataTable.
Merge	dataSet (DataSet)	Merges the DataSet into a specified DataSet.
Merge	dataSet (DataSet) preserveChanges (Boolean)	Merges the DataSet with a specified DataSet, preserving changes according to the specified argument.
Merge	rows[] (DataRow) preserveChanges (Boolean) missingSchemaAction (MissingSchemaAction)	Merges the DataSet with an array of DataRow objects, preserving changes, and handling incompatible schema according to the specified arguments.
Merge	dataSet (DataSet) preserveChanges (Boolean) missingSchemaAction (MissingSchemaAction)	Merges the DataSet with a specified DataSet, preserving changes, and handling incompatible schema according to the specified arguments.
Merge	table (DataTable) preserveChanges (Boolean) missingSchemaAction (MissingSchemaAction)	Merges the DataSet with a specified DataTable, preserving changes, and handling incompatible schema according to the specified arguments.
ReadXml	reader (XmlReader)	Reads XML schema and data into the DataSet using the specified XMLReader object.
ReadXml	stream (Stream)	Reads XML schema and data into the DataSet using the specified Stream object.
ReadXml	reader (TextReader)	Reads XML schema and data into the DataSet using the specified TextReader object.
ReadXml	fileName (String)	Reads XML schema and data into the DataSet using the specified file.
ReadXml	stream (Stream) Mode (XmlReadMode)	Reads XML schema and data into the DataSet using the specified Stream and XmlReadMode.
ReadXml	fileName (String) Mode (XmlReadMode)	Reads XML schema and data into the DataSet using the specified file and XmlReadMode.

Table B.9: continued

Name	Parameters	Description
ReadXml	reader (TextReader) Mode (XmlReadMode)	Reads XML schema and data into the DataSet using the specified TextReader and XmlReadMode.
ReadXml	reader (XmlReader) Mode (XmlReadMode)	Reads XML schema and data into the DataSet using the specified XmlReader and XmlReadMode.
ReadXmlSchema	reader (XmlReader)	Reads the XML schema into the DataSet from the specified XmlReader object.
ReadXmlSchema	stream (Stream)	Reads the XML schema into the DataSet from the specified Stream object.
ReadXmlSchema	reader (TextReader)	Reads the XML schema into the DataSet from the specified TextReader object.
ReadXmlSchema	fileName (String)	Reads the XML schema into the DataSet from the specified file.
RejectChanges	none	Rolls back all changes made to the DataSet since it was loaded or the last time the AcceptChanges method was called.
Reset	none	Resets the DataSet to its original state.
ToString	none	Returns a string that represents the current object.
WriteXml	writer (XmlWriter)	Writes the current schema and data for the DataSet using the specified XMLWriter object.
WriteXml	fileName (String)	Writes the current schema and data for the DataSet using the specified file.
WriteXml	stream (Stream)	Writes the current schema and data for the DataSet using the specified Stream object.
WriteXml	writer (TextWriter)	Writes the current schema and data for the DataSet using the specified TextWriter object.

Name	Parameters	Description
WriteXml	stream (Stream) mode (XmlWriteMode)	Reads XML schema and data into the DataSet using the specified XmlReader and XmlReadMode.
WriteXml	fileName (String) mode (XmlWriteMode)	Reads XML schema and data into the DataSet using the specified XmlReader and XmlReadMode.
WriteXml	writer (TextWriter) mode (XmlWriteMode)	Reads XML schema and data into the DataSet using the specified XmlReader and XmlReadMode.
WriteXml	writer (XmlWriter) mode (XmlWriteMode)	Reads XML schema and data into the DataSet using the specified XmlReader and XmlReadMode.
WriteXmlSchema	writer (TextWriter)	Writes the DataSet structure as an XML schema to the specified TextWriter object.
WriteXmlSchema	stream (Stream)	Writes the DataSet structure as an XML schema to the specified Stream object.
WriteXmlSchema	fileName (String)	Writes the DataSet structure as an XML schema to the specified file.
WriteXmlSchema	writer (XMLWriter)	Writes the DataSet structure as an XML schema to the XMLWriter object.

Table B.10: **DataSet** *Events*

Name	Description
MergeFailed	Fires when a target and source DataRow have the same primary key value and EnforceConstraints is set to true.
Disposed	Adds an event handler to listen to the Dispose event on the component.

DataTable Object Members

The DataTable class represents one table of in-memory data. Tables B.11 through B.14 list the constructor, properties, methods, and events of the DataTable class.

Table B.11: **DataTable** *Constructor*

Name	Parameters	Description
DataTable	none	Initializes a new instance of the DataTable class.
DataTable	tableName (String)	Initializes a new instance of the DataTable class with the specified name.
DataTable	info (SerializationInfo) context (StreamingContext)	Initializes a new instance of the DataTable class with the SerializationInfo and StreamingContext.

Table B.12: **DataTable** *Properties*

Name	Type	Description
CaseSensitive	Boolean	Indicates whether string comparisons within the table are case sensitive.
ChildRelations	DataRelationCollection	Retrieves the collection of child relations for the DataTable.
Columns	DataColumnCollections	Retrieves the collection of columns for the DataTable.
Constraints	ConstraintCollection	Retrieves the collection of constraints for the DataTable.
Container	IContainer	Retrieves the container for the component.
DataSet	DataSet	Retrieves the DataSet that the table belongs to.
DefaultView	DataView	Retrieves a customized view of the table.
DesignMode	Boolean	Retrieves a value indicating whether the component is in design mode.
DisplayExpression	String	Retrieves or sets the expression that will return a value used to represent the table in the UI.
ExtendedProperties	PropertyCollection	Retrieves the collection of customized user information.
HasErrors	Boolean	Retrieves a value indicating whether there are errors in any of the rows in the tables in the DataSet to which the table belongs.

Name	Type	Description
Locale	CultureInfo	Retrieves or sets the locale information used to compare strings within the table.
MinimumCapacity	Integer	Retrieves or sets the initial beginning capacity for the table.
Namespace	String	Retrieves or sets the namespace for the DataTable.
ParentRelations	DataRelationCollection	Retrieves the collection of parent relations for the DataTable.
Prefix	String	Gets or sets the namespace for the XML representation of the data stored in the DataTable.
PrimaryKey	DataColumn	Retrieves or sets an array of columns that function as primary keys for the DataTable.
Rows	DataRowCollection	Retrieves the collection of rows that belong to this table.
Site	ISite	Retrieves or sets the site of the component.
TableName	String	Retrieves or sets the table name.

Table B.13: **DataTable** *Methods*

Name	Parameters	Description
AcceptChanges	none	Commits all changes made to this table since the last time the AcceptChanges method was called.
BeginInit	none	Begins the initialization of a DataTable that is used on a form or used by another component.
Clear	none	Clears the table of all data.
Clone	none	Clones the structure of the DataTable, including all schemas, relations, and constraints.
Compute	expression (String) filter (String)	Computes the specified expression on the current rows that pass the filter criteria.
Dispose	none	Disposes the component.

Table B.13: continued

Name	Parameters	Description
Dispose	disposing (Boolean)	Releases the unmanaged resources used by the MarshalByValueComponent and optionally releases the managed resources.
EndInit	none	Ends the initialization of a DataTable that is used on a form or is used by another component.
Equals	obj (Object)	Determines whether the specified object is the same instance as the current object.
Equals	objA (Object) objB (Object)	Determines if the specified object instances are equal.
GetChanges	none	Gets a copy of the DataTable that contains all the changes made to it since it was loaded or AcceptChanges was last called.
GetChanges	rowState (DataRowState)	Gets a copy of the DataTable that contains all the changes made to it since it was loaded or AcceptChanges was last called, filtered by DataRowState.
GetErrors	none	Returns an array of DataRow objects that contain errors.
GetHashCode	none	Serves as a hash function for a particular type.
GetService	service (Type)	Returns the implementer of the IServiceProvider.
GetType	none	Retrieves the type of the object.
ImportRow	row (DataRow)	Copies a DataRow, including original and current values, DataRowState values, and errors, into a DataTable.
LoadDataRow	values[] (Object) acceptChanges (Boolean)	Finds and updates a specific row. If no matching row is found, then a new row is created using the given values.
NewRow	none	Creates a new DataRow with the same schema as the table.
RejectChanges	none	Rolls back all changes made to the table since the last time the AcceptChanges method was called.
Select	none	Retrieves an array of DataRow objects.

Name	Parameters	Description
Select	FilterExpression (String)	Retrieves an array of DataRow objects that match the filter criteria ordered by the primary key.
Select	FilterExpression (String) sort (String)	Retrieves an array of DataRow objects that match the filter criteria, in the specified sort order.
Select	FilterExpression (String) sort (String) recordState (DataViewRowState)	Retrieves an array of DataRow objects that match the filter criteria, in the specified sort order, and that match the specified state.
ToString	none	Returns a string that represents the current object.

Table B.14: **DataTable** *Events*

Name	Description
ColumnChanged	Occurs after a value has been changed for the specified DataColumn in a DataRow.
ColumnChanging	Occurs when a value is changing for a specified DataColumn in a DataRow.
Disposed	Adds an event handler to listen to the Disposed event on a component.
RowChanged	Fires after a row value has been edited successfully.
RowChanging	Fires when a value for a row is changing.
RowDeleted	Fires after a row has been deleted.
RowDeleting	Fires before a row in the table is about to be deleted.

DataView Object Members

The DataView class represents a databindable, customized view of a DataTable. Tables B.15 through B.18 list the constructor, properties, methods, and events for the DataView class.

Table B.15: **DataView** *Constructor*

Name	Parameters	Description
DataView	none	Initializes a new instance of the DataView class.
DataView	table (DataTable)	Initializes a new instance of the DataView class with the specified DataTable.

Table B.16: **DataView** *Properties*

Name	Type	Description
AllowDelete	Boolean	Retrieves or sets a value indicating whether deletes are allowed.
AllowEdit	Boolean	Retrieves or sets a value indicating whether edits are allowed.
AllowNew	Boolean	Retrieves or sets a value indicating whether new rows can be added.
ApplyDefaultSort	Boolean	Retrieves or sets a value indicating whether to use the default sort.
Container	IContainer	Retrieves the container for the component.
Count	Integer	Retrieves the number of records in the DataView after RowFilter and RowStateFilter have been applied.
DataViewManager	DataViewManager	Retrieves the DataView associated with this view.
DesignMode	Boolean	Retrieves a value indicating whether the component is currently in design mode.
Item	DataRowView	Retrieves a row of data from a specified table.
RowFilter	String	Retrieves or sets the expression used to filter which rows are viewed in the DataView.
RowStateFilter	DataViewRowState	Retrieves or sets the row state filter used in the DataView.
Site	ISite	Retrieves or sets the site of the component.
Sort	String	Retrieves or sets the sort column or columns and the sort order for the table.
Table	DataTable	Retrieves or sets the source table.

Table B.17: **DataView** *Methods*

Name	Parameters	Description
AddNew	none	Adds a new row to the DataView.
BeginInit	none	Begins the initialization of a DataView that is used on a form or used by another component.
Delete	index (Integer)	Deletes a row at the specified index.
Dispose	none	Disposes of the resources (other than memory) used by the DataView object.

Name	Parameters	Description
Dispose	disposing (Boolean)	Releases the unmanaged resources used by the MarshalByValueComponent and optionally releases the managed resources.
EndInit	none	Ends the initialization of a DataView that is used on a form or used by another component.
Equals	none	Determines whether the specified object is the same instance as the current object.
Equals	objA (Object) objB (Object)	Determines if the specified object instances are equal.
Find	key (Object)	Finds a row in the DataView using the specified primary key value.
Find	key[] (Object)	Finds a row in the DataView using the specified primary key values.
GetEnumerator	none	Retrieves an enumerator for this DataView.
GetHashCode	none	Serves as a hash function for a particular type.
GetService	service (Type)	Gets the implementer of the IServiceProvider.
GetType	none	Retrieves the type of the object.
ToString	none	Returns a string that represents the current object.

Table B.18: **DataView** *Events*

Name	Description
Disposed	Adds an event handler to listen to the Disposed event on a component.
ListChanged	Fires when the list managed by the DataView changes.

DataViewManager Object Members

Contains a default DataViewSettingCollection for each DataTable in a DataSet.

Table B.19: **DataViewManager** *Constructor*

Name	Parameters	Description
DataViewManager	none	Initializes a new instance of the DataViewManager class.
DataViewManager	dataSet (DataSet)	Initializes a new instance of the DataViewManger class for the specified DataSet.

Table B.20: **DataViewManager** *Properties*

Name	Type	Description
Container	IContainer	Retrieves the container for the component.
DataSet	DataSet	Retrieves or sets the name of the DataSet to use with the DataViewManager.
DataViewSetting-CollectionString	String	Retrieves or sets a value used for code persistence.
DataViewSettings	DataViewSettingCollection	Gets the DataViewSetting-Collection for each DataTable in the DataSet.
DesignMode	Boolean	Retrieves a value indicating whether the component is currently in design mode.
Site	ISite	Retrieves or sets the site of the component.

Table B.21: **DataViewManager** *Methods*

Name	Parameters	Description
CreateDataView	table (DataView)	Creates a DataView for the specified DataTable.
Dispose	none	Disposes of the resources (other than memory) used by the DataView object.
Dispose	disposing (Boolean)	Releases the unmanaged resources used by the MarshalByValueComponent and optionally releases the managed resources.
Equals	none	Determines whether the specified object is the same instance as the current object.
Equals	objA (Object) objB (Object)	Determines if the specified object instances are equal.
GetHashCode	none	Serves as a hash function for a particular type.
GetService	service (Type)	Gets the implementer of the IServiceProvider.
GetType	none	Retrieves the type of the object.
ToString	none	Returns a string that represents the current object.

Table B.22: **DataViewManager** *Events*

Name	Description
Disposed	Adds an event handler to listen to the Disposed event on a component.
ListChanged	Fires when a row is added or deleted from a DataView.

System.Data.OleDb Namespace

The System.Data.OleDb namespace is the Ole DB .NET Data Provider.

OleDbCommand Object Members

The OleDbCommand class represents a query command to be made to a data source. Tables B.23 through B.26 list the constructor, properties, methods, and events for the OleDbCommand class.

Table B.23: **OleDbCommand** *Constructor*

Name	Parameters	Description
OleDbCommand	none	Initializes a new instance of the OleDbCommand class.
OleDbCommand	cmdText (String)	Initializes a new instance of the OleDbCommand class with the specified command text.
OleDbCommand	cmdText (String) connection (OleDbConnection)	Initializes a new instance of the OleDbCommand class with the specified command text and OleDbConnection.
OleDbCommand	cmdText (String) connectionString (String) Transaction (OleDbTransaction)	Initializes a new instance of the OleDbCommand class with the specified command text and connection string.

Table B.24: **OleDbCommand** *Properties*

Name	Type	Description
CommandText	String	Retrieves or sets the SQL command text or the provider-specific syntax to run against the data source.
CommandTimeout	Integer	Retrieves or sets the time to wait while executing the command before terminating the attempt and generating an error.
CommandType	CommandType	Retrieves or sets how the CommandText property is interpreted.

Table B.24: continued

Name	Type	Description
Connection	OleDbConnection	Retrieves or sets the OleDbConnection used by this instance of the the OleDbCommand.
Container	IContainer	Returns container for this component.
DesignTimeVisible	Boolean	Retrieves or sets a value indicating whether the command object should be visible in a customized Windows Form designer control.
Parameters	OleDbParameterCollection	Retrieves the OleDbParameterCollection.
Site	ISite	Retrieves or sets the site for the component.
Transaction	OleDbTransaction	Retrieves or sets the transaction in which the OleDbCommand executes.
UpdatedRowSource	UpdateRowSource	Retrieves or sets how command results are applied to the DataRow when used by the Update method of a DBDataSetCommand.

Table B.25: **OleDbCommand** *Methods*

Name	Parameters	Description
Cancel	none	Cancels the execution of a command.
CreateObjRef	requestedType (Type)	Creates an object that contains all information necessary to generate a proxy used for communicating with a remote object.
CreateParameter	none	Creates a new instance of an OleDbParameter object.
Dispose	none	Releases all resources held by the component.
Dispose	disposing (Boolean)	Releases the unmanaged resources used by the MarshalByValueComponent and optionally releases the managed resources.

Name	Parameters	Description
Equals	obj (Object)	Determines whether the specified Object is the same instance as the current Object.
Equals	objA (Object) objB (Object)	Determines if the specified object instances are equal.
ExecuteNonQuery	none	Executes a SQL command against the data source that does not return any rows.
ExecuteReader	none	Sends the CommandText to the Conenction and builds an OleDbReader.
ExecuteReader	behavior (CommandBehavior)	Sends the CommandText to the Connection and builds an OleDbReader using one of the CommandBehavior values.
ExecuteScalar	none	Executes the query, and returns the first column of the first row in the resultset returned by the query.
GetHashCode	none	Serves as a hash function for a particular type.
GetLifetime Service	none	Retrieves a lifetime service object that controls the lifetime policy for this instance.
GetType	none	Retrieves the Type of the Object.
Initialize LifetimeService	none	Allows object to provide its own lease and control its own lifetime.
Prepare	none	Creates a prepared version of the command on the data source.
ResetCommand Timeout	none	Resets the CommandTimeout property to the default value.
ToString	none	Returns a String representing the current object.

Table B.26: **OleDbCommand** *Events*

Name	Description
Disposed	Adds an event handler to listen to the Disposed event on a component.

`OleDbConnection` Object Members

The `OleDbConnection` class represents an open connection to a data source. Tables B.27 through B.31 list the constructor, properties, methods, shared methods, and events for the `OleDbConnection` class.

Table B.27: `OleDbConnection` *Constructor*

Name	Parameters	Description
OleDbConnection	none	Initializes a new instance of the `OleDbConnection` class.
OleDbConnection	connectionString (String)	Initializes a new instance of the `OleDbConnection` class with the specified connection string.

Table B.28: `OleDbConnection` *Properties*

Name	Type	Description
ConnectionString	String	Retrieves or sets the string used to open a data store.
ConnectionTimeout	Integer	Retrieves or sets the string used to open a data store.
Container	IContainer	Returns the `IContainer` that contains the component.
Database	String	Retrieves or sets the time to wait while establishing a connection.
DataSource	String	Retrieves or sets the name of the database to connect to.
Provider	String	Retrieves or sets the name of the provider.
ServerVersion	String	Retrieves a string containing the version of the server to which the client is connected.
Site	ISite	Retrieves or sets the site of the `Component`.
State	ConnectionState	Retrieves the current state of the connection.

Table B.29: `OleDbConnection` *Methods*

Name	Parameters	Description
BeginTransaction	none	Begins a database transaction.

Name	Parameters	Description
ChangeDatabase	value (String)	Changes the current database for an open OleDbConnection.
Close	none	Closes the connection to the database.
CreateCommand	none	Creates and returns an OleDbCommand object associated with the OleDbConnection.
CreateObjRef	requestedType (Type)	Creates an object that contains all information necessary to generate a proxy used for communicating with a remote object.
Dispose	none	Releases all resources held by the component.
Dispose	disposing (Boolean)	Releases the unmanaged resources used by the MarshalByValueComponent and optionally releases the managed resources.
Equals	obj (Object)	Determines whether the specified Object is the same instance as the current Object.
Equals	objA (Object) objB (Object)	Determines if the specified object instances are equal.
GetHashCode	none	Serves as a hash function for a particular type.
GetLifetimeService	none	Retrieves a lifetime service object that controls the lifetime policy for this instance.
GetOleDbSchemaTable	schema (Guid) Restrictions[] (Object)	Returns the schema table and associated restriction columns of the specified schema.
GetType	none	Retrieves the Type of the Object.
InitializeLifetime Service	none	Allows object to provide its own lease and control its own lifetime.

Table B.29: continued

Name	Parameters	Description
Open	none	Opens a database connection with the current property settings.
ToString	none	Returns a String object that represents the current object.

Table B.30: **OleDbConnection** *Static (Shared) Methods*

Name	Parameters	Description
ReleaseObjectPool	none	Indicates that the OleDbConnection object pooling can be cleared when the last underlying OLE DB Provider is released.

Table B.31: **OleDbConnection** *Events*

Name	Description
Disposed	Adds an event handler to listen to the Disposed event on a component.
InfoMessage	Fires when the provider sends a warning or a message.
StateChanged	Fires when the state of the connection changes.

OleDbDataReader Object Members

The OleDbDataReader class represents a way of reading a forward-only stream of data records from a data source. Tables B.32 and B.33 list the properties and methods for the OleDbDataReader class.

Table B.32: **OleDbDataReader** *Properties*

Name	Type	Description
Depth	Integer	Retrieves a value indicating the depth of nesting for the current row.
FieldCount	Integer	Indicates the number of fields within the current record. This is a read-only property.
IsClosed	Boolean	Indicates whether the data reader is closed. This is a read-only property.
Item	Object	Indicates the value for a column.
RecordsAffected	Integer	Retrieves the number of rows changed, inserted, or deleted by execution of a SQL statement.

Table B.33: **OleDbDataReader** *Methods*

Name	Parameters	Description
Close	none	Closes the data reader object.
CreateObjRef	requestedType (Type)	Creates an object that contains all information necessary to generate a proxy used for communicating with a remote object.
Equals	obj (Object)	Determines whether the specified Object is the same instance as the current Object.
Equals	objA (Object) objB (Object)	Determines if the specified object instances are equal.
GetBoolean	ordinal (Integer)	Retrieves the value of the specified column as a Boolean.
GetByte	ordinal (Integer)	Retrieves the value of the specified column as a byte.
GetBytes	ordinal (Integer) dataIndex (Long) buffer[] (Byte) bufferIndex (Integer) length (Integer)	Retrieves the value of the specified column as a byte array.
GetChar	ordinal (Integer)	Retrieves the value of the specified column as a character.
GetChars	ordinal (Integer) dataIndex (Long) buffer[] (Char) bufferIndex (Integer) length (Integer)	Retrieves the value of the specified column as a character array.
GetData	ordinal (Integer)	Not currently supported.
GetDataTypeName	index (Integer)	Retrieves the name of the back-end data type.
GetDateTime	ordinal (Integer)	Retrieves the value of the specified column as a DateTime object.
GetDecimal	ordinal (Integer)	Retrieves the value of the specified column as a Decimal object.
GetDouble	ordinal (Integer)	Retrieves the value of the specified column as a double-precision floating-point number.
GetFieldType	index (Integer)	Retrieves the Type that is the data type of the object.

Table B.33: continued

Name	Parameters	Description
GetFloat	ordinal (Integer)	Retrieves the value of the specified column as a single-precision floating-point number.
GetGuid	ordinal (Integer)	Retrieves the value of the specified column as a globally unique identifier.
GetHashCode	none	Serves as a hash function for a particular type.
GetInt16	ordinal (Integer)	Retrieves the value of the specified column as a 16-bit signed integer.
GetInt32	ordinal (Integer)	Retrieves the value of the specified column as a 32-bit signed integer.
GetInt64	ordinal (Integer)	Retrieves the value of the specified column as a 64-bit signed integer.
GetLifetime Service	none	Retrieves a lifetime service object that controls the lifetime policy for this instance.
GetName	index (Integer)	Retrieves the name of the specified column.
GetOrdinal	name (String)	Retrieves the column ordinal given the specified column name.
GetSchemaTable	none	Returns a DataTable that describes the column metadata of the OleDbDataReader.
GetString	ordinal (Integer)	Returns the value of the specified column as a string.
GetTimeSpan	ordinal (Integer)	Retrieves the value of the specified column as a TimeSpan object.
GetType	none	Retrieves the Type of the Object.
GetValue	ordinal (Integer)	Retrieves the value of the column with the specified index.
GetValues	values[] (Object)	Retrieves all the attribute fields in the collection for the current record.
Initialize LifetimeService	none	Allows object to provide its own lease and control its own lifetime.
IsDBNull	ordinal (Integer)	Retrieves a value indicating a non-existent value.
NextResult	none	Advances the data reader to the next result set.

Name	Parameters	Description
Read	none	Advances the data reader to the next record.
ToString	none	Returns a String representing the current Object.

OleDbDataAdapter Object Members

The OleDbDataAdapter class represents a set of data commands and a database connection that are used to populate a data set and update the data source. Tables B.34 through B.37 list the constructor, properties, methods, and events for the OleDbDataSetCommand class.

Table B.34: **OleDbDataAdapter** *Constructor*

Name	Parameters	Description
OleDbDataAdapter	none	Initializes a new instance of the OleDbDataSetCommand class.
OleDbDataAdapter	selectCommand (OleDbCommand)	Initializes a new instance of the OleDbDataSetCommand class with the specified select command.
OleDbDataAdapter	selectCommandText (String) selectConnection (OleDbConnection)	Initializes a new instance of the OleDbDataSetCommand class with the specified select statement and OleDbConnection object.
OleDbDataAdapter	selectCommandText (String) selectConnection String (String)	Initializes a new instance of the OleDbDataSetCommand class.

Table B.35: **OleDbDataAdapter** *Properties*

Name	Type	Description
AcceptChangesDuringFill	Boolean	Retrieves or sets a value indicating whether AcceptChanges is called on a DataRow after it is added to a DataTable.
Container	IContainer	Returns the IContainer that contains the component.
DeleteCommand	OleDbCommand	Retrieves or sets a command to delete records from the data set.

Table B.35: continued

Name	Type	Description
InsertCommand	OleDbCommand	Retrieves or sets a command to insert records into the data source.
MissingMappingAction	MissingMappingAction	Retrieves or sets whether unmapped source tables or columns are to be passed with their source names to be filtered.
MissingSchemaAction	MissingSchemaAction	Retrieves or sets whether missing source tables, columns, and their relationships are to be added to the data set schema or ignored or whether to raise an error.
SelectCommand	OleDbCommand	Retrieves or sets a command used to select records in the data source.
Site	ISite	Retrieves or sets the site of the Component.
TableMappings	DataTableMappings	Retrieves how a source table is to be mapped to a data set table.
UpdateCommand	OleDbCommand	Retrieves or sets a command used to update records in the data source.

Table B.36: **OleDbDataAdapter** *Methods*

Name	Parameters	Description
CreateObjRef	requestType (Type)	Creates an object that contains all information necessary to generate a proxy used for communicating with a remote object.
Dispose	none	Releases all resources held by the component.
Dispose	disposing (Boolean)	Releases the unmanaged resources used by the MarshalByValueComponent and optionally releases the managed resources.

Name	Parameters	Description
Equals	obj (Object)	Determines whether the specified Object is the same instance as the current Object.
Equals	objA (Object) objB (Object)	Determines whether the specified object instances are equal.
Fill	dataTable (DataTable) Adodb (Object)	Adds or refreshes rows in a DataTable to match those in an ADO recordset or Record object using the specified DataTable and ADO objects.
Fill	dataSet (DataSet) adodb (Object) srcTable (String)	Adds or refreshes rows in the DataSet to match those in an ADO Recordset or Record object using the specified DataSet, ADO object, and source table name.
Fill	dataSet (DataSet)	Fills the DataSet with records from the data source.
Fill	dataTable (DataTable)	Adds or refreshes rows in a DataTable to match those in the data source using the DataTable name.
Fill	dataSet (DataSet) srcTable (String)	Fills the DataSet with records from the source table specified.
Fill	dataTable(DataTable) dataReader (IDataReader)	Add or refreshes rows in a DataTable to match those in the data source using the specified DataTable and IDataReader.
Fill	dataTable (DataTable) Command (IDbCommand) Behavior (CommandBehavior)	Adds or refreshes rows in a DataTable to match those in the data source using the DataTable name, the specified SQL SELECT statement, and CommandBehavior.
Fill	dataSet (DataSet) startRecord (Integer) maxRecords (Integer) srcTable (String)	Fills the DataSet with records located between the given bounds from the specified source table.

Table B.36: continued

Name	Parameters	Description
Fill	dataSet (DataSet) srcTable (String) dataReader (IDataReader) startRecord (Integer) maxRecords (Integer)	Adds or refreshes rows in a specified range in the DataSet to match those in the data source using the DataSet, DataTable, and IDataReader names.
Fill	dataSet (DataSet) startRecord (Integer) maxRecords (Integer) srcTable (String) command (IDbCommand) behavior (CommandBehavior)	Adds or refreshes rows in a specified range in the DataSet to match those in the data source using the DataSet and source table names, command string, and command behavior.
FillSchema	dataSet (DataSet) schemaType (SchemaType)	Adds a DataTable named "Table" to the specified DataSet and configures the schema to match that in the data source based on the specified SchemaType.
FillSchema	dataTable (DataTable) schemaType (SchemaType)	Adds a DataTable and configures the schema of the table based on the specified SchemaType.
FillSchema	dataSet (DataSet) schemaType (SchemaType) srcTable (String)	Adds a DataTable to the specified DataSet and configures the schema to match that in the data source based on the specified SchemaType and DataTable.
FillSchema	dataSet (DataSet) schemaType (SchemaType) srcTable (String)	Adds a DataTable to the specified DataSet and configures the Schema to match that in the data source based upon the specified SchemaType and DataTable.
GetFill Parameters	none	Returns all parameters used when performing the select command.
GetHashCode	none	Serves as a hash function for a particular type.

Name	Parameters	Description
GetLifetimeService	none	Retrieves a lifetime service object that controls the lifetime policy for this instance.
GetType	none	Retrieves the `Type` of the `Object`.
InitializeLifetime Service	none	Allows object to provide its own lease and control its own life-time.
ToString	none	Returns a `String` representing the current object.
Update	datRows[] (DataRow)	Calls the respective `insert`, `update`, or `delete` commands for each inserted, updated, or deleted row in the given array of `DataRow` objects.
Update	dataset (DataSet)	Calls the respective `insert`, `update`, or `delete` commands for each inserted, updated, or deleted row in the specified data set.
Update	dataTable (DataTable)	Calls the respective `insert`, `update`, or `delete` statements for each inserted, updated, or deleted row in the specified DataTable.
Update	dataRows[] (DataRow) tableMapping (DataTableMapping)	Calls the respective `insert`, `update`, or `delete` statements for each inserted, updated, or deleted row in the specified array of DataRows.
Update	dataset (DataSet) srcTable (String)	Calls the respective `insert`, `update`, or `delete` commands for each inserted, updated, or deleted row in the specified data set with the given source table name.

Table B.37: **OleDbDataAdapter** *Events*

Name	Description
Disposed	Adds an event handler to listen to the Disposed event on a component.
FillError	Occurs when an error occurs during a fill operation.
RowUpdated	Fires during Update after a command is executed against the data source.
RowUpdating	Fires during Update before a command is executed against the data source.

OleDbError Object Members

The OleDbError class collects information relevant to a warning or error returned by the data source. Tables B.38 and B.39 list the properties and methods for the OleDbError class.

Table B.38: **OleDbError** *Properties*

Name	Type	Description
Message	String	Retrieves a short description of the error.
NativeError	Integer	Retrieves the database-specific error information.
Source	String	Retrieves the name of the object that generated the error.
SQLState	String	Retrieves the five-character error code following the ANSI SQL standard for the database.

Table B.39: **OleDbError** *Methods*

Name	Parameters	Description
Equals	obj (Object)	Determines whether the specified Object is the same instance as the current Object.
Equals	objA (Object) objB (Object)	Determines whether the specified object instances are equal.
GetHashCode	none	Serves as a hash function for a particular type.
GetType	none	Retrieves the Type of the Object.
ToString	none	Retrieves the complete text of the error message.

OleDbParameter Object Members

The OleDbParameter class represents a parameter to an OleDbCommand.
Tables B.40 through B.42 list the constructor, properties, and methods for
the OleDbParameter class.

Table B.40: **OleDbParameter** *Constructor*

Name	Parameters	Description
OleDbParameter	none	Initializes a new instance of the OleDbParameter class.
OleDbParameter	name (String) Value (Object)	Initializes a new instance of the OleDbParameter class with the parameter name and an OleDbParameter object.
OleDbParameter	name (String) dataType (OleDbType)	Initializes a new instance of the OleDbParameter class with the specified name and data type.
OleDbParameter	name (String) dataType (OleDbDBType) size (Integer)	Initializes a new instance of the OleDbParameter class with the specified name, data type, and size.
OleDbParameter	name (String) dataType (OleDbDBType) size (Integer) srcColumn (String)	Initializes a new instance of the OleDbParameter class with the specified name, data type, size, and source column name.
OleDbParameter	name (String) dataType (OleDbDBType) size (Integer) direction (ParameterDirection) isNullable (Boolean) precision (Byte) scale (Byte) srcColumn (String) srcVersion (DataRowVersion) value (Object)	Initializes a new instance of the OleDbParameter class with the specified name, data type, size, parameter direction, precision, parameter scale, source column name, DataRowVersion, and the value of the parameter.

Table B.41: **OleDbParameter** *Properties*

Name	Type	Description
DBType	DBType	Retrieves or sets the native data type from the data source.
Direction	ParameterDirection	Retrieves or sets whether the parameter is input only, output only, bidirectional, or a return value parameter.

Table B.41: continued

Name	Type	Description
IsNullable	Boolean	Retrieves or sets whether the parameter accepts null values.
OleDbType	OleDbType	Retrieves or sets the `OleDbType` for the parameter.
ParameterName	String	Retrieves or sets the name of the `OleDbParameter`.
Precision	Byte	Retrieves or sets the maximum number of digits used to represent the value.
Scale	Byte	Retrieves or sets the number of decimal places to which `Value` is resolved.
Size	Integer	Retrieves or sets the maximum size, in bytes, of the data within the field.
SourceColumn	String	Retrieves or sets the name of the source column mapped to the `DataSet`.
SourceVersion	DataRowVersion	Retrieves or sets the `DataRowVersion` to use when loading a `Value`.
Value	Object	Retrieves or sets the value of the parameter.

Table B.42: **OleDbParameter** *Methods*

Name	Parameters	Description
CreateObjRef	requestedType (Type)	Creates an object that contains all information necessary to generate a proxy used for communicating with a remote object.
Equals	obj (Object)	Determines whether the specified `Object` is the same instance as the current `Object`.
Equals	objA (Object) objB (Object)	Determines whether the specified object instances are equal.
GetHashCode	none	Serves as a hash function for a particular type.
GetLifetimeService	none	Retrieves a lifetime service object that controls the lifetime policy for this instance.
GetType	none	Retrieves the `Type` of the `Object`.

Name	Parameters	Description
InitializeLifetimeService	none	Allows object to provide its own lease and control its own life-time.
ToString	none	Returns a String representing the current object.

System.Data.SqlClient Namespace

The System.Data.SqlClient namespace is the .NET Data Provider for SQL Server. The classes in this namespace bypass OLE DB and communicate directly with SQL Server, therefore increasing performance tremendously when using SQL Server.

SqlCommand Object Members

The SqlCommand class represents a Transact-SQL query or stored procedure to execute at a SQL Server database. Tables B.43 through B.46 list the constructor, properties, methods, and events for the SqlCommand class.

Table B.43: **SqlCommand** *Constructor*

Name	Parameters	Description
SqlCommand	none	Initializes a new instance of the SqlCommand class.
SqlCommand	cmdText (String)	Initializes a new instance of the SqlCommand class with the specified command text.
SqlCommand	cmdText (String) connection (SqlConnection)	Initializes a new instance of the SqlCommand class with the specified command text and SqlConnection.
SqlCommand	cmdText (String) connection (SqlConnection) Transaction (SqlTransaction)	Initializes a new instance of the SqlCommand class with the text of the query, a SqlConnection, and the Transaction.

Table B.44: **SqlCommand** *Properties*

Name	Type	Description
CommandText	String	Retrieves or sets the Transact-SQL or stored procedure to execute at the data source.

Table B.44: continued

Name	Type	Description
CommandTimeout	Integer	Retrieves or sets the wait time before terminating the attempt to connect.
CommandType	CommandType	Retrieves or sets how the CommandText property is interpreted.
Connection	SqlConnection	Retrieves or sets the SqlConnection used by this instance of SqlCommand.
Container	IContainer	Returns the IContainer that contains this component.
DesignTimeVisible	Boolean	Retrieves or sets a value indicating whether the command object should be visible in a Windows Form designer control.
Parameters	SqlParameterCollection	Retrieves the SqlParameterCollection.
Site	ISite	Retrieves or sets the site for the component.
Transaction	SqlTransaction	Retrieves or sets the transaction in which the SqlCommand executes.
UpdatedRowSource	UpdateRowSource	Retrieves or sets how command results are applied to the DataRow when used by the Update method of a DbDataAdapter.

Table B.45: **SqlCommand** *Methods*

Name	Parameters	Description
Cancel	none	Cancels the execution of the SqlCommand.
CreateObjRef	requestedType (Type)	Creates an object that contains all information necessary to generate a proxy used for communicating with a remote object.
CreateParameter	none	Creates an instance of SqlParameter.
Dispose	none	Releases all resources held by the component.

Name	Parameters	Description
Dispose	disposing (Boolean)	Releases the unmanaged resources used by the MarshalByValueComponent and optionally releases the managed resources.
Equals	obj (Object)	Determines whether the specified Object is the same instance as the current Object.
Equals	objA (Object) objB (Object)	Determines whether the specified object instances are equal.
ExecuteNonQuery	none	Executes a Transact-SQL statement against the data source and returns the number of rows affected.
ExecuteReader	none	Sends the CommandText to the Connection and builds a SqlDataReader.
ExecuteReader	behavior (CommandBehavior)	Sends the CommandText to the Connection and builds a SqlDataReader using one of the CammandBehavior values.
ExecuteScalar	none	Executes the query and returns the value in the first column of the first row of the result set.
ExecuteXmlReader	none	Sends the CommandText to the Connection and builds an XmlReader object.
GetHashCode	none	Serves as a hash function for a particular type.
GetLifetimeService	none	Retrieves a lifetime service object that controls the lifetime policy for this instance.
GetType	none	Retrieves the Type of the object.
InitializeLifetime Service	none	Allows object to provide its own lease and control its own lifetime.
Prepare	none	Creates a prepared version of the command on an instance of SQL Server.

Table B.45: continued

Name	Parameters	Description
ResetCommandTimeout	none	Resets the Command time out back to its default value.
ToString	none	Returns a String that represents the current object.

Table B.46: **SqlCommand** *Events*

Name	Description
Disposed	Adds an event handler to listen to the Disposed event of the component.

SqlConnection Object Members

The SqlConnection class represents an open connection to a Sql Server database. Tables B.47 through B.50 list the constructor, properties, methods, and events for the SqlCollection class.

Table B.47: **SqlConnection** *Constructor*

Name	Parameters	Description
SqlConnection	none	Initializes a new instance of the SqlConnection class.
SqlConnection	connectionString (String)	Initializes a new instance of the SqlConnection class with the specified connection string.

Table B.48: **SqlConnection** *Properties*

Name	Type	Description
ConnectionString	String	Retrieves or sets the string used to open a data store in SQL Server.
ConnectionTimeout	Integer	Retrieves or sets the time to wait while establishing a connection before terminating the attempt and generating an error.
Container	IContainer	Returns the IContainer that contains the component.
Database	String	Retrieves or sets the name of the current database or the database to be used after a connection is opened.
DataSource	String	Retrieves or sets the name of the database to connect to.

Name	Type	Description
PacketSize	Integer	Gets the size (in bytes) of the network packets used for communicating with a SQL Server instance.
ServerVersion	String	Retrieves a string containing the version of the connected Sql Server.
Site	ISite	Retrieves or sets the site of the Component.
State	DBObjectState	Retrieves the current state of the connection.
WorkstationID	String	Retrieves a string that identifies the database client.

Table B.49: **SqlConnection** *Methods*

Name	Parameters	Description
BeginTransaction	none	Begins a database transaction.
BeginTransaction	iso (IsolationLevel)	Begins a database transaction with the specified isolation level.
BeginTransaction	transactionName (String)	Begins a database transaction with the specified transaction name.
BeginTransaction	iso (IsolationLevel) transactionName (String)	Begins a database transaction with the specifed isolation level and transaction name.
ChangeDatabase	database (String)	Changes the current database for an open SqlConnection.
Close	none	Closes the connection to the database.
CreateCommand	none	Creates and returns a SqlCommand object associated with the SqlConnection.
CreateObjRef	requestedType (Type)	Creates an object that contains all information necessary to generate a proxy used for communicating with a remote object.

Table B.49: continued

Name	Parameters	Description
Dispose	none	Releases all resources held by the component.
Dispose	disposing (Boolean)	Releases the unmanaged resources used by the MarshalByValueComponent and optionally releases the managed resources.
Equals	obj (Object)	Determines whether the specified Object is the same instance as the current Object.
Equals	objA (Object) objB (Object)	Determines whether the specified object instances are equal.
GetHashCode	none	Serves as a hash function for a particular type.
GetLifetimeService	none	Retrieves a lifetime service object that controls the lifetime policy for this instance.
GetType	none	Retrieves the Type of the Object.
InitializeLifetime Service	none	Allows object to provide its own lease and control its own lifetime.
Open	none	Opens a database connection with the current property settings.
ToString	none	Returns a String object that represents the current object.

Table B.50: **SqlConnection** *Events*

Name	Description
Disposed	Adds an event handler to listen to the Disposed event of the component.
InfoMessage	Fires when the provider sends a warning or a message.
StateChange	Fires when the state of the connection changes.

SqlDataReader Object Members

The SqlDataReader class represents a way of reading a forward-only stream of data records from a Sql Server. Tables B.51 and B.52 list the properties and methods for the SqlDataReader class.

Table B.51: **SqlDataReader** *Properties*

Name	Type	Description
Depth	Integer	Retrieves a value indicating the depth of the nesting for the current row.
FieldCount	Integer	Indicates the number of fields within the current record. This is a read-only property.
IsClosed	Boolean	Indicates whether the data reader is closed. This is a read-only property.
Item	Object	Indicates the value for a column.
RecordsAffected	Integer	Retrieves the number of rows changed, inserted, or deleted by execution of the Transact-SQL statement.

Table B.52: **SqlDataReader** *Methods*

Name	Parameters	Description
Close	none	Closes the data reader object.
CreateObjRef	requestedType (Type)	Creates an object that contains all information necessary to generate a proxy used for communicating with a remote object.
Equals	obj (Object)	Determines whether the specified Object is the same instance as the current Object.
Equals	objA (Object) objB (Object)	Determines whether the specified object instances are equal.
GetBoolean	ordinal (Integer)	Retrieves the value of the specified column as a Boolean.
GetByte	ordinal (Integer)	Retrieves the value of the specified column as a byte.
GetBytes	ordinal (Integer) (Long) buffer[] (Byte) bufferIndex (Integer) length (Integer)	Retrieves the dataIndex value of the specified column as a byte array.
GetChar	ordinal (Integer)	Retrieves the value of the specified column as a character.

Table B.52: continued

Name	Parameters	Description
GetChars	ordinal (Integer) dataIndex (Long) buffer[] (Char) bufferIndex (Integer) length (Integer)	Retrieves the value of the specified column as a character array.
GetData	ordinal (Integer)	Not currently supported.
GetDataTypeName	ordinal (Integer)	Retrieves the name of the back-end data type.
GetDateTime	ordinal (Integer)	Retrieves the value of the specified column as a DateTime object.
GetDecimal	ordinal (Integer)	Retrieves the value of the specified column as a Decimal object.
GetDouble	ordinal (Integer)	Retrieves the value of the specified column as a double-precision floating-point number.
GetFieldType	ordinal (Integer)	Retrieves the Type that is the data type of the object.
GetFloat	ordinal (Integer)	Retrieves the value of the specified column as a single-precision floating-point number.
GetGuid	ordinal (Integer)	Retrieves the value of the specified column as a globally unique identifier.
GetHashCode	none	Serves as a hash function for a particular type.
GetInt16	ordinal (Integer)	Retrieves the value of the specified column as a 16-bit signed integer.
GetInt32	ordinal (Integer)	Retrieves the value of the specified column as a 32-bit signed integer.
GetInt64	ordinal (Integer)	Retrieves the value of the specified column as a 64-bit signed integer.
GetName	ordinal (Integer)	Retrieves the name of the specified column.
GetOrdinal	name (String)	Retrieves the column ordinal given the specified column name.

Name	Parameters	Description
GetSchemaTable	none	Returns a DataTable that describes the column metadata of the SqlDataReader.
GetSqlBinary	ordinal (Integer)	Retrieves the value of the specified column as a SqlBinary object.
GetSqlBoolean	ordinal (Integer)	Retrieves the value of the specified column as a SqlBoolean object.
GetSqlByte	ordinal (Integer)	Retrieves the value of the specified column as a SqlByte object.
GetSqlDateTime	ordinal (Integer)	Retrieves the value of the specified column as a SqlDateTime object.
GetSqlDouble	ordinal (Integer)	Retrieves the value of the specified column as a SqlDouble object.
GetSqlGuid	ordinal (Integer)	Retrieves the value of the specified column as a SqlGuid object.
GetSqlInt16	ordinal (Integer)	Retrieves the value of the specified column as a SqlInt16 object.
GetSqlInt32	ordinal (Integer)	Retrieves the value of the specified column as a SqlInt32 object.
GetSqlInt64	ordinal (Integer)	Retrieves the value of the specified column as a SqlInt64 object.
GetSqlMoney	ordinal (Integer)	Retrieves the value of the specified column as a SqlMoney object.
GetSqlSingle	ordinal (Integer)	Retrieves the value of the specified column as a SqlSingle object.
GetSqlString	ordinal (Integer)	Retrieves the value of the specified column as a SqlString object.
GetSqlValue	ordinal (Integer)	Retrieves an Object that is a representation of the underlying SqlDbType Variant.

Table B.52: continued

Name	Parameters	Description
GetSqlValues	values[] (Object)	Retrieves all the attribute fields in the collection for the current column.
GetString	ordinal (Integer)	Returns the value of the specified column as a string.
GetType	none	Retrieves the Type of the Object.
GetValue	ordinal (Integer) value (Object)	Retrieves the value of the specified column.
GetValues	values[] (Object)	Retrieves all the attribute fields in the collection for the current record.
InitializeLifetime Service	none	Allows object to provide its own lease and control its own lifetime.
IsDBNull	ordinal (Integer)	Retrieves a value indicating a nonexistent value.
NextResult	none	Advances the data reader to the next result set.
Read	none	Advances the data reader to the next record.
ToString	none	Returns a String representing the current Object.

SqlDataAdapter Object Members

The SqlDataAdapter represents a set of data commands and a database connection that are used to fill a data set and update the data source. Tables B.53 through B.56 list the constructor, properties, methods, and events for the SqlDataAdapter class.

Table B.53: **SqlDataAdapter** *Constructor*

Name	Parameters	Description
SqlDataAdapter	none	Initializes a new instance of the SqlDataAdapter class.
SqlDataAdapter	selectCommand (SqlCommand)	Initializes a new instance of the SqlDataAdapter class with the specified select command.

Name	Parameters	Description
SqlDataAdapter	selectCommandText (String) selectConnection (SqlConnection)	Initializes a new instance of the SqlDataAdapter class with the specified select statement and SqlConnection object.
SqlDataAdapter	selectCommandText (String) selectConnectionString (String)	Initializes a new instance of the SqlDataAdapter class with the specified select statement and connection string.

Table B.54: **SqlDataAdapter** *Properties*

Name	Type	Description
AcceptChangesDuringFill	Boolean	Retrieves or sets a value indicating whether AcceptChanges is called on a DataRow after it is added to a DataTable.
Container	IContainer	Returns the IContainer that contains the component.
DeleteCommand	SqlCommand	Retrieves or sets a command to delete records from the data set.
InsertCommand	SqlCommand	Retrieves or sets a command to insert records into the data source.
MissingMappingAction	MissingMappingAction	Retrieves or sets whether unmapped source tables or columns are to be passed with their source names to be filtered.
MissingSchemaAction	MissingSchemaAction	Retrieves or sets whether missing source tables, columns, and their relationships are to be added to the data set schema or ignored or whether to raise an error.
SelectCommand	SqlCommand	Retrieves or sets a command used to select records in the data source.
Site	ISite	Retrieves or sets the site of the Component.
TableMappings	DataTableMappings	Retrieves how a source table is to be mapped to a data set table.

Table B.54: continued

Name	Type	Description
UpdateCommnad	SqlCommand	Retrieves or sets a command used to update records in the data source.

Table B.55: **SqlDataAdapter** *Methods*

Name	Parameters	Description
CreateObjRef	requestType (Type)	Creates an object that contains all information necessary to generate a proxy used for communicating with a remote object.
Dispose	none	Releases all resources held by the component.
Dispose	disposing (Boolean)	Releases the unmanaged resources used by the MarshalByValueComponent and optionally releases the managed resources.
Equals	obj (Object)	Determines whether the specified Object is the same instance as the current Object.
Equals	objA (Object) objB (Object)	Determines whether the specified object instances are equal.
Fill	dataSet (DataSet)	Fills the DataSet with records from the data source.
Fill	dataTable (DataTable)	Adds or refreshes rows in a DataTable to match those in the data source using the DataTable name.
Fill	dataSet (DataSet) srcTable (String)	Fills the DataSet with records from the specified source table.
Fill	dataTable(DataTable) dataReader (IDataReader)	Add or refreshes rows in a DataTable to match those in the data source using the specified DataTable and IDataReader.
Fill	dataTable (DataTable) Command (IDbCommand) Behavior (CommandBehavior)	Adds or refreshes rows in a DataTable to match those in the data source using the DataTable name, the specified SQL SELECT statement, and CommandBehavior.
Fill	dataSet (DataSet) startRecord (Integer) maxRecords (Integer) srcTable (String)	Fills the DataSet with records located between the given bounds from the specified source table.

Name	Parameters	Description
Fill	dataSet (DataSet) srcTable (String) dataReader (IDataReader) startRecord (Integer) maxRecords (Integer)	Adds or refreshes rows in a specified range in the DataSet to match those in the data source using the DataSet, DataTable, and IDataReader names.
Fill	dataSet (DataSet) startRecord (Integer) maxRecords (Integer) srcTable (String) command (IDbCommand) behavior (CommandBehavior)	Adds or refreshes rows in a specified range in the DataSet to match those in the data source using the DataSet and source table names, command string, and command behavior.
FillSchema	dataSet (DataSet) schemaType (SchemaType)	Adds a DataTable named "Table" to the specified DataSet and configures the schema to match that in the data source based on the specified SchemaType.
FillSchema	dataTable (DataTable) schemaType (SchemaType)	Adds a DataTable and configures the schema of the table based on the specified SchemaType.
FillSchema	dataSet (DataSet) schemaType (SchemaType) srcTable (String)	Adds a DataTable to the specified DataSet and configures the schema to match that in the data source based on the specified SchemaType and DataTable.
FillSchema	dataSet (DataSet) schemaType (SchemaType) command (IDBCommand) behavior (CommandBehavior)	Adds a DataTable to the specified DataSet and configures the schema to match that in the data source based on the specified SchemaType.
GetFill Parameters	none	Returns all parameters used when performing the select command.
GetHashCode	none	Serves as a hash function for a particular type.
GetLifetime Service	none	Retrieves a lifetime service object that controls the lifetime policy for this instance.
GetType	none	Retrieves the Type of the Object.
Initialize LifetimeService	none	Allows object to provide its own lease and control its own lifetime.
ToString	none	Returns a String representing the current object.

Table B.55: continued

Name	Parameters	Description
Update	dataRows[] (DataRow)	Calls the respective insert, update, or delete commands for each inserted, updated, or deleted row in the given array of DataRow objects.
Update	dataset (DataSet)	Calls the respective insert, update, or delete commands for each inserted, updated, or deleted row in the specified data set.
Update	dataTable (DataTable)	Calls the respective insert, update, or delete statements for each inserted, updated, or deleted row in the specified DataTable.
Update	dataRows[] (DataRow) tableMapping (DataTableMapping)	Calls the respective insert, update, or delete statements for each inserted, updated, or deleted row in the specified array of DataRows.
Update	dataset (DataSet) srcTable (String)	Calls the respective insert, update, or delete commands for each inserted, updated, or deleted row in the specified data set with the given source table name.

Table B.56: **SqlDataAdapter** *Events*

Name	Description
Disposed	Adds an event handler to listen to the Disposed event on a component.
FillError	Occurs when an error occurs during a fill operation.
RowUpdated	Fires during Update after a command is executed against the data source.
RowUpdating	Fires during Update before a command is executed against the data source.

SqlError Object Members

The SqlError class collects information relevant to a warning or error returned by Sql Server. Tables B.57 and B.58 list the properties and methods for the SqlError class.

Table B.57: **SqlError** *Properties*

Name	Type	Description
Class	Byte	Retrieves the severity level of the error returned from the Sql Server adapter.
LineNumber	Integer	Retrieves the line number within the Sql command batch or stored procedure that had the error.
Message	String	Retrieves the text describing the error.
Number	Integer	Retrieves the number that identifies the type of error.
Procedure	String	Retrieves the name of the stored procedure that generated the error.
Server	String	Retrieves the name of the database server that generated the error.
Source	String	Retrieves the line of source code that generated the error.
State	Byte	Retrieves the number modifying the error to provide additional information.

Table B.58: **SqlError** *Methods*

Name	Parameters	Description
Equals	obj (Object)	Determines whether the specified Object is the same instance as the current Object.
Equals	objA (Object) objB (Object)	Determines whether the specified object instances are equal.
GetHashCode	none	Serves as a hash function for a particular type.
GetType	none	Retrieves the Type of the Object.
ToString	none	Returns the entire text of the SqlError.

SqlParameter Object Members

The SqlParameter class represents a parameter to a SqlCommand object. Tables B.59 through B.61 list the constructor, properties, and methods for the SqlParameter class.

Table B.59: **SqlParameter** *Constructor*

Name	Parameters	Description
SqlParameter	none	Initializes a new instance of the SqlParameter class.
SqlParameter	name (String) Value (Object)	Initializes a new instance of the SqlParameter class with the parameter name and an SqlParameter object.

Table B.59: continued

Name	Parameters	Description
SqlParameter	parameterName (String) dbType (SqlDbType)	Initializes a new instance of the SqlParameter class with the specified name and SqlDbType.
SqlParameter	parameterName (String) dbType (SqlDbType) size (Integer)	Initializes a new instance of the SqlParameter class with the specified name, SqlDbType, and size.
SqlParameter	parameterName (String) dbType (SqlDbType) size (Integer) sourceColumn (String)	Initializes a new instance of the SqlParameter class with the specified name, SqlDbType, size, and source column name.
SqlParameter	parameterName (String) dbType (SqlDbType) size (Integer) direction (ParameterDirection) isNullable (Boolean) precision (Byte) scale (Byte) sourceColumn (String) sourceVersion (DataRowVersion) value (Object)	Initializes a new instance of the SqlParameter class with the specified name, direction, parameter precision, parameter scale, source column name, DataRowVersion, and the value of the parameter.SqlDbType, size, parameter.

Table B.60: **SqlParameter** *Properties*

Name	Type	Description
DbType	DbType	Retrieves or sets the native data type from the data source.
Direction	ParameterDirection	Retrieves or sets whether the parameter is input only, output only, bidirectional, or a return value parameter.
IsNullable	Boolean	Retrieves or sets whether the parameter accepts null values.
Offset	Integer	Retrieves or sets the offset to the value.

Name	Type	Description
ParameterName	String	Retrieves or sets the name of the `SqlParameter`.
Precision	Byte	Retrieves or sets the maximum number of digits used to represent the value.
Scale	Byte	Retrieves or sets the number of decimal places to which `Value` is resolved.
Size	Integer	Retrieves or sets the maximum size, in bytes, of the data within the field.
SourceColumn	String	Retrieves or sets the name of the source column mapped to the `DataSet`.
SourceVersion	DataRowVersion	Retrieves or sets the `DataRowVersion` to use when loading a `Value`.
SqlDbType	SqlDbType	Retrieves or sets the `SqlDbType` for the parameter.
Value	Object	Retrieves or sets the value of the parameter.

Table B.61: **SqlParameter** *Methods*

Name	Parameters	Description
CreateObjRef	requestedType (Type)	Creates an object that contains all information necessary to generate a proxy used for communicating with a remote object.
Equals	obj (Object)	Determines whether the specified `Object` is the same instance as the current `Object`.
Equals	objA (Object) objB (Object)	Determines whether the specified object instances are equal.
GetHashCode	none	Serves as a hash function for a particular type.
GetLifetimeService	none	Retrieves a lifetime service object that controls the lifetime policy for this instance.
GetType	none	Retrieves the `Type` of the `Object`.
InitializeLifetimeService	none	Allows object to provide its own lease and control its own lifetime.
ToString	none	Returns a String representing the current object.

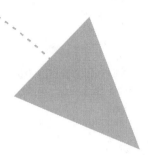
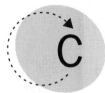

Visual Basic.NET Language Reference

With the latest version of the language, Visual Basic developers should now feel like first-class citizens. Microsoft has introduced a number of new features, including a number of object-oriented programming (OOP) improvements. This appendix does not serve as an exhaustive reference for the Visual Basic .NET language. As with previous versions of VB, entire books will be dedicated to this language. This appendix should serve as a primer and quick reference for VB.NET.

Changes from Previous Versions of VB

Although the advancements to the language make the language more powerful, they do come at a price. Developers now need to design their applications with these new features in mind.

General Changes

The sections that follow present the changes to declarations, variable assignments, and scope. You can save time in writing code and debugging if you are aware of these changes.

DECLARATIONS

In previous versions of Visual Basic, multiple variable declarations are permitted within a single statement; however, if the data type of each variable is not specified, the variable defaults to a Variant:

```
Dim a As Integer, b As Integer  ' a is an Integer, b is an Integer
Dim x, y as Integer             ' x is a Variant, y is an Integer
```

In VB.NET, repeating the data type name in the declaration is no longer necessary:

```
Dim x, y as Integer  ' Both x and y are Integers
```

VARIABLE ASSIGNMENTS

In addition to the enhancements made to multiple variable declarations as just outlined, variable assignment has been enhanced to permit variable declaration and assignment within a single statement:

```
Dim y as Integer = 3
```

SCOPE

Variable scope has been tweaked in VB.NET as well. In VB 6.0, variables declared within a procedure had procedure scope regardless of whether the variable was declared within a block. Consider the following:

EXAMPLE

```
For x = 100 To 1 Step -1
    ' y has procedure scope even though it was declared inside the block.
    Dim y As Integer
      y = y + x
Next
z = y    ' y is available outside the block
```

Note that y is available outside the block it was declared in. In VB.NET, y is unavailable at procedure scope.

Procedure Changes

The sections that follow present the changes to these areas: parentheses, `Static`, optional arguments, `ByRef` and `ByVal`, and `ParamArrays ByVal`.

USE OF PARENTHESES

One of the biggest headaches (in my opinion anyway) addressed in VB.NET is the use of parentheses when calling procedures. If you recall, in Visual Basic 6.0, when making `Function` calls, parentheses were required around argument lists. However, when calling a `Sub`, parentheses were forbidden unless the `Call` statement was used, in which case they were required:

EXAMPLE

```
Call SetCustomerLastName("Smith")
SetCustomerLastName "Smith"
```

You'll be glad to learn that parentheses are required around any non-empty argument list. When making calls with empty argument lists, parentheses are optional.

Static NOT SUPPORTED FOR PROCEDURES

Previous versions of Visual Basic allowed the shorthand practice of marking a procedure with the `Static` modifier. This allowed all local variables in the procedure to maintain state between calls to the procedure. VB.NET does not support this shortcut, instead requiring the developer to mark every local variable as `Static` as required.

Optional Arguments

Another change to procedures in VB.NET is in the way optional parameters are handled. In VB 6.0, default values were not required for optional parameters. Developers were able to detect missing parameters via the IsMissing function. In VB.NET, all optional parameters require default values. Therefore, IsMissing is no longer needed and no longer supported.

ByRef versus ByVal

Passing parameters ByRef allows the procedure to modify the value of the parameter in the calling program, potentially leading to unexpected results. In Visual Basic 6.0, parameters that were not explicitly marked ByVal defaulted to ByRef. In VB.NET, all parameters are passed ByVal unless marked ByRef. This change should be inconsequential to the studious developer who marks his parameters either ByVal or ByRef explicitly anyway to avoid confusion.

ParamArrays ByVal

In VB 6.0, procedures could accept a variable number of arguments by specifying the ParamArray keyword on the last argument for the procedure. This array was always of type Variant and passed ByRef because you could not specify ByVal.

In VB.NET, a ParamArray is always passed ByVal and all arguments in the array must be of the type specified for the ParamArray.

Return Statement

In Visual Basic 6.0, values were returned from functions simply by setting the name of the function to the value to be returned:

```
Function TestFunction As Integer
    TestFunction = 1
End Function
```

Many developers found this syntax confusing, so Microsoft has included the new Return statement to provide an alternate means of returning a value from a function:

```
Function TestFunction As Integer
    Return 1
End Function
```

Property Changes

The sections that follow discuss the changes in the handling of properties. The areas affected are the default properties, property declarations, and ByRef arguments.

DEFAULT PROPERTIES

Visual Basic 6.0 supported default properties for objects, which often led to shorter though more confusing code. Consider the following example:

```
rs.Fields.Item("FirstName").Value = "Jack"
```

In VB 6.0, because the `Fields` collection is the default property on the `Recordset` object, and because the `Value` property is the default property for the `Item` property of the collection, this assignment is functionally equivalent to the following:

```
rs("FirstName") = "Jack"
```

To help reduce confusion, but at the expense of shorter code, VB.NET supports only parameterized default properties:

```
rs.Fields("FirstName").Value = "Jack"   '  valid because Item is parameterized
```

PROPERTY DECLARATIONS

One of the more confusing aspects of previous versions of Visual Basic, especially for programmers making the jump to VB from other languages, was property declaration syntax. VB 6.0 included both `Property Get` and `Property Set` statements. Further, either `Property Let` or `Property Set` had to be used depending upon whether an object reference or default property was to be assigned. VB.NET introduces a unified property declaration syntax, which includes both a `Get` and a `Set` clause:

EXAMPLE

```
Dim m_PhoneNumber As String
Property PhoneNumber As Integer
    Get
        PhoneNumber = FormatPhone(m_PhoneNumber)
    End Get
    Set  ' The implicit variable Value represents value being set
      m_PhoneNumber = Strip(Value)
    End Set
End Property  ' PhoneNumber
```

As a consequence of this new unified syntax, `Property Let` is no longer supported.

PROPERTIES ByRef

As covered previously, VB.NET now supports only parameterized default properties. Arguments for parameterized default properties must be specified `ByVal` because `ByRef` arguments are no longer supported for parameterized queries.

Changes to Arrays

Two array-related statements were impacted by the changes in VB.NET: `Size` and `LBound`. It is important to note these changes or else your program may yield unexpected results.

Size

Visual Basic 6.0 allowed the creation of fixed-size arrays with the following syntax:

```
Dim MyArray(0 to 4) As Integer
```

EXAMPLE

An array created in this fashion could not be resized with the `ReDim` statement. VB.NET no longer supports fixed-size arrays such as this. The preceding array can be created in VB.NET with any of the following statements:

```
Dim MyArray(5) As Integer
Dim MyArray() As New Integer(5) {}
Dim MyArray() As Integer {0, 1, 2, 3, 4}
```

Multidimensional arrays are supported and created in the following manner:

```
Dim MyArray( , , ) As Integer
```

Note that although arrays can no longer be fixed-size, multidimensional arrays are fixed-dimension. Although the individual dimensions can be resized with the `ReDim` statements, the number of dimensions cannot change.

LBound

In Visual Basic 6.0, the default lower bound for an array was 0. This could be changed to a default lower bound of 1 by using the `Option Base` statement. In VB.NET, however, all arrays have a lower bound of 0 and the `Option Base` statement is not supported.

Data Type Changes

The `Variant` type is now a reserved keyword, and all types derive from the `Object` type. Short, Long, and Integer types have also been modified in VB.NET.

Object Versus Variant

In Visual Basic 6.0, the `Variant` type served as the universal data type. This type supported any kind of data the developer wanted to put in a variable of this type. VB.NET introduces a universal type system in that all types derive from the `Object` type. The `Variant` type is no longer supported; however, it is still a reserved keyword.

Short, Integer, AND Long

Fundamental changes have been made to the treatment of integers in VB.NET. In previous versions of Visual Basic, the `Integer` type was 16 bits, the `Long` type was 32 bits, and the language did not support a 64-bit integer type. In VB.NET this changes with the introduction of the Short type for 16-bit values, Integer now handles 32-bit values, and now VB supports 64-bit values with the Long type. These types correspond to the CLR types of System.Int16, System.Int32, and System.Int64 respectively.

No Fixed-Length Strings

Visual Basic 6.0 supported the concept of fixed-length strings with the following syntax:

EXAMPLE

```
Dim MyString As String * 25 'Defines a fixed-length string
```

In VB.NET, fixed-length strings are no longer supported. The length of the string assigned to it determines the size of the string variable.

No Currency Data Type

In an effort to handle more places on both sides of the decimal point when dealing with monetary values, the Currency data type in Visual Basic 6.0 has been retired in favor of the new Decimal data type, which maps to the System.Decimal type in the CLR.

New Features in VB.NET

VB.NET introduces some new features that many developers have been asking for. While these features can provide greater functionality for your programs, they make programming in VB.NET more complex, so it is essential that you understand these new features before putting them to use.

Error Handling

One of the most anticipated new features found in VB.NET is support for structured exception handling. In addition to the unstructured exception handling supported in previous versions of Visual Basic using On Error statements, VB.NET now supports robust structured exception handling via the Try...Catch...Finally statement:

EXAMPLE

```
Try
    Customer = CustomerList(1)
Catch e as IndexOutOfRangeException
    'Handle error gracefully
    Customer = New Customer()
Finally
    'Do any final clean up here
    CustomerList = Nothing
End Try
```

In this example, the Try block of the Try...Catch...Finally statement contains the code to monitor for errors. When an error is raised, each of the

`Catch` block expressions is evaluated to find a match. If a matching `Catch` block is found, control is transferred to that block. Otherwise, control is passed back up to any enclosing `Catch` blocks. If a match still does not exist, the error is not caught and is raised as usual. Note that multiple `Catch` blocks are allowed within a single `Try...Catch...Finally` statement.

Structures Replace UDTs

Another major change in the language is the evolution of User-Defined Types (UDTs). In Visual Basic 6.0, UDTs and their members had public access and were created using the `Type...End Type` declaration.

In VB.NET, UDTs have been evolved into (or replaced with, depending on your view of things) *structures*. Structures are created with the `Structure...End Structure` construction and their members must have an access modifier (`Public`, `Protected`, and so on).

Constructors and Destructors

A powerful new feature of VB.NET that has been long available in other OOP languages is that of class constructors and destructors. These special methods, `Sub New` and `Sub Finalize`, allow for the initialization and disposal of resources associated with the instantiation of classes such as database connections or network connections. These methods replace the `Class_Initialize` and `Class_Terminate` methods from VB 6.0 and run before any other code from the class is executed. Coupled with the new overloading feature, multiple parameterized constructors may be created for added flexibility. Declaration of constructors and destructors is discussed in the section on classes.

Overloading

One of the more powerful features of VB.NET that C and C++ developers should be familiar with is that of overloading. Methods can be *overloaded*, meaning that they share the same name but have unique signatures. This is a useful means of providing computation on different kinds of parameters while avoiding creating unique method names for a variety of different input combinations. Consider the following example:

EXAMPLE

```
Class Shape
    Public Height, Width As Integer
    Public Function Perimeter() As Integer
        Return ((Height * 2) + (Width * 2))
    End Function
    Public Function Perimeter(Length As Integer) As Integer
        ' assume square
        Return (Length * 4)
    End Function
```

```
        Public Function Perimeter(Length As Integer, Width As Integer) As Integer
            ' assume rectangle
            Return ((Length * 2) + (Width * 2))
        End Function
End Class
```

In this example, we are able to calculate the perimeter of a variety of shapes using the overloaded method `Perimeter`.

Namespaces and Assemblies

In Visual Basic 6.0, the VB project name served as the hierarchical organization of classes in the project. VB.NET extends this concept to include robust capabilities to organize types into namespace hierarchies and file assemblies. This topic is discussed in depth later in this appendix.

Inheritance

Visual Basic.NET supports *inheritance*, the ability to derive classes from pre-existing classes. Derived classes extend the members of the base class by overriding inherited members or by adding functionality by adding members. All classes created with Visual Basic.NET are inheritable by default.

Threading Model

One of the drawbacks of the VB 6.0 language was the threading models available. With Visual Basic.NET, you can write multithreaded and free-threaded applications that perform multiple tasks simultaneously. This becomes very useful when developing scalable applications. Please consult another text on VB.NET or the .NET Framework docs for a complete discussion of this topic.

Memory Management

Like the C# language, VB.NET employs *automatic memory management*. Transparent to developers, the language uses garbage collection to move objects around in memory and clean up after unused objects.

Getting Started

In keeping with programming tradition, Listing C.1 outlines our first "Hello, world" program.

EXAMPLE

Listing C.1: The classic "hello, world" program, hello.vb.

```
Imports System.WinForms
Module Hello
    Sub Main() {
```

Listing C.1: continued

```
        ' write "Hello, world!" to the screen
        MessageBox.Show("Hello, World!")
    End Sub
End Module
```

By following convention, the source code for our program is saved with a
.vb file extension, hello.vb. We can compile our program using the VB.NET
command-line compiler, vbc.exe, using the following syntax:

```
vbc hello.vb
```

The output of this directive produces our executable program, hello.exe.
The output of the program is

```
Hello, World!
```

OUTPUT

From this basic example, we can glean several important points:

- The entry point of a VB.NET program is a subroutine named Main.

- You can write to the console using the System.WinForms.MessageBox
  class found in the .NET platform framework classes.

- C, C++, and C# developers may notice that our Main is not enclosed
  within a class. In the example, Sub Main is found within Module Hello.
  Modules are a special reference type whose members are implicitly
  shared. Modules are further explained later in the appendix.

- You can use the Imports statement to symbolically handle library
  dependencies. Users of VisualStudio.NET can still use the Add
  Reference option in the Project menu from within the IDE; however,
  references may now be set inline with your code. Please consult
  Appendix E for an introduction to the VisualStudio.NET IDE.

Variables

Variables are storage locations and in VB.NET must have a specific type.
When declared within method, property, or indexer declarations, variables
are said to be *local*. Variables are declared in the following way:

```
Dim variablename As Type
```

So, to create an integer variable, we could write this:

```
Dim x As Integer
```

Variables must be assigned a value before they can be used, and we can
both declare and assign a value to a variable in one step:

```
Dim x as Integer = 1
```

Parameters

Another way to define variables is through the use of formal method parameters. Table C.1 outlines the four types of method parameters.

Table C.1: Parameter Types in VB.NET

Parameter Type	Modifier	Description
value	ByVal	Modifications do not impact original argument passed into the method
reference	ByRef	Modifications directly impact original argument passed into the method
optional	Optional	Does not require the argument to be supplied; however, a default value must be supplied in the argument declaration
parameter array	ParamArray	Enables variable length parameter lists

Consider the following class that employs each of the parameter types:

EXAMPLE

```
Imports System
Class Test
    Sub ValueParamMethod(a As Integer)
        a = a + 2 ' the orginal parameter is not modified
    End Sub
    Sub RefParamMethod(ByRef a As Integer)
        a = a + 2 ' the orginal parameter is not modified
    End Sub
    Sub OptionalParamMethod(Optional a As Integer = 3)
        a = a + 2 ' if a is not supplied, defaults to 3
    End Sub
    Sub ParamArrayMethod(ParamArray args As Integer)
        ' provides flexibility through indefinite number of arguments
    End Sub
End Class
```

Expressions and Operators

Table C.2 outlines the operators found in VB.NET.

Table C.2: Operator Types in VB.NET

Category	Operators
Primary	All nonoperator expressions.
Exponentiation	^
Unary Negation	+, -
Multiplicative	*, /

Table C.2: continued

Category	Operators
Integer Division	\
Modulus	%
Additive	+ -
Concatenation	&
Relational	=,<,>,<=,>=, Like, Is, TypeOf
Conditional NOT	Not
Conditional AND	And, AndAlso
Conditional OR	Or, OrElse
Conditional XOR	XOr

Expressions are evaluated in order of operator precedence. This precedence is based upon the *associativity* of the operators:

- Except for assignment operators, all binary operators are performed from left to right.

- Assignment operators and the conditional operator are evaluated from right to left.

- Precedence may be controlled through the use of parentheses.

Statements

In VB.NET, statements represent executable code. The next section outlines the statements found and VB.NET and their usage.

Blocks

A block statement allows multiple statements to be written in contexts where a single statement is allowed. A *block statement* consists of a statement list enclosed by braces:

```
Sub Main

End Sub
```

Statement Lists

A *statement list is* simply one or more statements written in sequence and enclosed in blocks as outlined following:

EXAMPLE

```
Sub Main
    Refresh()
    Repaint()
End Sub
```

Labeled

A *labeled statement* allows a statement to be referenced by a Goto statement. The scope of the label is the block that encloses it, including any nested blocks:

EXAMPLE

```
Sub Main
    If (X>0) Then Goto MyLabel
    X = X + 1
    MyLabel:
        return X
End Sub
```

Declarations

A *declaration statement* declares a local variable or constant:

```
Dim X as Integer = 3
Dim Const pi As Decimal = 3.14
```

Expressions

As expected, an *expression statement* evaluates a given statement:

EXAMPLE

```
Return (x * y)
Repaint(Me)
```

Selection

Selection statements allow for the execution of one of a list of possible statements based upon the value of a controlling expression. Selection statements include the If...Then...Else and Select...Case statements.

If

The If statement selects a statement for execution based on a Boolean expression:

EXAMPLE

```
If (x > 0) Then
    x = x -1
End If
```

This statement may be coupled with an else clause in order to specify a statement for execution if the condition fails:

EXAMPLE

```
If (x > 0) Then
    x = x - 1
Else
    return x
End If
```

If statements may also be nested:

EXAMPLE

```
If (x <> 3) Then
    If (x > 0) Then
        x = x - 1
    Else
        Return x
    End If
End If
```

Select Case

To provide multiple statements for possible execution based upon the value of a condition, we use the `Select Case` statement:

EXAMPLE

```
Select Case (x)
    Case 1
        MessageBox.Show("X = 1")
    Case 2
        MessageBox.Show("X = 2")
    Case 3
        MessageBox.Show("X = 3")
    Case Else
        MessageBox.Show("X does not equal 1,2, or 3")
End Select
```

The `Select...Case` statement evaluates the expression and looks for a match with a constant value from one of the labeled statements. When a match is found, execution control is transferred to the statement list for the matching label. If no match is found, control is transferred to the `Case Else` block and its statement list.

Loops

Loop statements allow for the execution of a statement list as long as some expression evaluates `True`. VB.NET includes four such iteration statements: `While...End While`, `Do...Loop`, `For...Next`, and `For Each...Next`.

While...End While

The `While...End While` statement executes a statement list zero or more times, depending on the value of the conditional expression:

EXAMPLE

```
While (x < 100)
    MessageBox.Show(x)
    X = X + 1
End While
```

Do...Loop

Similar to the While statement, the Do...Loop statement executes one or more times:

EXAMPLE

```
Do
    MessageBox.Show(x)
    X = X + 1
Loop While(X < 100)
```

Note that the Do...Loop statement can use the While keyword as used above, which breaks the loop if the expression evaluates to False or the Until keyword, which breaks the loop if the expression evaluates to True.

For...Next

The For...Next statement loops on a set of bounds. The statement specifies a lower bound, an upper bound, and an optional step for the iteration. Upon commencement of the loop, the three values are evaluated. If the step is omitted, the iteration defaults to a step of 1:

EXAMPLE

```
For x = 0 to 100
    MessageBox.Show(x)
Next
For x = 100 to 0 Step -1
    MessageBox.Show(x)
Next
```

For Each...Next

Very similar to the For...Next statement, the For Each...Next statement enumerates a collection and executes the statement list once for each item in the collection:

EXAMPLE

```
For Each x in Args
    MessageBox.Show(x)
Next
```

Control-Flow Statements

Another type of statement, the *control-flow* statement allows the unconditional transfer of control execution in a VB.NET program. These statements include Goto, Exit, Stop, Return, and End statements.

Goto

The Goto statement transfers control to the statement matching the specified label:

EXAMPLE

```
Sub Main
    If (X>0) Then Goto MyLabel
    X = X + 1
    MyLabel:
        return X
End Sub
```

Exit

An Exit statement transfers control to the next statement after the end of the enclosing block statement. If the block is a method, execution is transferred back to the caller of the method.

EXAMPLE

```
Do
    x = x + 10
    If x > 35 Then Exit Do
Loop While (x > 0)
```

Return

The Return statement returns control to the caller of the procedure in which the Return statement appears. If enclosed within a function, the Return statement may take a return value argument:

EXAMPLE

```
Function GetStudentID(FullName As String) As Integer
    Return "Jim Smith"
End Function
```

Stop

Using the Stop statement permits putting breakpoints in your code:

EXAMPLE

```
Dim x As Integer
For x = 1 To 5
    Debug.WriteLine (x)
    Stop 'Stop during each iteration.
Next I
```

END

Similar to the Stop statement, the End statement terminates program execution and can only appear in executables (.exes) and not libraries (.dlls).

Try

The try statement provides exception handling during execution of a statement block. The try block may be followed by one or more catch blocks and may be followed by one finally block:

EXAMPLE

```
Try
    Repaint()
Catch (e As Exception)
    'handle gracefully
    If(x < 0) Then ' out of range
```

```
        Throw New Exception("Index out of Range")
    End If
Finally
    ' any clean-up code here
End Try
```

Types

Two kinds of types are supported in VB.NET, value types and reference types. The difference between these two kinds of types is in the way the variables of each type behave.

Value Types

Unlike reference types, variables of value types contain the actual data they represent. Value types consist of primitives (except Object and String), enumerations, and structures.

PRIMITIVE TYPES

Primitive types are shorthand for CLR types found in the .NET platform. Table C.3 outlines each of the value types found in VB.NET as well as the system-provided type to which it corresponds.

Table C.3: Primitive Value Types in VB.NET

Type Name	Category	Description
Short	System.Int16	16-bit signed integral type
Integer	System.Int32	32-bit signed integral type
Long	System.Int64	64-bit signed integral type
Byte	System.Byte	8-bit unsigned integral type
Single	System.Single	Single-precision floating point type
Double	System.Double	Double-precision floating point type
Boolean	System.Boolean	Boolean type containing either True or False
Char	System.Char	Containing value is one Unicode character
Decimal	System.Decimal	New decimal type to replace less robust Currency type from previous versions of VB

ENUMERATIONS

A second kind of value type is the *Enumeration*, which is a user-defined type name for a group of related constants. This type is often used when a runtime decision is made from a fixed number of choices created at compile-time:

```
Enum Material
    Pine,
    Oak,
    Maple,
    Mahogany
End Enum
```

STRUCTURES

Structures are value types that share many similarities with classes. Like classes, structure definitions can include constants, fields, methods, events, operators, constructors, destructors, and even nested type declarations. See the definition of classes for a more complete definition of these items.

When used strategically, structures can often boost performance because structure values are stored on the stack. A structure can be declared in the following manner:

```
Structure Point
    Public x, y, z As Integer

    Public Sub New(x As Integer, y As Integer, z As Integer)
        Me.x = x
        Me.y = y
        Me.z = z
    End Sub
End Structure
```

We can use the structure in this way:

```
Dim Graph As Point() = new Point(1000)
For a = 1 to 1000
    Graph(a) = new Point(a, a, a + a)
Next
```

By using a structure instead of a class, the calling program instantiates just one object for an array of our `Point` struct instead of creating 1001 new objects as it would have if we had used a class declaration.

CONVERSIONS

As mentioned before, VB.NET includes a number of primitive value types. These types also have predefined conversions between them. These conversions are either implicit or explicit.

Implicit Conversions

Implicit conversions are those that can be performed without loss of data and without careful observation. For instance, consider a conversion from `Short` to `Integer`. Because this conversion requires no loss of data, it never fails.

Explicit Conversions

Unlike implicit conversions, *explicit conversions* may result in loss of data and must be handled by using a cast expression:

```
CInt(MyLongVariable)
```

The complete list of conversion functions include: CBool, CByte, CDate, CDbl, CDec, CInt, CLng, CSng, CShort, CStr, Fix, and Int.

Reference Types

Reference types are types whose variables store only references to the actual objects they represent. Because of this, operations made on one reference type variable may affect another reference type variable if it references the same object. Reference types include arrays, classes, interfaces, delegates, and the primitive type String. The primitive type Object, the class from which all classes are ultimately derived, is neither a reference type nor a value type.

ARRAY TYPES

VB.NET supports both single-dimensional and multidimensional arrays. Array types are reference types, so array declarations merely set aside space for the array. Array instances are actually created by initializing the array with array creation expressions:

EXAMPLE

```
Dim arr as Integer() ' declare single-dimension array
Dim arr As New Integer {10, 20, 30} ' initialize the array

Dim arr2(,) As Integer ' declare multi-dimension array
arr2 = New Integer[,] {10, 20, 30}, {30, 40, 50} ' initialize the array
```

Note that the preceding arrays are *rectangular arrays* because their shape is known. However, VB.NET also supports *jagged arrays*, also known as "arrays of arrays":

```
Dim jagged As New Integer(5)() ' declare multi-dimension array
```

CLASSES

Class declarations allow the programmer to create new reference types and to help employ the OOP principle of data hiding. Class declarations can include any of the following that are defined later in the appendix: fields, constants, properties, methods, events, constructors, destructors, and nested type declarations.

Member Access

Each member defined in the class declaration is accessible to one of five degrees. Table C.4 outlines the five degrees of accessibility of class members.

Table C.4: Degrees of Accessibility of Class Members

Degree	Definition
Public	Unlimited access
Protected	Access limited to the containing class or types derived from the containing class
Friend	Access limited to this program
Protected Friend	Access limited to this program or types derived from the containing class
Private	Access limited to the containing type

Constants

A *constant* is a member that represents a value computed at compile-time, which does not change. A simple class with two constants might look like this:

EXAMPLE

```
Class Test
    Public Const x As Integer = 1
    Public Const y As Integer = x + 2
End Class
```

Note that constant values can depend upon other constants as long as no circular references are created. With the appropriate access level, constants can be accessed via dot notation like any other member, as follows:

```
Dim A As Integer = Test.x
```

Fields

A *field member* is a variable associated with an object or class. Fields can be declared in the following way:

EXAMPLE

```
Class Student
    Public FirstName As String
    Public LastName As String
    Public Static ReadOnly HomeRoom As Integer

    Public Sub New(First As String, Last As String, Room As Integer)
        Me.FirstName = First
        Me.LastName = Last
        Me.HomeRoom = Room
    End Sub
End Class
```

In this example, we have created FirstName and LastName, two *instance fields*, or variables for which storage is allocated with each instance of the class that is created. We have also created a third field, this time a *shared field* by using the Static keyword. In doing so, we have created storage for the HomeRoom field in only the class level, so all instances of the Student class will share this field. To prevent unexpected results by inadvertently overwriting data, we have used the ReadOnly keyword, which allows the field to be changed only during its declaration or a constructor of its containing class.

Properties

Like fields, *properties* are named members with associated types. However, properties do not designate storage locations for their associated values. Instead, they define accessors that denote the statements to execute to read or write their values. A simple class with a property declaration would resemble the following:

EXAMPLE

```
Public Class PhoneNumber
    Private m_PhoneNumber As String
    Public Property Text As String
        Get
            Return m_PhoneNumber
        End Get
        Set
            m_PhoneNumber = FormatPhone(Value)
        End Set
    End Property
    Public Sub New(Phone As String)
        m_PhoneNumber = FormatPhone(Phone)
    End Sub
    ...
End Class
```

In this skeleton example of a phone number formatting class, we define both Get and Set accessors for the Text property. The Get accessor is called when the Text property is read and, conversely, the Set accessor is called when the property's value is changed. Note the implicit Value parameter of the Set accessor.

We can use this class and its properties in the following manner:

EXAMPLE

```
Dim pn As New PhoneNumber("8675309") 'constructor formats
TextBox1.Text = pn.Text ' Get accessor returns formatted number
pn.Text = TextBox1.Text ' Set accessor, number is formatted and stored
```

Methods

A *method* is a member that implements an action that can be performed by an object or class. Methods have a signature that consists of the number, types, and modifiers of the list of its parameters. Methods may or may not have a return type and value. For methods returning a type, the procedure is created with the Function keyword; otherwise, the Sub keyword is used. Like fields, methods may be *shared methods* (accessed through the class) or *instance methods* (which are accessed through instances of the class). We declare methods in this way:

EXAMPLE

```
Public Class SportsTicker
    Public Sub Start()
        ' implementation goes here
    End Sub
    Public Shared Sub Reset()
        ' implementation goes here
    End Sub
    Public Function GetScoreByTeam(Team As String) As GameInfo
        ' implementation goes here
    End Function
End Class
```

In this framework example, we've defined three methods. Start is an instance method with no return value, which initiates scrolling on our sports ticker. Reset is a shared method, which returns the ticker to its original state. Finally, GetScoreByTeam is an instance method, which returns a GameInfo class (defined separately) containing all the game information for the given team on the current day.

One of the more powerful features of VB.NET that developers of other languages might be familiar with is that of overloading. Methods may be *overloaded*, meaning they share the same name but have unique signatures. This is a useful means of providing computation on different kinds of parameters while avoiding creating unique method names for a variety of different input combinations. Consider the following example:

EXAMPLE

```
Class Shape
    Public Height, Width As Integer
    Public Function Perimeter() As Integer
        Return ((Height * 2) + (Width * 2))
    End Function
    Public Function Perimeter(length As Integer) As Integer
        ' assume square
        Return (length * 4)
    End Function
    Public Function Perimeter(length As Integer, width As Integer) As Integer
        ' assume rectangle
        Return ((length * 2) + (width * 2))
    End Function
    Public Function Perimeter(sides As Integer()) As Integer
        ' unknown shape, calculate
        Dim p as Integer = 0
        For x = 0 to sides.length
            p = p + sides[x]
        Next
        Return p
```

```
        End Function
End Class
```

In this example, we are able to calculate the perimeter of a variety of shapes using the overloaded method `Perimeter`.

Events

An *event* is a special member that enables a class to provide notifications to the calling program. Events are declared much like fields with an added Event keyword as follows:

EXAMPLE

```
Class TestClass
    Public Event MouseOver As MouseOverHandler
End Class
```

The declaration type is always that of a delegate, in this case `MouseOverHandler`, which we define as follows:

```
Public Delegate Sub MouseOverHandler(Sender As Object, e As System.EventArgs)
```

Delegates and their other uses are discussed later in this reference.

To hook up the event handler for our event, we use the `AddHandler` operator from the calling program:

EXAMPLE

```
Public Class TestForm
    Public Sub New()
        AddHandler TestClass1.MouseOver , AddressOf TestClass1_MouseOver
    End Sub
    Dim TestClass1  As New TestClass()
    Sub TestClass1_MouseOver(Sender As Object, e As EventArgs)
        ' handle event here
    End Sub
    Sub RemoveHandler()
        ' removes the handler
        RemoveHandler TestClass1.MouseOver , AddressOf TestClass1_MouseOver
    End Sub
End Class
```

Instance Constructors

Constructors are members, which provide any initialization operations for an instance of a class. Similar in many ways to methods, constructors may be overloaded as well to provide alternate ways of instantiating a class. Constructors are created by adding a procedure named `Sub New` to your class. The following is an extension of our `Shape` class to include two constructors to allow initialization of the `Height` and `Width` fields upon instantiation.

EXAMPLE

```
Class Shape
    Public Height, Width As Integer
    Public Sub New(h As Integer, w As Integer)
        Height = h
        Width = w
    End Sub
    Public Sub New(h As Integer)
        MyBase.New()
        ' assume square
        Height = h
        Width = h
    End Sub
    Public Function Perimeter() As Integer
        Return ((Height * 2) + (Width * 2))
    End Function
    Public Function Perimeter(length As Integer) As Integer
        ' assume square
        Return (length * 4)
    End Function
End Class
```

Note that the first line of a constructor must make a call to the constructor of the base class or another constructor within the class. Because we had no constructors in our class beforehand, you may have guessed that the use of constructors is optional. If no constructor is provided, the compiler automatically generates an empty constructor with no parameters.

Destructors

A *destructor* is a member that performs the actions required to terminate an instance of a class. Destructors have no accessibility level, take no parameters, and cannot be called explicitly. Instead, destructors are called implicitly by the system during regular garbage collection. We add destructors to a class by adding a Sub Finalize procedure.

```
Sub Finalize()
    'add any clean-up code here
End Sub
```

Shared Constructors

Shared constructors perform the required actions to initialize a class the same way as instance constructors initialize an instance of a class. However, like destructors, shared constructors have no accessibility level, take no parameters, and cannot be call explicitly. A shared constructor looks like this:

```
Shared Sub New()
    ' implementation code
End Sub
```

Inheritance

Inheritance is the mechanism that allows one type to derive from another. Classes support single inheritance and all classes ultimately derive from the object type. Consider a generic form of our Shape class once again:

EXAMPLE

```
Class Shape
    Public Function Perimeter(sides As Integer()) As Integer
        ' unknown shape, calculate
        Dim p As Integer = 0
        For x = 0 to Sides.Length - 1
            p = P + sides(x)
        Next
        Return p
    End Function
End Class
```

Now let's derive a new type from this class:

EXAMPLE

```
Class Rectangle
    Inherits Shape
    Public Function Area(h As Integer, w As Integer) As Integer
        Return h * w
    End Function
End Class
```

Our new class inherits the Perimeter method from Shape while adding its own Area method. However, inheritance doesn't have to be verbatim. By adding the Overridable keyword to a method or property in the base class, we may override its implementation in the derived class:

EXAMPLE

```
Class Shape
    Public Overridable Function Perimeter(Sides As Integer()) As Integer
        ' unknown shape, calculate
        Dim p As Integer = 0
        For x = 0 to Sides.Length - 1
            p = P + sides(x)
        Next
        Return p
    End Function
End Class
```

Now let's derive a new type from this class and override the Perimeter method:

EXAMPLE

```
Class Square
    Inherits Shape
    Public Overrides Function Perimeter(sides As Integer()) As Integer
        Return p * 4
    End Function
    Public Function Area(h As Integer, w As Integer) As Integer
        Return h * w
```

```
        End Function
End Class
```

Often, it may be prudent to design the base class with no implementation details and stipulate that the derived class provide its own implementation. This is accomplished by marking the class as MustInherit as follows:

```
MustInherit Class Shape
        Public Function MustInherit Perimeter() As Integer

        End Function
End Class
```

Our derived class is created in the same manner as in the previous example:

EXAMPLE

```
Class Square
        Inherits Shape
        Public Overrides Function Perimeter(sides As Integer()) As Integer
            Return p * 4
        End Function
        Public Function Area(h As Integer, w As Integer) As Integer
            Return h * w
        End Function
End Class
```

INTERFACES

Interfaces are contracts that a class (or structure) implementing the interface must adhere to. Interface members may include methods, properties, and events and interfaces support multiple inheritance. They contain no implementation details because this is left to the implementing class or struct:

EXAMPLE

```
Interface IValidation
        Sub Validate(text As String)
        End Sub
End Interface
Class PhoneNumber
        Inherits IValidation
        Sub Validate(text As String)
            ' validation code goes here
        End Sub
End Class
```

DELEGATES

Delegates are the VB.NET answer to function pointers in C++. However, delegates are type-safe and secure. *Delegates* derive from the System. Delegate type and encapsulate a callable entity, either a method on an instance class or a shared method on a class. A delegate can reference any object as long as the method's signature matches its own signature. Delegates are declared much like methods; after all, they are essentially just method signatures:

```
Delegate Sub MyDelegate()
```

After the delegate is declared, it must be instantiated:

EXAMPLE

```
Class MyClass
    Sub TestMethod()
        MessageBox.Show("Calling MyClass.TestMethod")
    End Sub
    Shared Sub TestDelegateCall(d As MyDelegate)
        d() ' calls TestMethod() anonymously
    End Sub
End Class
```

Component-Based Features

Until this point we've focused on programs and even program fragments in introducing the concepts of the language. However, VB.NET has several features that enable building component-based applications.

Namespaces and Assemblies

Namespaces provide a logical organizational system both internally within the program and externally to other programs. Consider the following example:

EXAMPLE

```
Namespace Que.ByExample
    Class Book
        ...
    End Class
End Namespace
```

Because namespaces may be nested, the preceding example is functionally equivalent to the following:

EXAMPLE

```
Namespace Que
    Namespace ByExample
        Class Book
            ...
        End Class
    End Namespace
End Namespace
```

In either case, we can reference the Book class via its fully qualified namespace:

```
Que.ByExample.Book
```

We can avoid using the fully qualified namespace by using the `Imports` statement as we have seen with the `System` namespace in prior examples:

```
Imports Que.ByExample
```

Assemblies are used for physical packaging and deployment by acting as containers for types. *Assemblies* take two forms, .exe files, which include a main entry point, and .dll libraries, which do not have a main entry point. The VB.NET compiler produces .exe applications by default. The compiler produces libraries by specifying the `target` switch as follows:

```
vbc /target:library filename.vb
```

Attributes

VB.NET supports `attributes` whereby programmers can specify declarative information for program entities and retrieve this information at runtime via reflection. In fact, the .NET Framework provides a number of special case attribute types already. Take the following example for instance:

EXAMPLE

```
< WebMethod(Description="Returns the stock price", EnableSession=true)>
Public Function GetCurrentStockPrice() As Desimal
...
End Function
```

In this fragment from a stock lookup Web service, we have marked the `GetCurrentStockPrice` method with the `WebMethod` attribute, which denotes it as callable via Web services. Just as the .NET Framework team developed the `WebMethod` attribute, we can derive our own custom attributes from the `System.Attribute` class:

```
Imports System
[AttributeUsage(AttributeTargets.All)]
Public Class HelpDocAttribute
    Inherits Attribute
    Public Keywords As String
    Private url As String
    Private topic As String
    Public Sub New(url As String, topic As String)
        Me.url = url
        Me.topic = topic
    End Sub
    Public Property Url As String
        Get
            Return url
        End Get
    End Property
    Public Property Topic As String
        Get
            Return topic
        End Get
```

```
        End Property
End Class
```

In creating our custom attribute, we first have to denote on which targets our attribute can be used. We do this, ironically, by using another attribute on our class declaration, the `AttributeUsage` class. Note that we specify our attribute to be available on any elements by passing the enumerated value `AttributeTargets.All` to the `AttributeUsage` constructor. Please consult the .NET Framework docs for available values of the `AttributeTargets` enumeration.

After designating which targets our attribute will be used on, we next set up our positional and named parameters. For custom attributes, *positional parameters* are those corresponding to the arguments for the public constructors of the attribute. *Named parameters* are those defined by public read/write properties of the class. Note that in our example we have created two positional parameters, `Url` and `Topic`, and one named parameter, `Keywords`.

Once declared, our custom attribute may be employed in this way:

EXAMPLE

```
<HelpDocAttribute("http:'help.xyzcompany.com/docs/SportsTicker.aspx", _
    "SportsTicker Class")>
Public Class SportsTicker
    <HelpDocAttribute("http:'help.xyzcompany.com/docs/SportsTicker.aspx", _
        "SportsTicker Constructor", Keywords="SportsTicker")>
    Public Sub New()
    ...
    End Sub
End Class
```

Notice that for the `SportsTicker` class itself, we pass the positional parameters of `Url` and `Topic`, and for the public constructor, we add a third parameter for a keyword search.

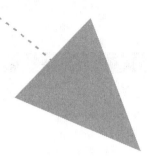

C# Language Reference

C# is a new type-safe, object-oriented language introduced by Microsoft that aspires to combine the rapid development features of Microsoft Visual Basic with the performance and power of C++. Because C# was derived from C and C++ and because of some similarities to Sun's Java language, developers with experience in any of these languages should find the C# syntax and concepts familiar.

Unlike Java, C# does not offer its own class library. Instead, it enables access to the Microsoft .NET platform, which provides a common runtime engine and class library. This appendix covers the fundamental aspects of this new language.

Getting Started

In keeping with programming tradition, Listing D.1 outlines our first program: "Hello, world".

EXAMPLE

Listing D.1: The classic "Hello, world" program, hello.cs.

```
using System;

class Hello
{
        static void Main() {
            // write "Hello, world!" to the screen
            Console.WriteLine("Hello, world!");
        }
}
```

Developers with experience in ASP/VBScript should note that the C# language is case sensitive and requires a semicolon at the end of statements like JavaScript. By following convention, we save the source code for our program with a .cs file extension, hello.cs. We can compile our program using the .NET command-line compiler, csc.exe, using the following syntax:

```
csc hello.cs
```

The output of this directive produces our executable program, hello.exe. The output of the program is as follows:

```
Hello, world!
```

OUTPUT

From this basic example, we can glean several important points:

- The entry point of a C# program is a static method named Main.

- As mentioned before, C# does not include a class library. We are able to write to the console using the System.Console class found in the .NET platform framework classes.

- C, C++, and Java developers may notice that Main is not a global method. This is because C# does not support global methods and variables. These elements must be enclosed within a type declaration such as classes and structs.

- The Using statement symbolically handles library dependencies instead of importing source with the #include statement found in C and C++.

Variables

Variables are storage locations and in C# must have a specific type. When declared within method, property, or indexer declarations, variables are said to be *local*. Variables are declared in the following way:

```
type variablename;
```

To create an integer variable, we would write the following:

```
int x;
```

Variables must be assigned a value before they can be used, and we can both declare and assign a value to a variable in one step:

```
int x = 1;
```

Parameters

Another way to define variables is through the use of formal method parameters. Table D.1 outlines the four types of method parameters.

Table D.1: Parameter Types in C#

Parameter Type	Modifier	Description
value	none	Modifications do not impact original argument passed into the method.
reference	ref	Modifications directly impact original argument passed into the method.
output	out	Used for passing values out of a method. Initial value is inconsequential.
parameter array	params	Enables variable length parameter lists.

Consider the following class, which employs each of the parameter types:

```
using System;
class Test
{
    public void ValueParamMethod(int a)
    {
        a += 2; // the original parameter is not modified
    }
    public void RefParamMethod(ref int a)
    {
        a += 2; // the original parameter is not modified
    }
    public void OutParamMethod(out int a)
    {
        a = 2; // original value unimportant, a set to 2 and passed out
    }
    public void ParamArrayMethod(params int[] args)
    {
        // provides flexibility through indefinite number of arguments
    }
}
```

Memory Management

Like the Java language, C# employs *automatic memory management.* Transparently to developers, the language uses garbage collection to move objects around in memory and clean up after unused objects. For more fine-grained control over memory management, C# provides developers with the ability to write "unsafe" code. Please refer to a C# text for a more complete discussion of memory management and unsafe code.

Operators and Expressions

C# includes unary, binary, and ternary operators. Table D.2 outlines these operators.

Table D.2: Operator Types in C#

Category	Operators
Primary	`(x) x.y f(x) a[x] x++ x` `new typeof sizeof checked unchecked`
Unary	`+ - ! ~ ++x --x (T)x`
Multiplicative	`* / %`
Additive	`+ -`
Shift	`<< >>`
Relational	`< > <= >= is`
Equality	`== !=`
Logical AND	`&`
Logical XOR	`^`
Logical OR	`|`
Conditional AND	`&&`
Conditional OR	`||`
Conditional	`?:`
Assignment	`= *= /= %= += -= <<= >>= &= ^= |=`

Expressions are evaluated in order of operator precedence. This precedence is based upon the *associativity* of the operators:

- Except for assignment operators, all binary operators are performed from left to right.

- Assignment operators and the conditional operator are evaluated from right to left.

- Precedence may be controlled through the use of parentheses.

Statements

As a derivation of C and C++, C# borrows most of its statements from these two languages. The next section outlines the statements found in C# and their usage.

Blocks

A *block* statement allows multiple statements to be written in contexts where a single statement is allowed. A *block* statement consists of a statement list enclosed by braces:

```
\
static void main
{

}
```

EXAMPLE

Statement Lists

A *statement list* is simply one or more statements written in sequence and enclosed in blocks as outlined in the preceding section:

```
static void main
{
    refresh();
    repaint();
}
```

EXAMPLE

Empty Statement

An *empty statement* performs no operations and is used where a statement is required, as in this while loop with a null body:

```
while (x > 0)
{
    ;
}
```

EXAMPLE

Labeled

A *labeled statement* allows a statement to be referenced by a goto statement. The scope of the label is the block that encloses it, including any nested blocks:

```
static void main
{
    if(x>0) goto MyLabel;
    x++;
    MyLabel:
        return x;
}
```

EXAMPLE

Declarations

A *declaration statement* declares a local variable or constant:

```
int x = 3;
const decimal pi = 3.14;
```

EXAMPLE

Expressions

As expected, an *expression statement* evaluates a given statement:

EXAMPLE

```
return (x * y);
repaint(this);
```

Selection

Selection statements allow for the execution of one of a list of possible statements based upon the value of a controlling expression. Selection statements include the `if` and `switch` statements.

if

The `if` statement selects a statement for execution based on a Boolean expression:

EXAMPLE

```
if (x > 0)
{
    x--;
}
```

This statement can be coupled with an `else` clause to specify a statement for execution if the condition fails:

EXAMPLE

```
if (x > 0)
{
    x--;
}
else
{
return x;
}
```

`if` statements can also be nested:

EXAMPLE

```
if (x !=3)
{
    if (x > 0)
    {
        x--;
    }
    else
    {
    return x;
    }
}
```

switch

To provide multiple statements for possible execution based upon the value of the condition expression, we use the `switch` statement:

EXAMPLE

```
switch (x)
{
    case 1:
        Console.WriteLine("X = 1");
        break;
    case 2:
        Console.WriteLine("X = 2");
        break;
    case 3:
        Console.WriteLine("X = 3");
        break;
    default:
        Console.WriteLine("X does not equal 1,2, or 3");
        break;
}
```

The switch statement evaluates the expression and looks for a match with a constant value from one of the labeled statements. Upon finding a match, execution control is transferred to the statement list for the matching label. If no match is found, control is transferred to the default label and its statement list. Note that the statement list of the switch statement must end in a construct that renders the end point of the statement list unreachable, usually break.

Iteration

Iteration statements allow for the execution of a statement list as long as some expression evaluates true. C# includes four such iteration statements: while, do, for, and foreach.

while

The while statement executes a statement list zero or more times, depending on the value of the conditional expression:

EXAMPLE

```
while (x < 100)
{
    Console.WriteLine(x);
    x++
}
```

do

Similar to the while statement, the do statement executes one or more times:

EXAMPLE

```
do
{
    Console.WriteLine(x);
    x++
}
while(x < 100)
```

for

The for statement evaluates a series of initialization expressions and repeats execution based on evaluation of these expressions. In addition to the statement list to be executed, the for statement has three parts: initializer, condition, and iterator.

EXAMPLE

```csharp
for (int x = 0; x < 100; x++)
{
    Console.WriteLine(x);
}
```

foreach

Very similar to the for statement, the foreach statement enumerates a collection and executes the statement list once for each item in the collection:

EXAMPLE

```csharp
foreach (int x in args)
{
    Console.WriteLine(x);
}
```

jump

Another type of statement, the jump statement, allows the unconditional transfer of control execution in a C# program. Jump statements include break, continue, goto, return, and throw statements.

break

The break statement unconditionally exits the nearest enclosing switch, while, do, for, or foreach statement:

EXAMPLE

```csharp
switch (x)
{
    case 1:
        Console.WriteLine("X = 1");
        break;
    default:
        Console.WriteLine("X does not equal 1");
        break;
}
```

continue

The continue statement restarts the nearest enclosing while, do, for, or foreach statement:

EXAMPLE

```csharp
while(true)
    Console.WriteLine(x);
    if(x < 100) continue;
    break;
}
```

goto

As mentioned during the discussion of labeled statements, the goto statement transfers control to a labeled statement:

EXAMPLE

```
static void main
{
    if(x>0) goto MyLabel;
    x++;
    MyLabel:
        return x;
}
```

return

The return statement returns control to the caller of the function in which the return statement appears:

EXAMPLE

```
int GetStudentID(string FullName)
{
    return x;
}
```

throw

The throw statement throws an exception. See the try statement for usage.

try

The try statement provides exception handling during execution of a statement block. The try block may be followed by one or more catch blocks and may be followed by one finally block:

EXAMPLE

```
try
{
    repaint();
}
catch (Exception e)
{
    //handle gracefully
    if(x < 0) // out of range
    {
        throw new Exception("Index out of Range");
    }
}
finally
{
    // any clean-up code here
}
```

checked **and** unchecked

The checked and unchecked statements are used to control the overflow checking context for integral-type arithmetic operations and conversions:

EXAMPLE

```
int x = 1000000;
int y = 1000000;
Console.WriteLine(unchecked(x^2));
Console.WriteLine(checked(y^2));
```

lock

The lock statement obtains the mutual-exclusion lock for a given object, executes a statement list, and then releases the lock:

EXAMPLE

```
lock(MyResource)
{
    MyResource.Name = "Bob";
}
```

using

The using statement obtains one or more resources, executes a statement list, and then disposes of the resource:

EXAMPLE

```
using (MyResource r = new MyResource())
{
    r.Update();
```

Types

Two kinds of types are supported in C#, value types and reference types. The difference between these two kinds of types is in the way the variables of each type behave.

Value Types

Unlike reference types, variables of *value types* contain the actual data they represent. Value types consist of predefined types, enums, and structs.

PREDEFINED TYPES

Predefined types are shorthand for system types found in the .NET platform. Table D.3 outlines each of the value types found in C# as well as the system-provided type to which it corresponds.

Table D.3: Predefined Value Types in C#

Type Name	Category	Description
object	System.Object	The absolute base class of all other types
string	System.String	Unicode character sequence

Table D.3: continued

Type Name	Category	Description
sbyte	System.SByte	8-bit signed integral type
short	System.Int16	16-bit signed integral type
int	System.Int32	32-bit signed integral type
long	System.Int64	64-bit signed integral type
byte	System.Byte	8-bit unsigned integral type
ushort	System.UInt16	16-bit unsigned integral type
uint	System.UInt32	32-bit unsigned integral type
ulong	System.UInt64	64-bit unsigned integral type
float	System.Single	Single-precision floating point type
double	System.Double	Double-precision floating point type
bool	System.Boolean	Boolean type containing either true or false
char	System.Char	Containing value is one Unicode character

ENUMS

A second kind of value type is the enum, which is a user-defined type name for a group of related constants. This type is often used when a runtime decision is made from a fixed number of choices created at compile time.

EXAMPLE

```
enum Material
{
    Pine,
    Oak,
    Maple,
    Mahogany
}
```

Structs

Structs are value types that share many similarities with classes. Like classes, struct definitions can include constants, fields, methods, events, operators, constructors, destructors, and even nested type declarations. See the definition of classes for a more complete definition of these items.

When used strategically, a struct can often boost performance because its values are stored on the stack.

EXAMPLE

```
struct Point
{
    public int x, y, z;

    public Student(int x, int y, int z)
    {
```

```
        this.x = x;
        this.y = y;
        this.z = z;
    }
}
```

We can use the struct in this way:

EXAMPLE

```
Point[] graph = new Point[1000];
for (int a = 0; a < 1000; a++){
    graph[a] = new Point(a, a, a + a);
}
```

By using a struct instead of a class, the calling program instantiates just one object for an array of our Point struct instead of creating 1001 new objects as it would have if we had used a class declaration.

CONVERSIONS

As mentioned before, C# includes a number of predefined value types. These types also have predefined conversions between them. These conversions are either implicit or explicit.

Implicit Conversions

Implicit conversions are those that may be performed without loss of data and without careful observation, for instance, from int to long. Because this conversion requires no loss of data, it never fails.

Explicit Conversions

Unlike implicit conversions, *explicit conversions* may result in loss of data and must be handled by using a cast expression:

```
(int)MyLongVariable
```

EXAMPLE

Reference Types

Reference types are types whose variables store only references to the actual objects they represent. Because of this, operations made on one reference type variable may affect another reference type variable if it references the same object. Reference types include arrays, classes, interfaces, and delegates.

ARRAY TYPES

C# supports both single-dimensional and multidimensional arrays. Array types are reference types, so array declarations merely set aside space for the array. Array instances are actually created by initializing the array with array creation expressions:

EXAMPLE

```
int[] arr; // declare single-dimension array
arr = new int[] {10, 20, 30}; // initialize the array
int[,] arr2; // declare multi-dimension array
arr2 = new int[,] {10, 20, 30}, {30, 40, 50}; // initialize the array
```

Also, as with other variables, we can declare the array and initialize it in a single step:

EXAMPLE

```
int[] arr = new int[] {10, 20, 30}; // initialize the array
int[,] arr2 = new int[,] {10, 20, 30}, {30, 40, 50}; // initialize the array
```

Note that the preceding arrays are *rectangular arrays* because their shape is known. However, C# also supports *jagged arrays*, also known as "arrays of arrays":

```
int[][] jagged = new int[5][]; // declare single-dimension array
```

EXAMPLE

CLASSES

Class declarations allow the programmer to create new reference types and to help employ the OOP principle of data hiding. Class declarations can include any of the following, which are defined later in the appendix: fields, constants, properties, methods, indexers, operators, events, constructors, destructors, and nested type declarations.

Member Access

Each member defined in the class declaration is accessible to one of five possible degrees. Table D.4 outlines the five degrees of accessibility of class members.

Table D.4: Degrees of accessibility of class members.

Degree	Definition
public	Unlimited access
protected internal	Access limited to the current program or types derived from the containing class
protected	Access limited to the containing class or types derived from the containing class
internal	Access limited to this program
private	Access limited to the containing type

Constants

A *constant* is a member that represents a value computed at compile time that does not change. A simple class with two constants might look like this:

```
class Test
{
    public const int x = 1;
    public const int y = x + 2;
}
```

Note that constant values can depend upon other constants as long as no circular references are created. With the appropriate access level, constants can be accessed via dot notation as can any other member, like this:

```
int A = Test.x;
```

Fields

A field member is a variable associated with an object or class. Fields can be declared in the following fashion:

```
class Student
{
    public string FirstName;
    public string LastName;
    public static readonly int HomeRoom;

    public Student(string First, string Last, int Room)
    {
        FirstName = First;
        LastName = Last;
        HomeRoom = Room;
    }
}
```

In this example, we have created FirstName and LastName, two *instance fields*, or variables for which storage is allocated with each instance of the class that is created. We have also created a third field, this time a *static field* by using the static keyword. In doing so, we have created storage for the HomeRoom field in only the class level, so all instances of the Student class will share this field. To prevent unexpected results by inadvertently overwriting data, we have used the readonly keyword, which allows the field to be changed only during its declaration or a constructor of its containing class.

Properties

Like fields, *properties* are named members with associated types. However, properties do not designate storage locations for their associated values. Instead, they define accessors that denote the statements to execute to read or write their values. A simple class with a property declaration would resemble the following:

EXAMPLE

```
public class PhoneNumber
{
    private string m_PhoneNumber;
    public string Text
    {
        get
        {
            return m_PhoneNumber;
        }
        set
        {
            m_PhoneNumber = FormatPhone(value);
        }
    }
    public PhoneNumber(string Phone)
    {
        m_PhoneNumber = FormatPhone(Phone);
    }
    ...
}
```

In this skeleton example of a phone number formatting class, we define both get and set accessors for the Text property. The get accessor is called when the Text property is read and, conversely, the set accessor is called when the property's value is changed. Note the implicit value parameter of the set accessor.

We can use this class and its properties in the following manner:

EXAMPLE

```
PhoneNumber pn = new PhoneNumber("8675309"); //constructor formats
TextBox1.Text = pn.Text; // get accessor returns formatted number
pn.Text = TextBox1.Text; // set accessor, number is formatted and stored
```

Methods

A *method* is a member that implements an action that can be performed by an object or class. Methods have a signature that consists of the name of the method and the number, types, and modifiers of the list of parameters. Methods may have a return type and value or may be void. Like fields, methods may be *static methods* (accessed through the class) or *instance methods* (which are accessed through instances of the class). We declare methods in this way:

EXAMPLE

```
public class SportsTicker
{
    public void Start()
    {
        //implementation goes here
    }
    public static void Reset()
```

```
    {
        //implementation goes here
    }
    public GameInfo GetScoreByTeam(string Team)
    {
        //implementation goes here
    }
}
```

In this framework example, we've defined three methods. Start is an instance method with no return value, which initiates scrolling on our sports ticker. Reset is a static method, which returns the ticker to its original state. Finally, GetScoreByTeam is an instance method, which returns a GameInfo class (defined separately) containing all the game information for the given team on the current day.

One of the more powerful features of C# that C and C++ developers should be familiar with is that of overloading. Methods may be *overloaded*, meaning they share the same name but have unique signatures. This is a useful means of providing computation on different kinds of parameters while avoiding creating unique method names for a variety of different input combinations. Consider the following example:

EXAMPLE

```
class Shape
{
    public int Height, Width;
    public int Perimeter()
    {
        return ((Height * 2) + (Width * 2));
    }
    public int Perimeter(int length)
    {
        // assume square
        return (length * 4);
    }
    public int Perimeter(int length, int width)
    {
        // assume rectangle
        return ((length * 2) + (width * 2));
    }
    public int Perimeter(int[] sides)
    {
        // unknown shape, calculate
        int p = 0;
        for (int x = 0; x < sides.length; x++)
        {
            p += sides[x];
        }
```

```
        return p;
    }
}
```

In this example, we are able to calculate the perimeter of a variety of shapes using the overloaded method `Perimeter`.

Events

An *event* is a special member that enables a class to provide notifications to the calling program. Events are declared much like fields with an added event keyword as follows:

EXAMPLE

```
class TestClass
{
    public event MouseOverHandler MouseOver;
}
```

The declaration type is always that of a delegate, in this case `ClickHandler`, which we define as follows:

EXAMPLE

```
public delegate void MouseOverHandler(object sender, System.EventArgs e);
```

Delegates and their other uses are discussed later in this reference.

To hook up the event handler for our event, we use the += operator from the calling program:

EXAMPLE

```
public class TestForm
{
    public TestForm()
    {
        TestClass1.MouseOver += new    MouseOverHandler(TestClass1_MouseOver);
    }
    TestClass TestClass1 = new TestClass();
    void TestClass1_MouseOver(object sender, EventArgs e)
    {
        Console.WriteLine("Mouseover!");
    }
    public void RemoveHandler()
    {
        // removes the handler
        TestClass1.MouseOver -= new    MouseOverHandler(TestClass1_MouseOver);
    }
}
```

Operators

An `operator` is a member that defines the meaning of an expression operator that can be applied to instances of the class. Table D.5 outlines the forms of operators.

Table D.5: Class Member Operators

Operator Form	Operators	Implementation
Unary	+, -, !, ~	Takes single parameter of same type as containing type and returns any type
Unary	++ or --	Takes single parameter of same type as containing type and returns same type as containing type
Unary	true or false	Takes single parameter of same type as containing type and returns type
boolBinary	==,!=,>,<,>=,<=	Takes two parameters, at least one of same type as containing type and returns any type
Conversion	N/A	Converts from source type to target type, one of which must be of same type as containing type

An example of a unary operator using the + operator would be declared as follows:

EXAMPLE

```
public static TestClass operator+(TestClass x, TestClass y)
{
    return new TestClass(x.value + y.value);
}
```

Of course, implementation within the operator is up to the programmer, but additional unary operators would resemble the preceding example. Although a binary operator may return any type, the most often used return type is that of bool. An example of such an operator follows:

EXAMPLE

```
public static bool TestClass operator==(TestClass x, TestClass y)
{
    return  x.value ==  y.value;
}
```

The third type of operator is the conversion operator. This type of operator allows the programmer to create user-defined conversions from one type to another. A conversion between two types is valid if

- the source type and the target types differ

- either the source type or the target types is of type declaring the conversion

- neither the source type nor the target type is of type object or an interface type

- the source type is not a base class of the target type and the target type is not a base class of the source type

After making sure these conditions are met, we must determine whether the conversion must be *implicit* or *explicit*. As a rule, implicit conversions are designed to never throw exceptions or lose data. This conversion lends itself to scenarios where data is being converted from a subset type to a super type, as in from char to string. Conversely, explicit conversions are designed to handle situations where loss of data could occur. Conversion operators are defined in the following manner:

EXAMPLE

```
public static implicit operator MyChar(String s)
{
    return  s.value;
}
public static explicit operator String(MyChar c)
{
    return  new MyChar(c);
}
```

Indexers

An *indexer* is a member that enables for...each traversal much like an array. Indexer declarations resemble property declarations except that they are nameless and include indexing parameters. If we built a Bucket class to hold a set of Shape objects we created earlier, we could do so in the following way:

EXAMPLE

```
class Bucket
{
    Shape[] shapes;
    int length;
    public Bucket(int length)
    {
        if (length < 0) throw new ArgumentException();
        shapes = new Shape[((length - 1)];
        this.length = length;
    }
    public int Length
    {
        get
        {
            return length;
        }
    }
    public Shape this[int index]
    {
        get
        {
            if (index < 0 || index >= length)
            {
                throw new IndexOutOfRangeException();
```

```
        }
        return (shapes[index]);
    }
    set
    {
        if (index < 0 || index >= length)
        {
            throw new IndexOutOfRangeException();
        }
        shapes[index] = value;
    }
    }
}
```

This allows us to traverse the class in the same way we do an array:

EXAMPLE

```
Bucket Shapes(5);
for (int x = 0; x < 20; x++)
{
    Shapes[x].Height = x;
    Shapes[x].Width = x;
    Console.WriteLine(Shapes[x].Perimeter());
}
```

Instance Constructors

Constructors are members that provide any initialization operations for an instance of a class. Similar in many ways to methods, constructors may be overloaded as well to provide alternate ways of instantiating a class. Constructors have the same name as the class and have no return type. The following example is an extension of our Shape class to include two constructors to allow initialization of the Height and Width fields upon instantiation.

EXAMPLE

```
class Shape
{
    public int Height, Width;
    public Shape(int h, int w)
    {
        Height = h;
        Width = w;
    }
    public Shape(int h)
    {
        // assume square
        Height = h;
        Width = h;
    }
    public int Perimeter()
    {
```

```
            return ((Height * 2) + (Width * 2));
    }
    public int Perimeter(int length)
    {
        // assume square
        return (length * 4);
    }
    public int Perimeter(int length, int width)
    {
        // assume rectangle
        return ((length * 2) + (width * 2));
    }
    public int Perimeter(int[] sides)
    {
        // unknown shape, calculate
        int p = 0;
        for (int x = 0; x < sides.length; x++)
        {
            p += sides[x];
        }
        return p;
    }
}
```

Because we had no constructors in our class beforehand, you might have guessed that the use of constructors is optional. If no constructor is provided, the compiler automatically generates an empty constructor with no parameters.

Destructors

A *destructor* is a member that performs the actions required to terminate an instance of a class. Destructors have no accessibility level, take no parameters, and cannot be called explicitly. Instead, destructors are called implicitly by the system during regular garbage collection. Destructors, like constructors, have the same name as the class and are created in this way:

EXAMPLE

```
~Shape(){
    //add any clean-up code here
}
```

Static Constructors

Static constructors perform the required actions to initialize a class the same way as instance constructors initialize an instance of a class. However, like destructors, static constructors have no accessibility level, take no parameters, and cannot be called explicitly. A static constructor looks like this:

EXAMPLE

```
Static Shape()
{
    // implementation code
}
```

Inheritance

Inheritance is the mechanism that allows one type to derive from another. Classes support single inheritance and all classes ultimately derive from the object type. Consider a generic form of our Shape class once again:

EXAMPLE

```
class Shape
{
    public int Perimeter(int[] sides)
    {
        // unknown shape, calculate
        int p = 0;
        for (int x = 0; x < sides.length; x++)
        {
            p += sides[x];
        }
        return p;
    }
}
```

Now let's derive a new type from this class:

EXAMPLE

```
class Rectangle:Shape
{
    public Area(int h, int w)
    {
        return h * w;
    }
}
```

Our new class inherits the Perimeter method from Shape while adding its own Area method. However, inheritance doesn't have to be verbatim. By adding the virtual keyword to a method, property, or indexer in the base class, we can override its implementation in the derived class:

EXAMPLE

```
class Shape
{
    public virtual int Perimeter(int[] sides)
    {
        // unknown shape, calculate
        int p = 0;
        for (int x = 0; x < sides.length; x++)
        {
            p += sides[x];
        }
```

```
        return p;
    }
}
```

Now let's derive a new type from this class and override the `Perimeter` method:

EXAMPLE

```
class Square:Shape
{
    public override int Perimeter(int[] sides)
    {
        return (sides[x] * 4);
    }
    public Area(int h)
    {
        return h * h;
    }
}
```

Often, it may be prudent to design the base class with no implementation details and stipulate that the derived class provides its own implementation. This is accomplished by marking the class as `abstract`, as follows:

EXAMPLE

```
abstract class Shape
{
    public abstract int Perimeter()
    {
    }
}
```

Our derived class is created in the same manner as in the previous example:

EXAMPLE

```
class Square:Shape
{
    public override int Perimeter()
    {
        return (sides[x] * 4);
    }
    public Area(int h)
    {
        return h * h;
    }
}
```

INTERFACES

Interfaces are contracts that a class (or struct) implementing the interface must adhere to. Interface members may include methods, properties, indexers, and events and interfaces support multiple inheritance. They contain no implementation details because that is left to the implementing class or struct:

EXAMPLE

```
interface IValidation
{
    void Validate(string text);
}
class PhoneNumber:IValidation
{
    void Validate(string text)
    {
        // validation code goes here
    }
}
```

DELEGATES

Delegates are the C# answer to function pointers in C++. However, delegates are type-safe and secure. Delegates derive from the System.Delegate and encapsulate a callable entity, either a method on an instance class or a static method on a class. A delegate can reference any object as long as the method's signature matches its own signature. Delegates are declared much like methods; after all, they are essentially just method signatures:

```
delegate void MyDelegate();
```

After the delegate is declared, it must be instantiated:

EXAMPLE

```
class MyClass
{
    void TestMethod()
    {
        Console.WriteLine("Calling MyClass.TestMethod");
    }
    static void TestDelegateCall(MyDelegate d)
    {
        d(); // calls TestMethod() anonymously
    }
}
```

Component-Based Features

Up to this point, we've focused on programs and even program fragments in introducing the concepts of the language. However, C# has several features that enable building component-based applications: namespaces, assemblies, and attributes.

Namespaces and Assemblies

Namespaces provide a logical organizational system, both internally within the program and externally to other programs. Consider the following example:

EXAMPLE

```
namespace Que.ByExample
{
    class Book
    {...}
```

Because namespaces may be nested, the preceding example is functionally equivalent to

EXAMPLE

```
namespace Que
{
    namespace ByExample
    {
        class Book
        {...}
    }
}
```

In either case, we can reference the Book class via its fully qualified namespace:

EXAMPLE

```
Que.ByExample.Book
```

We can avoid using the fully qualified namespace by using the using directive as we have seen with the System namespace in prior examples:

```
using Que.ByExample;
```

Assemblies are used for physical packaging and deployment by acting as containers for types. Assemblies take two forms, .exe files, which include a main entry point, and .dll libraries, which do not have a main entry point. The C# compiler produces .exe applications by default. The compiler produces libraries by specifying the target switch as follows:

```
csc /target:library filename.cs
```

Attributes

C# supports *attributes* whereby programmers can specify declarative information for program entities and retrieve this information at runtime via reflection. In fact, the .NET Framework provides a number of special case attribute types already. Take the following example for instance:

EXAMPLE

```
[ WebMethod(Description="Returns the stock price", EnableSession=true)]
public decimal GetCurrentStockPrice() {...}
```

In this fragment from a stock lookup Web service, we have marked the GetCurrentStockPrice method with the WebMethod attribute, which denotes it as callable via Web services. Just as the .NET Framework team developed the WebMethod attribute, we can derive our own custom attributes from the System.Attribute class:

EXAMPLE

```
using System;
[AttributeUsage(AttributeTargets.All)]
public class HelpDocAttribute : Attribute
{
    public string Keywords;
    private string url;
    private string topic;
    public HelpDocAttribute(string url, string topic)
    {
        this.url = url;
        this.topic = topic;
    }
    public string Url
    {
        get
        {
            return url;
        }
    }
    public string Topic
    {
        get
        {
            return topic;
        }
    }
}
```

In creating our custom attribute, we first have to denote on which targets our attribute can be used. We do this, ironically, by using another attribute on our class declaration, the AttributeUsage class. Note that we specify our attribute to be available on any elements by passing the enumerated value AttributeTargets.All to the AttributeUsage constructor. Please consult the .NET Framework documentation for available values of the AttributeTargets enumeration.

After designating which targets our attribute will be used on, we next set up our positional and named parameters. For custom attributes, *positional parameters* are those corresponding to the arguments for the public constructors of the attribute. *Named parameters* are those defined by public read/write properties of the class. Note that in our example we have created two positional parameters, Url and Topic, and one named parameter, Keywords.

Once declared, our custom attribute may be employed in this way:

EXAMPLE

```
[HelpDocAttribute("http://help.xyzcompany.com/docs/SportsTicker.aspx",
    "SportsTicker Class")]
public class SportsTicker
{
    [HelpDocAttribute("http://help.xyzcompany.com/docs/SportsTicker.aspx",
        "SportsTicker Constructor", Keywords="SportsTicker")]
    public SportsTicker(){...}
}
```

Notice that for the SportsTicker class itself, we pass the positional parameters of Url and Topic, and for the public constructor, we add a third parameter for a keyword search.

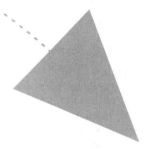

Index

V

validate( ), 43
validation, validation controls, 27, 42-50, 195-225
ASPSmith VControls in, 310
BaseValidator class in, 199-200
built-in controls for, 47
client side, 196-197
ClientTarget property in, 197, 216
CompareValidator in, 203-206, 219
ControlToValidate in, 201-202, 204, 208
CustomValidator in, 213-215
DownLevel and UpLevel settings in, 197, 216
Dynamic HTML (DHTML) vs., 197
in e-commerce Web site example, 378
e-mail application for, 210-213
EmailBox VControl in, 220-224
error handling for, 47
ErrorMessage in, 199
Form Validation Example for, 217-219
forms and, 196
HtmlControls, 120
inserting, 197-200
IsValid methods for, 203
NET Framework and, 196
OnServerValidate in, 213
properties for, 199-200, 199
RangeValidator for, 47-50, 201-203, 206
RegularExpressionValidator in, 206, 207-213, 219
RequiredFieldValidator for, 47-50, 198-201, 219
ValidationExpression in, 219
ValidationSummary for, 47-50, 199, 215-217
VControl or Validated Control in, 220-224
WebUIValidation.js file for, 196-197
zip code, 212
ValidationExpression, 219
ValidationSummary, 47-50, 199, 215-217
variables, scope of, 233, 248-249

VB.NET (Visual Basic .NET), 8, 25, 139
language reference, 459-486
VB/VBScript syntax errors 360
VBScript, 2, 22, 26, 34, 42, 207
VControl or Validated Control, 220-224
vdisco files, 301
verification service, for credit card, 277
Vertigo Software, 366
ViewState, 326-329, 372-373
Visual Basic, 2, 8, 21, 27-28, 31, 110, 182
in user controls, 227
language reference, 459-486
viewing database query results, 58-62
Visual Studio, 9, 21
Visual Studio .NET (VS .NET), 2, 9, 20, 25, 28, 110, 247, 260, 271, 279
debug/in debugging, 359
deployment, 312-313
in validation controls, 197
in Web services, 296-304, 296

W

Warren, Susan, 366
Web controls, 109
Web Form with Event Handlers example, 243-244
web hosting, 26, 304
Web pages, 247
Web services, 9, 11, 20, 28, 247, 275-305
advanced topics in, 288-296
architecture of, 279
asynchronous processing in, 293-295
blocking in, 294
client for, 286-288
client proxy for, 283-286
compiling of, 281, 286
complex types in, 288-293
debugging, 303
definition of, 277-278
deploying, 303-304
Disco discovery protocol for, 279, 301
distributed computing and, 276-277

distributed object applications in, 276
in e-commerce Web site example, 381-382
event handlers and, 280
file extensions of, 280
interface for, 281
interoperability using, 277, 293
Java development of, 304
Microsoft Message Queue Server (MSMQ) and, 288
Microsoft Transaction Server (MTS) and, 288
namespace for, 281
naming, 280
pipeline architecture for, 280
processor directives in, 280
protocol bindings for, 282
publishing to Internet, 277
serialization in XML for, 285, 289-293
Simple Object Access Protocol (SOAP) and, 278, 282, 285-295
testing, 283
transaction support in, 295-296
Universal Description, Discovery, and Integration (UDDI) for, 277, 279, 301-302, 304
URLs in, 284, 301-302
verification services, 277
Visual Studio .NET for, 296-304
asmx and .asmx.cs / .asmx.vb files in, 299-301
vsdisco files in, 301
consuming, 301-304
debugging, 303
deployment, 303-304
preliminary setup for, 296-298
project structure in, 298-301
Web Hosting and, 304
Web Services Description Language (WSDL) for, 278-279, 282, 284
[WebMethod] attribute in, 281-283
Windows DNA model and, 288
writing, 279-288
XML and, 277, 285, 289-293
Web Services Description Language (WSDL), 278-279, 282, 284